Windows PowerShell Cookbook™

Other Microsoft .NET resources from O'Reilly

Related titles   Windows PowerShell Quick   Windows Vista
                     Reference   Administration
                     Windows Server 2008: The   Windows Vista: The
                     Definitive Guide   Definitive Guide

.NET Books   *dotnet.oreilly.com* is a complete catalog of O'Reilly's books on
Resource Center .NET and related technologies, including sample chapters and
                     code examples.

ONDotnet.com provides independent coverage of fundamental,
interoperable, and emerging Microsoft .NET programming and
web services technologies.

Conferences   O'Reilly brings diverse innovators together to nurture the ideas
                     that spark revolutionary industries. We specialize in document-
                     ing the latest tools and systems, translating the innovator's
                     knowledge into useful skills for those in the trenches. Visit *con-
                     ferences.oreilly.com* for our upcoming events.

Safari Bookshelf (*safari.oreilly.com*) is the premier online reference library for programmers and IT professionals. Conduct
searches across more than 1,000 books. Subscribers can zero in
on answers to time-critical questions in a matter of seconds.
Read the books on your Bookshelf from cover to cover or simply flip to the page you need. Try it today for free.

Windows PowerShell Cookbook™

Lee Holmes

O'REILLY®

Beijing · Cambridge · Farnham · Köln · Sebastopol · Taipei · Tokyo

Windows PowerShell Cookbook™
by Lee Holmes

Copyright © 2008 Lee Holmes. All rights reserved.
Printed in the United States of America.

Published by O'Reilly Media, Inc., 1005 Gravenstein Highway North, Sebastopol, CA 95472.

O'Reilly books may be purchased for educational, business, or sales promotional use. Online editions are also available for most titles (*safari.oreilly.com*). For more information, contact our corporate/institutional sales department: (800) 998-9938 or *corporate@oreilly.com*.

Editor: John Osborn

Production Editor: Laurel R.T. Ruma

Production Services: Tolman Creek Design

Cover Designer: Karen Montgomery

Interior Designer: David Futato

Illustrators: Robert Romano and Jessamyn Read

Printing History:

October 2007:   First Edition.

 This book uses RepKover™, a durable and flexible lay-flat binding.

ISBN: 978-0-596-52849-2

[M]   [8/08]

Table of Contents

Part III. Common Tasks

Part IV. Administrator Tasks

Foreword

When Lee asked me to write the foreword to his new book I was pleasantly surprised. I was under the impression that forewords were written by people who were respected and accomplished in their chosen field. Apparently, that isn't the case at all. My closest brush with accomplishment and respect came at a New Year's celebration long ago and involved hairspray and a butane lighter. I guess it doesn't matter too much—I mean, who reads the foreword to a scripting book anyways, right?

Lee wanted one of the Microsoft Scripting Guys to write the foreword. He wrote this book for the same hard-working admin scripters who frequent the TechNet Script Center. Lee thought it would make sense to have an original member of that team provide some perspective on where Windows admin scripting has been and where, with Windows PowerShell, it is going.

A lot has happened since Lee and I first spoke about this. I've left the Microsoft Scripting Guys team to work on the WMI SDK, and the Scripting Guys name has become a bit of a joke given that the current driving force behind the team is a slight, half-sandwich-eating lady named Jean Ross. For now, Jean is keeping Greg around to do menial labor like packing up and shipping Dr. Scripto bobblehead dolls, but we'll just see what happens when he finally runs out of topics for his "Hey, Scripting Guy" column. The future of scripting could very well be The Scripting Girl.

Glue, Enablers, and a WSH

Whenever I think "perspective" and "scripting"—which is far too often—I think Bob Wells. Bob takes his scripting very seriously and has been promoting it inside and outside of Microsoft for years. When I joined the Scripting Guys team, Bob would preach to me about "glue" and "enablers." It took some time before I understood why he was talking about it so often and why finding just the right term for enablers was so important to him. I now know that it's because crisply defining these two concepts establishes a simple, useful framework in which to think about admin scripting. The glue part is the scripting language itself—the *foreachs*, *ifs*, and *vars*.

It's what you use to orchestrate, or glue together, the set of subtasks you need to do to complete a larger task. The enablers (and, no, we never came up with a better term for them) are the instruments that actually accomplish each of the subtasks.

This table lists the glue and enablers that we, as Windows scripters, have had available to us over the years.

Glue	Enabler
Cmd.exe batch language	Command-line tools (OS, ResKit, Support Tools)
WSH	Command-line tools (OS, ResKit, Support Tools)
	Automation-enabled COM objects (WMI, ADSI)
Windows PowerShell	Command-line tools (OS, ResKit, Support Tools
	Automation-enabled COM objects (WMI, ADSI)
	.NET Framework Class Library

Notice how each new environment lets you work with the enablers of the previous environment. This is important because it lets you carry forward your hard-earned knowledge. Objectively, we can say that WSH scripting is more powerful than batch scripting because it provides access to more enablers. You can automate more tasks because you have access to the additional functionality exposed by automatable COM objects. Less objectively, you could argue that even if you're only going to use command-line tools as enablers, WSH is a better choice than batch because it provides some really useful glue functionality; advances in available enablers make more things possible while advances in glue (sometimes) make things more convenient.

WSH scripting is a pretty capable environment. The WMI and ADSI COM libraries alone provide admins around the world with countless cycles of pain and elation. But there's always that pesky task that you just can't do with WSH, or that requires you to download some tool from some strangely named web site at 2 a.m. when you really shouldn't be making decisions about what to install on your production servers. If only VBScript included the infamous Win32 API among its enablers, then, like those strange creatures known as developers, you could do *anything*.

Well, in developer land these days, the .NET Framework Class Library (FCL) is the new Win32 API. So, what we really need is a scripting environment that includes the FCL as an enabler. That's exactly what Windows PowerShell does. In fact, Windows PowerShell runs in the same environment as that library and, as a result, works seamlessly with it. I read a lot of press about the object-pipelining capabilities of Windows PowerShell. Those capabilities are very cool and represent an excellent advance in the glue department—an advance that certainly makes working with the FCL more natural. But the addition of the FCL as an enabler is the thing that makes Jeffrey et al.'s creation objectively more powerful than WSH. And even if you don't run into anything in the FCL that you need right away, it's comforting to know that when you make an investment and develop expertise in this latest environment, you gain access to all the enablers that your developer counterparts currently have or will have in the foreseeable future. It should also be comforting to know that if you spend the time to learn Windows PowerShell, that knowledge should last you as long as the .NET Framework lasts Microsoft.

Windows PowerShell follows in the tradition of WSH by improving on the glue aspect of its predecessor. One of the real pain points of working with COM objects in WSH was finding out what properties and methods were available. Unless you shelled out the bucks for a smart editor, you lost a lot of productivity context switching from writing a script and consulting documentation. Not so when working with objects in Windows PowerShell. Type this at a Windows PowerShell prompt:

```
$objShell = New-Object -com Shell.Application
$objShell | Get-Member
```

It does a scripter good, does it not?

That Lee Guy

Hopefully my rambling has convinced you that Windows PowerShell is a good thing and that it's worth your time to learn it. Now, why do I think you should learn it by buying and reading this book?

First off, I should tell you that the Windows PowerShell team is a bunch of odd ducks.[*] These folks are obsessed. From Jeffrey Snover on down, they are incredible teachers who love and believe in their technology so much that it's difficult to *stop* them from teaching you! Even among that bunch of quackers, Lee stands out. Have you ever heard the sound an Exchange server makes when it cringes? Well, ours cringe when Lee comes to work and starts answering questions on our internal Windows PowerShell mailing list. Lee has amassed unique knowledge about how to leverage Windows PowerShell to address problems that arise in the real world. And he and O'Reilly have done us a great service by capturing and sharing some of that knowledge in this book.

Windows system admin scripters are the coolest people on the planet. It continues to be a pleasure to work for you and I sincerely hope you enjoy the book.

—Dean Tsaltas
Microsoft Scripting Guy Emeritus

---

[*] Canadian ducks (Canuck ducks) in many cases.

Preface

In late 2002, Slashdot posted a story about a "next generation shell" rumored to be in development at Microsoft. As a longtime fan of the power unlocked by shells and their scripting languages, the post immediately captured my interest. Could this shell possibly provide the command-line power and productivity that I'd long loved on Unix systems?

Since I had just joined Microsoft six months earlier, I jumped at the chance to finally get to the bottom of a Slashdot-sourced Microsoft Mystery. The post talked about strong integration with the .NET Framework, so I posted a query to an internal C# mailing list. I got a response that the project was called "Monad," which I then used to track down an internal prototype build.

Prototype was a generous term. In its early stages, the build was primarily a proof of concept. Want to clear the screen? No problem! Just lean on the Enter key until your previous commands and output scroll out of view! But even at these early stages, it was immediately clear that Monad marked a revolution in command-line shells. As with many things of this magnitude, its beauty was self-evident. Monad passed full-fidelity .NET objects between its commands. For even the most complex commands, Monad abolished the (until now, standard) need for fragile text-based parsing. Simple and powerful data manipulation tools supported this new model, creating a shell both powerful, and easy to use.

I joined the Monad development team shortly after that to help do my part to bring this masterpiece of technology to the rest of the world. Since then, Monad has grown to become a real, tangible, product—now called Windows PowerShell.

So why write a book about it? And why *this* book?

Many users have picked up (and will continue to pick up) PowerShell for the sake of learning PowerShell. Any tangible benefits come by way of side effect. For others, though, you might prefer to opportunistically learn a new technology as it solves your needs. How do you use PowerShell to navigate the filesystem? How can you manage files and folders? Retrieve a web page?

This book focuses squarely on helping you learn PowerShell through task-based solutions to your most pressing problems. Read a recipe, read a chapter, or read the entire book—either way, you're bound to learn something.

Who This Book Is For

This book helps you use PowerShell to *get things done*. It contains hundreds of solutions to specific, real-world problems. For systems management, you'll find plenty examples that show how to manage the filesystem, Windows Registry, event logs, processes, and more. For enterprise administration, you'll find two entire chapters devoted to WMI, Active Directory, and other enterprise-focused tasks.

For administrators of Exchange 2007 or Operations Manager 2007 (MOM), you'll find a chapter devoted to each that covers the getting started information and top tasks for those groundbreaking new products.

Along the way, you'll also learn an enormous amount about PowerShell: its features, its commands, and its scripting language—but you'll most importantly solve problems.

How This Book Is Organized

This book consists of five main sections: a guided tour of PowerShell, PowerShell fundamentals, common tasks, administrator tasks, and a detailed reference.

Part 1: Tour

A Guided Tour of Windows PowerShell breezes through PowerShell at a high level. It introduces PowerShell's core features:

- An interactive shell
- A new command model
- An object-based pipeline
- A razor-sharp focus on administrators
- A consistent model for learning and discovery
- Ubiquitous scripting
- Integration with critical management technologies
- A consistent model for interacting with data stores

The guided tour lets you orient yourself and become familiar with PowerShell as a whole. This familiarity helps create a mental framework for you to understand the details and solutions from the rest of the book.

Part 2: Fundamentals

Chapters 1 through 6 cover the PowerShell fundamentals that underpin many of the solutions used throughout the book. The solutions in this section introduce you to the PowerShell interactive shell, fundamental pipeline and object concepts, and many features of the PowerShell scripting language.

Part 3: Common Tasks

Chapters 7 through 16 cover the tasks you will run into most commonly when starting to tackle more complex problems in PowerShell. This includes working with simple and structured files, Internet-connected scripts, code reuse, user interaction, and more.

Part 4: Administrator Tasks

Chapters 17 through 26 focus on the most common tasks in systems and enterprise management. Chapters 17 through 22 focus on individual systems: the filesystem, registry, event logs, processes, services, and more. Chapters 23 and 24 focus on Active Directory, as well as the typical tasks most common in managing networked or domain-joined systems.

Chapters 25 and 26 are devoted to managing Exchange 2007 and Operations Manager 2007 (MOM), respectively.

Part 5: References

Many books belch useless information into their appendix simply to increase page count. In this book, however, the detailed reference underpins an integral and essential resource for learning and using PowerShell. It covers:

- The PowerShell language and environment
- Regular expression syntax and PowerShell-focused examples
- PowerShell's automatic and default variables
- PowerShell's standard verbs
- Administrator-friendly .NET classes and their uses
- Administrator-friendly WMI classes and their uses
- Administrator-friendly COM objects and their uses
- .NET string formatting syntax and PowerShell-focused examples
- .NET DateTime formatting syntax and PowerShell-focused examples

What You Need to Use This Book

The majority of this book requires only a working installation of Windows Power-Shell. If you do not yet have PowerShell installed, you may obtain it by following the download link at *http://www.microsoft.com/PowerShell*. This link provides download instructions for PowerShell on Windows XP, Windows Server 2003, and Windows Vista. For Windows Server 2008, PowerShell comes installed as an optional component that you can enable through the Control Panel like other optional components.

The Active Directory scripts given in "Active Directory" are most useful when applied to an enterprise environment, but Recipe 23.1, "Test Active Directory Scripts on a Local Installation" shows how to install additional software (*Active Directory Application Mode*) that lets you run these scripts against a local installation.

Chapters 26 and 27 require that you have access to an Exchange or Operations Manager 2007 environment. If you do not have access to these environments, Recipe 25.1, "Experiment with Exchange Management Shell" and Recipe 26.1, "Experiment with the Command Shell" show you how to use Microsoft Virtual Labs for Exchange and Operations Manager as a viable alternative.

Conventions Used in This Book

The following typographical conventions are used in this book:

Plain text
> Indicates menu titles, menu options, menu buttons, and keyboard accelerators (such as Alt and Ctrl)

Italic
> Indicates new terms, URLs, email addresses, filenames, file extensions, path-names, directories, and Unix utilities

`Constant width`
> Indicates commands, options, switches, variables, attributes, keys, functions, types, classes, namespaces, methods, modules, properties, parameters, values, objects, events, event handlers, XML tags, HTML tags, macros, the contents of files, or the output from commands

`Constant width bold`
> Shows commands or other text that should be typed literally by the user

`Constant width italic`
> Shows text that should be replaced with user-supplied values

This icon signifies a tip, suggestion, or general note.

 This icon indicates a warning or caution.

Code Examples

Obtaining Code Examples

To obtain electronic versions of the programs and examples given in this book, visit the *Examples* link at:

http://www.oreilly.com/catalog/9780596528492

Using Code Examples

This book is here to help you get your job done. In general, you may use the code in this book in your programs and documentation. You do not need to contact us for permission unless you're reproducing a significant portion of the code. For example, writing a program that uses several chunks of code from this book does not require permission. Selling or distributing a CD-ROM of examples from O'Reilly books *does* require permission. Answering a question by citing this book and quoting example code does not require permission. Incorporating a significant amount of example code from this book into your product's documentation *does* require permission.

We appreciate, but do not require, attribution. An attribution usually includes the title, author, publisher, and ISBN. For example: "*Windows PowerShell Cookbook* by Lee Holmes. Copyright 2007 Lee Holmes, 978-0-596-52849-2."

If you feel your use of code examples falls outside fair use or the permission given above, feel free to contact us at *permissions@oreilly.com*.

Comments and Questions

Please address comments and questions concerning this book to the publisher:

O'Reilly Media, Inc.
1005 Gravenstein Highway North
Sebastopol, CA 95472
800-998-9938 (in the United States or Canada)
707-829-0515 (international or local)
707-829-0104 (fax)

We have a web page for this book, where we list errata, examples, and any additional information. You can access this page at:

http://www.oreilly.com/catalog/9780596528492

To comment or ask technical questions about this book, send email to:

bookquestions@oreilly.com

For more information about our books, conferences, Resource Centers, and the O'Reilly Network, see our web site at:

http://www.oreilly.com

Acknowledgments

"I do not like writing, but I do like having written."
—William Zinsser
On Writing Well

Writing is the task of crafting icebergs. The heft of the book you hold in your hands is just a hint of the effort it took to get it there—by a cast much larger than me.

The groundwork started decades ago. My parents nurtured my interest in computers and software, supported an evening-only bulletin board service, put up with "viruses" that told them to buy a new computer for Christmas, and even listened to me blather about batch files or how PowerShell compares to Excel. Without their support, who knows where I'd be.

My family and friends helped keep me sane for the past year. Ariel: you are the light of my life. Robin: thinking of you reminds me each day that serendipity is still alive and well in this busy world. Thank you to all of my friends and family for being there for me. You can have me back now. :)

I would not have written this book without the tremendous influence of Guy Allen, visionary of University of Toronto's Professional Writing program. Guy: your mentoring forever changed me, just as it molds thousands of others from English hackers into writers.

Of course, members of the PowerShell team (both new and old) are the ones that made this a book about PowerShell. Building this product with you has been a unique challenge and experience—but most of all, a distinct pleasure. In addition to the PowerShell team, the entire PowerShell community defined this book's focus. From MVPs, to early adopters, to newsgroup lurkers: your support, questions, and feedback have been the inspiration behind each page.

Converting thoughts into print always involves a cast of unsung heroes, even though each author tries their best to convince the world how important these heroes are.

Thank you to my technical reviewers: Christina Lemaire, Dean Tsaltas, Debbie Timmins, James Manning, Jeffrey Tadlock, June Blender, Markus Lindemann, Michael Dragone, and Michael Howard. I truly appreciate you donating your nights and weekends to help craft something of which we can all be proud.

To the awesome staff at O'Reilly—John Osborn, Laurel Ruma, Kyley Caldwell, and the production team—your patience and persistence helped craft a book that holds true to its original vision. It also ensured that the book didn't just knock around in my head, but actually got out the door.

This book would not be possible without the support from each and every one of you.

## PART I

Tour

A Guided Tour of Windows PowerShell

A Guided Tour of Windows PowerShell

Introduction

Windows PowerShell promises to revolutionize the world of system management and command-line shells. From its object-based pipelines, to its administrator focus, to its enormous reach into other Microsoft management technologies, PowerShell drastically improves the productivity of administrators and power-users alike.

When learning a new technology, it is natural to feel bewildered at first by all the unfamiliar features and functionality. This perhaps rings especially true for users new to Windows PowerShell, because it may be their first experience with a fully featured command-line shell. Or worse, they've heard stories of PowerShell's fantastic integrated scripting capabilities and fear being forced into a world of programming that they've actively avoided until now.

Fortunately, these fears are entirely misguided: PowerShell is a shell that both grows with you and grows on you. Let's take a tour to see what it is capable of:

- PowerShell works with standard Windows commands and applications. You don't have to throw away what you already know and use.

- PowerShell introduces a powerful new type of command. PowerShell commands (called *cmdlets*) share a common *Verb-Noun* syntax and offer many usability improvements over standard commands.

- PowerShell understands objects. Working directly with richly structured objects makes working with (and combining) PowerShell commands immensely easier than working in the plain-text world of traditional shells.

- PowerShell caters to administrators. Even with all its advances, PowerShell focuses strongly on its use as an interactive shell: the experience of entering commands in a running PowerShell application.

- PowerShell supports discovery. Using three simple commands, you can learn and discover almost anything PowerShell has to offer.

- PowerShell enables ubiquitous scripting. With a fully fledged scripting language that works directly from the command line, PowerShell lets you automate tasks with ease.
- PowerShell bridges many technologies. By letting you work with .NET, COM, WMI, XML, and Active Directory, PowerShell makes working with these previously isolated technologies easier than ever before.
- PowerShell simplifies management of data stores. Through its provider model, PowerShell lets you manage data stores using the same techniques you already use to manage files and folders.

We'll explore each of these pillars in this introductory tour of PowerShell.

An Interactive Shell

At its core, PowerShell is first and foremost an interactive shell. While it supports scripting and other powerful features, its focus as a shell underpins everything.

Getting started in PowerShell is a simple matter of launching *PowerShell.exe* rather than *cmd.exe*—the shells begin to diverge as you explore the intermediate and advanced functionality, but you can be productive in PowerShell immediately.

To launch Windows PowerShell

Click Start → All Programs → Windows PowerShell 1.0 → Windows PowerShell

or alternatively,

Click Start → Run, and then type "PowerShell".

A PowerShell prompt window opens that's nearly identical to the traditional command prompt window of Windows XP, Windows Server 2003, and their many ancestors. The `PS C:\Documents and Settings\Lee>` prompt indicates that Power-Shell is ready for input, as shown in Figure T-1.

Once you've launched your PowerShell prompt, you can enter DOS-style and Unix-style commands for navigating around the filesystem just as you would with any Windows or Unix command prompt—as in the interactive session shown in Example T-1.

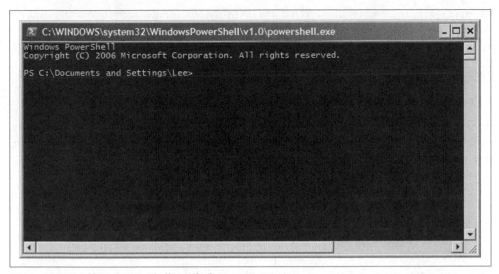

Figure T-1. Windows PowerShell, ready for input

Example T-1. Entering many standard DOS and UNIX-style file manipulation commands produces the same results you get when you use them with any other Windows shell

```
PS C:\Documents and Settings\Lee> function Prompt { "PS >" }
PS >pushd .
PS >cd \
PS >dir


    Directory: Microsoft.PowerShell.Core\FileSystem::C:\


Mode                LastWriteTime     Length Name
----                -------------     ------ ----
d----        11/2/2006    4:36 AM            $WINDOWS.~BT
d----         5/8/2007    8:37 PM            Blurpark
d----       11/29/2006    2:47 PM            Boot
d----       11/28/2006    2:10 PM            DECCHECK
d----        10/7/2006    4:30 PM            Documents and Settings
d----        5/21/2007    6:02 PM            F&SC-demo
d----         4/2/2007    7:21 PM            Inetpub
d----        5/20/2007    4:59 PM            Program Files
d----        5/21/2007    7:26 PM            temp
d----        5/21/2007    8:55 PM            Windows
-a---         1/7/2006   10:37 PM          0 autoexec.bat
-ar-s       11/29/2006    1:39 PM       8192 BOOTSECT.BAK
-a---         1/7/2006   10:37 PM          0 config.sys
-a---         5/1/2007    8:43 PM      33057 RUU.log
-a---         4/2/2007    7:46 PM       2487 secedit.INTEG.RAW


PS >popd
```

Example T-1. Entering many standard DOS and UNIX-style file manipulation commands produces the same results you get when you use them with any other Windows shell (continued)

```
PS >pwd

Path
----
C:\Documents and Settings\Lee
```

As shown in Example T-1, you can use the pushd, cd, dir, pwd, and popd commands to store the current location, navigate around the filesystem, list items in the current directory, and then return to your original location. Try it!

 The pushd command is an alternative name (alias) to the much more descriptively named PowerShell command, Push-Location. Likewise, the cd, dir, popd, and pwd commands all have more memorable counterparts.

Although navigating around the filesystem is helpful, so is running the tools you know and love, such as ipconfig and notepad. Type the command name and you'll see results like those shown in Example T-2.

Example T-2. Windows tools and applications such as ipconfig run in PowerShell just as they do in the cmd.exe

```
PS >ipconfig

Windows IP Configuration


Ethernet adapter Wireless Network Connection 4:

        Connection-specific DNS Suffix  . : hsd1.wa.comcast.net.
        IP Address. . . . . . . . . . . : 192.168.1.100
        Subnet Mask . . . . . . . . . . : 255.255.255.0
        Default Gateway . . . . . . . . : 192.168.1.1
PS >notepad
(notepad launches)
```

Entering ipconfig displays the IP addresses of your current network connections. Entering notepad runs—as you'd expect—the Notepad editor that ships with Windows. Try them both on your own machine.

Structured Commands (Cmdlets)

In addition to supporting traditional Windows executables, PowerShell introduces a powerful new type of command called a *cmdlet* (pronounced *command-let*). All cmdlets are named in a *Verb-Noun* pattern, such as Get-Process, Get-Content, and Stop-Process.

```
PS >Get-Process -Name lsass

Handles  NPM(K)    PM(K)     WS(K) VM(M)   CPU(s)     Id ProcessName
-------  ------    -----     ----- -----   ------     -- -----------
    668      13     6228      1660    46            932 lsass
```

In this example, you provide a value to the `ProcessName` parameter to get a specific process by name.

 Once you know the handful of common verbs in PowerShell, learning how to work with new nouns becomes much easier. While you may never have worked with a certain object before (such as a Service), the standard `Get`, `Set`, `Start`, and `Stop` actions still apply. For a list of these common verbs, see Table D-1.

You don't always have to type these full cmdlet names, however. PowerShell lets you use the Tab key to auto-complete cmdlet names and parameter names:

```
PS >Get-Pr<TAB> -N<TAB> lsass
```

For quick interactive use, even that may be too much typing. To help improve your efficiency, PowerShell defines aliases for all common commands and lets you define your own. In addition to alias names, PowerShell only requires that you type enough of the parameter name to disambiguate it from the rest of the parameters in that cmdlet. PowerShell is also case-insensitive. Using the built-in `gps` alias (that represents the `Get-Process` cmdlet) along with parameter shortening, you can instead type:

```
PS >gps -n lsass
```

Going even further, PowerShell supports *positional parameters* on cmdlets. Positional parameters let you provide parameter values in a certain position on the command line, rather than having to specify them by name. The `Get-Process` cmdlet takes a process name as its first positional parameter. This parameter even supports wildcards:

```
PS >gps l*s
```

Deep Integration of Objects

PowerShell begins to flex more of its muscle as you explore the way it handles structured data and richly functional objects. For example, the following command generates a simple text string. Since nothing captures that output, PowerShell displays it to you:

```
PS >"Hello World"
Hello World
```

The string you just generated is, in fact, a fully functional object from the .NET Framework. For example, you can access its `Length` property, which tells you how many characters are in the string. To access a property, you place a dot between the object and its property name:

```
PS >"Hello World".Length
11
```

All PowerShell commands that produce output generate that output as objects, as well. For example, the Get-Process cmdlet generates a System.Diagnostics.Process object, which you can store in a variable. In PowerShell, variable names start with a $ character. If you have an instance of *Notepad* running, the following command stores a reference to it:

```
$process = Get-Process notepad
```

Since this is a fully functional Process object from the .NET Framework, you can call methods on that object to perform actions on it. This command calls the Kill() method, which stops a process. To access a method, you place a dot between the object and its method name:

```
$process.Kill()
```

PowerShell supports this functionality more directly through the Stop-Process cmdlet, but this example demonstrates an important point about your ability to interact with these rich objects.

Administrators As First-Class Users

While PowerShell's support for objects from the .NET Framework quickens the pulse of most users, PowerShell continues to focus strongly on administrative tasks. For example, PowerShell supports MB (for megabyte) and GB (for gigabyte) as some of the standard administrative constants. For example, how many disks will it take to back up a 40GB hard drive to CD-ROM?

```
PS >40GB / 650MB
63.0153846153846
```

Just because PowerShell is an administrator-focused shell doesn't mean you can't still use the .NET Framework for administrative tasks though! In fact, PowerShell makes a great calendar. For example, is 2008 a leap year? PowerShell can tell you:

```
PS >[DateTime]::IsLeapYear(2008)
True
```

Going further, how might you determine how much time remains until summer? The following command converts "06/21/2008" (the start of summer) to a date, and then subtracts the current date from that. It stores the result in the $result variable, and then accesses the TotalDays property.

```
PS >$result = [DateTime] "06/21/2008" - [DateTime]::Now
PS >$result.TotalDays
283.0549285662616
```

Composable Commands

Whenever a command generates output, you can use a *pipeline character* (|) to pass that output directly to another command as input. If the second command understands the objects produced by the first command, it can operate on the results. You can chain together many commands this way, creating powerful compositions out of a few simple operations. For example, the following command gets all items in the Path1 directory and moves them to the Path2 directory:

```
Get-Item Path1\* | Move-Item -Destination Path2
```

You can create even more complex commands by adding additional cmdlets to the pipeline. In Example T-3, the first command gets all processes running on the system. It passes those to the Where-Object cmdlet, which runs a comparison against each incoming item. In this case, the comparison is $_.Handles -ge 500, which checks whether the Handles property of the current object (represented by the $_ variable) is greater than or equal to 500. For each object in which this comparison holds true, you pass the results to the Sort-Object cmdlet, asking it to sort items by their Handles property. Finally, you pass the objects to the Format-Table cmdlet to generate a table that contains the Handles, Name, and Description of the process.

Example T-3. You can build more complex PowerShell commands by using pipelines to link cmdlets, as shown in this example with Get-Process, Where-Object, Sort-Object, and Format-Table

```
PS >Get-Process |
>>    Where-Object { $_.Handles -ge 500 } |
>>    Sort-Object Handles |
>>    Format-Table Handles,Name,Description -Auto
>>

Handles Name     Description
------- ----     -----------
    588 winlogon
    592 svchost
    667 lsass
    725 csrss
    742 System
    964 WINWORD  Microsoft Office Word
   1112 OUTLOOK  Microsoft Office Outlook
   2063 svchost
```

Techniques to Protect You from Yourself

While aliases, wildcards, and composable pipelines are powerful, their use in commands that modify system information can easily be nerve-wracking. After all, what does this command do? Think about it, but don't try it just yet:

```
PS >gps [b-t]*[c-r] | Stop-Process
```

It appears to stop all processes that begin with the letters b through t and end with the letters c through r. How can you be sure? Let PowerShell tell you. For commands that modify data, PowerShell supports –WhatIf and –Confirm parameters that let you see what a command *would* do:

```
PS >gps [b-t]*[c-r] | Stop-Process -whatif
What if: Performing operation "Stop-Process" on Target "ctfmon (812)".
What if: Performing operation "Stop-Process" on Target "Ditto (1916)".
What if: Performing operation "Stop-Process" on Target "dsamain (316)".
What if: Performing operation "Stop-Process" on Target "ehrecvr (1832)".
What if: Performing operation "Stop-Process" on Target "ehSched (1852)".
What if: Performing operation "Stop-Process" on Target "EXCEL (2092)".
What if: Performing operation "Stop-Process" on Target "explorer (1900)".
(...)
```

In this interaction, using the –whatif parameter with the Stop-Process pipelined command lets you preview which processes on your system will be stopped before you actually carry out the operation.

Note that this example is not a dare! In the words of one reviewer:

> Not only did it stop everything, but on Vista, it forced a shutdown with only one minute warning!
>
> It was very funny though... At least I had enough time to save everything first!

Common Discovery Commands

While reading through a guided tour is helpful, I find that most learning happens in an ad hoc fashion. To find all commands that match a given wildcard, use the Get-Command cmdlet. For example, by entering the following, you can find out which PowerShell commands (and Windows applications) contain the word *process*.

```
PS >Get-Command *process*

CommandType     Name              Definition
-----------     ----              ----------
Cmdlet          Get-Process       Get-Process [[-Name] <Str...
Application     qprocess.exe      c:\windows\system32\qproc...
Cmdlet          Stop-Process      Stop-Process [-Id] <Int32...
```

To see what a command such as Get-Process does, use the Get-Help cmdlet, like this:

```
PS >Get-Help Get-Process
```

Since PowerShell lets you work with objects from the .NET Framework, it provides the Get-Member cmdlet to retrieve information about the properties and methods that an object, such as a .NET System.String, supports. Piping a string to the Get-Member command displays its type name and its members:

```
PS >"Hello World" | Get-Member


    TypeName: System.String

Name                MemberType           Definition
----                ----------           ----------
(...)
PadLeft             Method               System.String PadLeft(Int32 tota...
PadRight            Method               System.String PadRight(Int32 tot...
Remove              Method               System.String Remove(Int32 start...
Replace             Method               System.String Replace(Char oldCh...
Split               Method               System.String[] Split(Params Cha...
StartsWith          Method               System.Boolean StartsWith(String...
Substring           Method               System.String Substring(Int32 st...
ToCharArray         Method               System.Char[] ToCharArray(), Sys...
ToLower             Method               System.String ToLower(), System....
ToLowerInvariant    Method               System.String ToLowerInvariant()
ToString            Method               System.String ToString(), System...
ToUpper             Method               System.String ToUpper(), System....
ToUpperInvariant    Method               System.String ToUpperInvariant()
Trim                Method               System.String Trim(Params Char[]...
TrimEnd             Method               System.String TrimEnd(Params Cha...
TrimStart           Method               System.String TrimStart(Params C...
Chars               ParameterizedProperty System.Char Chars(Int32 index) {...
Length              Property             System.Int32 Length {get;}
```

Ubiquitous Scripting

PowerShell makes no distinction between the commands typed at the command line and the commands written in a script. Your favorite cmdlets work in scripts and your favorite scripting techniques (e.g., the foreach statement) work directly on the command line. For example, to add up the handle count for all running processes:

```
PS >$handleCount - 0
PS >foreach($process in Get-Process) { $handleCount += $process.Handles }
PS >$handleCount
19403
```

While PowerShell provides a command (Measure-Object) to measure statistics about collections, this short example shows how PowerShell lets you apply techniques that normally require a separate scripting or programming language.

In addition to using PowerShell scripting keywords, you can also create and work directly with objects from the .NET Framework. PowerShell becomes almost like the C# immediate mode in Visual Studio. Example T-4 shows how PowerShell lets you easily interact with the .NET Framework.

Example T-4. Using objects from the .NET Framework to retrieve a web page and process its content

```
PS >$webClient = New-Object System.Net.WebClient
PS >$content = $webClient.DownloadString("http://blogs.msdn.com/PowerShell/rss.aspx")
PS >$content.Substring(0,1000)
```

Example T-4. Using objects from the .NET Framework to retrieve a web page and process its content

```
<?xml version="1.0" encoding="UTF-8" ?>
<?xml-stylesheet type="text/xsl" href="http://blogs.msdn.com/utility/FeedS
tylesheets/rss.xsl" media="screen"?><rss version="2.0" xmlns:dc="http://pu
rl.org/dc/elements/1.1/" xmlns:slash="http://purl.org/rss/1.0/modules/slas
h/" xmlns:wfw="http://wellformedweb.org/CommentAPI/"><channel><title>Windo
(...)
```

Ad Hoc Development

By blurring the lines between interactive administration and writing scripts, the history buffer of PowerShell sessions quickly become the basis for ad-hoc script development. In this example, you call the Get-History cmdlet to retrieve the history of your session. For each of those items, you get its CommandLine property (the thing you typed) and send the output to a new script file.

```
PS >Get-History | Foreach-Object { $_.CommandLine } > c:\temp\script.ps1
PS >notepad c:\temp\script.ps1
(save the content you want to keep)
PS >c:\temp\script.ps1
```

 If this is the first time you've run a script in PowerShell, you will need to configure your Execution Policy. For more information about selecting an execution policy, see Recipe 16.1, Enable Scripting Through an Execution Policy" in Chapter 16.

Bridging Technologies

We've seen how PowerShell lets you to fully leverage the .NET Framework in your tasks, but its support for common technologies stretches even further. As Example T-5 shows, PowerShell supports XML:

Example T-5. Working with XML content in PowerShell

```
PS >$xmlContent = [xml] $content
PS >$xmlContent

xml                     xml-stylesheet          rss
---                     --------------          ---
                                                rss


PS >$xmlContent.rss


version : 2.0
dc      : http://purl.org/dc/elements/1.1/
slash   : http://purl.org/rss/1.0/modules/slash/
wfw     : http://wellformedweb.org/CommentAPI/
```

```
channel : channel


PS >$xmlContent.rss.channel.item | select Title

title
-----
CMD.exe compatibility
Time Stamping Log Files
Microsoft Compute Cluster now has a PowerShell Provider and Cmdlets
The Virtuous Cycle: .NET Developers using PowerShell
(...)
```

Powershell also lets you work with Windows Management Instrumentation (WMI):

```
PS >Get-WmiObject Win32_Bios


SMBIOSBIOSVersion : ASUS A7N8X Deluxe ACPI BIOS Rev 1009
Manufacturer      : Phoenix Technologies, LTD
Name              : Phoenix - AwardBIOS v6.00PG
SerialNumber      : xxxxxxxxxxx
Version           : Nvidia - 42302e31
```

or, as Example T-6 shows, Active Directory Service Interfaces (ADSI):

Example T-6. Working with Active Directory in PowerShell

```
PS >[ADSI] "WinNT://./Administrator" | Format-List *


UserFlags            : {66113}
MaxStorage           : {-1}
PasswordAge          : {19550795}
PasswordExpired      : {0}
LoginHours           : {255 255 255 255 255 255 255 255 255 255 255
                       255 255 255 255 255 255 255 255 255 255}
FullName             : {}
Description          : {Built-in account for administering the compu
                       ter/domain}
BadPasswordAttempts  : {0}
LastLogin            : {5/21/2007 3:00:00 AM}
HomeDirectory        : {}
LoginScript          : {}
Profile              : {}
HomeDirDrive         : {}
Parameters           : {}
PrimaryGroupID       : {513}
Name                 : {Administrator}
MinPasswordLength    : {0}
MaxPasswordAge       : {3710851}
MinPasswordAge       : {0}
```

```
PasswordHistoryLength      : {0}
AutoUnlockInterval         : {1800}
LockoutObservationInterval : {1800}
MaxBadPasswordsAllowed     : {0}
RasPermissions             : {1}
objectSid                  : {1 5 0 0 0 0 0 5 21 0 0 0 121 227 252 83 122
                             130 50 34 67 23 10 50 244 1 0 0}
```

or, as Example T-7 shows, even scripting traditional COM objects:

Example T-7. Working with COM objects in PowerShell

```
PS >$firewall = New-Object -com HNetCfg.FwMgr
PS >$firewall.LocalPolicy.CurrentProfile


Type                                          : 1
FirewallEnabled                               : True
ExceptionsNotAllowed                          : False
NotificationsDisabled                         : False
UnicastResponsesToMulticastBroadcastDisabled  : False
RemoteAdminSettings                           : System.__ComObject
IcmpSettings                                  : System.__ComObject
GloballyOpenPorts                             : {Media Center Extender Serv
                                                ice, Remote Media Center Ex
                                                perience, Adam Test Instanc
                                                e, QWAVE...}
Services                                      : {File and Printer Sharing,
                                                UPnP Framework, Remote Desk
                                                top}
AuthorizedApplications                        : {Remote Assistance, Windows
                                                 Messenger, Media Center, T
                                                rillian...}
```

Namespace Navigation Through Providers

Another avenue PowerShell provides for working with the system is *providers*. PowerShell providers let you navigate and manage data stores using the same techniques you already use to work with the filesystem, as illustrated in Example T-8.

Example T-8. Navigating the filesystem

```
PS >Set-Location c:\
PS >Get-ChildItem


    Directory: Microsoft.PowerShell.Core\FileSystem::C:\
```

Example T-8. Navigating the filesystem (continued)

```
Mode              LastWriteTime      Length Name
----              -------------      ------ ----
d----        11/2/2006    4:36 AM           $WINDOWS.~BT
d----         5/8/2007    8:37 PM           Blurpark
d----        11/29/2006   2:47 PM           Boot
d----        11/28/2006   2:10 PM           DECCHECK
d----        10/7/2006    4:30 PM           Documents and Settings
d----         5/21/2007   6:02 PM           F&SC-demo
d----         4/2/2007    7:21 PM           Inetpub
d----         5/20/2007   4:59 PM           Program Files
d----         5/21/2007  11:47 PM           temp
d----         5/21/2007   8:55 PM           Windows
-a---         1/7/2006   10:37 PM         0 autoexec.bat
-ar-s        11/29/2006   1:39 PM      8192 BOOTSECT.BAK
-a---         1/7/2006   10:37 PM         0 config.sys
-a---         5/1/2007    8:43 PM     33057 RUU.log
-a---         4/2/2007    7:46 PM      2487 secedit.INTEG.RAW
```

This also works on the registry, as shown in Example T-9:

Example T-9. Navigating the registry

```
PS >Set-Location HKCU:\Software\Microsoft\Windows\
PS >Get-ChildItem


    Hive: Microsoft.PowerShell.Core\Registry::HKEY_CURRENT_USER\Software\Mi
crosoft\Windows

SKC  VC Name                        Property
---  -- ----                        --------
 30   1 CurrentVersion              {ISC}
  3   1 Shell                       {BagMRU Size}
  4   2 ShellNoRoam                 {(default), BagMRU Size}


PS >Set-Location CurrentVersion\Run
PS >Get-ItemProperty .


(...)
FolderShare            : "C:\Program Files\FolderShare\FolderShare.exe" /ba
                         ckground
TaskSwitchXP           : d:\lee\tools\TaskSwitchXP.exe
ctfmon.exe             : C:\WINDOWS\system32\ctfmon.exe
Ditto                  : C:\Program Files\Ditto\Ditto.exe
(...)
```

Or even the machine's certificate store, as Example T-10 illustrates.

Example T-10. Navigating the certificate store

```
PS >Set-Location cert:\CurrentUser\Root
PS >Get-ChildItem


    Directory: Microsoft.PowerShell.Security\Certificate::CurrentUser\Root


Thumbprint                               Subject
----------                               -------
CDD4EEAE6000AC7F40C3802C171E30148030C072 CN=Microsoft Root Certificate...
BE36A4562FB2EE05DBB3D32323ADF445084ED656 CN=Thawte Timestamping CA, OU...
A43489159A520F0D93D032CCAF37E7FE20A8B419 CN=Microsoft Root Authority, ...
9FE47B4D05D46E8066BAB1D1BFC9E48F1DBE6B26 CN=PowerShell Local Certifica...
7F88CD7223F3C813818C994614A89C99FA3B5247 CN=Microsoft Authenticode(tm)...
245C97DF7514E7CF2DF8BE72AE957B9E04741E85 OU=Copyright (c) 1997 Microso...
(...)
```

Much, Much More

As exciting as this guided tour was, it barely scratches the surface of how you can use PowerShell to improve your productivity and systems management skills. For more information about getting started in PowerShell, see Chapter 1, *The Windows Power-Shell Interactive Shell*.

Fundamentals

The Windows PowerShell Interactive Shell

1.0   Introduction

Above all else, the design of Windows PowerShell places priority on its use as an efficient and powerful interactive shell. Even its scripting language plays a critical role in this effort, as it too heavily favors interactive use.

What surprises most people when they first launch PowerShell is its similarity to the command prompt that has long existed as part of Windows. Familiar tools continue to run. Familiar commands continue to run. Even familiar hotkeys are the same. Supporting this familiar user interface, though, is a powerful engine that lets you accomplish once cumbersome administrative and scripting tasks with ease.

This chapter introduces PowerShell from the perspective of its interactive shell.

1.1   Run Programs, Scripts, and Existing Tools

Problem

You rely on a lot of effort invested in your current tools. You have traditional executables, Perl scripts, VBScript, and of course, a legacy build system that has organically grown into a tangled mess of batch files. You want to use PowerShell, but don't want to give up everything you already have.

Solution

To run a program, script, batch file, or other executable command in the system's path, enter its filename. For these executable types, the extension is optional:

```
Program.exe arguments
ScriptName.ps1 arguments
BatchFile.cmd arguments
```

To run a command that contains a space in its name, enclose its filename in single-quotes (') and precede the command with an ampersand (&), known in PowerShell as the *Invoke operator*:

```
& 'C:\Program Files\Program\Program.exe' arguments
```

To run a command in the current directory, place .\ in front of its filename:

```
.\Program.exe arguments
```

To run a command with spaces in its name from the current directory, precede it with both an ampersand and .\:

```
& '.\Program With Spaces.exe' arguments
```

Discussion

In this case, the solution is mainly to use your current tools as you always have. The only difference is that you run them in the PowerShell interactive shell, rather than *cmd.exe*.

The final three tips in the solution merit special attention. They are the features of PowerShell that many new users stumble on when it comes to running programs. The first is running commands that contain spaces. In *cmd.exe*, the way to run a command that contains spaces is to surround it with quotes:

```
"C:\Program Files\Program\Program.exe"
```

In PowerShell, though, placing text inside quotes is part of a feature that lets you evaluate complex expressions at the prompt, as shown in Example 1-1.

Example 1-1. Evaluating expressions at the PowerShell prompt

```
PS >1 + 1
2
PS >26 * 1.15
29.9
PS >"Hello" + " World"
Hello World
PS >"Hello World"
Hello World
PS >"C:\Program Files\Program\Program.exe"
C:\Program Files\Program\Program.exe
PS >
```

So, a program name in quotes is no different from any other string in quotes. It's just an expression. As shown previously, the way to run a command in a string is to precede that string with the *invoke* (&) operator. If the command you want to run is a batch file that modifies its environment, see Recipe 1.8, "Program: Retain Changes to Environment Variables Set by a Batch File."

By default, PowerShell's security policies prevent scripts from running. Once you begin writing or using scripts, though, you should configure this policy to something less restrictive. For information on how to configure your execution policy, see Recipe 16.1, "Enable Scripting Through an Execution Policy."

The second command that new users (and seasoned veterans before coffee!) sometimes stumble on is running commands from the current directory. In *cmd.exe*, the current directory is considered part of the path—the list of directories that Windows searches to find the program name you typed. If you are in the *C:\Programs* directory, cmd.exe looks in *C:\Programs* (among other places) for applications to run.

PowerShell, like most Unix shells, requires that you explicitly state your desire to run a program from the current directory. To do that, you use the .\Program.exe syntax, as shown previously. This prevents malicious users on your system from littering your hard drive with evil programs that have names similar to (or the same as) commands you might run while visiting that directory.

To save themselves from having to type the location of commonly used scripts and programs, many users put these utilities along with their PowerShell scripts in a "tools" directory, which they add to their system's path. If PowerShell can find a script or utility in your system's path, you do not need to explicitly specify its location.

Scripts and examples from this book are available at *http://www.oreilly.com/catalog/9780596528492*.

To learn how to write a PowerShell script, see Recipe 10.1, "Write a Script.

See Also

- Recipe 1.8, "Program: Retain Changes to Environment Variables Set by a Batch File"
- Recipe 10.1, "Write a Script
- Recipe 16.1, "Enable Scripting Through an Execution Policy"

1.2   Run a PowerShell Command

Problem

You want to run a PowerShell command.

Solution

To run a PowerShell command, type its name at the command prompt. For example:

```
PS >Get-Process

Handles  NPM(K)    PM(K)    WS(K) VM(M)   CPU(s)     Id ProcessName
-------  ------    -----    ----- -----   ------     -- -----------
    133       5    11760     7668    46          1112 audiodg
    184       5    33248      508    93          1692 avgamsvr
    143       7    31852      984    97          1788 avgemc
```

Discussion

The Get-Process command is an example of a native PowerShell command, called a *cmdlet*. As compared to traditional commands, cmdlets provide significant benefits to both administrators and developers:

- They share a common and regular command-line syntax.
- They support rich pipeline scenarios (using the output of one command as the input of another).
- They produce easily manageable object-based output, rather than error-prone plain text output.

Because the Get-Process cmdlet generates rich object-based output, you can use its output for many process-related tasks.

The Get-Process cmdlet is just one of the many that PowerShell supports. See Recipe 1.4, "Find a Command to Accomplish a Task" to learn techniques for finding additional commands that PowerShell supports.

For more information about working with classes from the .NET Framework, see Recipe 3.4, "Work with .NET Objects."

See Also

- Recipe 1.4, "Find a Command to Accomplish a Task"
- Recipe 3.4, "Work with .NET Objects"

1.3   Customize Your Shell, Profile, and Prompt

Problem

You want to customize PowerShell's interactive experience with a personalized prompt, aliases, and more.

Solution

When you want to customize aspects of PowerShell, place those customizations in your personal profile script. PowerShell provides easy access to this profile script by storing its location in the $profile variable.

By default, PowerShell's security policies prevent scripts (including your profile) from running. Once you begin writing scripts, though, you should configure this policy to something less restrictive. For information on how to configure your execution policy, see Recipe 16.1, "Enable Scripting Through an Execution Policy."

To create a new profile (and overwrite one if it already exists):

```
New-Item -type file -force $profile
```

To edit your profile:

```
notepad $profile
```

To see your profile file:

```
Get-ChildItem $profile
```

Once you create a profile script, you can add a function called Prompt that returns a string. PowerShell displays the output of this function as your command-line prompt.

```
function Prompt
{
    "PS [$env:COMPUTERNAME] >"
}
```

This example prompt displays your computer name, and look like: PS [LEE-DESK]>

You may also find it helpful to add aliases to your profile. Aliases let you to refer to common commands by a name that you choose. Personal profile scripts let you automatically define aliases, functions, variables, or any other customizations that you might set interactively from the PowerShell prompt. Aliases are among the most common customizations, as they let you refer to PowerShell commands (and your own scripts) by a name that is easier to type.

If you want to define an alias for a command but also need to modify the parameters to that command, then define a function instead.

For example:

```
Set-Alias new New-Object
Set-Alias iexplore 'C:\Program Files\Internet Explorer\iexplore.exe'
```

Your changes will become effective once you save your profile and restart Power-Shell. To reload your profile immediately, run the command:

```
. $profile
```

Functions are also very common customizations, with the most popular of those being the Prompt function.

Discussion

Although the Prompt function returns a simple string, you can also use the function for more complex tasks. For example, many users update their console window title (by changing the $host.UI.RawUI.WindowTitle variable) or use the Write-Host cmdlet to output the prompt in color. If your prompt function handles the screen output itself, it still needs to return a string (for example, a single space) to prevent Power-Shell from using its default. If you don't want this extra space to appear in your prompt, add an extra space at the end of your Write-Host command and return the backspace ("`b") character, as shown in Example 1-2.

Example 1-2. An example PowerShell prompt

```
function Prompt
{
    $id = 1
    $historyItem = Get-History -Count 1
    if($historyItem)
    {
        $id = $historyItem.Id + 1
    }

    Write-Host -ForegroundColor DarkGray "`n[$(Get-Location)]"
    Write-Host -NoNewLine "PS:$id > "
    $host.UI.RawUI.WindowTitle = "$(Get-Location)"

    "`b"
}
```

In addition to showing the current location, this prompt also shows the ID for that command in your history. This lets you locate and invoke past commands with relative ease:

```
[C:\]
PS:73 >5 * 5
25

[C:\]
PS:74 >1 + 1
2

[C:\]
PS:75 >Invoke-History 73
5 * 5
```

```
25

[C:\]
PS:76 >
```

Although the profile referenced by $profile is the one you will almost always want
to use, PowerShell actually supports four separate profile scripts. For further details
of these scripts (along with other shell customization options), see "Common Customization Points" in Appendix A.

See Also

- Recipe 16.1, "Enable Scripting Through an Execution Policy."
- "Common Customization Points" in Appendix A

1.4   Find a Command to Accomplish a Task

Problem

You want to accomplish a task in PowerShell but don't know the command or
cmdlet to accomplish that task.

Solution

Use the Get-Command cmdlet to search for and investigate commands.

To get the summary information about a specific command, specify the command
name as an argument:

```
Get-Command CommandName
```

To get the detailed information about a specific command, pipe the output of Get-
Command to the Format-List cmdlet:

```
Get-Command CommandName | Format-List
```

To search for all commands with a name that contains *text*, surround the text with
asterisk characters:

```
Get-Command *text*
```

To search for all commands that use the Get verb, supply Get to the -Verb parameter:

```
Get-Command -Verb Get
```

To search for all commands that act on a service, supply Service to the -Noun
parameter:

```
Get-Command -Noun Service
```

Discussion

One of the benefits that PowerShell provides administrators is the consistency of its command names. All PowerShell commands (called *cmdlets*) follow a regular *Verb-Noun* pattern. For example: Get-Process, Get-EventLog, and Set-Location. The verbs come from a relatively small set of standard verbs (as listed in Appendix D, *Standard PowerShell Verbs*), and describe what action the cmdlet takes. The nouns are specific to the cmdlet and describe what the cmdlet acts on.

Knowing this philosophy, you can easily learn to work with groups of cmdlets. If you want to start a service on the local machine, the standard verb for that is Start. A good guess would be to first try Start-Service (which in this case would be correct), but typing Get-Command -Verb Start would also be an effective way to see what things you can start. Going the other way, you can see what actions are supported on services by typing Get-Command -Noun Service.

See Recipe 1.5, "Get Help on a Command" for a way to list all commands along with a brief description of what they do.

The Get-Command cmdlet is one of the three commands you will use most commonly as you explore Windows PowerShell. The other two commands are Get-Help and Get-Member.

There is one important point when it comes to looking for a PowerShell command to accomplish a task. Many times, that PowerShell command does not exist, because the task is best accomplished the same way it always was—shutdown.exe to reboot a machine, netstat.exe to list protocol statistics and current TCP/IP network connections, and many more.

For more information about the Get-Command cmdlet, type **Get-Help Get-Command**.

See Also

- Recipe 1.5, "Get Help on a Command"

1.5   Get Help on a Command

Problem

You want to learn about how a specific command works and how to use it.

Solution

The command that provides help and usage information about a command is called Get-Help. It supports several different views of the help information, depending on your needs.

To get the summary of help information for a specific command, provide the command's name as an argument to the Get-Help cmdlet. This primarily includes its synopsis, syntax, and detailed description:

```
Get-Help CommandName
```

or

```
CommandName -?
```

To get the detailed help information for a specific command, supply the –Detailed flag to the Get-Help cmdlet. In addition to the summary view, this also includes its parameter descriptions and examples:

```
Get-Help CommandName -Detailed
```

To get the full help information for a specific command, supply the –Full flag to the Get-Help cmdlet. In addition to the detailed view, this also includes its full parameter descriptions and additional notes:

```
Get-Help CommandName -Full
```

To get only the examples for a specific command, supply the –Examples flag to the Get-Help cmdlet:

```
Get-Help CommandName -Examples
```

Discussion

The Get-Help cmdlet is the primary way to interact with the help system in PowerShell. Like the Get-Command cmdlet, the Get-Help cmdlet supports wildcards. If you want to list all commands that match a certain pattern (for example, *process*), you can simply type **Get-Help *process***.

 To generate a list of all cmdlets along with a brief synopsis, run the following command:

```
Get-Help * | Select-Object Name,Synopsis | Format-Table -Auto
```

If the pattern matches only a single command, PowerShell displays the help for that command. Although wildcarding is a helpful way to search PowerShell help, see Recipe 1.6, "Program: Search Help for Text" for a script that lets you search the help content for a specified pattern.

The Get-Help cmdlet is one of the three commands you will use most commonly as you explore Windows PowerShell. The other two commands are Get-Command and Get-Member.

For more information about the Get-Help cmdlet, type **Get-Help Get-Help**.

See Also

- Recipe 1.6, "Program: Search Help for Text"

1.6 Program: Search Help for Text

Both the Get-Command and Get-Help cmdlets let you search for command names that match a given pattern. However, when you don't know exactly what portions of a command name you are looking for, you will more often have success searching through the help *content* for an answer. On Unix systems, this command is called Apropos. Similar functionality does not exist as part of the PowerShell's help facilities, however.

That doesn't need to stop us, though, as we can write the functionality ourselves.

To run this program, supply a search string to the Search-Help script (given in Example 1-3). The search string can be either simple text or a regular expression. The script then displays the name and synopsis of all help topics that match. To see the help content for that topic, use the Get-Help cmdlet.

Example 1-3. Search-Help.ps1

```
##############################################################################
##
## Search-Help.ps1
##
## Search the PowerShell help documentation for a given keyword or regular
## expression.
##
## Example:
##    Search-Help hashtable
##    Search-Help "(datetime|ticks)"
##############################################################################

param($pattern = $(throw "Please specify content to search for"))

$helpNames = $(Get-Help * | Where-Object { $_.Category -ne "Alias" })

foreach($helpTopic in $helpNames)
{
   $content = Get-Help -Full $helpTopic.Name | Out-String
   if($content -match $pattern)
   {
      $helpTopic | Select-Object Name,Synopsis
   }
}
```

For more information about running scripts, see Recipe 1.1, "Run Programs, Scripts, and Existing Tools."

See Also

- Recipe 1.1, "Run Programs, Scripts, and Existing Tools"

1.7 Invoke a PowerShell Script From Outside PowerShell

Problem

You want to invoke a PowerShell script from a batch file, a logon script, scheduled task, or any other non-PowerShell application.

Solution

Launch PowerShell.exe in the following way:

```
PowerShell "& 'full path to script' arguments"
```

For example,

```
PowerShell "& 'c:\shared scripts\Get-Report.ps1' Hello World"
```

Discussion

Supplying a single string argument to *PowerShell.exe* invokes PowerShell, runs the command as though you had typed it in the interactive shell, and then exits. Since the path to a script often contains spaces, you invoke the script by placing its name between single quotes, and after the & character. If the script name does not contain spaces, you can omit the single quotes and & character. This technique lets you invoke a PowerShell script as the target of a logon script, advanced file association, scheduled task and more.

> If you are the author of the program that needs to run PowerShell scripts or commands, PowerShell lets you call these scripts and commands much more easily than calling its command-line interface. For more information about this approach, see Recipe 15.13, "Add PowerShell Scripting to Your Own Program."

If the command becomes much more complex than a simple script call, special characters in the application calling PowerShell (such as *cmd.exe*) might interfere with the command you want to send to PowerShell. For this situation, PowerShell supports an EncodedCommand parameter: a Base64 encoded representation of the Unicode string you want to run. Example 1-4 demonstrates how to convert a string containing PowerShell commands to a Base64 encoded form.

Example 1-4. Converting PowerShell commands into a Base64 encoded form

```
$commands = '1..10 | % { "PowerShell Rocks" }'
$bytes = [System.Text.Encoding]::Unicode.GetBytes($commands)
$encodedString = [Convert]::ToBase64String($bytes)
```

Once you have the encoded string, you can use it as the value of the EncodedCommand parameter, as shown in Example 1-5.

Example 1-5. Launching PowerShell with an encoded command from cmd.exe

```
Microsoft Windows [Version 6.0.6000]
Copyright (c) 2006 Microsoft Corporation.  All rights reserved.

C:\Users\Lee>PowerShell -EncodedCommand MQAuAC4AMQAwACAAfAAgACUAIAB7ACAAIgBQAG8A↵
dwBlAHIAUwBoAGUAbABsACAAUgBvAGMAawBzACIAIAB9AA==
PowerShell Rocks
PowerShell Rocks
PowerShell Rocks
PowerShell Rocks
PowerShell Rocks
PowerShell Rocks
PowerShell Rocks
PowerShell Rocks
PowerShell Rocks
PowerShell Rocks
```

For more information about how to invoke PowerShell scripts, see Recipe 1.1, "Run Programs, Scripts, and Existing Tools."

See Also

- Recipe 1.1, "Run Programs, Scripts, and Existing Tools"
- Recipe 15.13, "Add PowerShell Scripting to Your Own Program"

1.8   Program: Retain Changes to Environment Variables Set by a Batch File

When a batch file modifies an environment variable, *cmd.exe* retains this change even after the script exits. This often causes problems, as one batch file can accidentally pollute the environment of another. That said, batch file authors sometimes intentionally change the global environment to customize the path and other aspects of the environment to suit a specific task.

However, environment variables are private details of a process and disappear when that process exits. This makes the environment customization scripts mentioned above stop working when you run them from PowerShell—just as they fail to work when you run them from another *cmd.exe* (for example, cmd.exe /c MyScript.cmd).

The script in Example 1-6 lets you run batch files that modify the environment and retain their changes even after *cmd.exe* exits. It accomplishes this by storing the environment variables in a text file once the batch file completes, and then setting all those environment variables again in your PowerShell session.

To run this script, type **Invoke-CmdScript** *Scriptname.cmd* or **Invoke-CmdScript** *Scriptname.bat*—whichever extension the batch files uses.

 If this is the first time you've run a script in PowerShell, you will need to configure your Execution Policy. For more information about selecting an execution policy, see Recipe 16.1, "Enable Scripting Through an Execution Policy."

Notice that this script uses the full names for cmdlets: Get-Content, Foreach-Object, Set-Content, and Remove-Item. This makes the script readable and is ideal for scripts that somebody else will read. It is by no means required, though. For quick scripts and interactive use, shorter aliases (such as gc, %, sc, and ri) can make you more productive.

Example 1-6. Invoke-CmdScript.ps1

```
##############################################################################
##
## Invoke-CmdScript.ps1
##
## Invoke the specified batch file (and parameters), but also propagate any
## environment variable changes back to the PowerShell environment that
## called it.
##
## i.e., for an already existing 'foo-that-sets-the-FOO-env-variable.cmd':
##
## PS > type foo-that-sets-the-FOO-env-variable.cmd
## @set FOO=%*
## echo FOO set to %FOO%.
##
## PS > $env:FOO
##
## PS > Invoke-CmdScript "foo-that-sets-the-FOO-env-variable.cmd" Test
##
## C:\Temp>echo FOO set to Test.
## FOO set to Test.
##
## PS > $env:FOO
## Test
##
##############################################################################

param([string] $script, [string] $parameters)
```

Example 1-6. Invoke-CmdScript.ps1 (continued)

```
$tempFile = [IO.Path]::GetTempFileName()

## Store the output of cmd.exe.  We also ask cmd.exe to output
## the environment table after the batch file completes
cmd /c " `"$script`" $parameters && set > `"$tempFile`" "

## Go through the environment variables in the temp file.
## For each of them, set the variable in our local environment.
Get-Content $tempFile | Foreach-Object {
    if($_ -match "^(.*?)=(.*)$")
    {
        Set-Content "env:\$($matches[1])" $matches[2]
    }
}

Remove-Item $tempFile
```

For more information about running scripts, see Recipe 1.1, "Run Programs, Scripts, and Existing Tools."

See Also

- Recipe 1.1, "Run Programs, Scripts, and Existing Tools"
- Recipe 16.1, "Enable Scripting Through an Execution Policy"

1.9   Get the System Date and Time

Problem

You want to get the system date.

Solution

To get the system date, run the command Get-Date.

Discussion

The Get-Date command generates rich object-based output, so you can use its result for many date-related tasks. For example, to determine the current day of the week:

```
PS >$date = Get-Date
PS >$date.DayOfWeek
Sunday
```

For more information about the Get-Date cmdlet, type **Get-Help Get-Date**.

For more information about working with classes from the .NET Framework, see Recipe 3.4, "Work with .NET Objects."

See Also

- Recipe 3.4, "Work with .NET Objects"

1.10   Determine the Status of the Last Command

Problem

You want to get status information about the last command you executed, such as whether it succeeded.

Solution

Use one of the two variables PowerShell provides to determine the status of the last command you executed: the $lastExitCode variable and the $? variable.

$lastExitCode
: A number that represents the exit code/error level of the last script or application that exited

$? (*pronounced "dollar hook"*)
: A Boolean value that represents the success or failure of the last command

Discussion

The $lastExitCode PowerShell variable is similar to the %errorlevel% variable in DOS. It holds the exit code of the last application to exit. This lets you continue to interact with traditional executables (such as ping, findstr, and choice) that use exit codes as a primary communication mechanism. PowerShell also extends the meaning of this variable to include the exit codes of scripts, which can set their status using the exit statement. Example 1-7 demonstrates this interaction.

Example 1-7. Interacting with the $lastExitCode and $? variables

```
PS >ping localhost

Pinging MyComputer [127.0.0.1] with 32 bytes of data:

Reply from 127.0.0.1: bytes=32 time<1ms TTL=128
Reply from 127.0.0.1: bytes=32 time<1ms TTL=128
Reply from 127.0.0.1: bytes=32 time<1ms TTL=128
Reply from 127.0.0.1: bytes=32 time<1ms TTL=128

Ping statistics for 127.0.0.1:
    Packets: Sent = 4, Received = 4, Lost = 0 (0% loss),
Approximate round trip times in milliseconds:
    Minimum = 0ms, Maximum = 0ms, Average = 0ms
PS >$?
True
PS >$lastExitCode
```

Example 1-7. Interacting with the $lastExitCode and $? variables (continued)

```
0
PS >ping missing-host
Ping request could not find host missing-host. Please check the name and try again.
PS >$?
False
PS >$lastExitCode
1
```

The $? variable describes the exit status of the last application in a more general manner. PowerShell sets this variable to False on error conditions such as when:

- An application exits with a non-zero exit code.
- A cmdlet or script writes anything to its error stream.
- A cmdlet or script encounters a terminating error or exception.

For commands that do not indicate an error condition, PowerShell sets the $? variable to True.

1.11 Measure the Duration of a Command

Problem

You want to know how long a command takes to execute.

Solution

To measure the duration of a command, use the Measure-Command cmdlet:

```
PS >Measure-Command { Start-Sleep -Milliseconds 337 }


Days              : 0
Hours             : 0
Minutes           : 0
Seconds           : 0
Milliseconds      : 339
Ticks             : 3392297
TotalDays         : 3.92626967592593E-06
TotalHours        : 9.42304722222222E-05
TotalMinutes      : 0.00565382833333333
TotalSeconds      : 0.3392297
TotalMilliseconds : 339.2297
```

Discussion

In interactive use, it is common to want to measure the duration of a command. An example of this might be running a performance benchmark on an application you've developed. The Measure-Command cmdlet makes this easy to do. Because the command generates rich object-based output, you can use its output for many date-related tasks. See Recipe 3.4, "Work with .NET Objects," for more information.

For more information about the Measure-Command cmdlet, type **Get-Help Measure-Command**.

See Also

*   Recipe 3.4, "Work with .NET Objects"

1.12   Customize the Shell to Improve Your Productivity

Problem

You want to use the PowerShell console more efficiently for copying, pasting, history management, and scrolling.

Solution

Run the commands shown in Example 1-8 to permanently customize your Power-Shell console windows and make many tasks easier.

Example 1-8. Set-ConsoleProperties.ps1

```
Push-Location
Set-Location HKCU:\Console
New-Item '.\%SystemRoot%_system32_WindowsPowerShell_v1.0_powershell.exe'
Set-Location '.\%SystemRoot%_system32_WindowsPowerShell_v1.0_powershell.exe'

New-ItemProperty . ColorTable00 -type DWORD -value 0x00562401
New-ItemProperty . ColorTable07 -type DWORD -value 0x00f0edee
New-ItemProperty . FaceName -type STRING -value "Lucida Console"
New-ItemProperty . FontFamily -type DWORD -value 0x00000036
New-ItemProperty . FontSize -type DWORD -value 0x000c0000
New-ItemProperty . FontWeight -type DWORD -value 0x00000190
New-ItemProperty . HistoryNoDup -type DWORD -value 0x00000000
New-ItemProperty . QuickEdit -type DWORD -value 0x00000001
New-ItemProperty . ScreenBufferSize -type DWORD -value 0x0bb80078
New-ItemProperty . WindowSize -type DWORD -value 0x00320078
Pop-Location
```

These commands customize the console color, font, history storage properties, QuickEdit mode, buffer size, and window size.

With these changes in place, you can also improve your productivity by learning some of the hotkeys for common tasks, as listed in Table 1-1. PowerShell uses the same input facilities as *cmd.exe*, and so brings with it all the input features that you are already familiar with—and some that you aren't!

Table 1-1. Partial list of Windows PowerShell hotkeys

Hotkey	Meaning
Up arrow	Scan backward through your command history.
Down arrow	Scan forward through your command history.
PgUp	Display the first command in your command history.
PgDown	Display the last command in your command history.
Left arrow	Move cursor one character to the left on your command line.
Right arrow	Move cursor one character to the right on your command line.
Home	Move the cursor to the beginning of the command line.
End	Move the cursor to the end of the command line.
Control + Left arrow	Move the cursor one word to the left on your command line.
Control + Right arrow	Move the cursor one word to the right on your command line.

Discussion

When you launch PowerShell from the link on your Windows Start menu, it customizes several aspects of the console window:

- Foreground and background color, to make the console more visually appealing
- QuickEdit mode, to make copying and pasting with the mouse easier
- Buffer size, to make PowerShell retain the output of more commands in your console history

By default, these customizations do not apply when you run PowerShell from the Start → Run dialog. The commands given in the solution section improve the experience by applying these changes to all PowerShell windows that you open.

The hotkeys do, however, apply to all PowerShell windows (and any other application that uses Windows' *cooked* input mode). The most common are given in the in the solution section, but "Common Customization Points" in Appendix A provides the full list.

See Also

- "Common Customization Points" in Appendix A

1.13   Program: Learn Aliases for Common Commands

In interactive use, full cmdlet names (such as Get-ChildItem) are cumbersome and slow to type. Although aliases are much more efficient, it takes awhile to discover them. To learn aliases more easily, you can modify your prompt to remind you of the shorter version of any aliased commands that you use.

This involves two steps:

1. Add the program, `Get-AliasSuggestion.ps1`, shown in Example 1-9, to your tools directory or other directory.

Example 1-9. Get-AliasSuggestion.ps1

```
##############################################################################
##
## Get-AliasSuggestion.ps1
##
## Get an alias suggestion from the full text of the last command
##
## ie:
##
## PS > Get-AliasSuggestion Remove-ItemProperty
## Suggestion: An alias for Remove-ItemProperty is rp
##
##############################################################################

param($lastCommand)

$helpMatches = @()

## Get the alias suggestions
foreach($alias in Get-Alias)
{
    if($lastCommand -match ("\b" +
        [System.Text.RegularExpressions.Regex]::Escape($alias.Definition) + "\b"))
    {
        $helpMatches += "Suggestion: An alias for $($alias.Definition) is $($alias.Name)"
    }
}

$helpMatches
```

2. Add the text from Example 1-10 to the `Prompt` function in your profile. If you do not yet have a `Prompt` function, see Recipe 1.3, "Customize Your Shell, Profile, and Prompt" to learn how to add one. If you already have a prompt function, you only need to add the content from inside the prompt function of Example 1-10.

Example 1-10. A useful prompt to teach you aliases for common commands

```
function Prompt
{
    ## Get the last item from the history
    $historyItem = Get-History -Count 1

    ## If there were any history items
    if($historyItem)
    {
        ## Get the training suggestion for that item
        $suggestions = @(Get-AliasSuggestion $historyItem.CommandLine)
```

Example 1-10. A useful prompt to teach you aliases for common commands (continued)

```
    ## If there were any suggestions
    if($suggestions)
    {
        ## For each suggestion, write it to the screen
        foreach($aliasSuggestion in $suggestions)
        {
            Write-Host "$aliasSuggestion"
        }
        Write-Host ""
    }
}

## Rest of prompt goes here
"PS [$env:COMPUTERNAME] >"
}
```

For more information about running scripts, see Recipe 1.1, "Run Programs, Scripts, and Existing Tools."

See Also

- Recipe 1.1, "Run Programs, Scripts, and Existing Tools"
- Recipe 1.3, "Customize Your Shell, Profile, and Prompt"

1.14   Access and Manage Your Console History

Problem

After working in the shell for awhile, you want to invoke commands from your history, view your command history, and save your command history.

Solution

The shortcuts given in Recipe 1.12, "Customize the Shell to Improve Your Productivity" let you manage your history, but PowerShell offers several features to help you work with your console in even more detail.

To get the most recent commands from your session, use the Get-History cmdlet:

```
Get-History
```

To rerun a specific command from your session history, provide its *Id* to the Invoke-History cmdlet:

```
Invoke-History Id
```

To increase (or limit) the number of commands stored in your session history, assign a new value to the $MaximumHistoryCount variable:

```
$MaximumHistoryCount = Count
```

To save your command history to a file, pipe the output of Get-History to the Export-CliXml cmdlet:

```
Get-History | Export-CliXml Filename
```

To add a previously saved command history to your current session history, call the Import-CliXml cmdlet and then pipe that output to the Add-History cmdlet:

```
Import-CliXml Filename | Add-History
```

Discussion

Unlike the console history hotkeys discussed in Recipe 1.12, "Customize the Shell to Improve Your Productivity" the Get-History cmdlet produces rich objects that represent information about items in your history. Each object contains that item's ID, command line, start of execution time, and end of execution time.

Once you know the ID of a history item (as shown in the output of Get-History), you can pass it to Invoke-History to execute that command again. The example prompt function shown in Recipe 1.3, "Customize Your Shell, Profile, and Prompt" makes working with prior history items easy—as the prompt for each command includes the history ID that will represent it.

The IDs provided by the Get-History cmdlet differ from the IDs given by the Windows console common history hotkeys (such as F7), because their history management techniques differ.

By default, PowerShell stores only the last 64 entries of your command history. If you want to raise or lower this amount, set the $MaximumHistoryCount variable to the size you desire. To make this change permanent, set the variable in your PowerShell profile script. To clear your history, either restart the shell, or temporarily set the $MaximumHistoryCount variable to 1.

See Also

- Recipe 1.3, "Customize Your Shell, Profile, and Prompt"
- Recipe 1.12, "Customize the Shell to Improve Your Productivity"

1.15   Store the Output of a Command into a File

Problem

You want to redirect the output of a pipeline into a file.

Solution

To redirect the output of a command into a file, use either the `Out-File` cmdlet or one of the redirection operators.

`Out-File`:

```
Get-ChildItem | Out-File unicodeFile.txt
Get-Content filename.cs | Out-File -Encoding ASCII file.txt
Get-ChildItem | Out-File-Width 120 unicodeFile.cs
```

Redirection operators:

```
Get-ChildItem > files.txt
Get-ChildItem 2> errors.txt
```

Discussion

The `Out-File` cmdlet and redirection operators share a lot in common—and for the most part, you can use either. The redirection operators are unique because they give the greatest amount of control over redirecting individual streams. The `Out-File` cmdlet is unique primarily because it lets you easily configure the formatting width and encoding.

The default formatting width and the default output encoding are two aspects of output redirection that can sometimes cause difficulty.

The default formatting width sometimes causes problems because redirecting Power-Shell-formatted output into a file is designed to mimic what you see on the screen. If your screen is 80 characters wide, the file will be 80 characters wide as well. Examples of PowerShell-formatted output include directory listings (that are implicitly formatted as a table) as well as any commands that you explicitly format using one of the `Format-*` set of cmdlets. If this causes problems, you can customize the width of the file with the –Width parameter on the `Out-File` cmdlet.

The default output encoding sometimes causes unexpected results because Power-Shell creates all files using the UTF-16 Unicode encoding by default. This allows PowerShell to fully support the entire range of international characters, cmdlets, and output. Although this is a great improvement to traditional shells, it may cause an unwanted surprise when running large search and replace operations on ASCII source code files, for example. To force PowerShell to send its output to a file in the ASCII encoding, use the –Encoding parameter on the `Out-File` cmdlet.

For more information about the `Out-File` cmdlet, type **Get-Help Out-File**. For a full list of supported redirection operators, see "Capturing Output" in Appendix A.

See Also

- "Capturing Output" in Appendix A

1.16   Add Information to the End of a File

Problem

You want to redirect the output of a pipeline into a file but add the information to the end of that file.

Solution

To redirect the output of a command into a file, use either the -Append parameter of the Out-File cmdlet, or one of the appending redirection operators as described in "Capturing Output" in Appendix A. Both support options to append text to the end of a file.

Out-File:

```
Get-ChildItem | Out-File -Append files.txt
```

Redirection operators:

```
Get-ChildItem >> files.txt
```

Discussion

The Out-File cmdlet and redirection operators share a lot in common—and for the most part, you can use either. See the discussion in Recipe 1.15, "Store the Output of a Command into a File" for a more detailed comparison of the two approaches, including reasons that you would pick one over the other.

See Also

- Recipe 1.15, "Store the Output of a Command into a File"
- "Capturing Output" in Appendix A

1.17   Record a Transcript of Your Shell Session

Problem

You want to record a log or transcript of your shell session.

Solution

To record a transcript of your shell session, run the command Start-Transcript *Path*. *Path* is optional and defaults to a filename based on the current system time. By default, PowerShell places this file in the My Documents directory. To stop recording the transcript of your shell system, run the command Stop-Transcript.

Discussion

Although the Get-History cmdlet is helpful, it does not record the output produced during your PowerShell session. To accomplish that, use the Start-Transcript cmdlet. In addition to the Path parameter described previously, the Start-Transcript cmdlet also supports parameters that let you control how PowerShell interacts with the output file.

1.18   Display the Properties of an Item As a List

Problem

You have an item (for example, an error record, directory item, or .NET object), and you want to display detailed information about that object in a list format.

Solution

To display detailed information about an item, pass that item to the Format-List cmdlet. For example, to display an error in list format, type the commands:

```
$currentError = $error[0]
$currentError | Format-List -Force
```

Discussion

The Format-List cmdlet is one of the three PowerShell formatting cmdlets. These cmdlets include Format-Table, Format-List, and Format-Wide. The Format-List cmdlet takes input and displays information about that input as a list. By default, PowerShell takes the list of properties to display from the *.format.ps1xml* files in PowerShell's installation directory. To display all properties of the item, type **Format-List ***. Sometimes, you might type Format-List * but still not get a list of the item's properties. This happens when the item is defined in the *.format.ps1xml* files, but does not define anything to be displayed for the list command. In that case, type **Format-List -Force.**

For more information about the Format-List cmdlet, type **Get-Help Format-List**.

1.19   Display the Properties of an Item As a Table

Problem

You have a set of items (for example, error records, directory items, or .NET objects), and you want to display summary information about them in a table format.

Solution

To display summary information about a set of items, pass those items to the `Format-Table` cmdlet. This is the default type of formatting for sets of items in PowerShell and provides several useful features.

To use PowerShell's default formatting, pipe the output of a cmdlet (such as the *Get-Process* cmdlet) to the `Format-Table` cmdlet:

```
Get-Process | Format-Table
```

To display specific properties (such as *Name* and *WorkingSet*,) in the table formatting, supply those property names as parameters to the `Format-Table` cmdlet:

```
Get-Process | Format-Table Name,WS
```

To instruct PowerShell to format the table in the most readable manner, supply the -Auto flag to the `Format-Table` cmdlet. PowerShell defines "WS" as an alias of the WorkingSet for processes:

```
Get-Process | Format-Table Name,WS -Auto
```

To define a custom column definition (such as a process's *Working Set* in megabytes), supply a custom formatting expression to the `Format-Table` cmdlet:

```
$fields = "Name",@{Label = "WS (MB)"; Expression = {$_.WS / 1mb}; Align = "Right"}
Get-Process | Format-Table $fields -Auto
```

Discussion

The `Format-Table` cmdlet is one of the three PowerShell formatting cmdlets. These cmdlets include `Format-Table`, `Format-List`, and `Format-Wide`. The `Format-Table` cmdlet takes input and displays information about that input as a table. By default, PowerShell takes the list of properties to display from the **.format.ps1xml* files in PowerShell's installation directory. You can display all properties of the items if you type **Format-Table ***, although this is rarely a useful view.

The -Auto parameter to `Format-Table` is a helpful way to automatically format the table to use screen space as efficiently as possible. It does come at a cost, however. To figure out the best table layout, PowerShell needs to examine each item in the incoming set of items. For small sets of items, this doesn't make much difference, but for large sets (such as a recursive directory listing) it does. Without the -Auto parameter, the `Format-Table` cmdlet can display items as soon as it receives them. With the -Auto flag, the cmdlet can only display results after it receives all the input.

Perhaps the most interesting feature of the `Format-Table` cmdlet is illustrated by the last example—the ability to define completely custom table columns. You define a custom table column similarly to the way that you define a custom column list. Rather than specify an existing property of the items, you provide a hashtable. That hashtable includes up to three keys: the column's label, a formatting expression, and alignment. The `Format-Table` cmdlet shows the label as the column header and uses your expression to generate data for that column. The label must be a string, the expression must be a script block, and the alignment must be either "Left", "Center", or "Right". In the expression script block, the $_ variable represents the current item being formatted.

The expression shown in the last example takes the working set of the current item and divides it by 1 megabyte (1 MB).

For more information about the Format-Table cmdlet, type **Get-Help Format-Table**.

For more information about hashtables, see Recipe 11.12, "Create a Hashtable or Associative Array."

For more information about script blocks, see Recipe 10.3, "Write a Script Block."

See Also

- Recipe 10.3, "Write a Script Block"
- Recipe 11.12, "Create a Hashtable or Associative Array"

1.20   Manage the Error Output of Commands

Problem

You want to display detailed information about errors that come from commands.

Solution

To list all errors (up to $MaximumErrorCount) that have occurred in this session, access the $error array:

```
$error
```

To list the last error that occurred in this session, access the first element in the $error array:

```
$error[0]
```

To list detailed information about an error, pipe the error into the Format-List cmdlet with the -Force parameter:

```
$currentError = $error[0]
$currentError | Format-List -Force
```

To list detailed information about the command that caused an error, access its InvocationInfo property:

```
$currentError = $error[0]
$currentError.InvocationInfo
```

To display errors in a more succinct category-based view, change the $errorView variable to "CategoryView":

```
$errorView = "CategoryView"
```

To clear the list of errors collected by PowerShell so far, call the `Clear( )` method on the `$error` variable:

```
$error.Clear( )
```

Discussion

Errors are a simple fact of life in the administrative world. Not all errors mean disaster, though. Because of this, PowerShell separates errors into two categories: nonterminating and terminating.

Nonterminating errors are the most common type of error. They indicate that the cmdlet, script, function, or pipeline encountered an error that it was able to recover from or was able to continue past. An example of a nonterminating error comes from the `Copy-Item` cmdlet. If it fails to copy a file from one location to another, it can still proceed with the rest of the files specified.

A terminating error, on the other hand, indicates a deeper, more fundamental error in the operation. An example of this can again come from the `Copy-Item` cmdlet when you specify invalid command-line parameters.

For more information on how to handle both nonterminating and terminating errors, see Chapter 13, *Tracing and Error Management*.

See Also

- Chapter 13, *Tracing and Error Management*

1.21   Configure Debug, Verbose, and Progress Output

Problem

You want to manage the detailed debug, verbose, and progress output generated by cmdlets and scripts.

Solution

To enable debug output for scripts and cmdlets that generate it:

```
$debugPreference = "Continue"
Start-DebugCommand
```

To enable verbose mode for a cmdlet that checks for the -Verbose parameter:

```
Copy-Item c:\temp\*.txt c:\temp\backup\ -Verbose
```

To disable progress output from a script or cmdlet that generates it:

```
$progressPreference = "SilentlyContinue"
Get-Progress.ps1
```

Discussion

In addition to error output (as described in Recipe 1.20, "Manage the Error Output of Commands"), many scripts and cmdlets generate several other types of output. This includes:

Debug output

Helps you diagnose problems that may arise and can provide a view into the inner workings of a command. You can use the `Write-Debug` cmdlet to produce this type of output in a script or the `WriteDebug( )` method to produce this type of output in a cmdlet. PowerShell displays this output in yellow, unless you customize it through the `$host.PrivateData.Debug*` color configuration variables.

Verbose output

Helps you monitor the actions of commands at a finer level than the default. You can use the `Write-Verbose` cmdlet to produce this type of output in a script or the `WriteVerbose( )` method to produce this type of output in a cmdlet. PowerShell displays this output in yellow, unless you customize it through the `$host.PrivateData.Verbose*` color configuration variables.

Progress output

Helps you monitor the status of long-running commands. You can use the `Write-Progress` cmdlet to produce this type of output in a script or the `WriteProgress( )` method to produce this type of output in a cmdlet. PowerShell displays this output in yellow, unless you customize it through the `$host.PrivateData.Progress*` color configuration variables.

Some cmdlets generate verbose and debug output only if you specify the -Verbose and -Debug parameters, respectively.

To configure the debug, verbose, and progress output of a script or cmdlet, modify the $debugPreference, $verbosePreference, and $progressPreference shell variables. These variables can accept the following values:

SilentlyContinue

Do not display this output.

Stop

Treat this output as an error.

Continue

Display this output.

Inquire

Display a continuation prompt for this output.

See Also

- Recipe 1.20, "Manage the Error Output of Commands"

1.22   Extend Your Shell with Additional Snapins

Problem

You want to use PowerShell cmdlets and providers written by a third party.

Solution

In PowerShell, extensions that contain additional cmdlets and providers are called *snapins*. The author might distribute them with an automated installer but can also distribute them as a standalone PowerShell assembly. PowerShell identifies each snapin by the filename of its assembly and by the snapin name that its author provides.

To use a snapin:

1. Obtain the snapin assembly.

2. Copy it to a secure location on your computer. Since snapins are equivalent to executable programs, pick a location (such as the `Program Files` directory) that provides users read access but not write access.

3. Register the snapin. From the directory that contains the snapin assembly, run `InstallUtil` *SnapinFilename.dll*. This command lets all users on the computer load and run commands defined by the snapin. You can find the `InstallUtil` utility in the .NET Framework's installation directory—commonly `C:\WINDOWS\Microsoft.NET\Framework\v2.0.50727\InstallUtil.exe`.

4. Add the snapin. At a PowerShell prompt (or in your profile file), run the command `Add-PsSnapin  SnapinIdentifier`. To see all available snapin identifiers, review the names listed in the output of the command:

   `Get-PsSnapin -Registered`

5. Use the cmdlets and providers contained in that snapin.

To remove the snapin registration from your system, type `InstallUtil /u` *SnapinFilename.dll*. Once uninstalled, you may delete the files associated with the snapin.

Discussion

For interactive use (or in a profile), the `Add-PsSnapin` cmdlet is the most common way to load an individual snapin. To load a preconfigured list of snapins, though, the following section Recipe 1.23, "Use Console Files to Load and Save Sets of Snapins" offers another option.

One popular source of additional snapins is the PowerShell Community Extensions project, located at *http://www.codeplex.com/PowerShellCX*.

See Also

- Recipe 1.23, "Use Console Files to Load and Save Sets of Snapins"

1.23   Use Console Files to Load and Save Sets of Snapins

Problem

You want to load PowerShell with a set of additional snapins, but do not want to modify your (or the user's) profile.

Solution

Once you register a snapin on your system, you can add its snapin identifier to a PowerShell *console file* to load it. When you specify that file as the -PsConsoleFile parameter of *PowerShell.exe*, PowerShell loads all snapins defined by the console file into the new session.

Save the list of currently loaded snapins to a console file:

```
Export-Console Filename.psc1
```

Load PowerShell with the set of snapins defined in the file *Filename.psc1*:

```
PowerShell -PsConsoleFile Filename.psc1
```

Discussion

PowerShell console files are simple XML files that list the identifiers of already-installed snapins to load. A typical console file looks like Example 1-11.

Example 1-11. A typical PowerShell console file

```xml
<?xml version="1.0" encoding="utf-8"?>
<PSConsoleFile ConsoleSchemaVersion="1.0">
  <PSVersion>1.0</PSVersion>
  <PSSnapIns>
    <PSSnapIn Name="CustomSnapin" />
    <PSSnapIn Name="SecondSnapin" />
  </PSSnapIns>
</PSConsoleFile>
```

Console files should be saved with the file extension *.psc1*.

Although it is common to load the console file with PowerShell's command-line options (in scripts and automated tasks), you can also double-click on the console file to load it interactively.

For more information on how to manage snapins, see Recipe 1.22, "Extend Your Shell with Additional Snapins".

See Also

- Recipe 1.22, "Extend Your Shell with Additional Snapins"

## CHAPTER 2

Pipelines

2.0 Introduction

One of the fundamental concepts in a shell is called the *pipeline*. It also forms the basis of one of the most significant advances that PowerShell brings to the table. A pipeline is a big name for a simple concept—a series of commands where the output of one becomes the input of the next. A pipeline in a shell is much like an assembly line in a factory: it successively refines something as it passes between the stages, as shown in Example 2-1.

Example 2-1. A PowerShell pipeline
```
Get-Process | Where-Object { $_.WorkingSet -gt 500kb } | Sort-Object -Descending Name
```

In PowerShell, you separate each stage in the pipeline with the pipe (|) character.

In Example 2-1, the Get-Process cmdlet generates objects that represent actual processes on the system. These process objects contain information about the process's name, memory usage, process id, and more. The Where-Object cmdlet, then, gets to work directly with those processes, testing easily for those that use more than 500 kb of memory. It passes those along, allowing the Sort-Object cmdlet to also work directly with those processes, sorting them by name in descending order. This brief example illustrates a significant advancement in the power of pipelines: PowerShell passes full-fidelity objects along the pipeline, not their text representations.

In contrast, all other shells pass data as plain text between the stages. Extracting meaningful information from plain-text output turns the authoring of pipelines into a black art. Expressing the previous example in a traditional Unix-based shell is exceedingly difficult and nearly impossible in *cmd.exe*.

Traditional text-based shells make writing pipelines so difficult because they require you to deeply understand the peculiarities of output formatting for each command in the pipeline, as shown in Example 2-2.

Example 2-2. A traditional text-based pipeline

```
lee@trinity:~$ ps -F | awk '{ if($5 > 500) print }' | sort -r -k 64,70
UID          PID  PPID  C    SZ    RSS PSR STIME TTY          TIME CMD
lee         8175  7967  0   965  1036   0 21:51 pts/0    00:00:00 ps -F
lee         7967  7966  0  1173  2104   0 21:38 pts/0    00:00:00 -bash
```

In this example, you have to know that, for every line, group number five represents the memory usage. You have to know another language (that of the awk tool) to filter by that column. Finally, you have to know the column range that contains the process name (columns 64 to 70 on this system) and then provide that to the sort command. And that's just a simple example.

An object-based pipeline opens up enormous possibilities, making system administration both immensely more simple and more powerful.

2.1   Filter Items in a List or Command Output

Problem

You want to filter the items in a list or command output.

Solution

Use the Where-Object cmdlet (which has the standard aliases, where and ?) to select items in a list (or command output) that match a condition you provide.

To list all running processes that have "*search*" in their name, use the -like operator to compare against the process's Name property:

```
Get-Process | Where-Object { $_.Name -like "*Search*" }
```

To list all directories in the current location, test the PsIsContainer property:

```
Get-ChildItem | Where-Object { $_.PsIsContainer }
```

To list all stopped services, use the -eq operator to compare against the service's Status property:

```
Get-Service | Where-Object { $_.Status -eq "Stopped" }
```

Discussion

For each item in its input (which is the output of the previous command), the Where-Object cmdlet evaluates that input against the script block that you specify. If the script block returns True, then the Where-Object cmdlet passes the object along. Otherwise, it does not. A script block is a series of PowerShell commands enclosed by the { and } characters. You can write any PowerShell commands inside the script block. In the script block, the $_ variable represents the current input object. For each item in the incoming set of objects, PowerShell assigns that item to the $_ variable, and then runs your script block. In the preceding examples, this incoming object represents the process, file, or service that the previous cmdlet generated.

This script block can contain a great deal of functionality, if desired. It can combine multiple tests, comparisons, and much more. For more information about script blocks, see Recipe 10.3, "Write a Script Block." For more information about the type of comparisons available to you, see "Comparison Operators" in Appendix A.

For simple filtering, the syntax of the Where-Object cmdlet may sometimes seem overbearing. The following section, Recipe 2.2, "Program: Simplify Most Where-Object Filters," shows a script that can make simple filtering (such as the previous examples) easier to work with.

For complex filtering (for example, the type you would normally rely on a mouse to do with files in an Explorer window), writing the script block to express your intent may be difficult or even infeasible. If this is the case Recipe 2.3, "Program: Interactively Filter Lists of Objects" shows a script that can make manual filtering easier to accomplish.

For more information about the Where-Object cmdlet, type **Get-Help Where-Object**.

See Also

- Recipe 2.2, "Program: Simplify Most Where-Object Filters"
- Recipe 2.3, "Program: Interactively Filter Lists of Objects"
- Recipe 10.3, "Write a Script Block"
- "Comparison Operators" in Appendix A

2.2   Program: Simplify Most Where-Object Filters

The Where-Object cmdlet is incredibly powerful, in that it allows you to filter your output based on arbitrary criteria. For extremely simple filters (such as filtering based only on a comparison to a single property), though, the syntax can get a little ungainly:

```
Get-Process | Where-Object { $_.Handles -gt 1000 }
```

For this type of situation, it is easy to write a script (as shown in Example 2-3) to off-load all the syntax to the script itself:

```
Get-Process | Compare-Property Handles gt 1000
Get-ChildItem | Compare-Property PsIsContainer
```

With a shorter alias, this becomes even easier to type:

```
PS >Set-Alias wheres Compare-Property
PS >Get-ChildItem | wheres Length gt 100
```

Example 2-3 implements this "simple where" functionality. Note that supplying a non-existing operator as the $operator parameter will generate an error message.

Example 2-3. Compare-Property.ps1

```
##############################################################################
## Compare-Property.ps1
##
## Compare the property you provide against the input supplied to the script.
## This provides the functionality of simple Where-Object comparisons without
## the syntax required for that cmdlet.
##
## Example:
##    Get-Process | Compare-Property Handles gt 1000
##    dir | Compare-Property PsIsContainer
##############################################################################
param($property, $operator = "eq", $matchText = "$true")

Begin { $expression = "`$_.$property -$operator `"$matchText`"" }
Process { if(Invoke-Expression $expression) { $_ } }
```

For more information about running scripts see Recipe 1.1, "Run Programs, Scripts,
and Existing Tools."

See Also

- Recipe 1.1, "Run Programs, Scripts, and Existing Tools"

2.3   Program: Interactively Filter Lists of Objects

There are times when the Where-Object cmdlet is too powerful. In those situations,
the Compare-Property script shown in Recipe 2.2, "Program: Simplify Most Where-
Object Filters" provides a much simpler alternative. There are also times when the
Where-Object cmdlet is too simple—when expressing your selection logic as code is
more cumbersome than selecting it manually. In those situations, an interactive filter
can be much more effective.

Example 2-4 implements this interactive filter. It uses several concepts not covered
yet in the book, so feel free to just consider it a neat script for now. To learn more
about a part that you don't yet understand, look it up in the table of contents or the
index.

Example 2-4. Select-FilteredObject.ps1

```
##############################################################################
##
## Select-FilteredObject.ps1
##
## Provides an interactive window to help you select complex sets of objects.
## To do this, it takes all the input from the pipeline, and presents it in a
## notepad window.  Keep any lines that represent objects you want to pass
## down the pipeline, delete the rest, then save the file and exit notepad.
##
```

Example 2-4. Select-FilteredObject.ps1 (continued)

```
## The script then passes the original objects that you kept along the
## pipeline.
##
## Example:
##    Get-Process | Select-FilteredObject | Stop-Process -WhatIf
##
##############################################################################

## PowerShell runs your "begin" script block before it passes you any of the
## items in the pipeline.
begin
{
    ## Create a temporary file
    $filename = [System.IO.Path]::GetTempFileName()

    ## Define a header in a "here-string" that explains how to interact with
    ## the file
    $header = @"
############################################################
## Keep any lines that represent objects you want to pass
## down the pipeline, and delete the rest.
##
## Once you finish selecting objects, save this file and
## exit.
############################################################

"@

    ## Place the instructions into the file
    $header > $filename

    ## Initialize the variables that will hold our list of objects, and
    ## a counter to help us keep track of the objects coming down the
    ## pipeline
    $objectList = @()
    $counter = 0
}

## PowerShell runs your "process" script block for each item it passes down
## the pipeline. In this block, the "$_" variable represents the current
## pipeline object
process
{
    ## Add a line to the file, using PowerShell's format (-f) operator.
    ## When provided the ouput of Get-Process, for example, these lines look
    ## like:
    ## 30: System.Diagnostics.Process (powershell)
    "{0}: {1}" -f $counter,$_.ToString() >> $filename

    ## Add the object to the list of objects, and increment our counter.
    $objectList += $_
    $counter++
}
```

Example 2-4. Select-FilteredObject.ps1 (continued)

```
## PowerShell runs your "end" script block once it completes passing all
## objects down the pipeline.
end
{
    ## Start notepad, then call the process's WaitForExit() method to
    ## pause the script until the user exits notepad.
    $processStartInfo = New-Object System.Diagnostics.ProcessStartInfo "notepad"
    $processStartInfo.Arguments = $filename
    $process = [System.Diagnostics.Process]::Start($processStartInfo)
    $process.WaitForExit()

    ## Go over each line of the file
    foreach($line in (Get-Content $filename))
    {
        ## Check if the line is of the special format: numbers, followed by
        ## a colon, followed by extra text.
        if($line -match "^(\d+?):.*")
        {
            ## If it did match the format, then $matches[1] represents the
            ## number -- a counter into the list of objects we saved during
            ## the "process" section.
            ## So, we output that object from our list of saved objects.
            $objectList[$matches[1]]
        }
    }

    ## Finally, clean up the temporary file.
    Remove-Item $filename
}
```

For more information about running scripts, see Recipe 1.1, "Run Programs, Scripts, and Existing Tools."

See Also

- Recipe 1.1, "Run Programs, Scripts, and Existing Tools"
- Recipe 2.2, "Program: Simplify Most Where-Object Filters"

2.4 Work with Each Item in a List or Command Output

Problem

You have a list of items and want to work with each item in that list.

Solution

Use the `Foreach-Object` cmdlet (which has the standard aliases `foreach` and `%`) to work with each item in a list.

To apply a calculation to each item in a list, use the `$_` variable as part of a calculation in the scriptblock parameter:

```
PS >1..10 | Foreach-Object { $_ * 2 }
2
4
6
8
10
12
14
16
18
20
```

To run a program on each file in a directory, use the `$_` variable as a parameter to the program in the script block parameter:

```
Get-ChildItem *.txt | Foreach-Object { attrib -r $_ }
```

To access a method or property for each object in a list, access that method or property on the `$_` variable in the script block parameter. In this example, you get the list of running processes called notepad, and then wait for each of them to exit:

```
$notepadProcesses = Get-Process notepad
$notepadProcesses | Foreach-Object { $_.WaitForExit() }
```

Discussion

Like the `Where-Object` cmdlet, the `Foreach-Object` cmdlet runs the script block that you specify for each item in the input. A script block is a series of PowerShell commands enclosed by the { and } characters. For each item in the set of incoming objects, PowerShell assigns that item to the `$_` variable, one element at a time. In the examples given by the solution, the `$_` variable represents each file or process that the previous cmdlet generated.

This script block can contain a great deal of functionality, if desired. You can combine multiple tests, comparisons, and much more. For more information about script blocks, see Recipe 10.3, "Write a Script Block." For more information about the type of comparisons available to you, see "Comparison Operators" in Appendix A.

 The first example in the solution demonstrates a neat way to generate ranges of numbers:

```
1..10
```

This is PowerShell's array range syntax, which you can learn more about in Recipe 11.3, "Access Elements of an Array."

The Foreach-Object cmdlet isn't the only way to perform actions on items in a list. The PowerShell scripting language supports several other keywords, such as for, (a different) foreach, do, and while. For information on how to use those keywords, see Recipe 4.4, "Repeat Operations with Loops."

For more information about the Foreach-Object cmdlet, type **Get-Help Foreach-Object**.

For more information about dealing with pipeline input in your own scripts, functions, and script blocks, see Recipe 10.7, "Access Pipeline Input."

See Also

- Recipe 4.4, "Repeat Operations with Loops"
- Recipe 10.3, "Write a Script Block"
- Recipe 10.7, "Access Pipeline Input"
- Recipe 11.3, "Access Elements of an Array"
- "Comparison Operators" in Appendix A

2.5   Automate Data-Intensive Tasks

Problem

You want to invoke a simple task on large amounts of data.

Solution

If only one piece of data changes (such as a server name or user name), store the data in a text file. Use the Get-Content cmdlet to retrieve the items, and then use the Foreach-Object cmdlet (which has the standard aliases foreach and %) to work with each item in that list. Example 2-5 illustrates this technique.

Example 2-5. Using information from a text file to automate data-intensive tasks

```
PS >Get-Content servers.txt
SERVER1
SERVER2
PS >$computers = Get-Content servers.txt
PS >$computers | Foreach-Object { Get-WmiObject Win32_OperatingSystem -Computer $_ }


SystemDirectory : C:\WINDOWS\system32
Organization    :
BuildNumber     : 2600
Version         : 5.1.2600

SystemDirectory : C:\WINDOWS\system32
```

Example 2-5. Using information from a text file to automate data-intensive tasks (continued)

```
Organization    :
BuildNumber     : 2600
Version         : 5.1.2600
```

If it becomes cumbersome (or unclear) to include the actions in the Foreach-Object cmdlet, you can also use the foreach scripting keyword as illustrated by Example 2-6.

Example 2-6. Using the foreach scripting keyword to make a looping statement easier to read

```
$computers = Get-Content servers.txt

foreach($computer in $computers)
{
    ## Get the information about the operating system from WMI
    $system = Get-WmiObject Win32_OperatingSystem -Computer $computer

    ## Determine if it is running Windows XP
    if($system.Version -eq "5.1.2600")
    {
        "$computer is running Windows XP"
    }
}
```

If several aspects of the data change per task (for example, both the WMI class and the computer name for computers in a large report), create a CSV file with a row for each task. Use the Import-Csv cmdlet to import that data into PowerShell, and then use properties of the resulting objects as multiple sources of related data. Example 2-7 illustrates this technique.

Example 2-7. Using information from a CSV to automate data-intensive tasks

```
PS >Get-Content WmiReport.csv
ComputerName,Class
LEE-DESK,Win32_OperatingSystem
LEE-DESK,Win32_Bios
PS >$data = Import-Csv WmiReport.csv
PS >$data

ComputerName                     Class
------------                     -----
LEE-DESK                         Win32_OperatingSystem
LEE-DESK                         Win32_Bios


PS >$data |
>>      Foreach-Object { Get-WmiObject $_.Class -Computer $_.ComputerName }
>>


SystemDirectory : C:\WINDOWS\system32
Organization    :
```

```
BuildNumber     : 2600
Version         : 5.1.2600

SMBIOSBIOSVersion : ASUS A7N8X Deluxe ACPI BIOS Rev 1009
Manufacturer      : Phoenix Technologies, LTD
Name              : Phoenix - AwardBIOS v6.00PG
SerialNumber      : xxxxxxxxxxx
Version           : Nvidia - 42302e31
```

Discussion

One of the major benefits of PowerShell is its capability to automate repetitive tasks. Sometimes, these repetitive tasks are action-intensive (such as system maintenance through registry and file cleanup) and consist of complex sequences of commands that will always be invoked together. In those situations, you can write a script to combine these operations to save time and reduce errors.

Other times, you need only to accomplish a single task (for example, retrieving the results of a WMI query) but need to invoke that task repeatedly for a large amount of data. In those situations, PowerShell's scripting statements, pipeline support, and data management cmdlets help automate those tasks.

One of the options given by the solution is the Import-Csv cmdlet. The Import-Csv cmdlet reads a CSV file and, for each row, automatically creates an object with properties that correspond to the names of the columns. Example 2-8 shows the results of a CSV that contains a ComputerName and Class header.

Example 2-8. The Import-Csv cmdlet creating objects with ComputerName and Class properties

```
PS >$data = Import-Csv WmiReport.csv
PS >$data

ComputerName                          Class
------------                          -----
LEE-DESK                              Win32_OperatingSystem
LEE-DESK                              Win32_Bios


PS >
PS >$data[0].ComputerName
LEE-DESK
```

As the solution illustrates, you can use the Foreach-Object cmdlet to provide data from these objects to repetitive cmdlet calls. It does this by specifying each parameter name, followed by the data (taken from a property of the current CSV object) that applies to it.

While this is the most general solution, many cmdlet parameters can automatically retrieve their value from incoming objects if any property of that object has the same name. This can let you to omit the `Foreach-Object` and property mapping steps altogether. Parameters that support this feature are said to support *Value from pipeline by property name*. The `Move-Item` cmdlet is one example of a cmdlet with parameters that support this, as shown by the `Accept pipeline input` rows inExample 2-9.

Example 2-9. Help content of the Move-Item showing a parameter that accepts value from pipeline by property name

```
PS >Get-Help Move-Item -Full
(...)
PARAMETERS
    -path <string[]>
        Specifies the path to the current location of the items. The default
        is the current directory. Wildcards are permitted.

        Required?                 true
        Position?                 1
        Default value             <current location>
        Accept pipeline input?    true (ByValue, ByPropertyName)
        Accept wildcard characters? true

    -destination <string>
        Specifies the path to the location where the items are being moved.
        The default is the current directory. Wildcards are permitted, but
        the result must specify a single location.

        To rename the item being moved, specify a new name in the value of
        Destination.

        Required?                 false
        Position?                 2
        Default value             <current location>
        Accept pipeline input?    true (ByPropertyName)
        Accept wildcard characters? True
(...)
```

If you purposefully name the columns in the CSV to correspond to parameters that take their value from pipeline by property name, PowerShell can do some (or all) of the parameter mapping for you. Example 2-10 demonstrates a CSV file that moves items in bulk.

Example 2-10. Using the Import-Csv cmdlet to automate a cmdlet that accepts value from pipeline by property name

```
PS >Get-Content ItemMoves.csv
Path,Destination
test.txt,Test1Directory
test2.txt,Test2Directory
PS >dir test.txt,test2.txt | Select Name

Name
----
```

Example 2-10. Using the Import-Csv cmdlet to automate a cmdlet that accepts value from pipeline by property name (continued)

```
test.txt
test2.txt


PS >Import-Csv ItemMoves.csv | Move-Item
PS >dir Test1Directory | Select Name

Name
----
test.txt


PS >dir Test2Directory | Select Name

Name
----
test2.txt
```

For more information about the Foreach-Object cmdlet and foreach scripting key-word, see Recipe 2.4, "Work with Each Item in a List or Command Output." For more information about working with CSV files, see Recipe 8.6, "Import Structured Data from a CSV File." For more information about working with Windows Man-agement Instrumentation (WMI), see Recipe 15.1, "Access Windows Management Instrumentation Data."

See Also

- Recipe 2.4, "Work with Each Item in a List or Command Output"
- Recipe 8.6, "Import Structured Data from a CSV File"
- Recipe 15.1, "Access Windows Management Instrumentation Data"

## CHAPTER 3

Variables and Objects

3.0   Introduction

As touched on in Chapter 2, *Pipelines*, PowerShell makes life immensely easier by keeping information in its native form: *objects*. Users expend most of their effort in traditional shells just trying to resuscitate information that the shell converted from its native form to plain text. Tools have evolved that ease the burden of working with plain text, but that job is still significantly more difficult than it needs to be.

Since PowerShell builds on Microsoft's .NET Framework, native information comes in the form of .NET *objects*—packages of information, and functionality closely related to that information.

Let's say that you want to get a list of running processes on your system. In other shells, your command (such as tlist.exe or /bin/ps) generates a plain-text report of the running processes on your system. To work with that output, you send it through a bevy of text processing tools—if you are lucky enough to have them available.

PowerShell's Get-Process cmdlet generates a list of the running processes on your system. In contrast to other shells, though, these are full-fidelity System.Diagnostics. Process objects straight out of the .NET Framework. The .NET Framework documentation describes them as objects that *"... [provide] access to local and remote processes, and [enable] you to start and stop local system processes."* With those objects in hand, PowerShell makes it trivial for you to access properties of objects (such as their process name or memory usage) and to access functionality on these objects (such as stopping them, starting them, or waiting for them to exit).

3.1 Store Information in Variables

Problem

You want to store the output of a pipeline or command for later use, or to work with it in more detail.

Solution

To store output for later use, store the output of the command in a variable. You can access this information later, or even pass it down the pipeline as though it was the output of the original command:

```
PS >$result = 2 + 2
PS >$result
4
PS >$processes = Get-Process
PS >$processes.Count
85
PS >$processes | Where-Object { $_.ID -eq 0 }

Handles  NPM(K)   PM(K)     WS(K) VM(M)   CPU(s)     Id ProcessName
-------  ------   -----     ----- -----   ------     -- -----------
      0       0       0        16     0                0 Idle
```

Discussion

Variables in PowerShell (and all other scripting and programming languages) let you store the output of something so that you can use it later. A variable name starts with a dollar sign ($) and can be followed by nearly any character. A small set of characters have special meaning to PowerShell, so PowerShell provides a way to make variable names that include even these.

You can store the result of any pipeline or command in a variable to use it later. If that command generates simple data (such as a number or string), then the variable contains simple data. If the command generates rich data (such as the objects that represent system processes from the Get-Process cmdlet), then the variable contains that list of rich data. If the command (such as a traditional executable) generates plain text (such as the output of traditional executable), then the variable contains plain text.

 If you've stored a large amount of data into a variable, but no longer need that data, assign the value $null (or anything else) to that variable so that PowerShell can release the memory it was using to store that data.

For more information about the syntax and types of PowerShell variables, see "Variables" in Appendix A.

In addition to variables that you create, PowerShell automatically defines several variables that represent things such as the location of your profile file, the process ID of PowerShell, and more. For a full list of these automatic variables, see Appendix C, *PowerShell Automatic Variables*.

See Also

- "Variables" in Appendix A
- Appendix C, *PowerShell Automatic Variables*

3.2 Access Environment Variables

Problem

You want to use an environment variable (such as the system path, or current user's name) in your script or interactive session.

Solution

PowerShell offers several ways to access environment variables.

To list all environment variables, list the children of the env drive:

```
Get-ChildItem env:
```

To get an environment variable using a more concise syntax, precede its name with `$env:`

```
$env:variablename
```

i.e.: *$env:username*

To get an environment variable using its Provider path, supply `env:` or `Environment::` to the `Get-ChildItem` cmdlet:

```
Get-ChildItem env:variablename
Get-ChildItem Environment::variablename
```

Discussion

PowerShell provides access to environment variables through its *environment provider*. Providers let you work with data stores (such as the registry, environment variables, and aliases) much as you would access the filesystem.

By default, PowerShell creates a drive (called env) that works with the *environment provider* to let you access environment variables. The environment provider lets you access items in the env: drive as you would any other drive: dir env:*variablename* or dir env:*variablename*. If you want to access the provider directly (rather than go through its drive), you can also type **dir Environment::*variablename***.

However, the most common (and easiest) way to work with environment variables is by typing $env:*variablename*. This works with any provider but is most typically used with environment variables.

This is because the environment provider shares something in common with several other providers—namely support for the *-Content set of core cmdlets (see Example 3-1).

Example 3-1. Working with content on different providers

```
PS >"hello world" > test
PS >Get-Content c:test
hello world
PS >Get-Content variable:ErrorActionPreference
Continue
PS >Get-Content function:more
param([string[]]$paths);  if(($paths -ne $null) -and ($paths.length -ne 0))  { ...
      Get-Content $local:file | Out-Host -p    }  }  else { $input | Out-Host ...
PS >Get-Content env:systemroot
C:\WINDOWS
```

For providers that support the content cmdlets, PowerShell lets you interact with this content through a special variable syntax (see Example 3-2).

Example 3-2. Using PowerShell's special variable syntax to access content

```
PS >$function:more
param([string[]]$paths);  if(($paths -ne $null) -and ($paths.length -ne 0))  { …
      Get-Content $local:file | Out-Host -p    }  }  else { $input | Out-Host …
PS >$variable:ErrorActionPreference
Continue
PS >$c:test
hello world
PS >$env:systemroot
C:\WINDOWS
```

This variable syntax for content management lets you to both get and set content:

```
    PS >$function:more = { $input | less.exe }
    PS >$function:more
    $input | less.exe
```

Now, when it comes to accessing complex provider paths using this method, you'll quickly run into naming issues (even if the underlying file exists):

```
    PS >$c:\temp\test.txt
    Unexpected token '\temp\test.txt' in expression or statement.
    At line:1 char:17
    + $c:\temp\test.txt <<<<
```

The solution to that lies in PowerShell's escaping support for complex variable names. To define a complex variable name, enclose it in braces:

```
PS >${1234123!@#$!@#$12$!@#$@!} = "Crazy Variable!"
PS >${1234123!@#$!@#$12$!@#$@!}
Crazy Variable!
PS >dir variable:\1*

Name                          Value
----                          -----
1234123!@#$!@#$12$!@#$@!       Crazy Variable!
```

... and the content equivalent (assuming that the file exists):

```
PS >${c:\temp\test.txt}
hello world
```

Since environment variable names do not contain special characters, this Get-Content *variable syntax* is the best (and easiest) way to access environment variables.

For more information about working with PowerShell variables, see "Variables" in Appendix A. For more information about working with environment type **Get-Help About_Environment_Variable**.

See Also

- "Variables" in Appendix A

3.3 Control Access and Scope of Variables and Other Items

Problem

You want to control how you define (or interact with) the visibility of variables, aliases, functions, and drives.

Solution

PowerShell offers several ways to access variables.

To create a variable with a specific scope, supply that scope before the variable name:

```
$SCOPE:variable - value
```

To access a variable at a specific scope, supply that scope before the variable name:

```
$SCOPE:variable
```

To create a variable that remains even after the script exits, create it in the GLOBAL scope:

```
$GLOBAL:variable = value
```

To change a scriptwide variable from within a function, supply SCRIPT as its scope name:

```
$SCRIPT:variable = value
```

Discussion

PowerShell controls access to variables, functions, aliases, and drives through a mechanism known as *scoping*. The *scope* of an item is another term for its visibility. You are always in a scope (called the *current* or *local* scope), but some actions change what that means.

When your code enters a nested prompt, script, function, or script block, PowerShell creates a new scope. That scope then becomes the local scope. When it does this, PowerShell remembers the relationship between your old scope and your new scope. From the view of the new scope, the old scope is called the *parent scope*. From the view of the old scope, the new scope is called a *child scope*. Child scopes get access to all the variables in the parent scope, but changing those variables in the child scope doesn't change the version in the parent scope.

 Trying to change a scriptwide variable from a function is often a "gotcha," because a function is a new scope. As mentioned previously, changing something in a child scope (the function) doesn't affect the parent scope (the script). The rest of this discussion describes ways to change the value for the entire script.

When your code exits a nested prompt, script, function, or script block, the opposite happens. PowerShell removes the old scope, then changes the local scope to be the scope that originally created it—the parent of that old scope.

Some scopes are so common that PowerShell gives them special names:

Global
> The outermost scope. Items in the global scope are visible from all other scopes.

Script
> The scope that represents the current script. Items in the script scope are visible from all other scopes in the script.

Local
> The current scope.

When you define the scope of an item, PowerShell supports two additional scope names that act more like options: `Private` and `AllScope`. When you define an item to have a `Private` scope, PowerShell does not make that item directly available to child scopes. PowerShell does not *hide* it from child scopes, though, as child scopes can still use the `-Scope` parameter of the `Get-Variable` cmdlet to get variables from parent scopes. When you specify the `AllScope` option for an item (through one of the `*-Variable`, `*-Alias`, or `*-Drive` cmdlets), child scopes that change the item also affect the value in parent scopes.

With this background, PowerShell provides several ways for you to control access and scope of variables and other items.

Variables

To define a variable at a specific scope (or access a variable at a specific scope), use its scope name in the variable reference. For example:

```
$SCRIPT:myVariable = value
```

As illustrated in "Variables" in Appendix A, the *-Variable set of cmdlets also allow you to specify scope names through their –Scope parameter.

Functions

To define a function at a specific scope (or access a function at a specific scope), use its scope name when creating the function. For example:

```
function $GLOBAL:MyFunction { ... }
GLOBAL:MyFunction args
```

Aliases and drives

To define an alias or drive at a specific scope, use the Option parameter of the *-Alias and *-Drive cmdlets. To access an alias or drive at a specific scope, use the Scope parameter of the *-Alias and *-Drive cmdlets.

For more information about scopes, type **Get-Help About-Scope**.

See Also

* "Variables" in Appendix A

3.4   Work with .NET Objects

Problem

You want to use and interact with one of the features that make PowerShell so powerful—its intrinsic support for .NET objects.

Solution

PowerShell offers ways to access methods (both static and instance) and properties.

To call a static method on a class, place the type name in square brackets, and then separate the class name from the method name with two colons:

```
[ClassName]::MethodName(parameter list)
```

To call a method on an object, place a dot between the variable that represents that object and the method name:

```
$objectReference.MethodName(parameter list)
```

To access a static property on a class, place the type name in square brackets, and then separate the class name from the property name with two colons:

```
[ClassName]::PropertyName
```

To access a property on an object, place a dot between the variable that represents that object and the property name:

```
$objectReference.PropertyName
```

Discussion

One feature that gives PowerShell its incredible reach into both system administration and application development is its capability to leverage Microsoft's enormous and broad .NET Framework. The .NET Framework is a large collection of classes. Each class embodies a specific concept and groups closely related functionality and information. Working with the .NET Framework is one aspect of PowerShell that introduces a revolution to the world of management shells.

An example of a class from the .NET Framework is System.Diagnostics.Process—the grouping of functionality that *"provides access to local and remote processes, and enables you to start and stop local system processes."*

 The terms *type* and *class* are often used interchangeably.

Classes contain *methods* (which allow you to perform operations) and *properties* (which allow you to access information).

For example, the Get-Process cmdlet generates System.Diagnostics.Process objects, not a plain-text report like traditional shells. Managing these processes becomes incredibly easy, as they contain a rich mix of information (properties) and operations (methods). You no longer have to parse a stream of text for the ID of a process—you can just ask the object directly!

```
PS >$process = Get-Process Notepad
PS >$process.Id
3872
```

Static methods

```
[ClassName]::MethodName(parameter list)
```

Some methods apply only to the concept the class represents. For example, retrieving all running processes on a system relates to the general concept of processes, instead of a specific process. Methods that apply to the class/type as a whole are called *static methods*.

For example:

```
PS >[System.Diagnostics.Process]::GetProcessById(0)
```

This specific task is better handled by the Get-Process cmdlet, but it demonstrates PowerShell's capability to call methods on .NET classes. It calls the static GetProcessById method on the System.Diagnostics.Process class to get the process with the ID of 0. This generates the following output:

Handles	NPM(K)	PM(K)	WS(K)	VM(M)	CPU(s)	Id	ProcessName
0	0	0	16	0		0	Idle

Instance methods

```
$objectReference.MethodName(parameter list)
```

Some methods relate only to specific, tangible realizations (called instances) of a class. An example of this would be stopping a process actually running on the system, as opposed to the general concept of processes. If *$objectReference* refers to a specific System.Diagnostics.Process (as output by the GetProcess cmdlet, for example), you may call methods to start it, stop it, or wait for it to exit. Methods that act on instances of a class are called *instance methods*.

The term *object* is often used interchangeably with the term *instance*.

For example:

```
PS >$process = GetProcess Notepad
PS >$process.WaitForExit()
```

Stores the process with an ID of 0 into the $process variable. It then calls the WaitForExit() instance method on that specific process to pause PowerShell until the process exits.

To learn about the different sets of parameters (overloads) that a given method supports, type that method name without any parameters:

```
PS >$now = Get-Date
PS >$now.AddDays
```

```
MemberType          : Method
OverloadDefinitions : {System.DateTime AddDays(Double value)}
TypeNameOfValue     : System.Management.Automation.PSMethod
Value               : System.DateTime AddDays(Double value)
Name                : AddDays
IsInstance          : True
```

Static properties

```
[ClassName]::PropertyName
```

or

```
[ClassName]::PropertyName = value
```

Like static methods, some properties relate only to information about the concept that the class represents. For example, the System.DateTime class *"represents an instant in time, typically expressed as a date and time of day."* It provides a Now static property that returns the current time:

```
PS >[System.DateTime]::Now
Saturday, June 2, 2007 4:57:20 PM
```

This specific task is better handled by the Get-Date cmdlet, but it demonstrates PowerShell's capability to access properties on .NET objects.

Although relatively rare, some types allow you to set the value of some static properties as well: for example, the [System.Environment]::CurrentDirectory property. This property represents the process's current directory—which represents PowerShell's startup directory, as opposed to the path you see in your prompt.

Instance properties

```
$objectReference.PropertyName
```

or

```
$objectReference.PropertyName = value
```

Like instance methods, some properties relate only to specific, tangible realizations (called *instances*) of a class. An example of this would be the day of an actual instant in time, as opposed to the general concept of dates and times. If $objectReference refers to a specific System.DateTime (as output by the Get-Date cmdlet or [System.DateTime]::Now, for example), you may want to retrieve its day of week, day, or month. Properties that return information about instances of a class are called *instance properties*.

For example:

```
PS >$today = Get-Date
PS >$today.DayOfWeek
Saturday
```

This example stores the current date in the $today variable. It then calls the DayOfWeek instance property to retrieve the day of the week for that specific date.

With this knowledge, the next questions are: "How do I learn about the functionality available in the .NET Framework?" and "How do I learn what an object does?"

For an answer to the first question, see Appendix E, *Selected .NET Classes and Their Uses* for a hand-picked list of the classes in the .NET Framework most useful to system administrators. For an answer to the second, see Recipe 3.9, "Learn About Types and Objects" and Recipe 3.10, "Get Detailed Documentation About Types and Objects."

See Also

- Recipe 3.9, "Learn About Types and Objects"
- Recipe 3.10, "Get Detailed Documentation About Types and Objects"
- Appendix E, *Selected .NET Classes and Their Uses*

3.5   Create an Instance of a .NET Object

Problem

You want to create an instance of a .NET object to interact with its methods and properties.

Solution

Use the New-Object cmdlet to create an instance of an object.

To create an instance of an object using its default constructor, use the New-Object cmdlet with the class name as its only parameter:

```
PS >$generator = New-Object System.Random
PS >$generator.NextDouble()
0.853699042859347
```

To create an instance of an object that takes parameters for its constructor, supply those parameters to the New-Object cmdlet. In some instances, the class may exist in a separate library not loaded in PowerShell by default, such as the System.Windows. Forms assembly. In that case, you must first load the assembly that contains the class:

```
[Reflection.Assembly]::LoadWithPartialName("System.Windows.Forms")
$image = New-Object System.Drawing.Bitmap source.gif
$image.Save("source_converted.jpg","JPEG")
```

To create an object and use it at the same time (without saving it for later), wrap the call to New-Object in parentheses:

```
PS >(New-Object Net.WebClient).DownloadString("http://live.com")
```

Discussion

Many cmdlets (such as Get-Process and Get-ChildItem) generate live .NET objects that represent tangible processes, files, and directories. However, PowerShell supports much more of the .NET Framework than just the objects that its cmdlets produce.

These additional areas of the .NET Framework supply a huge amount of functionality that you can use in your scripts and general system administration tasks.

When it comes to using most of these classes, the first step is often to create an instance of the class, store that instance in a variable, and then work with the methods and properties on that instance. To create an instance of a class, you use the New-Object cmdlet. The first parameter to the New-Object cmdlet is the type name, and the second parameter is the list of arguments to the constructor, if it takes any. The New-Object cmdlet supports PowerShell's *type shortcuts*, so you never have to use the fully qualified type name. For more information about type shortcuts, see Recipe 3.4, "Work with .NET Objects."

Since the second parameter to the New-Object cmdlet is an array of parameters to the type's constructor, you might encounter difficulty when trying to specify a parameter that itself is a list. Assuming $byte is an array of bytes:

```
PS >$memoryStream = New-Object System.IO.MemoryStream $bytes
New-Object : Cannot find an overload for ".ctor" and the argument count: "11".
At line:1 char:27
+ $memoryStream = New-Object  <<<< System.IO.MemoryStream $bytes
```

To solve this, provide an array that contains an array:

```
PS >$parameters = ,$bytes
PS >$memoryStream = New-Object System.IO.MemoryStream $parameters
```

or

```
PS >$memoryStream = New-Object System.IO.MemoryStream @(,$bytes)
```

Load types from another assembly

PowerShell makes most common types available by default. However, many are available only after you load the library (called the assembly) that defines them. The MSDN documentation for a class includes the assembly that defines it.

To load an assembly, use the methods provided by the System.Reflection.Assembly class:

```
PS >[Reflection.Assembly]::LoadWithPartialName("System.Web")

GAC     Version         Location
---     -------         --------
True    v2.0.50727      C:\WINDOWS\assembly\GAC_32\(…)\System.Web.dll


PS >[Web.HttpUtility]::UrlEncode("http://search.msn.com")
http%3a%2f%2fsearch.msn.com
```

The `LoadWithPartialName` method is unsuitable for scripts that you want to share with others or use in a production environment. It loads the most current version of the assembly, which may not be the same as the version you used to develop your script. To load an assembly in the safest way possible, use its fully qualified name with the `[Reflection.Assembly]::Load()` method.

For a hand-picked list of the classes in the .NET Framework most useful to system administrators, see Appendix E, *Selected .NET Classes and Their Uses*. To learn more about the functionality that a class supports, see Recipe 3.9, "Learn About Types and Objects."

For more information about the `New-Object` cmdlet, type **Get-Help New-Object**.

See Also

- Recipe 3.4, "Work with .NET Objects"
- Recipe 3.9, "Learn About Types and Objects"
- Appendix E, *Selected .NET Classes and Their Uses*

3.6   Program: Create Instances of Generic Objects

When you work with the .NET Framework, you'll often run across classes that have the primary responsibility of managing other objects. For example, the `System.Collections.ArrayList` class lets you manage a dynamic list of objects. You can add objects to an `ArrayList`, remove objects from it, sort the objects inside, and more. These objects can be any type of object—`String` objects, integers, `DateTime` objects, and many more. However, working with classes that support arbitrary objects can sometimes be a little awkward. One example is *type safety*: if you accidentally add a `String` to a list of integers, you might not find out until your program fails.

Although the issue becomes largely moot when working only inside PowerShell, a more common complaint in strongly typed languages (such as C#) is that you have to remind the environment (through explicit casts) about the type of your object when you work with it again:

```
// This is C# code
System.Collections.ArrayList list =
    new System.Collections.ArrayList();
list.Add("Hello World");

string result = (String) list[0];
```

To address these problems, the .NET Framework introduced a feature called *generic types*: classes that support arbitrary types of objects, but allow you to specify *which type* of object. In this case, a collection of strings:

```
// This is C# code
System.Collections.ObjectModel.Collection<String> list =
    new System.Collections.ObjectModel.Collection<String>();
list.Add("Hello World");

string result = list[0];
```

Although the New-Object cmdlet is powerful, it doesn't yet handle creating generic types very elegantly. For a simple generic type, you can use the syntax that the .NET Framework uses under the hood:

```
$coll = New-Object 'System.Collections.ObjectModel.Collection`1[System.String]'
```

However, that begins to fall apart if you want to use types defined outside the main mscorlib assembly, or want to create complex generic types (for example, ones that refer to other generic types).

Example 3-3 lets you to easily create instances of generic types.

Example 3-3. New-GenericObject.ps1

```
##############################################################################
##
## New-GenericObject.ps1
##
## Creates an object of a generic type:
##
## Usage:
##
##    # Simple generic collection
##    New-GenericObject System.Collections.ObjectModel.Collection System.Int32
##
##    # Generic dictionary with two types
##    New-GenericObject System.Collections.Generic.Dictionary `
##        System.String,System.Int32
##
##    # Generic list as the second type to a generic dictionary
##    $secondType = New-GenericObject System.Collections.Generic.List Int32
##    New-GenericObject System.Collections.Generic.Dictionary `
##        System.String,$secondType.GetType()
##
##    # Generic type with a non-default constructor
##    New-GenericObject System.Collections.Generic.LinkedListNode `
##        System.String "Hi"
##
##############################################################################
```

3.7   Reduce Typing for Long Class Names

Problem

You want to reduce the amount of redundant information in your script when you interact with classes that have long type names.

Solution

To reduce typing for static methods, store the type name in a variable:

```
$math = [System.Math]
$math::Min(1,10)
$math::Max(1,10)
```

To reduce typing for multiple objects in a namespace, use the -f (*format*) operator:

```
$namespace = "System.Collections.{0}"
$arrayList = New-Object ($namespace -f "ArrayList")
$queue = New-Object ($namespace -f "Queue")
```

To reduce typing for static methods of multiple types in a namespace, use the -f (*format*) operator along with a cast:

```
$namespace = "System.Diagnostics.{0}"
([Type] ($namespace -f "EventLog"))::GetEventLogs()
([Type] ($namespace -f "Process"))::GetCurrentProcess()
```

Discussion

One thing you will notice when working with some .NET classes (or classes from a third-party SDK), is that it quickly becomes tiresome to specify their fully qualified type names. For example, many useful collection classes in the .NET Framework all start with "System.Collections". This is called the *namespace* of that class. Most programming languages solve this problem with a *using* directive that lets you to specify a list of namespaces for that language to search when you type a plain class name such as "ArrayList". PowerShell lacks a using directive, but there are several options to get the benefits of one.

If you are repeatedly working with static methods on a specific type, you can store that type in a variable to reduce typing as shown in the solution:

```
$math = [System.Math]
$math::Min(1,10)
$math::Max(1,10)
```

If you are creating instances of different classes from a namespace, you can store the namespace in a variable and then use the PowerShell -f (*format*) operator to specify the unique class name:

```
$namespace = "System.Collections.{0}"
$arrayList = New-Object ($namespace -f "ArrayList")
$queue = New-Object ($namespace -f "Queue")
```

If you are working with static methods from several types in a namespace, you can store the namespace in a variable, use the -f (*format*) operator to specify the unique class name, and then finally cast that into a type:

```
$namespace = "System.Diagnostics.{0}"
([Type] ($namespace -f "EventLog"))::GetEventLogs()
([Type] ($namespace -f "Process"))::GetCurrentProcess()
```

For more information about PowerShell's format operator, see Recipe 5.6, "Place Formatted Information in a String."

See Also

- Recipe 5.6, "Place Formatted Information in a String"

3.8   Use a COM Object

Problem

You want to create a COM object to interact with its methods and properties.

Solution

Use the New-Object cmdlet (with the –ComObject parameter) to create a COM object from its *ProgID*. You can then interact with the methods and properties of the COM object as you would any other object in PowerShell.

```
$object = New-Object -ComObject ProgId
```

For example:

```
PS >$sapi = New-Object -Com Sapi.SpVoice
PS >$sapi.Speak("Hello World")
```

Discussion

Historically, many applications have exposed their scripting and administration interfaces as COM objects. While .NET APIs (and PowerShell cmdlets) are becoming more common, interacting with COM objects is still a common administrative task.

As with classes in the .NET Framework, it is difficult to know what COM objects you can use to help you accomplish your system administration tasks. For a hand-picked list of the COM objects most useful to system administrators, see Appendix G, *Selected COM Objects and Their Uses*.

For more information about the New-Object cmdlet, type **Get-Help New-Object**.

See Also

- Appendix G, *Selected COM Objects and Their Uses*

3.9   Learn About Types and Objects

Problem

You have an instance of an object and want to know what methods and properties it supports.

Solution

The most common way to explore the methods and properties supported by an object is through the Get-Member cmdlet.

To get the instance members of an object you've stored in the $*object* variable, pipe it to the Get-Member cmdlet:

```
$object | Get-Member
Get-Member -InputObject $object
```

To get the static members of an object you've stored in the $*object* variable, supply the –Static flag to the Get-Member cmdlet:

```
$object | Get-Member -Static
Get-Member -Static -InputObject $object
```

To get the static members of a specific type, pipe that type to the Get-Member cmdlet, and also specify the –Static flag:

```
[Type] | Get-Member -Static
Get-Member -InputObject [Type]
```

To get members of the specified member type (for example, Method, Property) from an object you have stored in the $*object* variable, supply that member type to the –MemberType parameter:

```
$object | Get-Member -MemberType memberType
Get-Member -MemberType memberType -InputObject $object
```

Discussion

The Get-Member cmdlet is one of the three commands you will use most commonly as you explore Windows PowerShell. The other two commands are Get-Command and Get-Help.

If you pass the Get-Member cmdlet a collection of objects (such as an Array or ArrayList) through the pipeline, PowerShell extracts each item from the collection, and then passes them to the Get-Member cmdlet one-by-one. The Get-Member cmdlet then returns the members of each unique type that it receives. Although helpful the vast majority of the time, this sometimes causes difficulty when you want to learn about the members or properties of the collection class itself.

If you want to see the properties of a collection (as opposed to the elements it contains,) provide the collection to the –InputObject parameter, instead. Alternatively, you may wrap the collection in an array (using PowerShell's *unary comma operator*) so that the collection class remains when the Get-Member cmdlet unravels the outer array:

```
PS >$files = Get-ChildItem
PS >,$files | Get-Member


    TypeName: System.Object[]

Name            MemberType      Definition
----            ----------      ----------
Count           AliasProperty   Count = Length
Address         Method          System.Object& Address(Int32 )
(...)
```

For another way to learn detailed information about types and objects, see the following section, Recipe 3.10, "Get Detailed Documentation About Types and Objects."

For more information about the Get-Member cmdlet, type **Get-Help Get-Member**.

See Also

- Recipe 3.10, "Get Detailed Documentation About Types and Objects"

3.10 Get Detailed Documentation About Types and Objects

Problem

You have a type of object and want to know detailed information about the methods and properties it supports.

Solution

The documentation for the .NET Framework (available on *http://msdn.microsoft.com*) is the best way to get detailed documentation about the methods and properties supported by an object. That exploration generally comes in two stages:

1. Find the type of the object.

   To determine the type of an object, you can use either the type name shown by the Get-Member cmdlet (as described in Recipe 3.9, "Learn About Types and Objects"), or call the GetType() method of an object (if you have an instance of it):

   ```
   PS >$date = Get-Date
   PS >$date.GetType().ToString()
   System.DateTime
   ```

2. Enter that type name into the search box at *http://msdn.microsoft.com*.

Discussion

When the Get-Member cmdlet does not provide the information you need, the MSDN documentation for a type is a great alternative. It provides much more detailed information than the help offered by the Get-Member cmdlet—usually including detailed descriptions, related information, and even code samples. MSDN documentation focuses on developers using these types through a language such as C#, though, so you may find interpreting the information for use in PowerShell to be a little difficult at first.

Typically, the documentation for a class first starts with a general overview, and then provides a hyperlink to the members of the class—the list of methods and properties it supports.

 To get to the documentation for the members quickly, search for them more explicitly by adding the term "members" to your MSDN search term:

> ***typename*** members

Documentation for the members of a class lists its methods and properties, as does the output of the Get-Member cmdlet. The S icon represents static methods and properties. Click the member name for more information about that method or property.

Public constructors

This section lists the constructors of the type. You use a constructor when you create the type through the New-Object cmdlet. When you click on a constructor, the documentation provides all the different ways that you can create that object, including the parameter list that you will use with the New-Object cmdlet.

Public fields/public properties

This section lists the names of the fields and properties of an object. The S icon represents a static field or property. When you click on a field or property, the documentation also provides the type returned by this field or property.

For example, you might see the following in the definition for System.DateTime.Now:

```C#
public static DateTime Now { get; }
```

Public means that the Now property is public—that everybody can access it. Static means that the property is static (as described in Recipe 3.4, "Work with .NET Objects"). DateTime means that the property returns a DateTime object when you call it. Get; means that you can get information from this property but cannot set the information. Many properties support a Set; as well (such as the IsReadOnly property on System.IO.FileInfo), which means that you can change its value.

Public methods

This section lists the names of the methods of an object. The S icon represents a static method. When you click on a method, the documentation provides all the different ways that you can call that method, including the parameter list that you will use to call that method in PowerShell.

For example, you might see the following in the definition for System.DateTime.AddDays():

```
C#
public DateTime AddDays (
    double value
)
```

Public means that the AddDays method is public—that everybody can access it. DateTime means that the method returns a DateTime object when you call it. The text, double value, means that this method requires a parameter (of type double). In this case, that parameter determines the number of days to add to the DateTime object on which you call the method.

See Also

- Recipe 3.4, "Work with .NET Objects"
- Recipe 3.9, "Learn About Types and Objects"

3.11   Add Custom Methods and Properties to Objects

Problem

You have an object and want to add your own custom properties or methods (*members*) to that object.

Solution

Use the Add-Member cmdlet to add custom members to an object.

Discussion

The Add-Member cmdlet is extremely useful in helping you add custom members to individual objects. For example, imagine that you want to create a report from the files in the current directory, and that report should include each file's owner. The Owner property is not standard on the objects that Get-ChildItem produces, but you could write a small script to add them, as shown in Example 3-4.

Example 3-4. A script that adds custom properties to its output of file objects

```
##############################################################################
## Get-OwnerReport.ps1
##
## Gets a list of files in the current directory, but with their owner added
## to the resulting objects.
##
## Example:
##    Get-OwnerReport
##    Get-OwnerReport | Format-Table Name,LastWriteTime,Owner
##############################################################################

$files = Get-ChildItem
foreach($file in $files)
{
    $owner = (Get-Acl $file).Owner
    $file | Add-Member NoteProperty Owner $owner
    $file
}
```

For more information about running scripts, see Recipe 1.1, "Run Programs, Scripts, and Existing Tools."

Although it is most common to add static information (such as a NoteProperty), the Add-Member cmdlet supports several other property and method types—including AliasProperty, ScriptProperty, CodeProperty, CodeMethod, and ScriptMethod. For a more detailed description of these other property types, see "Working with the .NET Framework" in Appendix A, as well as the help documentation for the Add-Member cmdlet.

Although the Add-Member cmdlet lets you to customize specific objects, it does not let you to customize all objects of that type. For information on how to do that, see the following section Recipe 3.12, "Add Custom Methods and Properties to Types."

Calculated properties

Calculated properties are another useful way to add information to output objects. If your script or command uses a Format-Table or Select-Object command to generate its output, you can create additional properties by providing an expression that generates their value. For example:

```
Get-ChildItem |
    Select-Object Name,
        @{Name="Size (MB)"; Expression={ "{0,8:0.00}" -f ($_.Length / 1MB) } }
```

In this command, we get the list of files in the directory. We use the Select-Object command to retrieve its name and a calculated property called Size (MB). This calculated property returns the size of the file in megabytes, rather than the default (which is bytes).

For more information about the Add-Member cmdlet, type **Get-Help Add-Member**.

For more information about adding calculated properties, type **Get-Help Select-Object** or **Get-Help Format-Table**.

See Also

- Recipe 1.1, "Run Programs, Scripts, and Existing Tools"
- Recipe 3.12, "Add Custom Methods and Properties to Types
- "Working with the .NET Framework" in Appendix A

3.12   Add Custom Methods and Properties to Types

Problem

You want to add your own custom properties or methods to all objects of a certain type.

Solution

Use *custom type extension files* to add custom members to all objects of a type.

Discussion

Although the Add-Member cmdlet is extremely useful in helping you add custom members to individual objects, it requires that you add the members to each object that you want to interact with. It does not allow you to automatically add them to all objects of that type. For that purpose, PowerShell supports another mechanism—*custom type extension* files.

Type extensions are simple XML files that PowerShell interprets. They let you (as the administrator of the system) easily add your own features to any type exposed by the system. If you write code (for example, a script or function) that primarily interacts with a single type of object, then that code might be better suited as an extension to the type instead.

 Since type extension files are XML files, make sure that your customizations properly encode the characters that have special meaning in XML files—such as <, >, and &.

For example, imagine a script that returns the free disk space on a given drive. That might be helpful as a script, but you might find it easier to instead make PowerShell's PsDrive objects themselves tell you how much free space they have left.

Getting started

If you haven't already, the first step in creating a types extension file is to create an empty one. The best location for this is probably in the same directory as your custom profile, with the name Types.Custom.ps1xml, as shown in Example 3-5.

Example 3-5. Sample Types.Custom.ps1xml file

```
<?xml version="1.0" encoding="utf-8" ?>
<Types>
</Types>
```

Next, add a few lines to your PowerShell profile so that PowerShell loads your type extensions during startup:

```
$typeFile = (Join-Path (Split-Path $profile) "Types.Custom.ps1xml")
Update-TypeData -PrependPath $typeFile
```

By default, PowerShell loads several type extensions from the Types.ps1xml file in PowerShell's installation directory. The Update-TypeData cmdlet tells PowerShell to also look in your Types.Custom.ps1xml file for extensions. The -PrependPath para-meter makes PowerShell favor your extensions over the built-in ones in case of conflict.

Once you have a custom types file to work with, adding functionality becomes relatively straightforward. As a theme, these examples do exactly what we alluded to earlier: add functionality to PowerShell's PsDrive type.

To support this, you need to extend your custom types file so that it defines additions to the System.Management.Automation.PSDriveInfo type, as shown in Example 3-6. The System.Management.Automation.PSDriveInfo type is the type that the Get-PsDrive cmdlet generates.

Example 3-6. A template for changes to a custom types file

```
<?xml version="1.0" encoding="utf-8" ?>
<Types>
  <Type>
    <Name>System.Management.Automation.PSDriveInfo</Name>
    <Members>
        add members such as <ScriptProperty> here
    </Members>
  </Type>
</Types>
```

Add a ScriptProperty

A *ScriptProperty* lets you to add properties (that get and set information) to types, using PowerShell script as the extension language. It consists of three child elements: the Name of the property, the *Getter* of the property (via the GetScriptBlock child), and the *Setter* of the property (via the SetScriptBlock child).

In both the GetScriptBlock and SetScriptBlock sections, the $this variable refers to the current object being extended. In the SetScriptBlock section, the $args[0] variable represents the value that the user supplied as the right-hand side of the assignment.

Example 3-7 adds an AvailableFreeSpace ScriptProperty to PSDriveInfo, and should be placed within the members section of the template given in Example 3-6. When you access the property, it returns the amount of free space remaining on the drive. When you set the property, it outputs what changes you must make to obtain that amount of free space.

Example 3-7. A ScriptProperty for the PSDriveInfo type

```
<ScriptProperty>
  <Name>AvailableFreeSpace</Name>
  <GetScriptBlock>
    ## Ensure that this is a FileSystem drive
    if($this.Provider.ImplementingType -eq
       [Microsoft.PowerShell.Commands.FileSystemProvider])
    {
        ## Also ensure that it is a local drive
        $driveRoot = $this.Root
        $fileZone = [System.Security.Policy.Zone]::CreateFromUrl(`
                $driveRoot).SecurityZone
        if($fileZone -eq "MyComputer")
        {
            $drive = New-Object System.IO.DriveInfo $driveRoot
            $drive.AvailableFreeSpace
        }
    }
  </GetScriptBlock>
  <SetScriptBlock>
    ## Get the available free space
    $availableFreeSpace = $this.AvailableFreeSpace

    ## Find out the difference between what is available, and what they
    ## asked for.
    $spaceDifference = (([long] $args[0]) - $availableFreeSpace) / 1MB

    ## If they want more free space than they have, give that message
    if($spaceDifference -gt 0)
    {
        $message = "To obtain $args bytes of free space, " +
          " free $spaceDifference megabytes."
        Write-Host $message
    }
    ## If they want less free space than they have, give that message
    else
    {
        $spaceDifference = $spaceDifference * -1

        $message = "To obtain $args bytes of free space, " +
```

Example 3-7. A ScriptProperty for the PSDriveInfo type (continued)

```
              " use up $spaceDifference more megabytes."
          Write-Host $message
      }
    </SetScriptBlock>
  </ScriptProperty>
```

Add an AliasProperty

An *AliasProperty* gives an alternative name (alias) for a property. The referenced property does not need to exist when PowerShell processes your type extension file, since you (or another script) might later add the property through mechanisms such as the Add-Member cmdlet.

Example 3-8 adds a Free AliasProperty to PSDriveInfo, and should also be placed within the members section of the template given in Example 3-6. When you access the property, it returns the value of the AvailableFreeSpace property. When you set the property, it sets the value of the AvailableFreeSpace property.

Example 3-8. An AliasProperty for the PSDriveInfo type

```
  <AliasProperty>
    <Name>Free</Name>
    <ReferencedMemberName>AvailableFreeSpace</ReferencedMemberName>
  </AliasProperty>
```

Add a ScriptMethod

A *ScriptMethod* allows you to define an action on an object, using PowerShell script as the extension language. It consists of two child elements: the Name of the property and the Script.

In the script element, the $this variable refers to the current object you are extending. Like a standalone script, the $args variable represents the arguments to the method. Unlike standalone scripts, ScriptMethods do not support the param statement for parameters.

Example 3-9 adds a Remove ScriptMethod to PSDriveInfo. Like the other additions, place these customizations within the members section of the template given in Example 3-6. When you call this method with no arguments, the method simulates removing the drive (through the -WhatIf option to Remove-PsDrive). If you call this method with $true as the first argument, it actually removes the drive from the PowerShell session.

Example 3-9. A ScriptMethod for the PSDriveInfo type

```
  <ScriptMethod>
    <Name>Remove</Name>
    <Script>
      $force = [bool] $args[0]
```

Example 3-9. A ScriptMethod for the PSDriveInfo type (continued)

```
    ## Remove the drive if they use $true as the first parameter
    if($force)
    {
        $this | Remove-PSDrive
    }
    ## Otherwise, simulate the drive removal
    else
    {
        $this | Remove-PSDrive -WhatIf
    }
   </Script>
  </ScriptMethod>
```

Add other extension points

PowerShell supports several additional features in the types extension file, including CodeProperty, NoteProperty, CodeMethod, and MemberSet. Although not generally useful to end users, developers of PowerShell providers and cmdlets will find these features helpful. For more information about these additional features, see the Windows PowerShell SDK, or MSDN documentation.

## CHAPTER 4

Looping and Flow Control

4.0   Introduction

As you begin to write scripts or commands that interact with unknown data, the concepts of looping and flow control become increasingly important.

PowerShell's looping statements and commands let you perform an operation (or set of operations) without having to repeat the commands themselves. This includes, for example, doing something a specified number of times, processing each item in a collection, or working until a certain condition comes to pass.

PowerShell's flow control and comparison statements let you to adapt your script or command to unknown data. They let you execute commands based on the value of that data, skip commands based on the value of that data, and more.

Together, looping and flow control statements add significant versatility to your PowerShell toolbox.

4.1   Make Decisions with Comparison and Logical Operators

Problem

You want to compare some data with other data and make a decision based on that comparison.

Solution

Use PowerShell's logical operators to compare pieces of data and make decisions based on them.

Comparison operators:
```
-eq, -ne, -ge, -gt, -lt, -le, -like, -notlike, -match, -notmatch, -contains,
-notcontains, -is, -isnot
```
Logical operators:
```
-and, -or, -xor, -not
```

For a detailed description (and examples) of these operators, see "Comparison Operators" in Appendix A.

Discussion

PowerShell's logical and comparison operators let you compare pieces of data, or test data for some condition. An operator either compares two pieces of data (a *binary* operator) or tests one piece of data (a *unary* operator). All comparison operators are binary operators (they compare two pieces of data), as are most of the logical operators. The only unary logical operator is the -not operator, which returns the true/false opposite of the data that it tests.

Comparison operators compare two pieces of data and return a result that depends on the specific comparison operator. For example, you might want to check whether a collection has at least a certain number of elements:

```
PS >(dir).Count -ge 4
True
```

or, check whether a string matches a given regular expression:

```
PS >"Hello World" -match "H.*World"
True
```

Most comparison operators also adapt to the type of their input. For example, when you apply them to simple data such as a string, the -like and -match comparison operators determine whether the string matches the specified pattern. When you apply them to a collection of simple data, those same comparison operators return all elements in that collection that match the pattern you provide.

> The -match operator takes a regular expression as its argument. One of the more common regular expression symbols is the $ character, which represents the end of line. The $ character also represents the start of a PowerShell variable, though! To prevent PowerShell from interpreting characters as language terms or escape sequences, place the string in single quotes rather than double quotes:
>
> ```
> PS >"Hello World" -match "Hello"
> True
> PS >"Hello World" -match 'Hello$'
> False
> ```

For a detailed description of how the individual comparison operators adapt to their input, see "Comparison Operators" in Appendix A.

Logical operators combine true or false statements and return a result that depends on the specific logical operator. For example, you might want to check whether a string matches the wildcard pattern you supply, *and* that it is longer than a certain number of characters:

```
PS >$data = "Hello World"
PS >($data -like "*llo W*") -and ($data.Length -gt 10)
True
PS >($data -like "*llo W*") -and ($data.Length -gt 20)
False
```

Some of the comparison operators actually incorporate aspects of the logical operators. Since using the opposite of a comparison (such as -like) is so common, PowerShell provides comparison operators (such as -notlike) that save you from having to use the -not operator explicitly.

For a detailed description of the individual logical operators, see "Comparison Operators" in Appendix A.

Comparison operators and logical operators (when combined with flow control statements) form the core of how we write a script or command that adapts to its data and input.

See also "Conditional Statements" in Appendix A, for detailed information about these statements.

For more information about PowerShell's operators, type **Get-Help About_Operator**.

See Also

- "Comparison Operators" in Appendix A
- "Conditional Statements" in Appendix A

4.2   Adjust Script Flow Using Conditional Statements

Problem

You want to control the conditions under which PowerShell executes commands or portions of your script.

Solution

Use PowerShell's if, elseif, and else conditional statements to control the flow of execution in your script.

For example:

```
$temperature = 90

if($temperature -le 0)
```

```
{
    "Balmy Canadian Summer"
}
elseif($temperature -le 32)
{
    "Freezing"
}
elseif($temperature -le 50)
{
    "Cold"
}
elseif($temperature -le 70)
{
    "Warm"
}
else
{
    "Hot"
}
```

Discussion

Conditional statements include the following:

if *statement*
> Executes the script block that follows it if its *condition* evaluates to true

elseif *statement*
> Executes the script block that follows it if its *condition* evaluates to true, and none of the conditions in the if or elseif statements before it evaluate to true

else *statement*
> Executes the script block that follows it if none of the conditions in the if or elseif statements before it evaluate to true

For more information about these flow control statements, type **Get-Help About_ Flow_Control**.

4.3   Manage Large Conditional Statements with Switches

Problem

You want to find an easier or more compact way to represent a large if ... elseif ... else conditional statement.

Solution

Use PowerShell's switch statement to more easily represent a large if ... elseif ... else conditional statement.

For example:

```
$temperature = 20

switch($temperature)
{
    { $_ -lt 32 }    { "Below Freezing"; break }
    32               { "Exactly Freezing"; break }
    { $_ -le 50 }    { "Cold"; break }
    { $_ -le 70 }    { "Warm"; break }
    default          { "Hot" }
}
```

Discussion

PowerShell's switch statement lets you easily test its input against a large number of comparisons. The switch statement supports several options that allow you to configure how PowerShell compares the input against the conditions—such as with a wildcard, regular expression, or even arbitrary script block. Since scanning through the text in a file is such a common task, PowerShell's switch statement supports that directly. These additions make PowerShell switch statements a great deal more powerful than those in C and C++.

Although used as a way to express large conditional statements more cleanly, a switch statement operates much like a large sequence of if statements, as opposed to a large sequence of if ... elseif ... elseif ... else statements. Given the input that you provide, PowerShell evaluates that input against *each* of the comparisons in the switch statement. If the comparison evaluates to true, PowerShell then executes the script block that follows it. Unless that script block contains a break statement, PowerShell continues to evaluate the following comparisons.

For more information about PowerShell's switch statement, see "Conditional Statements" in Appendix A or type **Get-Help About_Switch**.

See Also

- "Conditional Statements" in Appendix A

4.4   Repeat Operations with Loops

Problem

You want to execute the same block of code more than once.

Solution

Use one of PowerShell's looping statements (for, foreach, while, and do), or PowerShell's Foreach-Object cmdlet to run a command or script block more than once. For a detailed description of these looping statements, see "Looping Statements" in Appendix A. For example:

for *loop*

```
for($counter = 1; $counter -le 10; $counter++)
{
    "Loop number $counter"
}
```

foreach *loop*

```
foreach($file in dir)
{
    "File length: " + $file.Length
}
```

Foreach-Object *cmdlet*

```
Get-ChildItem | Foreach-Object { "File length: " + $_.Length }
```

while *loop*

```
$response = ""
while($response -ne "QUIT")
{
    $response = Read-Host "Type something"
}
```

do..while *loop*

```
$response = ""
do
{
    $response = Read-Host "Type something"
} while($response -ne "QUIT")
```

Discussion

Although any of the looping statements can be written to be functionally equivalent to any of the others, each lends itself to certain problems.

You usually use a for loop when you need to perform an operation an exact number of times. Because using it this way is so common, it is often called a *counted for loop*.

You usually use a foreach loop when you have a collection of objects and want to visit each item in that collection. If you do not yet have that entire collection in memory (as in the dir collection from the foreach example above), the Foreach-Object cmdlet is usually a more efficient alternative.

Unlike the foreach loop, the Foreach-Object cmdlet allows you to process each element in the collection *as PowerShell generates it*. This is an important distinction; asking PowerShell to collect the entire output of a large command (such as Get-Content *hugefile.txt*) in a foreach loop can easily drag down your system.

A handy shortcut to repeat an operation on the command line is:

```
PS >1..10 | foreach { "Working" }
Working
Working
Working
Working
Working
Working
Working
Working
Working
Working
```

The while and do..while loops are similar, in that they continue to execute the loop as long as its condition evaluates to true. A while loop checks for this before ever running your script block, while a do..while loop checks the condition after running your script block.

For a detailed description of these looping statements, see "Looping Statements" in Appendix A or type **Get-Help About_For** or type **Get-Help About_Foreach**.

See Also

- "Looping Statements" in Appendix A

4.5   Add a Pause or Delay

Problem

You want to pause or delay your script or command.

Solution

To pause until the user presses ENTER, use the Read-Host cmdlet:

```
PS >Read-Host "Press ENTER"
Press ENTER:
```

To pause until the user presses a key, use the ReadKey() method on the $host object:

```
PS >$host.UI.RawUI.ReadKey()
```

To pause a script for a given amount of time, use the Start-Sleep cmdlet:

```
PS >Start-Sleep 5
PS >Start-Sleep -Milliseconds 300
```

Discussion

When you want to pause your script until the user presses a key or for a set amount of time, the Read-Host and Start-Sleep cmdlets are the two you are most likely to use. For more information about using the Read-Host cmdlet to read input from the user, see Recipe 12.1, "Read a Line of User Input." In other situations, you may sometimes want to write a loop in your script that runs at a constant speed—such as once per minute, or 30 times per second. That is typically a difficult task, as the commands in the loop might take up a significant amount of time, or even an inconsistent amount of time.

In the past, many computer games suffered from solving this problem incorrectly. To control their game speed, game developers added commands to slow down their game. For example, after much tweaking and fiddling, the developers might realize that the game plays correctly on a typical machine if they make the computer count to one million every time it updates the screen. Unfortunately, these commands (such as counting) depend heavily on the speed of the computer. Since a fast computer can count to 1 million much more quickly than a slow computer, the game ends up running much quicker (often to the point of incomprehensibility) on faster computers!

To make your loop run at a regular speed, you can measure how long the commands in a loop take to complete, and then delay for whatever time is left, as shown in Example 4-1.

Example 4-1. Running a loop at a constant speed

```
$loopDelayMilliseconds = 650
while($true)
{
   $startTime = Get-Date

   ## Do commands here
   "Executing"

   $endTime = Get-Date
   $loopLength = ($endTime - $startTime).TotalMilliseconds
   $timeRemaining = $loopDelayMilliseconds - $loopLength

   if($timeRemaining -gt 0)
   {
      Start-Sleep -Milliseconds $timeRemaining
   }
}
```

For more information about the Start-Sleep cmdlet, type **Get-Help Start-Sleep**.

See Also

- Recipe 12.1, "Read a Line of User Input

## CHAPTER 5

Strings and Unstructured Text

5.0 Introduction

Creating and manipulating text has long been one of the primary tasks of scripting languages and traditional shells. In fact, Perl (the language) started as a simple (but useful) tool designed for text processing. It has grown well beyond those humble roots, but its popularity provides strong evidence of the need it fills.

In text-based shells, this strong focus continues. When most of your interaction with the system happens by manipulating the text-based output of programs, powerful text processing utilities become crucial. These text parsing tools such as awk, sed, and grep form the keystones of text-based systems management.

In PowerShell's object-based environment, this traditional tool chain plays a less critical role. You can accomplish most of the tasks that previously required these tools much more effectively through other PowerShell commands. However, being an object-oriented shell does not mean that PowerShell drops all support for text processing. Dealing with strings and unstructured text continues to play an important part in a system administrator's life. Since PowerShell lets you to manage the majority of your system in its full fidelity (using cmdlets and objects,) the text processing tools can once again focus primarily on actual text processing tasks.

5.1 Create a String

Problem

You want to create a variable that holds text.

Solution

Use PowerShell string variables to give you a way to store and work with text.

To define a string that supports variable expansion and escape characters in its definition, surround it with double quotes:

```
$myString = "Hello World"
```

To define a literal string (that does not support variable expansion or escape characters), surround it with single quotes:

```
$myString = 'Hello World'
```

Discussion

String literals come in two varieties: *literal* (*nonexpanding*) and *expanding* strings. To create a literal string, place single quotes ($myString = 'Hello World') around the text. To create an expanding string, place double quotes ($myString = "Hello World") around the text.

In a literal string, all the text between the single quotes becomes part of your string. In an expanding string, PowerShell expands variable names (such as $myString) and escape sequences (such as `n) with their values (such as the content of $myString and the newline character, respectively).

For a detailed explanation of the escape sequences and replacement rules inside PowerShell strings, see "Strings" in Appendix A.

One exception to the *"all text in a literal string is literal"* rule comes from the quote characters themselves. In either type of string, PowerShell lets you to place two of that string's quote characters together to add the quote character itself:

```
$myString = "This string includes ""double quotes"" because it combined quote
characters."
$myString = 'This string includes ''single quotes'' because it combined quote
characters.'
```

This helps prevent escaping atrocities that would arise when you try to include a single quote in a single-quoted string. For example:

```
$myString = 'This string includes ' + "'" + 'single quotes' + "'"
```

 This example shows how easy PowerShell makes it to create new strings by adding other strings together. This is an attractive way to build a formatted report in a script but should be used with caution. Due to the way that the .NET Framework (and therefore PowerShell) manages strings, adding information to the end of a large string this way causes noticeable performance problems. If you intend to create large reports, see Recipe 5.13, "Generate Large Reports and Text Streams."

See Also

- Recipe 5.13, "Generate Large Reports and Text Streams"
- "Strings" in Appendix A

5.2 Create a Multiline or Formatted String

Problem

You want to create a variable that holds text with newlines or other explicit formatting.

Solution

Use a PowerShell *here string* to store and work with text that includes newlines and other formatting information.

```
$myString = @"
This is the first line
of a very long string. A "here string"
lets you to create blocks of text
that span several lines.
"@
```

Discussion

PowerShell begins a *here string* when it sees the characters @" followed by a newline. It ends the string when it sees the characters "@ on their own line. These seemingly odd restrictions allow you to create strings that include quote characters, newlines, and other symbols that you commonly use when you create large blocks of preformatted text.

 These restrictions, while useful, can sometimes cause problems when you copy and paste PowerShell examples from the Internet. Web pages often add spaces at the end of lines, which can interfere with the strict requirements of the beginning of a here string. If PowerShell produces an error when your script defines a here string, check that the here string does not include an errant space after its first quote character.

Like string literals, here strings may be literal (and use single quotes) or expanding (and use double quotes).

In addition to their usefulness in preformatted text variables, here strings also provide a useful way to temporarily disable lines in your script. Since PowerShell does not provide a first-class multiline comment, you can use a here string as you would use a multiline comment in other scripting or programming languages. Example 5-1 demonstrates this technique.

Example 5-1. Using here strings for multiline comments

```
## This is a regular comment
$null = @"
function MyTest
{
```

Example 5-1. Using here strings for multiline comments (continued)

```
    "This should not be considered a function"
}

$myVariable = 10;
"@

## This is regular script again
```

Using $null for the variable name tells PowerShell to not retain the information for your later use.

5.3   Place Special Characters in a String

Problem

You want to place special characters (such as tab and newline) in a string variable.

Solution

In an expanding string, use PowerShell's escape sequences to include special characters such as tab and newline.

```
    PS >$myString = "Report for Today`n----------------"
    PS >$myString
    Report for Today
    ----------------
```

Discussion

As discussed in Recipe 5.1, "Create a String," PowerShell strings come in two varieties: *literal* (or *nonexpanding*) and *expanding* strings. A literal string uses single quotes around its text, while an expanding string uses double quotes around its text.

In a literal string, all the text between the single quotes becomes part of your string. In an expanding string, PowerShell expands variable names (such as *$ENV: SystemRoot*) and escape sequences (such as `n) with their values (such as the SystemRoot environment variable and the newline character).

> Unlike many languages that use a backslash character (\) for escape sequences, PowerShell uses a back-tick (`) character. This stems from its focus on system administration, where backslashes are ubiquitous in path names.

For a detailed explanation of the escape sequences and replacement rules inside PowerShell strings, see "Strings" in Appendix A.

See Also

- Recipe 5.1, "Create a String"
- "Strings" in Appendix A

5.4 Insert Dynamic Information in a String

Problem

You want to place dynamic information (such as the value of another variable) in a string.

Solution

In an expanding string, include the name of a variable in the string to insert the value of that variable.

```
PS >$header = "Report for Today"
PS >$myString = "$header`n----------------"
PS >$myString
Report for Today
----------------
```

To include information more complex than just the value of a variable, enclose it in a subexpression:

```
PS >$header = "Report for Today"
PS >$myString = "$header`n$('-' * $header.Length)"
PS >$myString
Report for Today
----------------
```

Discussion

Variable substitution in an expanding string is a simple enough concept, but subexpressions deserve a little clarification.

A *subexpression* is the dollar sign character, followed by a PowerShell command (or set of commands) contained in parentheses:

```
$(subexpression)
```

When PowerShell sees a subexpression in an expanding string, it evaluates the subexpression and places the result in the expanding string. In the solution, the expression '-' * $header.Length tells PowerShell to make a line of dashes $header.Length long.

Another way to place dynamic information inside a string is to use PowerShell's string formatting operator, which is based on the rules of the .NET string formatting:

```
PS >$header = "Report for Today"
PS >$myString = "{0}`n{1}" -f $header,('-' * $header.Length)
```

```
PS >$myString
Report for Today
----------------
```

For an explanation of PowerShell's formatting operator, see Recipe 5.6, "Place Formatted Information in a String." For more information about PowerShell's escape characters, type **Get-Help About_Escape_Character** or type **Get-Help About_Special_ Character**.

See Also

- Recipe 5.6, "Place Formatted Information in a String"

5.5   Prevent a String from Including Dynamic Information

Problem

You want to prevent PowerShell from interpreting special characters or variable names inside a string.

Solution

Use a nonexpanding string to have PowerShell interpret your string exactly as entered. A nonexpanding uses the single quote character around its text.

```
PS >$myString = 'Useful PowerShell characters include: $, `, " and { }'
PS >$myString
Useful PowerShell characters include: $, `, " and { }
```

If you want to include newline characters as well, use a nonexpanding here string, as in Example 5-2.

Example 5-2. A nonexpanding here string that includes newline characters

```
PS >$myString = @'
>> Tip of the Day
>> --------------
>> Useful PowerShell characters include: $, `, ', " and { }
>> '@
>>
PS >$myString
Tip of the Day
--------------
Useful PowerShell characters include: $, `, ', " and { }
```

Discussion

In a literal string, all the text between the single quotes becomes part of your string. This is in contrast to an expanding string, where PowerShell expands variable names (such as $myString) and escape sequences (such as `n) with their values (such as the content of $myString and the newline character).

> Nonexpanding strings are a useful way to manage files and folders that contain special characters that might otherwise be interpreted as escape sequences. For more information about managing files with special characters in their name, see Recipe 17.6, "Manage Files That Include Special Characters."

As discussed in Recipe 5.1, "Create a String," one exception to the *all text in a literal string is literal* rule comes from the quote characters themselves. In either type of string, PowerShell let you place two of that string's quote characters together to include the quote character itself:

```
$myString = "This string includes ""double quotes"" because it combined quote characters."
$myString = 'This string includes ''single quotes'' because it combined quote characters.'
```

See Also

- Recipe 5.1, "Create a String"
- Recipe 17.6, "Manage Files That Include Special Characters"

5.6   Place Formatted Information in a String

Problem

You want to place formatted information (such as right-aligned text or numbers rounded to a specific number of decimal places) in a string.

Solution

Use PowerShell's formatting operator to place formatted information inside a string.

```
PS >$formatString = "{0,8:D4}  {1:C}`n"
PS >$report  = "Quantity  Price`n"
PS >$report += "---------------`n"
PS >$report += $formatString -f 50,2.5677
PS >$report += $formatString -f 3,9
PS >$report
Quantity  Price
---------------
    0050  $2.57
    0003  $9.00
```

Discussion

PowerShell's string formatting operator (-f) uses the same string formatting rules as the String.Format() method in the .NET Framework. It takes a format string on its left side, and the items you want to format on its right side.

In the solution, you format two numbers: a quantity and a price. The first number ({0}) represents the quantity and is right-aligned in a box of 8 characters (,8). It is formatted as a decimal number with 4 digits (:D4). The second number ({1}) represents the price, which you format as currency (:C).

For a detailed explanation of PowerShell's formatting operator, see "Simple Operators" in Appendix A, PowerShell Language and Environment. For a detailed list of the formatting rules, see Appendix H, *.NET String Formatting*.

Although primarily used to control the layout of information, the string-formatting operator is also a readable replacement for what is normally accomplished with string concatenation:

```
PS >$number1 = 10
PS >$number2 = 32
PS >"$number2 divided by $number1 is " + $number2 / $number1
32 divided by 10 is 3.2
```

The string formatting operator makes this much easier to read:

```
PS >"{0} divided by {1} is {2}" -f $number2, $number1, ($number2 / $number1)
32 divided by 10 is 3.2
```

In addition to the string formatting operator, PowerShell provides three formatting commands (Format-Table, Format-Wide, and Format-List) that lets you to easily generate formatted reports. For detailed information about those cmdlets, see "Formatting Output" in Appendix A.

See Also

- "Formatting Output" in Appendix A
- "Simple Operators" in Appendix A
- Appendix H, *.NET String Formatting*

5.7   Search a String for Text or a Pattern

Problem

You want to determine if a string contains another string, or want to find the position of a string within another string.

Solution

PowerShell provides several options to help you search a string for text.

Use the -like operator to determine whether a string matches a given DOS-like wildcard:

```
PS >"Hello World" -like "*llo W*"
True
```

Use the -match operator to determine whether a string matches a given regular expression:

```
PS >"Hello World" -match '.*l[l-z]o W.*$'
True
```

Use the Contains() method to determine whether a string contains a specific string:

```
PS >"Hello World".Contains("World")
True
```

Use the IndexOf() method to determine the location of one string within another:

```
PS >"Hello World".IndexOf("World")
6
```

Discussion

Since PowerShell strings are fully featured .NET objects, they support many string-oriented operations directly. The Contains() and IndexOf() methods are two examples of the many features that the String class supports. To learn what other functionality the String class supports, see Recipe 3.9, "Learn About Types and Objects."

Although they use similar characters, simple wildcards and regular expressions serve significantly different purposes. Wildcards are much more simple than regular expressions, and because of that, more constrained. While you can summarize the rules for wildcards in just four bullet points, entire books have been written to help teach and illuminate the use of regular expressions.

 A common use of regular expressions is to search for a string that spans multiple lines. By default, regular expressions do not search across lines, but you can use the *singleline* (?s) option to instruct them to do so:

```
PS >"Hello `n World" -match "Hello.*World"
False
PS >"Hello `n World" -match "(?s)Hello.*World"
True
```

Wildcards lend themselves to simple matches, while regular expressions lend themselves to more complex matches.

For a detailed description of the –like operator, see "Comparison Operators" in Appendix A. For a detailed description of the –match operator, see "Simple Operators" in Appendix A, PowerShell Language and Environment. For a detailed list of the regular expression rules and syntax, see Appendix B, *Regular Expression Reference*.

One difficulty sometimes arises when you try to store the result of a PowerShell command in a string, as shown in Example 5-3.

Example 5-3. Attempting to store output of a PowerShell command in a string

```
PS >Get-Help Get-ChildItem

NAME
    Get-ChildItem

SYNOPSIS
    Gets the items and child items in one or more specified locations.

(...)

PS >$helpContent = Get-Help Get-ChildItem
PS >$helpContent -match "location"
False
```

The –match operator searches a string for the pattern you specify but seems to fail in this case. This is because all PowerShell commands generate objects. If you don't store that output in another variable or pass it to another command, PowerShell converts to a text representation before it displays it to you. In Example 5-3, $helpContent is a fully featured object, not just its string representation:

```
PS >$helpContent.Name
Get-ChildItem
```

To work with the text-based representation of a PowerShell command, you can explicitly send it through the Out-String cmdlet. The Out-String cmdlet converts its input into the text-based form you are used to seeing on the screen:

```
PS >$helpContent = Get-Help Get-ChildItem | Out-String
PS >$helpContent -match "location"
True
```

See Also

- Recipe 3.9, "Learn About Types and Objects"
- "Comparison Operators" in Appendix A
- "Simple Operators" in Appendix A
- Appendix B, *Regular Expression Reference*

5.8   Replace Text in a String

Problem

You want to replace a portion of a string with another string.

Solution

PowerShell provides several options to help you replace text in a string with other text.

Use the `Replace()` method on the string itself to perform simple replacements:

```
PS >"Hello World".Replace("World", "PowerShell")
Hello PowerShell
```

Use PowerShell's regular expression –replace operator to perform more advanced regular expression replacements:

```
PS >"Hello World" -replace '(.*) (.*)','$2 $1'
World Hello
```

Discussion

The `Replace()` method and the –replace operator both provide useful ways to replace text in a string. The `Replace()` method is the quickest but also the most constrained. It replaces every occurrence of the exact string you specify with the exact replacement string that you provide. The –replace operator provides much more flexibility, since its arguments are regular expressions that can match and replace complex patterns.

> The regular expressions that you use with the –replace operator often contain characters that PowerShell normally interprets as variable names or escape characters. To prevent PowerShell from interpreting these characters, use a nonexpanding string (single quotes) as shown by the solution.

For more information about the –replace operator, see "Simple Operators" in Appendix A and Appendix H, *.NET String Formatting*.

See Also

- "Simple Operators" in Appendix A
- Appendix H, *.NET String Formatting*

5.9   Convert a String to Upper/Lowercase

Problem

You want to convert a string to uppercase or lowercase.

Solution

Use the `ToUpper()` and `ToLower()` methods of the string to convert it to uppercase and lowercase, respectively.

To convert a string to uppercase, use the `ToUpper()` method:

```
PS >"Hello World".ToUpper()
HELLO WORLD
```

To convert a string to lowercase, use the `ToLower()` method:

```
PS >"Hello World".ToLower()
hello world
```

Discussion

Since PowerShell strings are fully featured .NET objects, they support many string-oriented operations directly. The `ToUpper()` and `ToLower()` methods are two examples of the many features that the `String` class supports. To learn what other functionality the `String` class supports, see Recipe 3.9, "Learn About Types and Objects."

 Neither PowerShell nor the methods of the .NET `String` class directly support capitalizing only the first letter of a word. If you want to capitalize only the first character of a word or sentence, try the following commands:

```
PS >$text = "hello"
PS >$newText = $text.Substring(0,1).ToUpper() +
>>    $text.Substring(1)
>> $newText
>>
Hello
```

One thing to keep in mind as you convert a string to uppercase or lowercase is your motivation for doing it. One of the most common reasons is for comparing strings, as shown in Example 5-4.

Example 5-4. Using the ToUpper() method to normalize strings

```
## $text comes from the user, and contains the value "quit"
if($text.ToUpper() -eq "QUIT") { ... }
```

Unfortunately, explicitly changing the capitalization of strings fails in subtle ways when your script runs in different cultures. Many cultures follow different capitalization and comparison rules than you may be used to. For example, the Turkish language includes two types of the letter "I": one with a dot, and one without. The uppercase version of the lowercase letter "i" corresponds to the version of the capital I with a dot, not the capital I used in QUIT. Those capitalization rules cause the string comparison code in Example 5-4 to fail in the Turkish culture.

To compare some input against a hard-coded string in a case-insensitive manner, the better solution is to use PowerShell's –eq operator without changing any of the casing yourself. The –eq operator is case-insensitive and culture-neutral by default:

```
PS >$text1 = "Hello"
PS >$text2 = "HELLO"
PS >$text1 –eq $text2
True
```

For more information about writing culture-aware scripts, see Recipe 12.6, "Write Culture-Aware Scripts."

See Also

- Recipe 3.9, "Learn About Types and Objects"
- Recipe 12.6, "Write Culture-Aware Scripts"

5.10   Trim a String

Problem

You want to remove leading or trailing spaces from a string or user input.

Solution

Use the Trim() method of the string to remove all leading and trailing whitespace characters from that string.

```
PS >$text = " `t   Test String`t `t"
PS >"|" + $text.Trim() + "|"
|Test String|
```

Discussion

The Trim() method cleans all whitespace from the beginning *and* end of a string. If you want just one or the other, you can also call the TrimStart() or TrimEnd() method to remove whitespace from the beginning or the end of the string, respectively. If you want to remove specific characters from the beginning or end of a string, the Trim(), TrimStart(), and TrimEnd() methods provide options to support that. To trim a list of specific characters from the end of a string, provide that list to the method, as shown in Example 5-5.

Example 5-5. Trimming a list of characters from the end of a string

```
PS >"Hello World".TrimEnd('d','l','r','o','W',' ')
He
```

 At first blush, the following command that attempts to trim the text "World" from the end of a string appears to work incorrectly:

```
PS >"Hello World".TrimEnd(" World")

He
```

This happens because the TrimEnd() method takes a list of characters to remove from the end of a string. PowerShell automatically converts a string to a list of characters if required, so this command is in fact the same as the command in Example 5-5.

If you want to replace text anywhere in a string (and not just from the beginning or end), see Recipe 5.8, "Replace Text in a String."

See Also

- Recipe 5.8, "Replace Text in a String"

5.11 Format a Date for Output

Problem

You want to control the way that PowerShell displays or formats a date.

Solution

To control the format of a date, use one of the following options:

- The Get-Date cmdlet's –Format parameter:

  ```
  PS >Get-Date -Date "05/09/1998 1:23 PM" -Format "dd-MM-yyyy @ hh:mm:ss"
  09-05-1998 @ 01:23:00
  ```

- PowerShell's string formatting (-f) operator:

  ```
  PS >$date = [DateTime] "05/09/1998 1:23 PM"
  PS >"{0:dd-MM-yyyy @ hh:mm:ss}" -f $date
  09-05-1998 @ 01:23:00
  ```

- The object's ToString() method:

  ```
  PS >$date = [DateTime] "05/09/1998 1:23 PM"
  PS >$date.ToString("dd-MM-yyyy @ hh:mm:ss")
  09-05-1998 @ 01:23:00
  ```

- The Get-Date cmdlet's –UFormat parameter, which supports Unix date format strings:

  ```
  PS >Get-Date -Date "05/09/1998 1:23 PM" -UFormat "%d-%m-%Y @ %I:%M:%S"
  09-05-1998 @ 01:23:00
  ```

Discussion

Except for the -Uformat parameter of the Get-Date cmdlet, all date formatting in PowerShell uses the standard .NET DateTime format strings. These format strings let you display dates in one of many standard formats (such as your system's short or long date patterns), or in a completely custom manner. For more information on how to specify standard .NET DateTime format strings, see Appendix I, *.NET DateTime Formatting*.

If you are already used to the Unix-style date formatting strings (or are converting an existing script that uses a complex one), the -Uformat parameter of the Get-Date cmdlet may be helpful. It accepts the format strings accepted by the Unix date command, but does not provide any functionality that standard .NET date formatting strings cannot.

When working with the string version of dates and times, be aware that they are the most common source of internationalization issues—problems that arise from running a script on a machine with a different culture than the one it was written on. In North America "05/09/1998" means "May 9, 1998." In many other cultures, though, it means "September 5, 1998." Whenever possible use and compare DateTime objects (rather than strings) to other DateTime objects, as that avoids these cultural differences. Example 5-6 demonstrates this approach.

Example 5-6. Comparing DateTime objects with the -gt operator

```
PS >$dueDate = [DateTime] "01/01/2006"
PS >if([DateTime]::Now -gt $dueDate)
>> {
>>     "Account is now due"
>> }
>>
Account is now due
```

PowerShell *always* assumes the North American date format when it interprets a DateTime constant such as [DateTime] "05/09/1998". This is for the same reason that all languages interpret numeric constants (such as 12.34) in the North American format. If it did otherwise, nearly every script that dealt with dates and times would fail on international systems.

For more information about the Get-Date cmdlet, type **Get-Help Get-Date**.

See Also

- Appendix I, *.NET DateTime Formatting*

5.12   Program: Convert Text Streams to Objects

One of the strongest features of PowerShell is its object-based pipeline. You don't waste your energy creating, destroying, and recreating the object representation of your data. In other shells, you lose the full-fidelity representation of data when the pipeline converts it to pure text. You can regain some of it through excessive text parsing, but not all of it.

However, you still often have to interact with low-fidelity input that originates from outside PowerShell. Text-based data files and legacy programs are two examples.

PowerShell offers great support for two of the three text-parsing staples:

Sed
> Replaces text. For that functionality, PowerShell offers the -replace operator.

Grep
> Searches text. For that functionality, PowerShell offers the Select-String cmdlet, among others.

The third traditional text-parsing tool, *Awk*, lets you to chop a line of text into more intuitive groupings. PowerShell offers the Split() method on strings, but that lacks some of the power you usually need to break a string into groups.

The Convert-TextObject script presented in Example 5-7 lets you convert text streams into a set of objects that represent those text elements according to the rules you specify. From there, you can use all of PowerShell's object-based tools, which gives you even more power than you would get with the text-based equivalents.

Example 5-7. Convert-TextObject.ps1

```
##############################################################################
##
## Convert-TextObject.ps1 -- Convert a simple string into a custom PowerShell
## object.
##
##       Parameters:
##
##       [string] Delimiter
##          If specified, gives the .NET Regular Expression with which to
##          split the string. The script generates properties for the
##          resulting object out of the elements resulting from this split.
##          If not specified, defaults to splitting on the maximum amount
##          of whitespace: "\s+", as long as ParseExpression is not
##          specified either.
##
##       [string] ParseExpression
##          If specified, gives the .NET Regular Expression with which to
##          parse the string. The script generates properties for the
##          resulting object out of the groups captured by this regular
##          expression.
##
```

Example 5-7. Convert-TextObject.ps1 (continued)

```
##          ** NOTE ** Delimiter and ParseExpression are mutually exclusive.
##
##          [string[]] PropertyName
##              If specified, the script will pair the names from this object
##              definition with the elements from the parsed string.  If not
##              specified (or the generated object contains more properties
##              than you specify,) the script uses property names in the
##              pattern of Property1,Property2,...,PropertyN
##
##          [type[]] PropertyType
##              If specified, the script will pair the types from this list with
##              the properties from the parsed string.  If not specified (or the
##              generated object contains more properties than you specify,) the
##              script sets the properties to be of type [string]
##
##
##          Example usage:
##              "Hello World" | Convert-TextObject
##              Generates an Object with "Property1=Hello" and "Property2=World"
##
##              "Hello World" | Convert-TextObject -Delimiter "ll"
##              Generates an Object with "Property1=He" and "Property2=o World"
##
##              "Hello World" | Convert-TextObject -ParseExpression "He(ll.*o)r(ld)"
##              Generates an Objcct with "Property1-llo Wo" and "Property2=ld"
##
##              "Hello World" | Convert-TextObject -PropertyName FirstWord,SecondWord
##              Generates an Object with "FirstWord=Hello" and "SecondWord=World"
##
##              "123 456" | Convert-TextObject -PropertyType $([string],[int])
##              Generates an Object with "Property1=123" and "Property2=456"
##              The second property is an integer, as opposed to a string
##
###############################################################################
param(
    [string] $delimiter,
    [string] $parseExpression,
    [string[]] $propertyName,
    [type[]] $propertyType
    )

function Main(
    $inputObjects, $parseExpression, $propertyType,
    $propertyName, $delimiter)
{
    $delimiterSpecified = [bool] $delimiter
    $parseExpressionSpecified = [bool] $parseExpression

    ## If they've specified both ParseExpression and Delimiter, show usage
    if($delimiterSpecified -and $parseExpressionSpecified)
```

Example 5-7. Convert-TextObject.ps1 (continued)

```
    {
        Usage
        return
    }

    ## If they enter no parameters, assume a default delimiter of whitespace
    if(-not $($delimiterSpecified -or $parseExpressionSpecified))
    {
        $delimiter = "\s+"
        $delimiterSpecified = $true
    }

    ## Cycle through the $inputObjects, and parse it into objects
    foreach($inputObject in $inputObjects)
    {
        if(-not $inputObject) { $inputObject = "" }
        foreach($inputLine in $inputObject.ToString())
        {
            ParseTextObject $inputLine $delimiter $parseExpression `
                $propertyType $propertyName
        }
    }
}

function Usage
{
    "Usage: "
    " Convert-TextObject"
    " Convert-TextObject -ParseExpression parseExpression " +
        "[-PropertyName propertyName] [-PropertyType propertyType]"
    " Convert-TextObject -Delimiter delimiter " +
        "[-PropertyName propertyName] [-PropertyType propertyType]"
    return
}

## Function definition -- ParseTextObject.
## Perform the heavy-lifting -- parse a string into its components.
## for each component, add it as a note to the Object that we return
function ParseTextObject
{
    param(
        $textInput, $delimiter, $parseExpression,
        $propertyTypes, $propertyNames)

    $parseExpressionSpecified = -not $delimiter

    $returnObject = New-Object PSObject

    $matches = $null
    $matchCount = 0
    if($parseExpressionSpecified)
    {
```

Example 5-7. Convert-TextObject.ps1 (continued)

```
    ## Populates the matches variable by default
    [void] ($textInput -match $parseExpression)
    $matchCount = $matches.Count
}
else
{
    $matches = [Regex]::Split($textInput, $delimiter)
    $matchCount = $matches.Length
}

$counter = 0
if($parseExpressionSpecified) { $counter++ }
for(; $counter -lt $matchCount; $counter++)
{
    $propertyName = "None"
    $propertyType = [string]

    ## Parse by Expression
    if($parseExpressionSpecified)
    {
        $propertyName = "Property$counter"

        ## Get the property name
        if($counter -le $propertyNames.Length)
        {
            if($propertyName[$counter - 1])
            {
                $propertyName = $propertyNames[$counter - 1]
            }
        }

        ## Get the property value
        if($counter -le $propertyTypes.Length)
        {
            if($types[$counter - 1])
            {
                $propertyType = $propertyTypes[$counter - 1]
            }
        }
    }
    ## Parse by delimiter
    else
    {
        $propertyName = "Property$($counter + 1)"

        ## Get the property name
        if($counter -lt $propertyNames.Length)
        {
            if($propertyNames[$counter])
            {
                $propertyName = $propertyNames[$counter]
            }
        }
```

Example 5-7. Convert-TextObject.ps1 (continued)

```
        ## Get the property value
        if($counter -lt $propertyTypes.Length)
        {
            if($propertyTypes[$counter])
            {
                $propertyType = $propertyTypes[$counter]
            }
        }
    }

    Add-Note $returnObject $propertyName `
        ($matches[$counter] -as $propertyType)
}

$returnObject
}

## Add a note to an object
function Add-Note ($object, $name, $value)
{
    $object | Add-Member NoteProperty $name $value
}


Main $input $parseExpression $propertyType $propertyName $delimiter
```

For more information about running scripts, see Recipe 1.1, "Run Programs, Scripts, and Existing Tools."

See Also

- Recipe 1.1, "Run Programs, Scripts, and Existing Tools"

5.13   Generate Large Reports and Text Streams

Problem

You want to write a script that generates a large report or large amount of data

Solution

The best approach to generating a large amount of data is to take advantage of PowerShell's streaming behavior whenever possible. Opt for solutions that pipeline data between commands:

```
Get-ChildItem C:\ *.txt -Recurse | Out-File c:\temp\AllTextFiles.txt
```

rather than collect the output at each stage:

```
$files = Get-ChildItem C:\ *.txt -Recurse
$files | Out-File c:\temp\AllTextFiles.txt
```

If your script generates a large text report (and streaming is not an option), use the StringBuilder class:

```
$output = New-Object System.Text.StringBuilder
Get-ChildItem C:\ *.txt -Recurse |
    Foreach-Object { [void] $output.Append($_.FullName + "`n") }
$output.ToString()
```

rather than simple text concatenation:

```
$output = ""
Get-ChildItem C:\ *.txt -Recurse | Foreach-Object { $output += $_.FullName }
$output
```

Discussion

In PowerShell, combining commands in a pipeline is a fundamental concept. As scripts and cmdlets generate output, PowerShell passes that output to the next command in the pipeline as soon as it can. In the solution, the Get-ChildItem commands that retrieve all text files on the C: drive take a very long time to complete. However, since they *begin* to generate data almost immediately, PowerShell can pass that data onto the next command as soon as the Get-ChildItem cmdlet produces it. This is true of any commands that generate or consume data and is called *streaming*. The pipeline completes almost as soon as the Get-ChildItem cmdlet finishes producing its data and uses memory very efficiently as it does so.

The second Get-ChildItem example (that collects its data) prevents PowerShell from taking advantage of this streaming opportunity. It first stores all the files in an array, which, because of the amount of data, takes a long time and enormous amount of memory. Then, it sends all those objects into the output file, which takes a long time as well.

However, most commands can consume data produced by the pipeline directly, as illustrated by the Out-File cmdlet. For those commands, PowerShell provides streaming behavior as long as you combine the commands into a pipeline. For commands that do not support data coming from the pipeline directly, the Foreach-Object cmdlet (with the aliases of foreach and %) lets you to still work with each piece of data as the previous command produces it, as shown in the StringBuilder example.

Creating large text reports

When you generate large reports, it is common to store the entire report into a string, and then write that string out to a file once the script completes. You can usually accomplish this most effectively by streaming the text directly to its destination (a file or the screen), but sometimes this is not possible.

Since PowerShell makes it so easy to add more text to the end of a string (as in $output += $_.FullName), many initially opt for that approach. This works great for small-to-medium strings, but causes significant performance problems for large strings.

As an example of this performance difference, compare the following:

```
PS >Measure-Command {
>>     $output = New-Object Text.StringBuilder
>>     1..10000 |
>>         Foreach-Object { $output.Append("Hello World") }
>> }
>>


(...)
TotalSeconds     : 2.3471592

PS >Measure-Command {
>>     $output = ""
>>     1..10000 | Foreach-Object { $output += "Hello World" }
>> }
>>


(...)
TotalSeconds     : 4.9884882
```

In the .NET Framework (and therefore PowerShell), strings never change after you create them. When you add more text to the end of a string, PowerShell has to build a *new* string by combining the two smaller strings. This operation takes a long time for large strings, which is why the .NET Framework includes the System.Text.StringBuilder class. Unlike normal strings, the StringBuilder class assumes that you will modify its data—an assumption that allows it to adapt to change much more efficiently.

## CHAPTER 6

Calculations and Math

6.0   Introduction

Math is an important feature in any scripting language. Math support in a language includes addition, subtraction, multiplication, and division of course, but extends further into more advanced mathematical operations. So, it should not surprise you that PowerShell provides a strong suite of mathematical and calculation-oriented features.

Since PowerShell provides full access to its scripting language from the command line, though, this keeps a powerful and useful command-line calculator always at your fingertips!

In addition to its support for traditional mathematical operations, PowerShell also caters to system administrators by working natively with concepts such as megabytes and gigabytes, simple statistics (such as sum and average), and conversions between bases.

6.1   Perform Simple Arithmetic

Problem

You want to use PowerShell to calculate simple mathematical results.

Solution

Use PowerShell's arithmetic operators:

+	Addition
-	Subtraction
*	Multiplication
/	Division
%	Modulus

| += , -= , *= , /= , and %= | Assignment variations of the above |
| () | Precedence/Order of operations |

For a detailed description of these mathematical operators, see "Simple Operators" in Appendix A.

Discussion

One difficulty in many programming languages comes from the way that they handle data in variables. For example, this C# snippet stores the value of "1" in the result variable, when the user probably wanted the result to hold the floating point value of 1.5:

```
double result = 0;
result = 3/2;
```

This is because C# (along with many other languages) determines the result of the division from the type of data being used in the division. In the example above, it decides that you want the answer to be an integer since you used two integers in the division.

PowerShell, on the other hand, avoids this problem. Even if you use two integers in a division, PowerShell returns the result as a floating point number if required. This is called *widening*.

```
PS >$result = 0
PS >$result = 3/2
PS >$result
1.5
```

One exception to this automatic widening is when you explicitly tell PowerShell the type of result you want. For example, you might use an integer cast ([int]) to say that you want the result to be an integer after all:

```
PS >$result = [int] (3/2)
PS >$result
2
```

Many programming languages drop the portion after the decimal point when they convert them from floating point numbers to integers. This is called *truncation*. PowerShell, on the other hand, uses *banker's rounding* for this conversion. It converts floating point numbers to their nearest integer, rounding to the nearest even number in case of a tie.

Several programming techniques use truncation, though, so it is still important that a scripting language somehow support it. PowerShell does not have a built-in operator that performs a truncation-style division, but it does support it through the [Math]:: Truncate() method in the .NET Framework:

```
PS >$result = 3/2
PS >[Math]::Truncate($result)
1
```

If that syntax seems burdensome, the following example defines a trunc function that truncates its input:

```
PS >function trunc($number) { [Math]::Truncate($number) }
PS >$result = 3/2
PS >trunc $result
1
```

See Also

- "Simple Operators" in Appendix A

6.2   Perform Complex Arithmetic

Problem

You want to use PowerShell to calculate more complex or advanced mathematical results.

Solution

PowerShell supports more advanced mathematical tasks primarily through its support for the System.Math class in the .NET Framework.

To find the absolute value of a number, use the [Math]::Abs() method:

```
PS >[Math]::Abs(-10.6)
10.6
```

To find the power (such as the square or the cube) of a number, use the [Math]::Pow() method. In this case, finding 123 squared:

```
PS >[Math]::Pow(123, 2)
15129
```

To find the square root of a number, use the [Math]::Sqrt() method:

```
PS >[Math]::Sqrt(100)
10
```

To find the sine, cosine, or tangent of an angle (given in radians), use the [Math]::Sin(), [Math]::Cos(), or [Math]::Tan() method:

```
PS >[Math]::Sin( [Math]::PI / 2 )
1
```

To find the angle (given in radians) of a sine, cosine, or tangent value, use the [Math]::ASin(), [Math]::ACos(), or [Math]::ATan() method:

```
PS >[Math]::ASin(1)
1.5707963267949
```

See Recipe 3.9, "Learn About Types and Objects." to learn how to find out what other features the System.Math class provides.

Discussion

Once you start working with the System.Math class, it may seem as though its designers left out significant pieces of functionality. The class supports the square root of a number, but doesn't support other roots (such as the cube root). It supports sine, cosine, and tangent (and their inverses) in radians, but not in the more commonly used measure of degrees.

Working with any root

To determine any root (such as the cube root) of a number, you can use the function given in Example 6-1.

Example 6-1. A root function and some example calculations

```
PS >function root($number, $root) { [Math]::Exp($([Math]::Log($number) / $root)) }
PS >root 64 3
4
PS >root 25 5
1.90365393871588
PS >[Math]::Pow(1.90365393871588, 5)
25.0000000000001
PS >[Math]::Pow( $(root 25 5), 5)
25
```

This function applies the mathematical fact that you can express any root (such as the cube root) of a number as a series of operations with any other well-known root. Although you can pick 2 as a base (which generates square roots and powers of 2), the [Math]::Exp() and [Math]::Log() methods in the System.Math class use a more common mathematical base called *e*.

 The [Math]::Exp() and [Math]::Log() functions use *e* (approximately 2.718) as a base largely because the number appears so frequently in the type of mathematics that use these functions!

The example also illustrates a very important point about math on computers. When you use this function (or anything else that manipulates floating point numbers), always be aware that the results of floating point answers are only ever approximations of the actual result. If you combine multiple calculations in the same statement, programming and scripting languages can sometimes improve the accuracy of their answer (such as in the second [Math]::Pow() attempt), but that exception is rare.

Some mathematical systems avoid this problem by working with equations and calculations as symbols (and not numbers). Like humans, these systems know that taking the square of a number that you just took the square root of gives you the original number right back—so they don't actually have to do either of those operations. These systems, however, are extremely specialized and usually very expensive.

Working with degrees instead of radians

Converting radians (the way that mathematicians commonly measure angles) to degrees (the way that most people commonly measure angles) is much more straightforward than the root function. A circle has 2 * Pi radians if you measure in radians, and 360 degrees if you measure in degrees. That gives the following two functions:

```
PS >function Convert-RadiansToDegrees($angle) { $angle / (2 * [Math]::Pi) * 360 }
PS >function Convert-DegreesToRadians($angle) { $angle / 360 * (2 * [Math]::Pi) }
```

and their usage:

```
PS >Convert-RadiansToDegrees ([Math]::Pi)
180
PS >Convert-RadiansToDegrees ([Math]::Pi / 2)
90
PS >Convert-DegreesToRadians 360
6.28318530717959
PS >Convert-DegreesToRadians 45
0.785398163397448
PS >[Math]::Tan( (Convert-DegreesToRadians 45) )
1
```

See Also

- Recipe 3.9, "Learn About Types and Objects"

6.3   Measure Statistical Properties of a List

Problem

You want to measure the numeric (minimum, maximum, sum, average) or textual (characters, words, lines) features of a list of objects.

Solution

Use the Measure-Object cmdlet to measure these statistical properties of a list.

To measure the numeric features of a stream of objects, pipe those objects to the Measure-Object cmdlet:

```
PS >1..10 | Measure-Object –Average -Sum


Count    : 10
Average  : 5.5
Sum      : 55
Maximum  :
Minimum  :
Property :
```

To measure the numeric features of a specific property in a stream of objects, supply that property name to the -Property parameter of the Measure-Object cmdlet. For example, in a directory with files:

```
PS >Get-ChildItem | Measure-Object -Property Length -Max -Min -Average -Sum


Count    : 427
Average  : 10617025.4918033
Sum      : 4533469885
Maximum  : 647129088
Minimum  : 0
Property : Length
```

To measure the textual features of a stream of objects, use the -Character, -Word, and -Line parameters of the Measure-Object cmdlet:

```
PS >Get-ChildItem > output.txt
PS >Get-Content output.txt | Measure-Object -Character -Word -Line
```

Lines	Words	Characters	Property
964	6083	33484	

Discussion

By default, the Measure-Object cmdlet counts only the number of objects it receives. If you want to measure additional properties (such as the maximum, minimum, average, sum, characters, words, or lines) of those objects, then you need to specify them as options to the cmdlet.

For the numeric properties, though, you usually don't want to measure the objects themselves. Instead, you probably want to measure a specific property from the list—such as the Length property of a file. For that purpose, the Measure-Object cmdlet supports the -Property parameter to which you provide the property you want to measure.

Sometimes, you might want to measure a property that isn't a simple number—such as the LastWriteTime property of a file. Since the LastWriteTime property is a DateTime, you can't determine its average immediately. However, if any property allows you to convert it to a number and back in a meaningful way (such as the Ticks property of a DateTime), then you can still compute its statistical properties. Example 6-2 shows how to get the average LastWriteTime from a list of files.

Example 6-2. Using the Ticks property of the DateTime class to determine the average LastWriteTime of a list of files

```
PS >## Get the LastWriteTime from each file
PS >$times = dir | Foreach-Object { $_.LastWriteTime }

PS >## Measure the average Ticks property of those LastWriteTime
```

Example 6-2. Using the Ticks property of the DateTime class to determine the average LastWriteTime of a list of files (continued)

```
PS >$results = $times | Measure-Object Ticks -Average

PS >## Create a new DateTime out of the average Ticks
PS >New-Object DateTime $results.Average

Sunday, June 11, 2006 6:45:01 AM
```

For more information about the Measure-Object cmdlet, type **Get-Help Measure-Object**.

6.4   Work with Numbers As Binary

Problem

You want to work with the individual bits of a number, or work with a number built by combining a series of flags.

Solution

To directly enter a hexadecimal number, use the 0x prefix:

```
PS >$hexNumber = 0x1234
PS >$hexNumber
4660
```

To convert a number to its binary representation, supply a base of 2 to the [Convert]::ToString() method:

```
PS >[Convert]::ToString(1234, 2)
10011010010
```

To convert a binary number into its decimal representation, supply a base of 2 to the [Convert]::ToInt32() method:

```
PS >[Convert]::ToInt32("10011010010", 2)
1234
```

To manage the individual bits of a number, use PowerShell's binary operators. In this case, the Archive flag is just one of the many possible attributes that may be true of a given file:

```
PS >$archive = [System.IO.FileAttributes] "Archive"
PS >attrib +a test.txt
PS >Get-ChildItem | Where { $_.Attributes -band $archive } | Select Name

Name
----
test.txt
```

```
PS >attrib -a test.txt
PS >Get-ChildItem | Where { $_.Attributes -band $archive } | Select Name
PS >
```

Discussion

In some system administration tasks, it is common to come across numbers that seem to mean nothing by themselves. The attributes of a file are a perfect example:

```
PS >(Get-Item test.txt).Encrypt()
PS >(Get-Item test.txt).IsReadOnly = $true
PS >[int] (Get-Item test.txt -force).Attributes
16417
PS >(Get-Item test.txt -force).IsReadOnly = $false
PS >(Get-Item test.txt).Decrypt()
PS >[int] (Get-Item test.txt).Attributes
32
```

What can the numbers 16417 and 32 possibly tell us about the file?

The answer to this comes from looking at the attributes in another light—as a set of features that can be either True or False. Take, for example, the possible attributes for an item in a directory shown by Example 6-3.

Example 6-3. Possible attributes of a file

```
PS >[Enum]::GetNames([System.IO.FileAttributes])
ReadOnly
Hidden
System
Directory
Archive
Device
Normal
Temporary
SparseFile
ReparsePoint
Compressed
Offline
NotContentIndexed
Encrypted
```

If a file is ReadOnly, Archive, and Encrypted, then you might consider this as a succinct description of the attributes on that file:

```
ReadOnly = True
Archive = True
Encrypted = True
```

It just so happens that computers have an extremely concise way of representing sets of true and false values—a representation known as *binary*. To represent the attributes of a directory item as binary, you simply put them in a table. We give the item a "1" if the attribute applies to the item and a "0" otherwise (see Table 6-1).

Table 6-1. Attributes of a directory item

Attribute	True (1) or False (0)
Encrypted	1
NotContentIndexed	0
Offline	0
Compressed	0
ReparsePoint	0
SparseFile	0
Temporary	0
Normal	0
Device	0
Archive	1
Directory	0
<Unused>	0
System	0
Hidden	0
ReadOnly	1

If we treat those features as the individual binary digits in a number, that gives us the number 100000000100001. If we convert that number to its decimal form, it becomes clear where the number 16417 came from:

```
PS >[Convert]::ToInt32("100000000100001", 2)
16417
```

This technique sits at the core of many properties that you can express as a combination of features or flags. Rather than list the features in a table, though, documentation usually describes the number that would result from that feature being the only one active—such as FILE_ATTRIBUTE_REPARSEPOINT = 0x400. Example 6-4 shows the various representations of these file attributes.

Example 6-4. Integer, hexadecimal, and binary representations of possible file attributes

```
PS >$attributes = [Enum]::GetValues([System.IO.FileAttributes])
PS >$attributes | Select-Object `
>>     @{"Name"="Property";
>>         "Expression"= { $_ } },
>>     @{"Name"="Integer";
>>         "Expression"= { [int] $_ } },
>>     @{"Name"="Hexadecimal";
>>         "Expression"= { [Convert]::ToString([int] $_, 16) } },
>>     @{"Name"="Binary";
>>         "Expression"= { [Convert]::ToString([int] $_, 2) } } |
>>     Format-Table -auto
>>
```

Example 6-4. Integer, hexadecimal, and binary representations of possible file attributes (continued)

```
        Property Integer Hexadecimal Binary
        -------- ------- ----------- ------
        ReadOnly       1 1           1
          Hidden       2 2           10
          System       4 4           100
       Directory      16 10          10000
         Archive      32 20          100000
          Device      64 40          1000000
          Normal     128 80          10000000
       Temporary     256 100         100000000
      SparseFile     512 200         1000000000
    ReparsePoint    1024 400         10000000000
      Compressed    2048 800         100000000000
         Offline    4096 1000        1000000000000
NotContentIndexed   8192 2000        10000000000000
       Encrypted   16384 4000        100000000000000
```

Knowing how that 16417 number was formed, you can now use the properties in meaningful ways. For example, PowerShell's -band operator allows you to check if a certain bit has been set:

```
PS >$encrypted = 16384
PS >$attributes = (Get-Item test.txt -force).Attributes
PS >($attributes -band $encrypted) -eq $encrypted
True
PS >$compressed = 2048
PS >($attributes -band $compressed) -eq $compressed
False
PS >
```

Although the example above uses the numeric values explicitly, it would be more common to enter the number by its name:

```
PS >$archive = [System.IO.FileAttributes] "Archive"
PS >($attributes -band $archive) -eq $archive
True
```

For more information about PowerShell's binary operators, see "Simple Operators" in Appendix A.

See Also

- "Simple Operators" in Appendix A

6.5   Simplify Math with Administrative Constants

Problem

You want to work with common administrative numbers (that is, kilobytes, megabytes, and gigabytes) without having to remember or calculate those numbers.

Solution

Use PowerShell's administrative constants (KB, MB, and GB) to help work with these common numbers.

Calculate the download time (in seconds) of a 10.18 megabyte file over a connection that gets 215 kilobytes per second:

```
PS >10.18mb / 215kb
48.4852093023256
```

Discussion

PowerShell's administrative constants are based on powers of two, since those are the kind most commonly used when working with computers. Each is 1,024 times bigger than the one before it:

1kb = 1024
1mb = 1024 * 1 kb
1gb = 1024 * 1 mb

Some (such as hard drive manufacturers) prefer to call numbers based on powers of two "kibibytes," "mebibytes," and "gibibytes." They use the terms "kilobytes," "megabytes," and "gigabytes" to mean numbers that are 1,000 times bigger than the one before it—numbers based on powers of 10.

Although not represented by administrative constants, PowerShell still makes it easy to work with these numbers in powers of 10—for example, to figure out how big a "300 GB" hard drive is when reported by Windows:

```
PS >$kilobyte = [Math]::Pow(10,3)
PS >$kilobyte
1000
PS >$megabyte = [Math]::Pow(10,6)
PS >$megabyte
1000000
PS >$gigabyte = [Math]::Pow(10,9)
PS >$gigabyte
1000000000
PS >(300 * $gigabyte) / 1GB
279.396772384644
```

6.6   Convert Numbers Between Bases

Problem

You want to convert a number to a different base.

Solution

The PowerShell scripting language allows you to enter both decimal and hexadecimal numbers directly. It does not natively support other number bases, but its support for interaction with the .NET Framework enables conversion both to and from binary, octal, decimal, and hexadecimal.

To convert a hexadecimal number into its decimal representation, prefix the number by 0x to enter the number as hexadecimal:

```
PS >$myErrorCode = 0xFE4A
PS >$myErrorCode
65098
```

To convert a binary number into its decimal representation, supply a base of 2 to the [Convert]::ToInt32() method:

```
PS >[Convert]::ToInt32("10011010010", 2)
1234
```

To convert an octal number into its decimal representation, supply a base of 8 to the [Convert]::ToInt32() method:

```
PS >[Convert]::ToInt32("1234", 8)
668
```

To convert a number into its hexadecimal representation, use either the [Convert] class or PowerShell's format operator:

```
PS >## Use the [Convert] class
PS >[Convert]::ToString(1234, 16)
4d2

PS >## Use the formatting operator
PS >"{0:X4}" -f 1234
04D2
```

To convert a number into its binary representation, supply a base of 2 to the [Convert]::ToString() method:

```
PS >[Convert]::ToString(1234, 2)
10011010010
```

To convert a number into its octal representation, supply a base of 8 to the [Convert]::ToString() method:

```
PS >[Convert]::ToString(1234, 8)
2322
```

Discussion

It is most common to want to convert numbers between bases when you are dealing with numbers that represent binary combinations of data, such as the attributes of a file. For more information on how to work with binary data like this, see Recipe 7.4, "Parse and Manage Binary Files,"

See Also

- Recipe 7.4, "Parse and Manage Binary Files"

PART III
Common Tasks

## CHAPTER 7

Simple Files

7.0 Introduction

When administering a system, you naturally spend a significant amount of time working with the files on that system. Many of the things you want to do with these files are simple: get their content, search them for a pattern, or replace text inside them.

For even these simple operations, PowerShell's object-oriented flavor adds several unique and powerful twists.

7.1 Get the Content of a File

Problem

You want to get the content of a file.

Solution

Provide the filename as an argument to the Get-Content cmdlet:

```
PS >$content = Get-Content c:\temp\file.txt
```

Place the filename in a ${ } section to use the cmdlet Get-Content variable syntax:

```
PS >$content = ${c:\temp\file.txt}
```

Provide the filename as an argument to the ReadAllText() method to use the System.IO.File class from the .NET Framework:

```
PS >$content = [System.IO.File]::ReadAllText("c:\temp\file.txt")
```

Discussion

PowerShell offers three primary ways to get the content of a file. The first is the Get-Content cmdlet—the cmdlet designed for this purpose. In fact, the Get-Content cmdlet works on any PowerShell drive that supports the concept of items with content. This includes Alias:, Function:, and more. The second and third ways are the Get-Content variable syntax, and the ReadAllText() method.

When working against files, the Get-Content cmdlet returns the content of the file line-by-line. When it does this, PowerShell supplies additional information about that output line. This information, which PowerShell attaches as properties to each output line, includes the drive and path from where that line originated, among other things.

> If you want PowerShell to split the file content based on a string that you choose (rather than the default of newlines), the Get-Content cmdlet's –Delimiter parameter lets you provide one.

While useful, having PowerShell attach this extra information when you are not using it can sometimes slow down scripts that operate on large files. If you need to process a large file more quickly, the Get-Content cmdlet's ReadCount parameter lets you control how many lines PowerShell reads from the file at once. With a ReadCount of 1 (which is the default), PowerShell returns each line one-by-one. With a ReadCount of 2, PowerShell returns two lines at a time. With a ReadCount of less than 1, PowerShell returns all lines from the file at once.

> Beware of using a ReadCount of less than 1 for extremely large files. One of the benefits of the Get-Content cmdlet is its streaming behavior. No matter how large the file, you will still be able to process each line of the file without using up all your system's memory. Since a ReadCount of less than 1 reads the entire file before returning any results, large files have the potential to use up your system's memory. For more information about how to effectively take advantage of PowerShell's streaming capabilities, see Recipe 5.13, "Generate Large Reports and Text Streams."

If performance is a primary concern, the [File]::ReadAllText() method from the .NET Framework reads a file most quickly from the disk. Unlike the Get-Content cmdlet, it does not split the file into newlines, attach any additional information, or work against any other PowerShell drives. Like the Get-Content cmdlet with a ReadCount of less than 1, it reads all the content from the file before it returns it to you—so be cautious when using it on extremely large files.

For more information about the Get-Content cmdlet, type **Get-Help Get-Content**. For information on how to work with more structured files (such as XML and CSV), see Chapter 8, *Structured Files*. For more information on how to work with binary files, see Recipe 7.4, "Parse and Manage Binary Files."

See Also

- Recipe 5.13, "Generate Large Reports and Text Streams"
- Recipe 7.4, "Parse and Manage Binary Files"
- Chapter 8, *Structured Files*

7.2 Search a File for Text or a Pattern

Problem

You want to find a string or regular expression in a file.

Solution

To search a file for an exact (but case insensitive) match, use the –Simple parameter of the Select-String cmdlet:

```
PS >Select-String –Simple SearchText file.txt
```

To search a file for a regular expression, provide that pattern to the Select-String cmdlet:

```
PS >Select-String "\(...\) ...-...." phone.txt
```

To Recursively search all *.txt files for a regular expression, pipe the results of Get-ChildItem to the Select-String cmdlet:

```
PS >Get-ChildItem -Filter *.txt -Recurse | Select-String pattern
```

Discussion

The Select-String cmdlet is the easiest way to search files for a pattern or specific string. In contrast to the traditional text-matching utilities (such as grep) that support the same type of functionality, the matches returned by the Select-String cmdlet include detailed information about the match itself.

```
PS >$matches = Select-String "output file" transcript.txt
PS >$matches | Select LineNumber,Line

           LineNumber Line
           ---------- ----
                    7 Transcript started, output file...
```

If you want to search multiple files of a specific extension, the Select-String cmdlet lets you use wildcards (such as *.txt) on the filename. For more complicated lists of files (which includes searching all files in the directory), it is usually more useful to use the Get-ChildItem cmdlet to generate the list of files as shown previously.

By default, the Select-String cmdlet outputs the filename, line number, and matching line for every match it finds. In some cases, this output may be too much detail—

such as when you are searching for which binary file contains a specific string. Binary files rarely make sense when displayed as text, so your screen quickly fills with apparent garbage.

The solution to this problem comes from the Select-String's –Quiet switch. It simply returns True or False, depending on whether the file contains the string. So, to find the DLL in the current directory that contains the text "Debug":

```
Get-ChildItem | Where { $_ | Select-String "Debug" -Quiet }
```

Two other common tools used to search files for text are the –match operator and the switch statement with the –file option. For more information about those, see Recipe 5.7, "Search a String for Text or a Pattern" and Recipe 4.3, "Manage Large Conditional Statements with Switches." For more information about the Select-String cmdlet, type **Get-Help Select-String**.

See Also

- Recipe 4.3, "Manage Large Conditional Statements with Switches"
- Recipe 5.7, "Search a String for Text or a Pattern"

7.3   Parse and Manage Text-Based Logfiles

Problem

You want to parse and analyze a text-based logfile using PowerShell's standard object management commands.

Solution

Use the Convert-TextObject script given in Recipe 5.12, "Program: Convert Text Streams to Objects." to work with text-based logfiles. With your assistance, it converts steams of text into streams of objects, which you can then easily work with using PowerShell's standard commands.

The Convert-TextObject script primarily takes two arguments:

1. A regular expression that describes how to break the incoming text into groups
2. A list of property names that the script then assigns to those text groups

As an example, you can use patch logs from the Windows directory. These logs track the patch installation details from updates applied to the machine (except for Windows Vista). One detail included in these logfiles are the names and versions of the files modified by that specific patch, as shown in Example 7-1.

Example 7-1. Getting a list of files modified by hotfixes

```
PS >cd $env:WINDIR
PS >$parseExpression = "(.*): Destination:(.*) \((.*)\)"
PS >$files = dir kb*.log -Exclude *uninst.log
PS >$logContent = $files | Get-Content | Select-String $parseExpression
PS >$logContent

(...)
0.734: Destination:C:\WINNT\system32\shell32.dll (6.0.3790.205)
0.734: Destination:C:\WINNT\system32\wininet.dll (6.0.3790.218)
0.734: Destination:C:\WINNT\system32\urlmon.dll (6.0.3790.218)
0.734: Destination:C:\WINNT\system32\shlwapi.dll (6.0.3790.212)
0.734: Destination:C:\WINNT\system32\shdocvw.dll (6.0.3790.214)
0.734: Destination:C:\WINNT\system32\digest.dll (6.0.3790.0)
0.734: Destination:C:\WINNT\system32\browseui.dll (6.0.3790.218)
(...)
```

Like most logfiles, the format of the text is very regular but hard to manage. In this example, you have:

> A number (the number of seconds since the patch started)
> The text, ": Destination:"
> The file being patched
> An open parenthesis
> The version of the file being patched
> A close parenthesis

You don't care about any of the text, but the time, file, and file version are useful properties to track:

```
$properties = "Time","File","FileVersion"
```

So now, you use the Convert-TextObject script to convert the text output into a stream of objects:

```
PS >$logObjects = $logContent |
>> Convert-TextObject -ParseExpression $parseExpression -PropertyName $properties
>>
```

We can now easily query those objects using PowerShell's built-in commands. For example, you can find the files most commonly affected by patches and service packs, as shown by Example 7-2.

Example 7-2. Finding files most commonly affected by hotfixes

```
PS >$logObjects | Group-Object file | Sort-Object -Descending Count |
>> Select-Object Count,Name | Format-Table -Auto
>>

Count Name
----- ----
  152 C:\WINNT\system32\shdocvw.dll
  147 C:\WINNT\system32\shlwapi.dll
```

```
128 C:\WINNT\system32\wininet.dll
116 C:\WINNT\system32\shell32.dll
 92 C:\WINNT\system32\rpcss.dll
 92 C:\WINNT\system32\olecli32.dll
 92 C:\WINNT\system32\ole32.dll
 84 C:\WINNT\system32\urlmon.dll
(...)
```

Using this technique, you can work with most text-based logfiles.

Discussion

In Example 7-2, you got all the information you needed by splitting the input text into groups of simple strings. The time offset, file, and version information served their purposes as is. In addition to the features used by Example 7-2, however, the Convert-TextObject script also supports a parameter that lets you control the data types of those properties. If one of the properties should be treated as a number or a DateTime, you may get incorrect results if you work with that property as a string. For more information about this functionality, see the description of the –PropertyType parameter in the Convert-TextObject script.

Although most logfiles have entries designed to fit within a single line, some span multiple lines. When a logfile contains entries that span multiple lines, it includes some sort of special marker to separate log entries from each other. Take, for example:

```
PS >Get-Content AddressBook.txt
Name: Chrissy
Phone: 555-1212
----
Name: John
Phone: 555-1213
```

The key to working with this type of logfile comes from two places. The first is the –Delimiter parameter of the Get-Content cmdlet, which makes it split the file based on that delimiter instead of newlines. The second is to write a ParseExpression Regular Expression that ignores the newline characters that remain in each record.

```
PS >$records = gc AddressBook.txt -Delimiter "----"
PS >$parseExpression = "(?s)Name: (\S*).*Phone: (\S*).*"
PS >$records | Convert-TextObject -ParseExpression $parseExpression

Property1                                    Property2
---------                                    ---------
Chrissy                                      555-1212
John                                         555-1213
```

The parse expression in this example uses the *single line* option (?s) so that the (.*) portion of the regular expression accepts newline characters as well. For more information about these (and other) regular expression options, see Appendix B, *Regular Expression Reference*.

For extremely large logfiles, handwritten parsing tools may not meet your needs. In those situations, specialized log management tools can prove helpful. One example is Microsoft's free Log Parser (*http://www.logparser.com*). Another common alternative is to import the log entries to a SQL database, and then perform ad hoc queries on database tables, instead.

See Also

- Recipe 5.12, "Program: Convert Text Streams to Objects"
- Appendix B, *Regular Expression Reference*

7.4   Parse and Manage Binary Files

Problem

You want to work with binary data in a file.

Solution

Two main techniques are used when working with binary data in a file. The first is to read the file using the Byte encoding, so that PowerShell does not treat the content as text. The second is to use the BitConverter class to translate these bytes back and forth into numbers that you more commonly care about.

Example 7-3 displays the "characteristics" of a Windows executable. The beginning section of any executable (a *.DLL*, *.EXE*, and several others) starts with a binary section known as the *PE (portable executable) header*. Part of this header includes characteristics about that file—such as whether the file is a DLL.

For more information about the PE header format, see *http://www.microsoft.com/whdc/system/platform/firmware/PECOFF.mspx*.

Example 7-3. Get-Characteristics.ps1

```
##############################################################################
##
## Get-Characteristics.ps1
##
## Get the file characteristics of a file in the PE Executable File Format.
##
## ie:
##
## PS >Get-Characteristics $env:WINDIR\notepad.exe
## IMAGE_FILE_LOCAL_SYMS_STRIPPED
## IMAGE_FILE_RELOCS_STRIPPED
## IMAGE_FILE_EXECUTABLE_IMAGE
```

Example 7-3. Get-Characteristics.ps1 (continued)

```
## IMAGE_FILE_32BIT_MACHINE
## IMAGE_FILE_LINE_NUMS_STRIPPED
##
###############################################################################

param([string] $filename = $(throw "Please specify a filename."))

## Define the characteristics used in the PE file file header.
## Taken from http://www.microsoft.com/whdc/system/platform/firmware/PECOFF.mspx
$characteristics = @{}
$characteristics["IMAGE_FILE_RELOCS_STRIPPED"] = 0x0001
$characteristics["IMAGE_FILE_EXECUTABLE_IMAGE"] = 0x0002
$characteristics["IMAGE_FILE_LINE_NUMS_STRIPPED"] = 0x0004
$characteristics["IMAGE_FILE_LOCAL_SYMS_STRIPPED"] = 0x0008
$characteristics["IMAGE_FILE_AGGRESSIVE_WS_TRIM"] = 0x0010
$characteristics["IMAGE_FILE_LARGE_ADDRESS_AWARE"] = 0x0020
$characteristics["RESERVED"] = 0x0040
$characteristics["IMAGE_FILE_BYTES_REVERSED_LO"] = 0x0080
$characteristics["IMAGE_FILE_32BIT_MACHINE"] = 0x0100
$characteristics["IMAGE_FILE_DEBUG_STRIPPED"] = 0x0200
$characteristics["IMAGE_FILE_REMOVABLE_RUN_FROM_SWAP"] = 0x0400
$characteristics["IMAGE_FILE_NET_RUN_FROM_SWAP"] = 0x0800
$characteristics["IMAGE_FILE_SYSTEM"] = 0x1000
$characteristics["IMAGE_FILE_DLL"] = 0x2000
$characteristics["IMAGE_FILE_UP_SYSTEM_ONLY"] = 0x4000
$characteristics["IMAGE_FILE_BYTES_REVERSED_HI"] = 0x8000

## Get the content of the file, as an array of bytes
$fileBytes = Get-Content $filename -ReadCount 0 -Encoding byte

## The offset of the signature in the file is stored at location 0x3c.
$signatureOffset = $fileBytes[0x3c]

## Ensure it is a PE file
$signature = [char[]] $fileBytes[$signatureOffset..($signatureOffset + 3)]
if([String]::Join('', $signature) -ne "PE`0`0")
{
    throw "This file does not conform to the PE specification."
}

## The location of the COFF header is 4 bytes into the signature
$coffHeader = $signatureOffset + 4

## The characteristics data are 18 bytes into the COFF header. The BitConverter
## class manages the conversion of the 4 bytes into an integer.
$characteristicsData = [BitConverter]::ToInt32($fileBytes, $coffHeader + 18)

## Go through each of the characteristics. If the data from the file has that
## flag set, then output that characteristic.
foreach($key in $characteristics.Keys)
```

Example 7-3. Get-Characteristics.ps1 (continued)

```
{
    $flag = $characteristics[$key]
    if(($characteristicsData -band $flag) -eq $flag)
    {
        $key
    }
}
}
```

Discussion

For most files, this technique is the easiest way to work with binary data. If you actually modify the binary data, then you will also want to use the Byte encoding when you send it back to disk:

```
$fileBytes | Set-Content modified.exe -Encoding Byte
```

For extremely large files, though, it may be unacceptably slow to load the entire file into memory when you work with it. If you begin to run against this limit, the solution is to use file management classes from the .NET Framework. These classes include BinaryReader, StreamReader, and others. For more information about working with classes from the .NET Framework, see Recipe 3.4, "Work with .NET Objects." For more information about running scripts, see Recipe 1.1, "Run Programs, Scripts, and Existing Tools."

See Also

- Recipe 1.1, "Run Programs, Scripts, and Existing Tools"
- Recipe 3.4, "Work with .NET Objects"

7.5   Create a Temporary File

Problem

You want to create a file for temporary purposes and want to be sure that the file does not already exist.

Solution

Use the [System.IO.Path]::GetTempFilename() method from the .NET Framework to create a temporary file:

```
$filename = [System.IO.Path]::GetTempFileName()
 (... use the file ...)
Remove-Item -Force $filename
```

Discussion

It is common to want to create a file for temporary purposes. For example, you might want to search and replace text inside a file. Doing this to a large file requires a temporary file (see Recipe 7.6, "Search and Replace Text in a File"). Another example is the temporary file used by Recipe 2.3, "Program: Interactively Filter Lists of Objects."

Often, people create this temporary file wherever they can think of: in C:\, the script's current location, or any number of other places. Although this may work on the author's system, it rarely works well elsewhere. For example, if the user does not use their Administrator account for day-to-day tasks, your script will not have access to C:\ and will fail.

Another difficulty comes from trying to create a unique name for the temporary file. If your script just hardcodes a name (no matter how many random characters it has), it will fail if you run two copies at the same time. You might even craft a script smart enough to search for a filename that does not exist, create it, and then use it. Unfortunately, this could still break if another copy of your script creates that file after you see that it is missing—but before you actually create the file.

Finally, there are several security vulnerabilities that your script might introduce should it write its temporary files to a location that other users can read or write.

Luckily, the authors of the .NET Framework provided the [System.IO.Path]:: GetTempFilename() method to resolve these problems for you. It creates a unique filename in a reliable location in a secure manner. The method returns a filename, which you can then use as you want.

> Remember to delete this file when your script no longer needs it; otherwise, your script will waste disk space and cause needless clutter on your users' systems. Remember: your scripts should solve the administrator's problems, not cause them!

By default, the GetTempFilename() method returns a file with a *.tmp* extension. For most purposes, the file extension does not matter, and this works well. In the rare instances when you need to create a file with a specific extension, the [System.IO. Path]::ChangeExtension() method lets you change the extension of that temporary file. The following example creates a new temporary file that uses the *.cs* file extension:

```
$filename = [System.IO.Path]::GetTempFileName()
$newname = [System.IO.Path]::ChangeExtension($filename, ".cs")
Move-Item $filename $newname
(... use the file ...)
Remove-Item $newname
```

See Also

- Recipe 2.3, "Program: Interactively Filter Lists of Objects"
- Recipe 7.6, "Search and Replace Text in a File

7.6   Search and Replace Text in a File

Problem

You want to search for text in a file and replace that text with something new.

Solution

To search and replace text in a file, first store the content of the file in a variable, and then store the replaced text back in that file as shown in Example 7-4.

Example 7-4. Replacing text in a file

```
PS >$filename = "file.txt"
PS >$match = "source text"
PS >$replacement = "replacement text"
PS >
PS >$content = Get-Content $filename
PS >$content
This is some source text that we want
to replace. One of the things you may need
to be careful careful about with Source
Text is when it spans multiple lines,
and may have different Source Text
capitalization.
PS >
PS >$content = $content -creplace $match,$replacement
PS >$content
This is some replacement text that we want
to replace. One of the things you may need
to be careful careful about with Source
Text is when it spans multiple lines,
and may have different Source Text
capitalization.
PS >$content | Set-Content $filename
```

Discussion

Using PowerShell to search and replace text in a file (or many files!) is one of the best examples of using a tool to automate a repetitive task. What could literally take months by hand can be shortened to a few minutes (or hours, at most).

Notice that the solution uses the -creplace operator to replace text in a case-sensitive manner. This is almost always what you will want to do, as the replacement text uses the exact capitalization that you provide. If the text you want to replace is capitalized in several different ways (as in the term "Source Text" from the solution), then search and replace several times with the different possible capitalizations.

Example 7-4 illustrates what is perhaps the simplest (but actually most common) scenario:

- You work with an ASCII text file.
- You replace some literal text with a literal text replacement.
- You don't worry that the text match might span multiple lines.
- Your text file is relatively small.

If some of those assumptions don't hold true, then this discussion shows you how to tailor the way you search and replace within this file.

Work with files encoded in Unicode or another (OEM) code page

By default, the Set-Content cmdlet assumes that you want the output file to contain plain ASCII text. If you work with a file in another encoding (for example, Unicode or an OEM code page such as Cyrillic), use the -Encoding parameter of the Out-File cmdlet to specify that:

```
$content | Out-File -Encoding Unicode $filename
$content | Out-File -Encoding OEM $filename
```

Replace text using a pattern instead of plain text

Although it is most common to replace one literal string with another literal string, you might want to replace text according to a pattern in some advanced scenarios. One example might be swapping first name and last name. PowerShell supports this type of replacement through its support of regular expressions in its replacement operator:

```
PS >$content = Get-Content names.txt
PS >$content
John Doe
Mary Smith
PS >$content -replace '(.*) (.*)','$2, $1'
Doe, John
Smith, Mary
```

Replace text that spans multiple lines

The Get-Content cmdlet used in the solution retrieves a list of lines from the file. When you use the -replace operator against this array, it replaces your text in each of those lines individually. If your match spans multiple lines, as shown between lines 3 and 4 in Example 7-4, the –replace operator will be unaware of the match and will not perform the replacement.

If you want to replace text that spans multiple lines, then it becomes necessary to stop treating the input text as a collection of lines. Once you stop treating the input as a collection of lines, it is also important to use a replacement expression that can ignore line breaks, as shown in Example 7-5.

Example 7-5. Replacing text across multiple lines in a file

```
$filename = Get-Item file.txt
$singleLine = [System.IO.File]::ReadAllText($filename.FullName)
$content = $singleLine -creplace "(?s)Source(\s*)Text",'Replacement$1Text'
```

The first and second lines of Example 7-5 read the entire content of the file as a single string. It does this by calling the [System.IO.File]::ReadAllText() method from the .NET Framework, since the Get-Content cmdlet splits the content of the file into individual lines.

The third line of this solution replaces the text by using a regular expression pattern. The section, Source(\s*)Text, scans for the word Source followed optionally by some whitespace, followed by the word Text. Since the whitespace portion of the regular expression has parentheses around it, we want to remember exactly what that whitespace was. By default, regular expressions do not let newline characters count as whitespace, so the first portion of the regular expression uses the *single-line option* (?s) to allow newline characters to count as whitespace. The replacement portion of the –replace operator replaces that match with Replacement, followed by the exact whitespace from the match that we captured ($1), followed by Text. For more information, see "Simple Operators" in Appendix A.

Replace text in large files

The approaches used so far store the entire contents of the file in memory as they replace the text in them. Once we've made the replacements in memory, we write the updated content back to disk. This works well when replacing text in small, medium, and even moderately large files. For extremely large files (for example, more than several hundred megabytes), using this much memory may burden your system and slow down your script. To solve that problem, you can work on the files line-by-line, rather than with the entire file at once.

Since you're working with the file line-by-line, it will still be in use when you try to write replacement text back into it. You can avoid this problem if you write the replacement text into a temporary file until you've finished working with the main file. Once you've finished scanning through our file, you can delete it and replace it with the temporary file.

```
$filename = "file.txt"
$temporaryFile = [System.IO.Path]::GetTempFileName()

$match = "source text"
$replacement = "replacement text"

Get-Content $filename |
    Foreach-Object { $_ -creplace $match,$replacement | Add-Content $temporaryFile }

Remove-Item $filename
Move-Item $temporaryFile $filename
```

See Also

- "Simple Operators" in Appendix A

Structured Files

8.0   Introduction

In the world of text-only system administration, managing structured files is often a pain. For example, working with (or editing) an XML file means either loading it into an editor to modify by hand, or writing a custom tool that can do that for you. Even worse, it may mean modifying the file as though it were plain text while hoping to not break the structure of the XML itself.

In that same world, working with a file in CSV format means going through the file yourself, splitting each line by the commas in it. It's a seemingly great approach, until you find yourself faced with anything but the simplest of data.

Structure and structured files don't come only from other programs, either. When writing scripts, one common goal is to save structured data so that you can use it later. In most scripting (and programming) languages, this requires that you design a data structure to hold that data, design a way to store and retrieve it from disk, and bring it back to a usable form when you want to work with it again.

Fortunately, working with XML, CSVs, and even your own structured files becomes much easier with PowerShell at your side.

8.1   Access Information in an XML File

Problem

You want to work with and access information in an XML file.

Solution

Use PowerShell's XML cast to convert the plain-text XML into a form that you can more easily work with. In this case, the RSS feed downloaded from the Windows PowerShell blog:

```
PS >$xml = [xml] (Get-Content powershell_blog.xml)
```

See Recipe 9.1, "Download a File from the Internet" for an example of how to use PowerShell to download this file!

Like other rich objects, PowerShell displays the properties of the XML as you explore. These properties are child nodes and attributes in the XML, as shown by Example 8-1.

Example 8-1. Accessing properties of an XML document

```
PS >$xml

xml                     xml-stylesheet        rss
---                     --------------        ---
                                              rss


PS >$xml.rss


version : 2.0
dc      : http://purl.org/dc/elements/1.1/
slash   : http://purl.org/rss/1.0/modules/slash/
wfw     : http://wellformedweb.org/CommentAPI/
channel : channel
```

If more than one node shares the same name (as in the item nodes of an RSS feed), then the property name represents a collection of nodes:

```
PS >($xml.rss.channel.item).Count
15
```

You can access those items individually, like you would normally work with an array, as shown in Example 8-2.

Example 8-2. Accessing individual items in an XML document

```
PS >($xml.rss.channel.item)[0]

description : <P>Since a lot of people have been asking about it, yes - my
              (...)
guid        : guid
title       : "Windows PowerShell in Action" has been released
comment     : http://blogs.msdn.com/powershell/rsscomments.aspx?PostID=171
              8281
link        : http://blogs.msdn.com/powershell/archive/2007/02/19/windows-
              powershell-in-action-has-been-released.aspx
pubDate     : Mon, 19 Feb 2007 20:05:00 GMT
comments    : {4, http://blogs.msdn.com/powershell/comments/1718281.aspx}
commentRss  : http://blogs.msdn.com/powershell/commentrss.aspx?PostID=1718
              281
creator     : PowerShellTeam
```

You can access properties of those elements like you would normally work with an object:

```
PS >($xml.rss.channel.item)[0].title
"Windows PowerShell in Action" has been released
```

Since these are rich PowerShell objects, Example 8-3 demonstrates how you can use PowerShell's advanced object-based cmdlets for further work, such as sorting and filtering.

Example 8-3. Sorting and filtering items in an XML document

```
PS >$xml.rss.channel.item | Sort-Object title | Select-Object title

title
-----
"Windows PowerShell in Action" has been released
Controlling PowerShell Function (Re)Definition
Execution Policy and Vista
Executive Demo
It's All about Economics
NetCmdlets Beta 2 is now Available.
Payette Podcast
Port 25 interview with Bruce Payette
PowerShell Benefits Over  COM Scripting
PowerShell Cheat Sheet - Now in XPS
PowerShell Tip: How to "shift" arrays
Processing text, files and XML
Virtual Machine Manager's PowerShell Support
Windows PowerShell 1.0 for Windows Vista
Working With WMI Events
```

Discussion

PowerShell's native XML support provides an excellent way to easily navigate and access XML files. By exposing the XML hierarchy as properties, you can perform most tasks without having to resort to text-only processing, or custom tools.

In fact, PowerShell's support for interaction with XML goes beyond just presenting your data in an object-friendly way. The objects created by the [xml] cast in fact represent fully featured System.Xml.XmlDocument objects from the .NET Framework. Each property of the resulting objects represents a System.Xml.XmlElement object from the .NET Framework, as well. The underlying objects provide a great deal of additional functionality that you can use to perform both common and complex tasks on XML files.

The underlying System.Xml.XmlDocument and System.Xml.XmlElement objects that support your XML provide useful properties in their own right, as well: Attributes, Name, OuterXml, and more. Since these properties may interfere with the way you access properties from your XML file, PowerShell hides them by default. To access them, use the PsBase property on any node. The PsBase property works on any object in PowerShell, and represents the object underneath the PowerShell abstraction:

```
PS >$xml.rss.psbase.Attributes

#text
-----
2.0
http://purl.org/dc/elements/1.1/
http://purl.org/rss/1.0/modules/slash/
http://wellformedweb.org/CommentAPI/
```

For more information about using the underlying.NET objects for more advanced tasks, see the following section, Recipe 8.2, "Perform an XPath Query Against an XML File" and Recipe 8.3, "Modify Data in an XML File."

For more information about working with XML in PowerShell, see "XML" in Appendix A.

See Also

- Recipe 8.2, "Perform an XPath Query Against an XML File"
- Recipe 8.3, "Modify Data in an XML File"
- Recipe 9.1, "Download a File from the Internet"
- "XML" in Appendix A

8.2   Perform an XPath Query Against an XML File

Problem

You want to perform an advanced query against an XML file, using XML's standard *XPath* syntax.

Solution

Use PowerShell's XML cast to convert the plain-text XML into a form that you can more easily work with. In this case, the RSS feed downloaded from the Windows PowerShell blog:

```
PS >$xml = [xml] (Get-Content powershell_blog.xml)
```

Then use the SelectNodes() method on that variable to perform the query. For example, to find all post titles shorter than 20 characters:

```
PS >$query = "/rss/channel/item[string-length(title) < 20]/title"
PS >$xml.SelectNodes($query)
```

```
#text
-----
Payette Podcast
Executive Demo
```

Discussion

Although a language all its own, the XPath query syntax provides a powerful, XML-centric way to write advanced queries for XML files.

For simpler queries, you may find PowerShell's object-based XML navigation concepts easier to work with. For more information about working with XML through PowerShell's XML type, see "XML" in Appendix A.

See Also

- "XML" in Appendix A

8.3   Modify Data in an XML File

Problem

You want to use PowerShell to modify the data in an XML file.

Solution

To modify data in an XML file, load the file into PowerShell's XML data type, change the content you want, and then save the file back to disk. Example 8-4 demonstrates this approach.

Example 8-4. Modifying an XML file from PowerShell

```
PS >## Store the filename
PS >$filename = (Get-Item phone.xml).FullName
PS >
PS >## Get the content of the file, and load it
PS >## as XML
PS >Get-Content $filename
<AddressBook>
  <Person contactType="Personal">
    <Name>Lee</Name>
    <Phone type="home">555-1212</Phone>
    <Phone type="work">555-1213</Phone>
  </Person>
  <Person contactType="Business">
    <Name>Ariel</Name>
    <Phone>555-1234</Phone>
  </Person>
</AddressBook>
PS >$phoneBook = [xml] (Get-Content $filename)
PS >
```

Example 8-4. Modifying an XML file from PowerShell (continued)

```
PS >## Get the part with data we want to change
PS >$person = $phoneBook.AddressBook.Person[0]
PS >
PS >## Change the text part of the information,
PS >## and the type (which was an attribute)
PS >$person.Phone[0]."#text" = "555-1214"
PS >$person.Phone[0].type = "mobile"
PS >
PS >## Add a new phone entry
PS >$newNumber = [xml] '<Phone type="home">555-1215</Phone>'
PS >$newNode = $phoneBook.ImportNode($newNumber.Phone, $true)
PS >[void] $person.AppendChild($newNode)
PS >
PS >## Save the file to disk
PS >$phoneBook.Save($filename)
PS >Get-Content $filename
<AddressBook>
  <Person contactType="Personal">
    <Name>Lee</Name>
    <Phone type="mobile">555-1214</Phone>
    <Phone type="work">555-1213</Phone>
    <Phone type="home">555-1215</Phone>
  </Person>
  <Person contactType="Business">
    <Name>Ariel</Name>
    <Phone>555-1234</Phone>
  </Person>
</AddressBook>
```

Discussion

In the preceding solution, you change *Lee*'s phone number (which was the "text" portion of the XML's original first *Phone* node) from *555-1212* to *555-1214*. You also change the type of the phone number (which was an attribute of the *Phone* node) from "home" to "mobile".

Adding new information to the XML is nearly as easy. To add information to an XML file, you need to add it as a *child node* to another of the nodes in the file. The easiest way to get that child node is to write the string that represents the XML and then create a temporary PowerShell XML document from that. From that document, you use the main XML document's ImportNode() function to import the node you care about—specifically, the *Phone* node in this example.

Once we have the child node, you need to decide where to put it. Since we want this *Phone* node to be a child of the *Person* node for *Lee*, we will place it there. To add a child node ($newNode, in Example 8-4) to a destination node ($person, in the example), use the AppendChild() method from the destination node.

The Save() method on the XML document allows you to save to more than just files. For a quick way to convert XML into a "beautified" form, save it to the console:

```
$phoneBook.Save([Console]::Out)
```

Finally, we save the XML back to the file from which it came.

8.4 Easily Import and Export Your Structured Data

Problem

You have a set of data (such as a hashtable or array) and want to save it to disk so that you can use it later. Conversely, you have saved structured data to a file and want to import it so that you can use it.

Solution

Use PowerShell's Export-CliXml cmdlet to save structured data to disk, and the Import-CliXml cmdlet to import it again from disk.

For example, imagine storing a list of your favorite directories in a hashtable, so that you can easily navigate your system with a "Favorite CD" function. Example 8-5 shows this function.

Example 8-5. A function that requires persistent structured data

```
PS >$favorites = @{}
PS >$favorites["temp"] = "c:\temp"
PS >$favorites["music"] = "h:\lee\my music"
PS >function fcd {
>>     param([string] $location) Set-Location $favorites[$location]
>> }
>>
PS >Get-Location

Path
----
HKLM:\software


PS >fcd temp
PS >Get-Location

Path
----
C:\temp
```

Unfortunately, the $favorites variable vanishes whenever you close PowerShell.

To get around this, you could recreate the $favorites variable in your profile, but another way is to export it directly to a file. This command assumes that you have already created a profile, and places the file in the same location as that profile:

```
PS >$filename = Join-Path (Split-Path $profile) favorites.clixml
PS >$favorites | Export-CliXml $filename
PS >$favorites = $null
PS >$favorites
PS >
```

Once it's on disk, you can reload it using the Import-CliXml cmdlet, as shown in Example 8-6.

Example 8-6. Restoring structured data from disk

```
PS >$favorites = Import-CliXml $filename
PS >$favorites

Name                          Value
----                          -----
music                         h:\lee\my music
temp                          c:\temp


PS >fcd music
PS >Get-Location

Path
----
H:\lee\My Music
```

Discussion

PowerShell provides the Export-CliXml and Import-CliXml cmdlets to let you easily move structured data into and out of files. These cmdlets accomplish this in a very data-centric and future-proof way—by storing only the names, values, and basic data types for the properties of that data.

 By default, PowerShell stores one level of data: all directly accessible simple properties (such as the WorkingSet of a process) but a plain-text representation for anything deeper (such as a process's Threads collection). For information on how to control the depth of this export, type **Get-Help Export-CliXml** and see the explanation of the –Depth parameter.

After you import data saved by Export-CliXml, you again have access to the properties and values from the original data. PowerShell converts some objects back to their fully featured objects (such as System.DateTime objects), but for the most part does not retain functionality (for example, methods) from the original objects.

8.5 Store the Output of a Command in a CSV File

Problem

You want to store the output of a command in a CSV file for later processing. This is helpful when you want to export the data for later processing outside PowerShell.

Solution

Use PowerShell's Export-Csv cmdlet to save the output of a command into a CSV file. For example, to create an inventory of the patches applied to a system by KB number (on pre-Vista systems):

```
cd $env:WINDIR
Get-ChildItem KB*.log | Export-Csv c:\temp\patch_log.csv
```

You can then review this patch log in a tool such as Excel, mail it to others, or do whatever else you might want to do with a CSV file.

Discussion

The CSV file format is one of the most common formats for exchanging semistructured data between programs and systems.

PowerShell's Export-Csv cmdlet provides an easy way to export data from the PowerShell environment, while still allowing you to keep a fair amount of your data's structure. When PowerShell exports your data to the CSV, it creates a row for each object that you provide. For each row, PowerShell creates columns in the CSV that represent the values of your object's properties.

One thing to keep in mind is that the CSV file format supports only plain strings for property values. If a property on your object isn't actually a string, PowerShell converts it to a string for you. Having PowerShell convert rich property values (such as integers) to strings, however, does mean that a certain amount of information is not preserved. If your ultimate goal is to load this unmodified data again in PowerShell, the Export-CliXml cmdlet provides a much better alternative. For more information about the Export-CliXml cmdlet, see Recipe 8.4, "Easily Import and Export Your Structured Data."

For more information on how to import data from a CSV file into PowerShell, see the following section, Recipe 8.6, "Import Structured Data from a CSV File."

See Also

- Recipe 8.4, "Easily Import and Export Your Structured Data"
- Recipe 8.6, "Import Structured Data from a CSV File"

8.6   Import Structured Data from a CSV File

Problem

You want to import structured data that has been stored in a CSV file. This is helpful when you want to use structured data created by another program, or structured data modified by a person.

Solution

Use PowerShell's `Import-Csv` cmdlet to import structured data from a CSV file.

For example, imagine that you previously exported an inventory of the patches applied to a pre-Vista system by KB number:

```
cd $env:WINDIR
Get-ChildItem KB*.log | Export-Csv c:\temp\patch_log.csv
```

Somebody reviewed the CSV, and kept only lines from patch logs that they would like to review further. You would like to copy those actual patch logs to a directory so that you can share them.

```
PS >Import-Csv C:\temp\patch_log_reviewed.csv | Foreach-Object {
>>     Copy-Item -LiteralPath $_.FullName -Destination c:\temp\sharedlogs\ }
>>
```

Discussion

As mentioned in Recipe 8.5, "Store the Output of a Command in a CSV File," the CSV file format is one of the most common formats for exchanging semistructured data between programs and systems.

PowerShell's `Import-Csv` cmdlet provides an easy way to import semistructured data to the PowerShell environment from other programs. When PowerShell imports your data from the CSV, it creates a new object for each row in the CSV. For each object, PowerShell creates properties on the object from the values of the columns in the CSV.

> The preceding solution uses the `Foreach-Object` cmdlet to pass each object to the `Copy-Item` cmdlet. For each item, it uses the incoming object's `FullName` property as the source path, and uses *c:\temp\ sharedlogs* as the destination. However, the CSV includes a `PSPath` property that represents the source, and most cmdlets support `PSPath` as an alternative (*alias*) parameter name for `-LiteralPath`. Because of this, we could have also written
>
> ```
> PS >Import-Csv C:\temp\patch_log_reviewed.csv |
> >>     Copy-Item -Destination c:\temp\sharedlogs\
> >>
> ```
>
> For more information about this feature, see Recipe 2.5, "Automate Data-Intensive Tasks."

One thing to keep in mind is that the CSV file format supports only plain strings for property values. When you import data from a CSV, properties that look like dates will still only be strings. Properties that look like numbers will only be strings. Properties that look like any sort of rich data type will only be strings. That means that sorting on any property will always be an *alphabetical* sort, which is usually not the same as the sorting rules for the rich data types that the property might look like.

If your ultimate goal is to load rich unmodified data from something that you've previously exported from PowerShell, the `Import-CliXml` cmdlet provides a much better alternative. For more information about the `Import-CliXml` cmdlet, see Recipe 8.4, "Easily Import and Export Your Structured Data."

For more information on how to export data from PowerShell to a CSV file into PowerShell, see Recipe 8.5, "Store the Output of a Command in a CSV File."

See Also

- Recipe 2.5, "Automate Data-Intensive Tasks"
- Recipe 8.4, "Easily Import and Export Your Structured Data"
- Recipe 8.5, "Store the Output of a Command in a CSV File"

8.7 Use Excel to Manage Command Output

Problem

You want to use Excel to manipulate or visualize the output of a command.

Solution

Use PowerShell's `Export-Csv` cmdlet to save the output of a command in a CSV file, and then load that CSV in Excel. If you have Excel associated with *.CSV* files, the `Invoke-Item` cmdlet launches Excel when you provide it with a *.CSV* file as an argument.

Example 8-7 demonstrates how to generate a CSV containing the disk usage for subdirectories of the current directory.

Example 8-7. Using Excel to visualize disk usage on the system

```
PS >$filename = "c:\temp\diskusage.csv"
PS >
PS >$output = Get-ChildItem | Where-Object { $_.PsIsContainer } |
>>     Select-Object Name,
>>         @{ Name="Size";
>>             Expression={ ($_ | Get-ChildItem -Recurse |
>>                 Measure-Object -Sum Length).Sum + 0 } }
>>
```

Example 8-7. Using Excel to visualize disk usage on the system (continued)

```
PS >$output | Export-Csv $filename
PS >
PS >Invoke-Item $filename
```

In Excel, manipulate or format the data as you wish. As Figure 8-1 shows. we can manually create a pie chart:

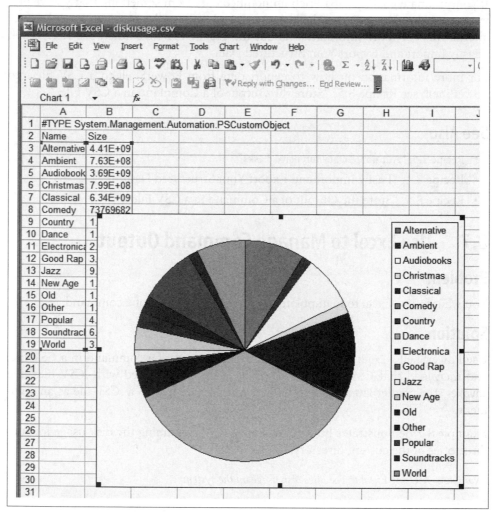

Figure 8-1. Visualizing data in Excel

Discussion

Although used only as a demonstration, Example 8-7 packs quite a bit into just a few lines.

The first Get-ChildItem line gets a list of all the files in the current directory and uses the Where-Object cmdlet to restrict those to directories. For each of those directories, you use the Select-Object cmdlet to pick out the Name and Size of that directory.

Directories don't have a Size property though. To get that, we use Select-Object's hashtable syntax to generate a *calculated property*. This calculated property (as defined by the Expression script block) uses the Get-ChildItem and Measure-Object cmdlets to add up the Length of all files in the given directory.

For more information about creating and working with calculated properties, see Recipe 3.11, "Add Custom Methods and Properties to Objects."

See Also

- Recipe 3.11, "Add Custom Methods and Properties to Objects"

CHAPTER 9

Internet-Enabled Scripts

9.0 Introduction

Although PowerShell provides an enormous benefit even when your scripts interact only with the local system, working with data sources from the Internet opens exciting and unique opportunities. For example, you might download files or information from the Internet, interact with a web service, store your output as HTML, or even send an email that reports the results of a long-running script.

Through its cmdlets and access to the networking support in the .NET Framework, PowerShell provides ample opportunities for Internet-enabled administration.

9.1 Download a File from the Internet

Problem

You want to download a file from a web site on the Internet.

Solution

Use the `DownloadFile()` method from the .NET Framework's `System.Net.WebClient` class to download a file:

```
PS >$source = "http://www.leeholmes.com/favicon.ico"
PS >$destination = "c:\temp\favicon.ico"
PS >
PS >$wc = New-Object System.Net.WebClient
PS >$wc.DownloadFile($source, $destination)
```

Discussion

The `System.Net.WebClient` class from the .NET Framework lets you easily upload and download data from remote web servers.

The WebClient class acts much like a web browser, in that you can specify a user agent, proxy (if your outgoing connection requires one), and even credentials.

All web browsers send a user agent identifier along with their web request. This identifier tells the web site what application is making the request—such as Internet Explorer, Firefox, or an automated crawler from a search engine. Many web sites check this user agent identifier to determine how to display the page. Unfortunately, many fail entirely if they can't determine the user agent for the incoming request. To make the System.Net.WebClient identify itself as Internet Explorer, use the following commands, instead:

```
$userAgent = "Mozilla/4.0 (compatible; MSIE 6.0; Windows NT 5.2;)"
$wc = New-Object System.Net.WebClient
$wc.Headers.Add("user-agent", $userAgent)
```

Notice that the solution uses a fully qualified path for the destination file. This is an important step, as the DownloadFile() method saves its files to the directory in which *PowerShell.exe* started (the root of your user profile directory by default) otherwise.

You can use the DownloadFile() method to download web pages just as easily as you download files—you need to supply only an URL as a source (such as *http://blogs. msdn.com/powershell/rss.xml*) instead of a filename. If you ultimately intend to parse or read through the downloaded page, the DownloadString() method may be more appropriate.

For more information on how to use download and parse web pages, see the following section, Recipe 9.2, "Download a Web Page from the Internet."

See Also

- Recipe 9.2, "Download a Web Page from the Internet"

9.2 Download a Web Page from the Internet

Problem

You want to download a web page from the Internet and work with the content as a plain string.

Solution

Use the DownloadString() method from the .NET Framework's System.Net.WebClient class to download a web page or plain text file into a string.

```
PS >$source = "http://blogs.msdn.com/powershell/rss.xml"
PS >
PS >$wc = New-Object System.Net.WebClient
PS >$content = $wc.DownloadString($source)
```

Discussion

Although web services are becoming increasingly popular, they are still far less common than web pages that display useful data. Because of this, retrieving data from services on the Internet often comes by means of *screen scraping*: downloading the HTML of the web page and then carefully separating out the content you want from the vast majority of the content that you do not.

 The technique of screen scraping has been around much longer than the Internet! As long as computer systems have generated output designed primarily for humans, screen scraping tools have risen to make this output available to other computer programs.

Unfortunately, screen scraping is an error-prone way to extract content. If the web page authors change the underlying HTML, your code will usually stop working correctly. If the site's HTML is written as valid XHTML, you may be able to use PowerShell's built in XML support to more easily parse the content.

For more information about PowerShell's built-in XML support, see Recipe 8.1, "Access Information in an XML File."

Despite its fragility, pure screen scraping is often the only alternative. In Example 9-1, you use this approach to easily fetch Encarta "Instant Answers" from MSN Search. If the script no longer works when you run it, I apologize—although it does demonstrate the perils of screen scraping.

Example 9-1. Get-Answer.ps1

```
##############################################################################
## Get-Answer.ps1
##
## Use Encarta's Instant Answers to answer your question
##
## Example:
##    Get-Answer "What is the population of China?"
##############################################################################
param([string] $question = $( throw "Please ask a question."))

function Main
{
    ## Load the System.Web.HttpUtility DLL, to let us URLEncode
    [void] [System.Reflection.Assembly]::LoadWithPartialName("System.Web")

    ## Get the web page into a single string with newlines between
    ## the lines.
    $encoded = [System.Web.HttpUtility]::UrlEncode($question)
    $url = "http://search.live.com/results.aspx?q=$encoded"
    $text = (new-object System.Net.WebClient).DownloadString($url)
```

Example 9-1. Get-Answer.ps1 (continued)

```
    ## Get the answer with annotations
    $startIndex = $text.IndexOf('<span class="answer_header">')
    $endIndex = $text.IndexOf('function YNC')

    ## If we found a result, then filter the result
    if(($startIndex -ge 0) -and ($endIndex -ge 0))
    {
        $partialText = $text.Substring($startIndex, $endIndex - $startIndex)

        ## Very fragile screen scraping here
        $pattern = '<script.+?<div (id="results"|class="answer_fact_body")>'
        $partialText = $partialText -replace $pattern,"`n"
        $partialText = $partialText -replace '<span class="attr.?.?.?">',"`n"
        $partialText = $partialText -replace '<BR ?/>',"`n"

        $partialText = clean-html $partialText
        $partialText = $partialText -replace "`n`n", "`n"

        "`n" + $partialText.Trim()
    }
    else
    {
        "`nNo answer found."
    }
}

## Clean HTML from a text chunk
function clean-html ($htmlInput)
{
    $tempString = [Regex]::Replace($htmlInput, "<[^>]*>", "")
    $tempString.Replace("  ", "")
}

. Main
```

For more information about running scripts, see Recipe 1.1, "Run Programs, Scripts, and Existing Tools."

See Also

- Recipe 1.1, "Run Programs, Scripts, and Existing Tools"
- Recipe 8.1, "Access Information in an XML File"

9.3   Program: Get-PageUrls

When working with HTML, it is common to require advanced regular expressions that separate the content you care about from the content you don't. A perfect example of this is extracting all the HTML links from a web page.

Links come in many forms, depending on how lenient you want to be. They may be well-formed according to the various HTML standards. They may use relative paths, or they may use absolute paths. They may place double quotes around the URL, or they may place single quotes around the URL. If you're really unlucky, they may accidentally include quotes on only one side of the URL.

Example 9-2 demonstrates some approaches for dealing with this type of advanced parsing task. Given a web page that you've downloaded from the Internet, it extracts all links from the page and returns a list of the URLs in that page. It also fixes URLs that were originally written as relative URLs (for example, /file.zip) to include the server from which they originated.

Example 9-2. Get-PageUrls.ps1

```
##############################################################################
## Get-PageUrls.ps1
##
## Parse all of the URLs out of a given file.
##
## Example:
##    Get-PageUrls microsoft.html http://www.microsoft.com
##
##############################################################################
param(
    ## The filename to parse
    [string] $filename = $(throw "Please specify a filename."),

    ## The URL from which you downloaded the page.
    ## For example, http://www.microsoft.com
    [string] $base = $(throw "Please specify a base URL."),

    ## The Regular Expression pattern with which to filter
    ## the returned URLs
    [string] $pattern = ".*"
     )

## Load the System.Web DLL so that we can decode URLs
[void] [Reflection.Assembly]::LoadWithPartialName("System.Web")

## Defines the regular expression that will parse an URL
## out of an anchor tag.
$regex = "<\s*a\s*[^>]*?href\s*=\s*[`"']*([^`"'>]+)[^>]*?>"

## Parse the file for links
function Main
{
    ## Do some minimal source URL fixups, by switching backslashes to
    ## forward slashes
    $base = $base.Replace("\", "/")

    if($base.IndexOf("://") -lt 0)
```

Example 9-2. Get-PageUrls.ps1 (continued)

```
    {
        throw "Please specify a base URL in the form of " +
            "http://server/path_to_file/file.html"
    }

    ## Determine the server from which the file originated.  This will
    ## help us resolve links such as "/somefile.zip"
    $base = $base.Substring(0,$base.LastIndexOf("/") + 1)
    $baseSlash = $base.IndexOf("/", $base.IndexOf("://") + 3)
    $domain = $base.Substring(0, $baseSlash)


    ## Put all of the file content into a big string, and
    ## get the regular expression matches
    $content = [String]::Join(' ', (get-content $filename))
    $contentMatches = @(GetMatches $content $regex)

    foreach($contentMatch in $contentMatches)
    {
        if(-not ($contentMatch -match $pattern)) { continue }

        $contentMatch = $contentMatch.Replace("\", "/")

        ## Hrefs may look like:
        ## ./file
        ## file
        ## ../../../file
        ## /file
        ## url
        ## We'll keep all of the relative paths, as they will resolve.
        ## We only need to resolve the ones pointing to the root.
        if($contentMatch.IndexOf("://") -gt 0)
        {
            $url = $contentMatch
        }
        elseif($contentMatch[0] -eq "/")
        {
            $url = "$domain$contentMatch"
        }
        else
        {
            $url = "$base$contentMatch"
            $url = $url.Replace("/./", "/")
        }

        ## Return the URL, after first removing any HTML entities
        [System.Web.HttpUtility]::HtmlDecode($url)
    }
}

function GetMatches([string] $content, [string] $regex)
```

Example 9-2. Get-PageUrls.ps1 (continued)

```
{
    $returnMatches = New-Object System.Collections.ArrayList

    ## Match the regular expression against the content, and
    ## add all trimmed matches to our return list
    $resultingMatches = [Regex]::Matches($content, $regex, "IgnoreCase")
    foreach($match in $resultingMatches)
    {
        $cleanedMatch = $match.Groups[1].Value.Trim()
        [void] $returnMatches.Add($cleanedMatch)
    }

    $returnMatches
}

. Main
```

For more information about running scripts, see Recipe 1.1, "Run Programs, Scripts, and Existing Tools."

See Also

- Recipe 1.1, "Run Programs, Scripts, and Existing Tools"

9.4 Program: Connect-WebService

Although screen scraping (parsing the HTML of a web page) is the most common way to obtain data from the Internet, web services are becoming increasingly common. Web services provide a significant advantage over HTML parsing, as they are much less likely to break when the web designer changes minor features in a design.

The only benefit to web services isn't their more stable interface, however. When working with web services, the .NET Framework lets you generate *proxies* that let you interact with the web service as easily as you would work with a regular .NET object. That is because to you, the web service user, these proxies act almost exactly the same as any other .NET object. To call a method on the web service, simply call a method on the proxy.

The primary differences you will notice when working with a web service proxy (as opposed to a regular .NET object) are the speed and Internet connectivity requirements. Depending on conditions, a method call on a web service proxy could easily take several seconds to complete. If your computer (or the remote computer) experiences network difficulties, the call might even return a network error message (such as a timeout) instead of the information you had hoped for.

Example 9-3 lets you connect to a remote web service if you know the location of its service description file (*WSDL*). It generates the web service proxy for you, allowing you to interact with it as you would any other .NET object.

Example 9-3. Connect-WebService.ps1

```
##############################################################################
## Connect-WebService.ps1
##
## Connect to a given web service, and create a type that allows you to
## interact with that web service.
##
## Example:
##
##      $wsdl = "http://terraserver.microsoft.com/TerraService2.asmx?WSDL"
##      $terraServer = Connect-WebService $wsdl
##      $place = New-Object Place
##      $place.City = "Redmond"
##      $place.State = "WA"
##      $place.Country = "USA"
##      $facts = $terraserver.GetPlaceFacts($place)
##      $facts.Center
##############################################################################
param(
    [string] $wsdlLocation = $(throw "Please specify a WSDL location"),
    [string] $namespace,
    [Switch] $requiresAuthentication)

## Create the web service cache, if it doesn't already exist
if(-not (Test-Path Variable:\Lee.Holmes.WebServiceCache))
{
    ${GLOBAL:Lee.Holmes.WebServiceCache} = @{}
}

## Check if there was an instance from a previous connection to
## this web service. If so, return that instead.
$oldInstance = ${GLOBAL:Lee.Holmes.WebServiceCache}[$wsdlLocation]
if($oldInstance)
{
    $oldInstance
    return
}

## Load the required Web Services DLL
[void] [Reflection.Assembly]::LoadWithPartialName("System.Web.Services")

## Download the WSDL for the service, and create a service description from
## it.
$wc = New-Object System.Net.WebClient

if($requiresAuthentication)
{
    $wc.UseDefaultCredentials = $true
}
```

Example 9-3. Connect-WebService.ps1 (continued)

```
$wsdlStream = $wc.OpenRead($wsdlLocation)

## Ensure that we were able to fetch the WSDL
if(-not (Test-Path Variable:\wsdlStream))
{
    return
}

$serviceDescription =
    [Web.Services.Description.ServiceDescription]::Read($wsdlStream)
$wsdlStream.Close()

## Ensure that we were able to read the WSDL into a service description
if(-not (Test-Path Variable:\serviceDescription))
{
    return
}

## Import the web service into a CodeDom
$serviceNamespace = New-Object System.CodeDom.CodeNamespace
if($namespace)
{
    $serviceNamespace.Name = $namespace
}

$codeCompileUnit = New-Object System.CodeDom.CodeCompileUnit
$serviceDescriptionImporter =
    New-Object Web.Services.Description.ServiceDescriptionImporter
$serviceDescriptionImporter.AddServiceDescription(
    $serviceDescription, $null, $null)
[void] $codeCompileUnit.Namespaces.Add($serviceNamespace)
[void] $serviceDescriptionImporter.Import(
    $serviceNamespace, $codeCompileUnit)

## Generate the code from that CodeDom into a string
$generatedCode = New-Object Text.StringBuilder
$stringWriter = New-Object IO.StringWriter $generatedCode
$provider = New-Object Microsoft.CSharp.CSharpCodeProvider
$provider.GenerateCodeFromCompileUnit($codeCompileUnit, $stringWriter, $null)

## Compile the source code.
$references = @("System.dll", "System.Web.Services.dll", "System.Xml.dll")
$compilerParameters = New-Object System.CodeDom.Compiler.CompilerParameters
$compilerParameters.ReferencedAssemblies.AddRange($references)
$compilerParameters.GenerateInMemory = $true

$compilerResults =
    $provider.CompileAssemblyFromSource($compilerParameters, $generatedCode)

## Write any errors if generated.
if($compilerResults.Errors.Count -gt 0)
```

Example 9-3. Connect-WebService.ps1 (continued)

```
{
    $errorLines = ""
    foreach($error in $compilerResults.Errors)
    {
        $errorLines += "`n`t" + $error.Line + ":`t" + $error.ErrorText
    }

    Write-Error $errorLines
    return
}
## There were no errors.  Create the web service object and return it.
else
{
    ## Get the assembly that we just compiled
    $assembly = $compilerResults.CompiledAssembly

    ## Find the type that had the WebServiceBindingAttribute.
    ## There may be other "helper types" in this file, but they will
    ## not have this attribute
    $type = $assembly.GetTypes() |
        Where-Object { $_.GetCustomAttributes(
            [System.Web.Services.WebServiceBindingAttribute], $false) }

    if(-not $type)
    {
        Write-Error "Could not generate web service proxy."
        return
    }

    ## Create an instance of the type, store it in the cache,
    ## and return it to the user.
    $instance = $assembly.CreateInstance($type)

    ## Many services that support authentication also require it on the
    ## resulting objects
    if($requiresAuthentication)
    {
        if(@($instance.PsObject.Properties |
            where { $_.Name -eq "UseDefaultCredentials" }).Count -eq 1)
        {
            $instance.UseDefaultCredentials = $true
        }
    }

    ${GLOBAL:Lee.Holmes.WebServiceCache}[$wsdlLocation] = $instance

    $instance
}
```

For more information about running scripts, see Recipe 1.1, "Run Programs, Scripts, and Existing Tools."

See Also

- Recipe 1.1, "Run Programs, Scripts, and Existing Tools"

9.5   Export Command Output As a Web Page

Problem

You want to export the results of a command as a web page so that you can post it to a web server.

Solution

Use PowerShell's `ConvertTo-Html` cmdlet to convert command output into a web page. For example, to create a quick HTML summary of PowerShell's commands:

```
PS >$filename = "c:\temp\help.html"
PS >
PS >$commands = Get-Command | Where { $_.CommandType -ne "Alias" }
PS >$summary = $commands | Get-Help | Select Name,Synopsis
PS >$summary | ConvertTo-Html | Set-Content $filename
```

Discussion

When you use the `ConvertTo-Html` cmdlet to export command output to a file, PowerShell generates an HTML table that represents the command output. In the table, it creates a row for each object that you provide. For each row, PowerShell creates columns to represent the values of your object's properties.

The `ConvertTo-Html` cmdlet lets you customize this table to some degree through parameters that allow you to add custom content to the head and body of the resulting page.

For more information about the `ConvertTo-Html` cmdlet, type **Get-Help ConvertTo-Html**.

9.6   Program: Send an Email

Example 9-4 shows how to easily send email messages from your scripts.

In addition to the fields shown in the script, the `System.Net.Mail.MailMessage` class supports properties that let you add attachments, set message priority, and much more. For more information about working with classes from the .NET Framework, see Recipe 3.4, "Work with .NET Objects."

Example 9-4. Send-MailMessage.ps1

```
##############################################################################
##
## Send-MailMessage.ps1
##
## Illustrate the techniques used to send an email in PowerShell.
##
## Example:
##
##   PS >$body = @"
##   >> Hi from another satisfied customer of The PowerShell Cookbook!
##   >> "@
##   >>
##   PS >$to = "guide_feedback@leeholmes.com"
##   PS >$subject = "Thanks for all of the scripts."
##   PS >$mailHost = "mail.leeholmes.com"
##   PS >Send-MailMessage $to $subject $body $mailHost
##
##############################################################################

param(
    [string[]] $to = $(throw "Please specify the destination mail address"),
    [string] $subject = "<No Subject>",
    [string] $body = $(throw "Please specify the message content"),
    [string] $smtpHost = $(throw "Please specify a mail server."),
    [string] $from = "$($env:UserName)@example.com"
  )

## Create the mail message
$email = New-Object System.Net.Mail.MailMessage

## Populate its fields
foreach($mailTo in $to)
{
    $email.To.Add($mailTo)
}

$email.From = $from
$email.Subject = $subject
$email.Body = $body

## Send the mail
$client = New-Object System.Net.Mail.SmtpClient $smtpHost
$client.UseDefaultCredentials = $true
$client.Send($email)
```

For more information about running scripts, see Recipe 1.1, "Run Programs, Scripts, and Existing Tools."

See Also

- Recipe 1.1, "Run Programs, Scripts, and Existing Tools"
- Recipe 3.4, "Work with .NET Objects"

9.7   Program: Interact with Internet Protocols

While it is common to work at an abstract level with web sites and web services, an entirely separate style of Internet-enabled scripting comes from interacting with the remote computer at a much lower level. This lower level (called the TCP level, for *Transmission Control Protocol*) forms the communication foundation of most Internet protocols—such as Telnet, SMTP (sending mail), POP3 (receiving mail), and HTTP (retrieving web content).

The .NET Framework provides classes that allow you to interact with many of the Internet protocols directly: the System.Web.Mail.SmtpMail class for SMTP, the System.Net.WebClient class for HTTP, and a few others. When the .NET Framework does not support an Internet protocol that you need, though, you can often script the application protocol directly if you know the details of how it works.

Example 9-5 shows how to receive information about mail waiting in a remote POP3 mailbox, using the Send-TcpRequest script given in Example 9-6.

Example 9-5. Interacting with a remote POP3 mailbox

```
## Get the user credential
if(-not (Test-Path Variable:\mailCredential))
{
    $mailCredential = Get-Credential
}
$address = $mailCredential.UserName
$password = $mailCredential.GetNetworkCredential().Password

## Connect to the remote computer, send the commands, and receive the
## output
$pop3Commands = "USER $address","PASS $password","STAT","QUIT"
$output = $pop3Commands | Send-TcpRequest mail.myserver.com 110
$inbox = $output.Split("`n")[3]

## Parse the output for the number of messages waiting and total bytes
$status = $inbox |
    Convert-TextObject -PropertyName "Response","Waiting","BytesTotal","Extra"
"{0} messages waiting, totaling {1} bytes." -f $status.Waiting, $status.BytesTotal
```

In Example 9-5, you connect to port 110 of the remote mail server. You then issue commands to request the status of the mailbox in a form that the mail server understands. The format of this network conversation is specified and required by the standard POP3 protocol. Example 9-5 uses the Convert-TextObject command, which is provided in Recipe 5.12, "Program: Convert Text Streams to Objects."

Example 9-6 supports the core functionality of Example 9-5. It lets you easily work with plain-text TCP protocols.

Example 9-6. Send-TcpRequest.ps1

```
##############################################################################
## Send-TcpRequest.ps1
##
## Send a TCP request to a remote computer, and return the response.
## If you do not supply input to this script (via either the pipeline, or the
## -InputObject parameter,) the script operates in interactive mode.
##
## Example:
##
##      $http = @"
##      GET / HTTP/1.1
##      Host:search.msn.com
##      `n`n
##      "@
##
##      $http | Send-TcpRequest search.msn.com 80
##############################################################################
param(
        [string] $remoteHost = "localhost",
        [int] $port = 80,
        [string] $inputObject,
        [int] $commandDelay = 100
    )

[string] $output = ""

## Store the input into an array that we can scan over. If there was no input,
## then we will be in interactive mode.
$currentInput = $inputObject
if(-not $currentInput)
{
    $SCRIPT:currentInput = @($input)
}
$scriptedMode = [bool] $currentInput

function Main
{
    ## Open the socket, and connect to the computer on the specified port
    if(-not $scriptedMode)
    {
        Write-Host "Connecting to $remoteHost on port $port"
    }

    trap { Write-Error "Could not connect to remote computer: $_"; exit }
    $socket = New-Object System.Net.Sockets.TcpClient($remoteHost, $port)

    if(-not $scriptedMode)
    {
        Write-Host "Connected.  Press ^D followed by [ENTER] to exit.`n"
    }

    $stream = $socket.GetStream()
    $writer = New-Object System.IO.StreamWriter($stream)
```

Example 9-6. Send-TcpRequest.ps1 (continued)

```
    ## Create a buffer to receive the response
    $buffer = New-Object System.Byte[] 1024
    $encoding = New-Object System.Text.AsciiEncoding


while($true)
{
    ## Receive the output that has buffered so far
    $SCRIPT:output += GetOutput

    ## If we're in scripted mode, send the commands,
    ## receive the output, and exit.
    if($scriptedMode)
    {
        foreach($line in $currentInput)
        {
            $writer.WriteLine($line)
            $writer.Flush()
            Start-Sleep -m $commandDelay
            $SCRIPT:output += GetOutput
        }

        break
    }
    ## If we're in interactive mode, write the buffered
    ## output, and respond to input.
    else
    {
        if($output)
        {
            foreach($line in $output.Split("`n"))
            {
                Write-Host $line
            }
            $SCRIPT:output = ""
        }

        ## Read the user's command, quitting if they hit ^D
        $command = Read-Host
        if($command -eq ([char] 4)) { break; }

        ## Otherwise, write their command to the remote host
        $writer.WriteLine($command)
        $writer.Flush()
    }
}

## Close the streams
$writer.Close()
$stream.Close()
```

Example 9-6. Send-TcpRequest.ps1 (continued)

```
    ## If we're in scripted mode, return the output
    if($scriptedMode)
    {
        $output
    }
}

## Read output from a remote host
function GetOutput
{
    $outputBuffer = ""
    $foundMore = $false

    ## Read all the data available from the stream, writing it to the
    ## output buffer when done.
    do
    {
        ## Allow data to buffer for a bit
        Start-Sleep -m 1000

        ## Read what data is available
        $foundmore = $false
        while($stream.DataAvailable)
        {
            $read = $stream.Read($buffer, 0, 1024)
            $outputBuffer += ($encoding.GetString($buffer, 0, $read))
            $foundmore = $true
        }
    } while($foundmore)

    $outputBuffer
}

. Main
```

For more information about running scripts, see Recipe 1.1, "Run Programs, Scripts, and Existing Tools."

See Also

- Recipe 1.1, "Run Programs, Scripts, and Existing Tools"
- Recipe 5.12, "Program: Convert Text Streams to Objects"

CHAPTER 10
Code Reuse

10.0 Introduction

What surprises many people is how much you can accomplish in PowerShell from the interactive prompt alone. Since PowerShell makes it so easy to join its powerful commands together into even more powerful combinations, enthusiasts grow to relish this brevity. In fact, there is a special place in the heart of most scripting enthusiasts set aside entirely for the most compact expressions of power: *one-liners*.

Despite its interactive efficiency, you obviously don't want to retype all your brilliant ideas anew each time you need them. When you want to save or reuse the commands that you've written, PowerShell provides many avenues to support you: scripts, libraries, functions, script blocks, and more.

10.1 Write a Script

Problem

You want to store your commands in a script, so that you can share them or reuse them later.

Solution

To write a PowerShell script, create a plain-text file with your editor of choice. Add your PowerShell commands to that script (the same PowerShell commands you use from the interactive shell) and then save it with a *.ps1* extension.

Discussion

One of the most important things to remember about PowerShell is that running scripts and working at the command line are essentially equivalent operations. If you see it in a script, you can type it or paste it at the command line. If you typed it on the command line, you can paste it into a text file and call it a script.

Once you write your script, PowerShell lets you call it in the same way that you call other programs and existing tools. Running a script does the same thing as running all the commands in that script.

> PowerShell introduces a few features related to running scripts and tools that may at first confuse you if you aren't aware of them. For more information about how to call scripts and existing tools, see Recipe 1.1, "Run Programs, Scripts, and Existing Tools."

The first time you try to run a script in PowerShell, PowerShell provides the error message:

```
File c:\tools\myFirstScript.ps1 cannot be loaded because the execution of scri
pts is disabled on this system. Please see "get-help about_signing" for more d
etails.
At line:1 char:12
+ myFirstScript <<<<
```

Since relatively few computer users write scripts, PowerShell's default security policies prevent scripts from running. Once you begin writing scripts, though, you should configure this policy to something less restrictive. For information on how to configure your execution policy, see Recipe 16.1, "Enable Scripting Through an Execution Policy."

When it comes to the filename of your script, picking a descriptive name is the best way to guarantee that you will always remember what that script does—or at least have a good idea. This is an issue that PowerShell tackles elegantly, by naming every cmdlet in the Verb-Noun pattern: a command that performs an action (*verb*) on an item (*noun*). As an example of the usefulness of this philosophy, consider the names of typical Windows commands given in Example 10-1:

Example 10-1. The names of some standard Windows commands

```
PS >dir $env:WINDIR\System32\*.exe | Select-Object Name

Name
----
accwiz.exe
actmovie.exe
ahui.exe
alg.exe
append.exe
arp.exe
asr_fmt.exe
asr_ldm.exe
asr_pfu.exe
at.exe
atmadm.exe
attrib.exe
(...)
```

Compare this to the names of some standard Windows PowerShell cmdlets given in Example 10-2.

Example 10-2. The names of some standard Windows PowerShell cmdlets

```
PS >Get-Command | Select-Object Name

Name
----
Add-Content
Add-History
Add-Member
Add-PSSnapin
Clear-Content
Clear-Item
Clear-ItemProperty
Clear-Variable
Compare-Object
ConvertFrom-SecureString
Convert-Path
ConvertTo-Html
(...)
```

As an additional way to improve discovery, PowerShell takes this even further with the philosophy (and explicit goal) that *"you can manage 80 percent of your system with less than 50 verbs."* As you learn the standard verbs for a concept (such as Get as the standard verb of *Read*, *Open*, and so on), you can often guess the verb of a command as the first step in discovering it.

When you name your script (*especially* if you intend to share it), make every effort to pick a name that follows these conventions. Appendix D, *Standard PowerShell Verbs* provides a list of PowerShell's standard verbs to help you name your scripts properly. As evidence of its utility for scripts, consider some of the scripts included in this book:

```
PS >dir | select Name

Name
----
Compare-Property.ps1
Connect-WebService.ps1
Convert-TextObject.ps1
Get-AliasSuggestion.ps1
Get-Answer.ps1
Get-Characteristics.ps1
Get-OwnerReport.ps1
Get-PageUrls.ps1
Invoke-CmdScript.ps1
New-GenericObject.ps1
Select-FilteredObject.ps1
(...)
```

Like the PowerShell cmdlets, the names of these scripts are clear, are easy to understand, and use verbs from PowerShell's standard verb list.

See Also

- Recipe 1.1, "Run Programs, Scripts, and Existing Tools"
- Recipe 16.1, "Enable Scripting Through an Execution Policy"
- Appendix D, *Standard PowerShell Verbs*

10.2 Write a Function

Problem

You have commands in your script that you want to call multiple times, or a section of your script that you consider to be a "helper" for the main purpose of your script.

Solution

Place this common code in a function, and then call that function instead. For example, this Celsius conversion code in a script:

```
param([double] $fahrenheit)

## Convert it to Celsius
$celsius = $fahrenheit - 32
$celsius = $celsius / 1.8

## Output the answer
"$fahrenheit degrees Fahrenheit is $celsius degrees Celsius."
```

could be placed in a function (itself in a script):

```
param([double] $fahrenheit)

## Convert Fahrenheit to Celsius
function ConvertFahrenheitToCelsius([double] $fahrenheit)
{
    $celsius = $fahrenheit - 32
    $celsius - $celsius / 1.8
    $celsius
}

$celsius = ConvertFahrenheitToCelsius $fahrenheit

## Output the answer
"$fahrenheit degrees Fahrenheit is $celsius degrees Celsius."
```

Although using a function arguably makes this specific script longer and more difficult to understand, the technique is extremely valuable (and used) in almost all nontrivial scripts.

Discussion

Once you define a function, any command after that definition can use it. This means that you must define your function *before* any part of your script that uses it. You might find this unwieldy if your script defines many functions, as the function definitions obscure the main logic portion of your script. If this is the case, you can put your main logic in a "Main" function, as described in "Writing Scripts, Reusing Functionality" in Appendix A.

> A common question that comes from those accustomed to batch scripting in `cmd.exe` is, "What is the PowerShell equivalent of a `GOTO`?" In situations where the `GOTO` is used to call subroutines or other isolated helper parts of the batch file, use a PowerShell function to accomplish that task. If the `GOTO` is used as a way to loop over something, PowerShell's looping mechanisms are more appropriate.

In PowerShell, calling a function is designed to feel just like calling a cmdlet or a script. As a user, you should not have to know whether a little helper routine was written as a cmdlet, script, or function. When you call a function, simply add the parameters after the function name, with spaces separating each one (as shown in the solution). This is in contrast to the way that you call functions in many programming languages (such as C#), where you use parentheses after the function name and commas between each parameter.

Also, notice that the return value from a function is anything that it writes to the output pipeline (such as $celsius in the solution). You can write `return $celsius` if you want, but it is unnecessary.

For more information about writing functions, see "Writing Scripts, Reusing Functionality" in Appendix A. For more information about PowerShell's looping statements, see Recipe 4.4, "Repeat Operations with Loops."

See Also

- Recipe 4.4, "Repeat Operations with Loops"
- "Writing Scripts, Reusing Functionality" in Appendix A

10.3   Write a Script Block

Problem

You have a section of your script that works nearly the same for all input, aside from a minor change in logic.

Solution

As shown in Example 10-3, place the minor logic differences in a script block, and then pass that script block as a parameter to the code that requires it. Use the invoke operator (&) to execute the script block.

Example 10-3. A script that applies a script block to each element in the pipeline

```
##############################################################################
## Map-Object.ps1
##
## Apply the given mapping command to each element of the input
##
## Example:
##    1,2,3 | Map-Object { $_ * 2 }
##############################################################################
param([ScriptBlock] $mapCommand)

process
{
    & $mapCommand
}
```

Discussion

Imagine a script that needs to multiply all the elements in a list by two:

```
function MultiplyInputByTwo
{
    process
    {
        $_ * 2
    }
}
```

but it also needs to perform a more complex calculation:

```
function MultiplyInputComplex
{
    process
    {
        ($_ + 2) * 3
    }
}
```

These two functions are strikingly similar, except for the single line that actually performs the calculation. As we add more calculations, this quickly becomes more evident. Adding each new seven line function gives us only one unique line of value!

```
PS >1,2,3 | MultiplyInputByTwo
2
4
6
PS >1,2,3 | MultiplyInputComplex
```

```
9
12
15
```

If we instead use a script block to hold this "unknown" calculation, we don't need to keep on adding new functions:

```
PS >1,2,3 | Map-Object { $_ * 2 }
2
4
6
PS >1,2,3 | Map-Object { ($_ + 2) * 3 }
9
12
15
PS >1,2,3 | Map-Object { ($_ + 3) * $_ }
4
10
18
```

In fact, the functionality provided by Map-Object is so helpful that it is a standard PowerShell cmdlet—called Foreach-Object. For more information about script blocks, see "Writing Scripts, Reusing Functionality" in Appendix A. For more information about running scripts, see Recipe 1.1, "Run Programs, Scripts, and Existing Tools."

See Also

- Recipe 1.1, "Run Programs, Scripts, and Existing Tools"
- "Writing Scripts, Reusing Functionality" in Appendix A

10.4 Return Data from a Script, Function, or Script Block

Problem

You want your script or function to return data to whatever called it.

Solution

To return data from a script or function, write that data to the output pipeline:

```
## Get-Tomorrow.ps1
## Get the date that represents tomorrow

function GetDate
{
    Get-Date
}

$tomorrow = (GetDate).AddDays(1)
$tomorrow
```

Discussion

In PowerShell, any data that your function or script generates gets sent to the output pipeline, unless something captures that output. The GetDate function generates data (a date) and does not capture it, so that becomes the output of the function. The portion of the script that calls the GetDate function captures that output and then manipulates it.

Finally, the script writes the $tomorrow variable to the pipeline without capturing it, so that becomes the return value of the script itself.

Some .NET methods—such as the System.Collections.ArrayList class produce output, even though you may not expect them to. To prevent them from sending data to the output pipeline, either capture the data or cast it to [void]:

```
PS >$collection = New-Object System.Collections.ArrayList
PS >$collection.Add("Hello")
0
PS >[void] $collection.Add("Hello")
```

Even with this *"pipeline output becomes the return value"* philosophy, PowerShell continues to support the traditional return keyword as a way to return from a function or script. If you specify anything after the keyword (such as return "Hello"), PowerShell treats that as a "Hello" statement followed by a return statement.

If you want to make your intention clear to other readers of your script, you can use the Write-Output cmdlet to explicitly send data down the pipeline. Both produce the same result, so this is only a matter of preference.

If you write a collection (such as an array or ArrayList) to the output pipeline, PowerShell in fact writes each element of that collection to the pipeline. To keep the collection intact as it travels down the pipeline, prefix it with a comma when you return it. This returns a collection (that will be unraveled) with one element: the collection you wanted to keep intact.

```
function WritesObjects
{
    $arrayList = New-Object System.Collections.ArrayList
    [void] $arrayList.Add("Hello")
    [void] $arrayList.Add("World")

    $arrayList
}

function WritesArrayList
```

```
{
    $arrayList = New-Object System.Collections.ArrayList
    [void] $arrayList.Add("Hello")
    [void] $arrayList.Add("World")

    ,$arrayList
}

$objectOutput = WritesObjects

# The following command would generate an error
# $objectOutput.Add("Extra")

$arrayListOutput = WritesArrayList
$arrayListOutput.Add("Extra")
```

Although relatively uncommon in PowerShell's world of fully structured data, you may sometimes want to use an exit code to indicate the success or failure of your script. For this, PowerShell offers the exit keyword.

For more information about the return and exit statements, see "Writing Scripts, Reusing Functionality" in Appendix A and Recipe 1.10, "Determine the Status of the Last Command.

See Also

- Recipe 1.10, "Determine the Status of the Last Command"
- "Writing Scripts, Reusing Functionality" in Appendix A

10.5   Place Common Functions in a Library

Problem

You've developed a useful set of functions and want to share them between multiple scripts.

Solution

First, place these common function definitions by themselves in a script, with a name that starts with Library. While the Library prefix is not required, it is a useful naming convention. Example 10-4 demonstrates this approach.

Example 10-4. A library of temperature functions

```
## LibraryTemperature.ps1
## Functions that manipulate and convert temperatures

## Convert Fahrenheit to Celsius
function ConvertFahrenheitToCelsius([double] $fahrenheit)
```

Example 10-4. A library of temperature functions (continued)

```
{
    $celsius = $fahrenheit - 32
    $celsius = $celsius / 1.8
    $celsius
}
```

Next, dot-source that library from any scripts that need to use those functions, as shown by Example 10-5.

Example 10-5. A script that uses a library

```
param([double] $fahrenheit)

$scriptDirectory = Split-Path $myInvocation.MyCommand.Path
. (Join-Path $scriptDirectory LibraryTemperature.ps1)

$celsius = ConvertFahrenheitToCelsius $fahrenheit

## Output the answer
"$fahrenheit degrees Fahrenheit is $celsius degrees Celsius."
```

Discussion

Although mostly used for libraries, you can dot-source any script or function. When you dot-source a script or function, PowerShell acts as though the calling script itself had included the commands from that script or function.

For more information about dot-sourcing, see "Writing Scripts, Reusing Functionality" in Appendix A.

See Also

- "Writing Scripts, Reusing Functionality" in Appendix A

10.6 Access Arguments of a Script, Function, or Script Block

Problem

You want to access the arguments provided to a script, function, or script block.

Solution

To access arguments by name, use a param statement:

```
param($firstNamedArgument, [int] $secondNamedArgument = 0)

"First named argument is: $firstNamedArgument"
"Second named argument is: $secondNamedArgument"
```

To access unnamed arguments by position, use the $args array:

```
"First positional argument is: " + $args[0]
"Second positional argument is: " + $args[1]
```

You can use these techniques in exactly the same way with scripts, functions, and script blocks, as illustrated by Example 10-6.

Example 10-6. Working with arguments in scripts, functions, and script blocks

```
##############################################################################
## Get-Arguments.ps1
##
## Use command-line arguments
##############################################################################
param($firstNamedArgument, [int] $secondNamedArgument = 0)

## Display the arguments by name
"First named argument is: $firstNamedArgument"
"Second named argument is: $secondNamedArgument"

function GetArgumentsFunction
{
## We could use a param statement here, as well
## param($firstNamedArgument, [int] $secondNamedArgument = 0)

## Display the arguments by position
"First positional function argument is: " + $args[0]
"Second positional function argument is: " + $args[1]
}

GetArgumentsFunction One Two

$scriptBlock =
{
    param($firstNamedArgument, [int] $secondNamedArgument = 0)

    ## We could use $args here, as well
    "First named scriptblock argument is: $firstNamedArgument"
    "Second named scriptblock argument is: $secondNamedArgument"
}

& $scriptBlock -First One -Second 4.5
```

Example 10-6 produces the following output:

```
PS >Get-Arguments First 2
First named argument is: First
Second named argument is: 2
First positional function argument is: One
Second positional function argument is: Two
First named scriptblock argument is: One
Second named scriptblock argument is: 4
```

Discussion

Although PowerShell supports both the param keyword and the $args array, you will most commonly want to use the param keyword to define and access script, function, and script block parameters.

 In most languages, the most common reason to access parameters through an $args-style array is to determine the name of the currently running script. For information about how to do this in PowerShell, see Recipe 14.2, "Access Information About Your Command's Invocation."

When you use the param keyword to define your parameters, PowerShell provides your script or function with many useful features that allow users to work with your script much like they work with cmdlets:

- Users need only to specify enough of the parameter name to disambiguate it from other parameters.
- Users can understand the meaning of your parameters much more clearly.
- You can specify the type of your parameters, which PowerShell uses to convert input if required.
- You can specify default values for your parameters.

The $args array is sometimes helpful, however, as a way to deal with all arguments at once. For example:

```
function Reverse
{
    $argsEnd = $args.Length - 1
    $args[$argsEnd..0]
}
```

produces

```
PS >Reverse 1 2 3 4
4
3
2
1
```

For more information about the param statement, see "Writing Scripts, Reusing Functionality" in Appendix A. For more information about running scripts, see Recipe 1.1, "Run Programs, Scripts, and Existing Tools.

See Also

- Recipe 14.2, "Access Information About Your Command's Invocation"
- Recipe 1.1, "Run Programs, Scripts, and Existing Tools"
- "Writing Scripts, Reusing Functionality" in Appendix A

10.7   Access Pipeline Input

Problem

You want to interact with input that a user sends to your function, script, or script block via the pipeline.

Solution

To access pipeline input, use the $input variable as shown by Example 10-7.

Example 10-7. Accessing pipeline input

```
function InputCounter
{
    $count = 0

    ## Go through each element in the pipeline, and add up
    ## how many elements there were.
    foreach($element in $input)
    {
        $count++
    }

    $count
}
```

which produces the following (or similar) output when run against your Windows system directory:

```
PS >dir $env:WINDIR | InputCounter
295
```

Discussion

In your scripts, functions, and script blocks, the $input variable represents an *enumerator* (as opposed to a simple array) for the pipeline input the user provides. An enumerator lets you use a foreach statement to efficiently scan over the elements of the input (as shown in Example 10-7) but does not let you directly access specific items (such as the fifth element in the input, for example).

 An enumerator only lets you to scan forward through its contents. Once you access an element, PowerShell automatically moves on to the next one. If you need to access an item that you've already accessed before, you must call $input.Reset() to scan through the list again from the beginning, or store the input in an array.

If you need to access specific elements in the input (or access items multiple times), the best approach is to store the input in an array. This prevents your script from taking advantage of the $input enumerator's streaming behavior, but is sometimes the only alternative. To store the input in an array, use PowerShell's list evaluation syntax (@()) to force PowerShell to interpret it as an array.

```
function ReverseInput
{
    $inputArray = @($input)
    $inputEnd = $inputArray.Count - 1

    $inputArray[$inputEnd..0]
}
```

which produces

```
PS >1,2,3,4 | ReverseInput
4
3
2
1
```

If dealing with pipeline input plays a major role in your script, function, or script block, PowerShell provides an alternative means of dealing with pipeline input that may make your script easier to write and understand. For more information, see the following section Recipe 10.8, "Write Pipeline-Oriented Scripts with Cmdlet Keywords."

See Also

• Recipe 10.8, "Write Pipeline-Oriented Scripts with Cmdlet Keywords"

10.8   Write Pipeline-Oriented Scripts with Cmdlet Keywords

Problem

Your script, function, or script block primarily takes input from the pipeline, and you want to write it in a way that makes this intention both easy to implement and easy to read.

Solution

To cleanly separate your script into regions that deal with the initialization, per-record processing, and cleanup portions, use the begin, process, and end keywords, respectively. For example, a pipeline-oriented conversion of the solution in the section Recipe 10.7, "Access Pipeline Input," looks like Example 10-8.

Example 10-8. A pipeline-oriented script that uses cmdlet keywords

```
function InputCounter
{
    begin
    {
        $count = 0
    }

    ## Go through each element in the pipeline, and add up
    ## how many elements there were.
    process
    {
        Write-Debug "Processing element $_"
        $count++
    }

    end
    {
        $count
    }
}
```

This produces the following output:

```
PS >$debugPreference = "Continue"
PS >dir | InputCounter
DEBUG: Processing element Compare-Property.ps1
DEBUG: Processing element Connect-WebService.ps1
DEBUG: Processing element Convert-TextObject.ps1
DEBUG: Processing element ConvertFrom-FahrenheitWithFunction.ps1
DEBUG: Processing element ConvertFrom-FahrenheitWithLibrary.ps1
DEBUG: Processing element ConvertFrom-FahrenheitWithoutFunction.ps1
DEBUG: Processing element Get-AliasSuggestion.ps1
(...)
DEBUG: Processing element Select-FilteredObject.ps1
DEBUG: Processing element Set-ConsoleProperties.ps1
20
```

Discussion

If your script, function, or script block deals primarily with input from the pipeline, the begin, process, and end keywords let you express your solution most clearly. Readers of your script (including you!) can easily see which portions of your script deal with initialization, per-record processing, and cleanup. In addition, separating your code into these blocks lets your script to consume elements from the pipeline as soon as the previous script produces them.

Take, for example, the Get-InputWithForeach and Get-InputWithKeyword functions shown in Example 10-9. The first visits each element in the pipeline with a foreach statement over its input, while the second uses the begin, process, and end keywords.

Example 10-9. Two functions that take different approaches to processing pipeline input

```
## Process each element in the pipeline, using a
## foreach statement to visit each element in $input
function Get-InputWithForeach($identifier)
{
    Write-Host "Beginning InputWithForeach (ID: $identifier)"

    foreach($element in $input)
    {
        Write-Host "Processing element $element (ID: $identifier)"
        $element
    }

    Write-Host "Ending InputWithForeach (ID: $identifier)"
}

## Process each element in the pipeline, using the
## cmdlet-style keywords to visit each element in $input
function Get-InputWithKeyword($identifier)
{
    begin
    {
        Write-Host "Beginning InputWithKeyword (ID: $identifier)"
    }

    process
    {
        Write-Host "Processing element $_ (ID: $identifier)"
        $_
    }

    end
    {
        Write-Host "Ending InputWithKeyword (ID: $identifier)"
    }
}
```

Both of these functions act the same when run individually, but the difference becomes clear when we combine them with other scripts or functions that take pipeline input. When a script uses the $input variable, it must wait until the previous script finishes producing output before it can start. If the previous script takes a long time to produce all its records (for example, a large directory listing), then your user must wait until the entire directory listing completes to see any results, rather than seeing results for each item as the script generates it.

If a script, function, or script block uses the cmdlet-style keywords, it must place all its code (aside from comments or its param statement if it uses one) inside one of the three blocks. If your code needs to define and initialize variables or define functions, place them in the begin block. Unlike most blocks of code contained within curly braces, the code in the begin, process, and end blocks has access to variables and functions defined within the blocks before it.

When we chain together two scripts that process their input with the begin, process, and end keywords, the second script gets to process input as soon as the first script produces it.

```
PS >1,2,3 | Get-InputWithKeyword 1 | Get-InputWithKeyword 2
Beginning InputWithKeyword (ID: 1)
Beginning InputWithKeyword (ID: 2)
Processing element 1 (ID: 1)
Processing element 1 (ID: 2)
1
Processing element 2 (ID: 1)
Processing element 2 (ID: 2)
2
Processing element 3 (ID: 1)
Processing element 3 (ID: 2)
3
Ending InputWithKeyword (ID: 1)
Ending InputWithKeyword (ID: 2)
```

When we chain together two scripts that process their input with the $input variable, the second script can't start until the first completes.

```
PS >1,2,3 | Get-InputWithForeach 1 | Get-InputWithForeach 2
Beginning InputWithForeach (ID: 1)
Processing element 1 (ID: 1)
Processing element 2 (ID: 1)
Processing element 3 (ID: 1)
Ending InputWithForeach (ID: 1)
Beginning InputWithForeach (ID: 2)
Processing element 1 (ID: 2)
1
Processing element 2 (ID: 2)
2
Processing element 3 (ID: 2)
3
Ending InputWithForeach (ID: 2)
```

When the first script uses the cmdlet-style keywords, and the second scripts uses the $input variable, the second script can't start until the first completes.

```
PS >1,2,3 | Get-InputWithKeyword 1 | Get-InputWithForeach 2
Beginning InputWithKeyword (ID: 1)
Processing element 1 (ID: 1)
Processing element 2 (ID: 1)
Processing element 3 (ID: 1)
```

```
Ending InputWithKeyword (ID: 1)
Beginning InputWithForeach (ID: 2)
Processing element 1 (ID: 2)
1
Processing element 2 (ID: 2)
2
Processing element 3 (ID: 2)
3
Ending InputWithForeach (ID: 2)
```

When the first script uses the $input variable and the second script uses the cmdlet-style keywords, the second script gets to process input as soon as the first script produces it.

```
PS >1,2,3 | Get-InputWithForeach 1 | Get-InputWithKeyword 2
Beginning InputWithKeyword (ID: 2)
Beginning InputWithForeach (ID: 1)
Processing element 1 (ID: 1)
Processing element 1 (ID: 2)
1
Processing element 2 (ID: 1)
Processing element 2 (ID: 2)
2
Processing element 3 (ID: 1)
Processing element 3 (ID: 2)
3
Ending InputWithForeach (ID: 1)
Ending InputWithKeyword (ID: 2)
```

For more information about dealing with pipeline input, see "Writing Scripts, Reusing Functionality" in Appendix A.

See Also

- Recipe 10.7, "Access Pipeline Input"
- "Writing Scripts, Reusing Functionality" in Appendix A

10.9   Write a Pipeline-Oriented Function

Problem

Your function primarily takes its input from the pipeline, and you want it to perform the same steps for each element of that input.

Solution

To write a pipeline-oriented function, define your function using the filter keyword, rather than the function keyword. PowerShell makes the current pipeline object available as the $_ variable.

```
filter Get-PropertyValue($property)
{
    $_.$property
}
```

Discussion

A filter is the equivalent of a function that uses the cmdlet-style keywords and has all its code inside the process section.

The solution demonstrates an extremely useful filter: one that returns the value of a property for each item in a pipeline:

```
PS >Get-Process | Get-PropertyValue Name
audiodg
avgamsvr
avgemc
avgrssvc
avgrssvc
avgupsvc
(...)
```

For more information about the cmdlet-style keywords, see Recipe 10.8, "Write Pipeline-Oriented Scripts with Cmdlet Keywords."

See Also

- Recipe 10.8, "Write Pipeline-Oriented Scripts with Cmdlet Keywords"

## CHAPTER 11

Lists, Arrays, and Hashtables

11.0 Introduction

Most scripts deal with more than one thing—lists of servers, lists of files, lookup codes, and more. To enable this, PowerShell supports many features to help you through both its language features and utility cmdlets.

PowerShell makes working with arrays and lists much like working with other data types: you can easily create an array or list and then add or remove elements from it. You can just as easily sort it, search it, or combine it with another array. When you want to store a mapping between one piece of data and another, a hashtable solves that need perfectly.

11.1 Create an Array or List of Items

Problem

You want to create an array or list of items.

Solution

To create an array that holds a given set of items, separate those items with commas:

```
PS >$myArray = 1,2,"Hello World"
PS >$myArray
1
2
Hello World
```

To create an array of a specific size, use the New-Object cmdlet:

```
PS >$myArray = New-Object string[] 10
PS >$myArray[5] = "Hello"
PS >$myArray[5]
Hello
```

To store the output of a command that generates a list, use variable assignment:

```
PS >$myArray = Get-Process
PS >$myArray
```

Handles	NPM(K)	PM(K)	WS(K)	VM(M)	CPU(s)	Id	ProcessName
274	6	1316	3908	33		3164	alg
983	7	3636	7472	30		688	csrss
69	4	924	3332	30	0.69	2232	ctfmon
180	5	2220	6116	37		2816	dllhost

(...)

To create an array that you plan to modify frequently, use an `ArrayList`, as shown by Example 11-1.

Example 11-1. Using an ArrayList to manage a dynamic collection of items

```
PS >$myArray = New-Object System.Collections.ArrayList
PS >[void] $myArray.Add("Hello")
PS >[void] $myArray.AddRange( ("World","How","Are","You") )
PS >$myArray
Hello
World
How
Are
You
PS >$myArray.RemoveAt(1)
PS >$myArray
Hello
How
Are
You
```

Discussion

Aside from the primitive data types (such as strings, integers, and decimals), lists of items are a common concept in the scripts and commands that you write. Most commands generate lists of data: the `Get-Content` cmdlet generates a list of strings in a file, the `Get-Process` cmdlet generates a list of processes running on the system, and the `Get-Command` cmdlet generates a list of commands, just to name a few.

The solution shows how to store the output of a command that generates a list. If a command outputs only one item (such as a single line from a file, a single process, or a single command), then that output is no longer a list. If you want to treat that output as a list even when it is not, use the list evaluation syntax (`@()`) to force PowerShell to interpret it as an array:

```
$myArray = @(Get-Process Explorer)
```

For more information on lists and arrays in PowerShell, see "Arrays and Lists" in Appendix A.

See Also

- "Arrays and Lists" in Appendix A

11.2 Create a Jagged or Multidimensional Array

Problem

You want to create an array of arrays, or an array of multiple dimensions.

Solution

To create a jagged multidimensional array (an **array** of arrays), use the @( ) array syntax:

```
PS >$jagged = @(
>>       (1,2,3,4),
>>       (5,6,7,8)
>>    )
>>
PS >$jagged[0][1]
>>2
PS >$jagged[1][3]
>>8
```

To create a (nonjagged) multidimensional array, **use the** New-Object cmdlet:

```
PS >$multidimensional = New-Object "int32[,]" 2,4
PS >$multidimensional[0,1] = 2
PS >$multidimensional[1,3] = 8
PS >
PS >$multidimensional[0,1]
>>2
PS >$multidimensional[1,3]
>>8
```

Discussion

Jagged and multidimensional arrays are useful for holding lists of lists/arrays of arrays. Jagged arrays are much easier to work with (and use less memory), while nonjagged multidimensional arrays are sometimes useful for dealing with large grids of data.

Since a jagged array is an array of arrays, creating an item in a jagged array follows the same rules as creating an item in a regular array. If any of the arrays are single-element arrays, use the unary comma operator. For example, to create a jagged array with one nested array of one element:

```
PS >$oneByOneJagged = @(
>>   ,(,1)
>>
PS >$oneByOneJagged[0][0]
```

For more information on lists and arrays in PowerShell, see "Arrays and Lists" in Appendix A.

See Also

- "Arrays and Lists" in Appendix A

11.3   Access Elements of an Array

Problem

You want to access the elements of an array.

Solution

To access a specific element of an array, use PowerShell's array access mechanism:

```
PS >$myArray = 1,2,"Hello World"
PS >$myArray[1]
2
```

To access a range of array elements, use array ranges and array slicing:

```
PS >$myArray = 1,2,"Hello World"
PS >$myArray[1..2 + 0]
2
Hello World
1
```

Discussion

PowerShell's array access mechanisms provide a convenient way to access either specific elements of an array or more complex combinations of elements in that array. In PowerShell (as with most other scripting and programming languages), the item at index 0 represents the first item in the array.

Although working with the elements of an array by their numerical index is helpful, you may find it useful to refer to them by something else—such as their name, or even a custom label. This type of array is known as an *associative array* (or *hashtable*). For more information about working with hashtables and associative arrays, see Recipe 11.12, "Create a Hashtable or Associative Array."

For more information on lists and arrays in PowerShell (including the array ranges and slicing syntax), see "Arrays and Lists" in Appendix A.

See Also

- Recipe 11.12, "Create a Hashtable or Associative Array
- "Arrays and Lists" in Appendix A

11.4 Visit Each Element of an Array

Problem

You want to work with each element of an array.

Solution

To access each item in an array one-by-one, use the Foreach-Object cmdlet:

```
PS >$myArray = 1,2,3
PS >$sum = 0
PS >$myArray | Foreach-Object { $sum += $_ }
PS >$sum
6
```

To access each item in an array in a more scriptlike fashion, use the foreach scripting keyword:

```
PS >$myArray = 1,2,3
PS >$sum = 0
PS >foreach($element in $myArray) { $sum += $element }
PS >$sum
6
```

To access items in an array by position, use a for loop:

```
PS >$myArray = 1,2,3
PS >$sum = 0
PS >for($counter = 0; $counter -lt $myArray.Count; $counter++) {
>>      $sum += $myArray[$counter]
>> }
>>
PS >$sum
6
```

Discussion

PowerShell provides three main alternatives to working with elements in an array. The Foreach-Object cmdlet and foreach scripting keyword techniques visit the items in an array one element at a time, while the for loop (and related looping constructs) lets you work with the items in an array in a less structured way.

For more information about the Foreach-Object cmdlet, see Recipe 2.4, "Work with Each Item in a List or Command Output."

For more information about the foreach scripting keyword, the for keyword, and other looping constructs, see Recipe 4.4, "Repeat Operations with Loops."

See Also

- Recipe 2.4, "Work with Each Item in a List or Command Output"
- Recipe 4.4, "Repeat Operations with Loops"

11.5 Sort an Array or List of Items

Problem

You want to sort the elements of an array or list.

Solution

To sort a list of items, use the Sort-Object cmdlet:

```
PS >Get-ChildItem | Sort-Object -Descending Length | Select Name,Length

Name                                                                Length
----                                                                ------
Convert-TextObject.ps1                                                6868
Connect-WebService.ps1                                                4178
Select-FilteredObject.ps1                                             3252
Get-PageUrls.ps1                                                      2878
Get-Characteristics.ps1                                               2515
Get-Answer.ps1                                                        1890
New-GenericObject.ps1                                                 1490
Invoke-CmdScript.ps1                                                  1313
```

Discussion

The Sort-Object cmdlet provides a convenient way for you to sort items by a property that you specify. If you don't specify a property, the Sort-Object cmdlet follows the sorting rules of those items if they define any.

In addition to sorting by a property in ascending or descending order, the Sort-Object cmdlet's –Unique switch also allows you to remove duplicates from the sorted collection.

For more information about the Sort-Object cmdlet, type **Get-Help Sort-Object**.

11.6 Determine Whether an Array Contains an Item

Problem

You want to determine whether an array or list contains a specific item.

Solution

To determine whether a list contains a specific item, use the –contains operator:

```
PS >"Hello","World" -contains "Hello"
True
PS >"Hello","World" -contains "There"
False
```

Discussion

The –contains operator is a useful way to quickly determine whether a list contains a specific element. To search a list for items that instead match a pattern, use the -match or -like operators.

For more information about the -contains, -match, and -like operators, see "Comparison Operators" in Appendix A.

See Also

- "Comparison Operators" in Appendix A

11.7 Combine Two Arrays

Problem

You have two arrays and want to combine them into one.

Solution

To combine PowerShell arrays, use the addition operator (+):

```
PS >$firstArray = "Element 1","Element 2","Element 3","Element 4"
PS >$secondArray = 1,2,3,4
PS >
PS >$result = $firstArray + $secondArray
PS >$result
Element 1
Element 2
Element 3
Element 4
1
2
3
4
```

Discussion

One common reason to combine two arrays is when you want to add data to the end of one of the arrays. For example:

```
PS >$array = 1,2
PS >$array = $array + 3,4
PS >$array
1
2
3
4
```

You can write this more clearly as:

```
PS >$array = 1,2
PS >$array += 3,4
PS >$array
1
2
3
4
```

When written in the second form, however, you might think that PowerShell simply adds the items to the end of the array while keeping the array itself intact. This is not true, since arrays in PowerShell (like most other languages) stay the same length once you create them. To combine two arrays, PowerShell creates a new array large enough to hold the contents of both arrays and then copies both arrays into the destination array.

If you plan to add and remove data from an array frequently, the System. Collections.ArrayList class provides a more dynamic alternative. For more information about using the ArrayList class, see Recipe 11.11, "Use the ArrayList Class for Advanced Array Tasks."

See Also

- Recipe 11.11, "Use the ArrayList Class for Advanced Array Tasks"

11.8   Find Items in an Array That Match a Value

Problem

You have an array and want to find all elements that match a given item or term—either exactly, by pattern, or by regular expression.

Solution

To find all elements that match an item, use the -eq, -like, and -match comparison operators:

```
PS >$array = "Item 1","Item 2","Item 3","Item 1","Item 12"
PS >$array -eq "Item 1"
Item 1
Item 1
PS >$array -like "*1*"
Item 1
Item 1
Item 12
PS >$array -match "Item .."
Item 12
```

Discussion

The -eq, -like, and -match operators are useful **ways** to find elements in a collection that match your given term. The -eq operator **returns** all elements that are equal to your term, the -like operator returns all elements that match the wildcard given in your pattern, and the -match operator returns **all** elements that match the regular expression given in your pattern.

For more information about the -eq, -like, and -match operators, see "Comparison Operators" in Appendix A.

See Also

- "Comparison Operators" in Appendix A

11.9   Remove Elements from an Array

Problem

You want to remove all elements from an array that match a given item or term—either exactly, by pattern, or by regular expression.

Solution

To remove all elements from an array that match a pattern, use the -ne, -notlike, and -notmatch comparison operators as shown in Example 11-2.

Example 11-2. Removing elements from an array using the -ne, -notlike, and -notmatch operators

```
PS >$array = "Item 1","Item 2","Item 3","Item 1","Item 12"
PS >$array -ne "Item 1"
Item 2
Item 3
Item 12
PS >$array -notlike "*1*"
Item 2
Item 3
PS >$array -notmatch "Item .."
Item 1
Item 2
Item 3
Item 1
```

To actually remove the items from the array, store the results back in the array:

```
PS >$array = "Item 1","Item 2","Item 3","Item 1","Item 12"
PS >$array = $array -ne "Item 1"
PS >$array
Item 2
Item 3
Item 12
```

Discussion

The -eq, -like, and -match operators are useful ways to find elements in a collection that match your given term. Their opposites—the –ne, -notlike, and –notmatch operators—return all elements that do not match that given term.

To remove all elements from an array that match a given pattern, then, you can save all elements that *do not* match that pattern.

For more information about the –ne, -notlike, and –notmatch operators, see "Comparison Operators" in Appendix A.

11.10 Find Items in an Array Greater or Less Than a Value

Problem

You have an array and want to find all elements greater or less than a given item or value.

Solution

To find all elements greater or less than a given value, use the –gt, -ge, -lt, and –le comparison operators:

```
PS >$array = "Item 1","Item 2","Item 3","Item 1","Item 12"
PS >$array -ge "Item 3"
Item 3
PS >$array -lt "Item 3"
Item 1
Item 2
Item 1
Item 12
```

Discussion

The -gt, -ge, -lt, and -le operators are useful ways to find elements in a collection that are greater or less than a given value. Like all other PowerShell comparison operators, these use the comparison rules of the items in the collection. Since the array in the solution is an array of strings, this result can easily surprise you:

```
PS >$array -lt "Item 2"
Item 1
Item 1
Item 12
```

The reason for this becomes clear when you look at the sorted array—"Item 12" comes before "Item 2" *alphabetically*, which is the way that PowerShell compares arrays of strings.

```
PS >$array | Sort-Object
Item 1
Item 1
Item 12
Item 2
Item 3
```

For more information about the -gt, -ge, -lt, and -le operators, see "Comparison Operators" in Appendix A.

See Also

- "Comparison Operators" in Appendix A

11.11 Use the ArrayList Class for Advanced Array Tasks

Problem

You have an array that you want to frequently add elements to, remove elements from, search, and modify.

Solution

To work with an array frequently after you define it, use the System.Collections.ArrayList class:

```
PS >$myArray = New-Object System.Collections.ArrayList
PS >[void] $myArray.Add("Hello")
PS >[void] $myArray.AddRange( ("World","How","Are","You") )
PS >$myArray
Hello
World
How
Are
You
PS >$myArray.RemoveAt(1)
PS >$myArray
Hello
How
Are
You
```

Discussion

Like most other languages, arrays in PowerShell stay the same length once you create them. PowerShell allows you to add items, remove items, and search for items in an array, but these operations may be time consuming when you are dealing with large amounts of data. For example, to combine two arrays, PowerShell creates a new array large enough to hold the contents of both arrays and then copies both arrays into the destination array.

In comparison, the ArrayList class is designed to let you easily add, remove, and search for items in a collection.

PowerShell passes along any data that your script generates, unless you capture it or cast it to [void]. Since it is designed primarily to be used from programming languages, the System.Collections.ArrayList class produces output, even though you may not expect it to. To prevent it from sending data to the output pipeline, either capture the data or cast it to [void]:

```
PS >$collection = New-Object System.Collections.ArrayList
PS >$collection.Add("Hello")
0
PS >[void] $collection.Add("World")
```

If you plan to add and remove data to and from an array frequently, the System.Collections.ArrayList class provides a more dynamic alternative.

For more information about working with classes from the .NET Framework, see Recipe 3.4, "Work with .NET Objects."

See Also

- Recipe 3.4, "Work with .NET Objects"

11.12 Create a Hashtable or Associative Array

Problem

You have a collection of items that you want to access through a label that you provide.

Solution

To define a mapping between labels and items, use a hashtable (associative array):

```
PS >$myHashtable = @{}
PS >
PS >$myHashtable = @{ Key1 = "Value1"; "Key 2" = 1,2,3 }
PS >$myHashtable["New Item"] = 5
PS >
PS >$myHashTable

Name                      Value
----                      -----
Key 2                     {1, 2, 3}
New Item                  5
Key1                      Value1
```

Discussion

Hashtables are much like arrays that allow you to access items by whatever label you want—not just through their index in the array. Because of that freedom, they form the keystone of a huge number of scripting techniques. Since they allow you to map names to values, they form the natural basis for lookup tables such as ZIP codes and area codes. Since they allow you to map names to fully featured objects and script blocks, they can often take the place of custom objects. Since you can map rich objects to other rich objects, they can even form the basis of more advanced data structures such as caches and object graphs.

This label and value mapping also proves helpful in interacting with cmdlets that support advanced configuration parameters, such as the calculated property parameters available on the Format-Table and Select-Object cmdlets.

For more information about working with hashtables, see "Hashtables (Associative Arrays)" in Appendix A.

See Also

- "Hashtables (Associative Arrays)" in Appendix A

11.13 Sort a Hashtable by Key or Value

Problem

You have a hashtable of keys and values, and want to get the list of values that result from sorting the keys in order.

Solution

To sort a hashtable, use the GetEnumerator() method on the hashtable to gain access to its individual elements. Then use the Sort-Object cmdlet to sort by Name or Value.

```
foreach($item in $myHashtable.GetEnumerator() | Sort Name)
{
    $item.Value
}
```

Discussion

Since the primary focus of a hashtable is to simply map keys to values, you should not depend on it to retain any ordering whatsoever—such as the order you added the items, the sorted order of the keys, or the sorted order of the values.

This becomes clear in Example 11-3.

Example 11-3. A demonstration of hashtable items not retaining their order

```
PS >$myHashtable = @{}
PS >$myHashtable["Hello"] = 3
PS >$myHashtable["Ali"] = 2
PS >$myHashtable["Alien"] = 4
PS >$myHashtable["Duck"] = 1
PS >$myHashtable["Hectic"] = 11
PS >$myHashtable

Name                          Value
----                          -----
Hectic                        11
Duck                          1
Alien                         4
Hello                         3
Ali                           2
```

However, the hashtable object supports a GetEnumerator() method that lets you deal with the individual hashtable entries—all of which have a Name and Value property. Once you have those, we can sort by them as easily as we can sort any other Power-Shell data. Example 11-4 demonstrates this technique.

Example 11-4. Sorting a hashtable by name and value

```
PS >$myHashtable.GetEnumerator() | Sort Name

Name                          Value
----                          -----
Ali                           2
Alien                         4
Duck                          1
Hectic                        11
Hello                         3


PS >$myHashtable.GetEnumerator() | Sort Value

Name                          Value
----                          -----
Duck                          1
Ali                           2
Hello                         3
Alien                         4
Hectic                        11
```

For more information about working with hashtables, see "Hashtables (Associative Arrays)" in Appendix A.

See Also

- "Hashtables (Associative Arrays)" in Appendix A

## CHAPTER 12

User Interaction

12.0 Introduction

While most scripts are designed to run automatically, you will frequently find it useful to have your scripts interact with the user.

 The best way to get input from your user is through the arguments and parameters to your script or function. This lets your users to run your script without having to be there as it runs!

If your script greatly benefits from (or requires) an interactive experience, PowerShell offers a range of possibilities. This might be simply waiting for a keypress, prompting for input, or displaying a richer choice-based prompt.

User input isn't the only aspect of interaction though. In addition to its input facilities, PowerShell supports output as well—from displaying simple text strings to much more detailed progress reporting and interaction with UI frameworks.

12.1 Read a Line of User Input

Problem

You want to use input from the user in your script.

Solution

To obtain user input, use the Read-Host cmdlet:

```
PS >$directory = Read-Host "Enter a directory name"
Enter a directory name: C:\MyDirectory
PS >$directory
C:\MyDirectory
```

Discussion

The Read-Host cmdlet reads a single line of input from the user. If the input contains sensitive data, the cmdlet supports an –AsSecureString parameter to read this input as a SecureString.

If the user input represents a date, time, or number, be aware that most cultures represent these data types differently. For more information about writing culturally aware scripts, see Recipe 12.6, "Write Culture-Aware Scripts."

For more information about the Read-Host cmdlet, type **Get-Help Read-Host**.

See Also

- Recipe 12.6, "Write Culture-Aware Scripts"

12.2   Read a Key of User Input

Problem

You want your script to get a single keypress from the user.

Solution

For most purposes, use the [Console]::ReadKey() method to read a key:

```
PS >$key = [Console]::ReadKey($true)
PS >$key


                   KeyChar                     Key            Modifiers
                   -------                     ---            ---------
                         h                       H                  Alt
```

For highly interactive use (for example, when you care about key down and key up), use:

```
PS >$key = $host.UI.RawUI.ReadKey("NoEcho,IncludeKeyDown")
PS >$key

      VirtualKeyCode          Character    ControlKeyState        KeyDown
      --------------          ---------    ---------------        -------
                  16                       ...ssed, NumLockOn         True


PS >$key.ControlKeyState
ShiftPressed, NumLockOn
```

Discussion

For most purposes, the [Console]::ReadKey() is the best way to get a keystroke from a user, as it accepts simple keypresses—as well as more complex keypresses that might include the Ctrl, Alt, and Shift keys.

The following function emulates the DOS pause command:

```
function Pause
{
    Write-Host -NoNewLine "Press any key to continue . . . "
    [Console]::ReadKey($true) | Out-Null
    Write-Host
}
```

If you need to capture individual key down and key up events (including those of the Ctrl, Alt, and Shift keys), use the $host.UI.RawUI.ReadKey() method.

12.3   Program: Display a Menu to the User

It is often useful to read input from the user but restrict it to a list of choices that you specify. The following script lets you access PowerShell's prompting functionality in a manner that is friendlier than what PowerShell exposes by default. It returns a number that represents the position of their choice from the list of options you provide.

PowerShell's prompting requires that you include an accelerator key (the & before a letter in the option description) to define the keypress that represents that option. Since you don't always control the list of options (for example, a list of possible directories), Example 12-1 automatically generates sensible accelerator characters for any descriptions that lack them.

Example 12-1. Read-HostWithPrompt.ps1

```
##############################################################################
##
## Read-HostWithPrompt.ps1
##
## Read user input, with choices restricted to the list of options you
## provide.
##
## ie:
##
##  PS >$caption = "Please specify a task"
##  PS >$message = "Specify a task to run"
##  PS >$option = "&Clean Temporary Files","&Defragment Hard Drive"
##  PS >$helptext = "Clean the temporary files from the computer",
##  >>               "Run the defragment task"
##  >>
##  PS >$default = 1
##  PS >Read-HostWithPrompt $caption $message $option $helptext $default
##
```

Example 12-1. Read-HostWithPrompt.ps1 (continued)

```
##  Please specify a task
##  Specify a task to run
##  [C] Clean Temporary Files  [D] Defragment Hard Drive  [?] Help
##  (default is "D"):?
##  C - Clean the temporary files from the computer
##  D - Run the defragment task
##  [C] Clean Temporary Files  [D] Defragment Hard Drive  [?] Help
##  (default is "D"):C
##  0
##
################################################################################

param(
    $caption = $null,
    $message = $null,
    $option = $(throw "Please specify some options."),
    $helpText = $null,
    $default = 0
    )

## Create the list of choices
[Management.Automation.Host.ChoiceDescription[]] $choices = @()

## Create a list of possible key accelerators for their options
$accelerators = New-Object System.Collections.ArrayList

## First, add a the list of numbers as possible choices
$startNumber = [int][char] '0'
$endNumber = [int][char] '9'
foreach($number in $startNumber..$endNumber)
{
    [void] $accelerators.Add([char] $number)
}

## Then, a list of characters as possible choices
$startLetter = [int][char] 'A'
$endLetter = [int][char] 'Z'
foreach($letter in $startLetter .. $endLetter)
{
    [void] $accelerators.Add([char] $letter)
}

## Go through each of the options, and add them to the choice collection
for($counter = 0; $counter -lt $option.Length; $counter++)
{
    $optionText = $option[$counter]

    ## If they didn't provide an accelerator, generate new option
    ## text for them
    if($optionText -notmatch '&')
    {
        $optionText = "&{0} - {1}" -f $accelerators[0],$optionText
    }
```

Example 12-1. Read-HostWithPrompt.ps1 (continued)

```
    ## Now, remove their option character from the list of possibilities
    $acceleratorIndex = $optionText.IndexOf('&')
    $optionCharacter = $optionText[$acceleratorIndex + 1]
    $accelerators.Remove($optionCharacter)

    ## Create the choice
    $choice = New-Object Management.Automation.Host.ChoiceDescription $optionText
    if($helpText -and $helpText[$counter])
    {
        $choice.HelpMessage = $helpText[$counter]
    }

    ## Add the choice to the list of possible choices
    $choices += $choice
}

## Prompt for the choice, returning the item the user selected
$host.UI.PromptForChoice($caption, $message, $choices, $default)
```

For more information about running scripts, see Recipe 1.1, "Run Programs, Scripts, and Existing Tools."

See Also

- Recipe 1.1, "Run Programs, Scripts, and Existing Tools"

12.4 Display Messages and Output to the User

Problem

You want to display messages and other information to the user.

Solution

To ensure that the output actually reaches the screen, call the Write-Host (or Out-Host) cmdlet:

```
PS >function Get-DirectorySize
>> {
>>     $size = (Get-ChildItem | Measure-Object -Sum Length).Sum
>>     Write-Host ("Directory size: {0:N0} bytes" -f $size)
>> }
>>
PS >Get-DirectorySize
Directory size: 46,581 bytes
PS >$size = Get-DirectorySize
Directory size: 46,581 bytes
```

If you want a message to help you (or the user) diagnose and debug your script, use the Write-Debug cmdlet. If you want a message to provide detailed trace-type output, use the Write-Verbose cmdlet, as shown in Example 12-2.

Example 12-2. A function that provides debug and verbose output

```
PS >function Get-DirectorySize
>> {
>>     Write-Debug "Current Directory: $(Get-Location)"
>>
>>     Write-Verbose "Getting size"
>>     $size = (Get-ChildItem | Measure-Object -Sum Length).Sum
>>     Write-Verbose "Got size: $size"
>>
>>     Write-Host ("Directory size: {0:N0} bytes" -f $size)
>> }
>>
PS >$DebugPreference = "Continue"
PS >Get-DirectorySize
DEBUG: Current Directory: D:\lee\OReilly\Scripts\Programs
Directory size: 46,581 bytes
PS >$DebugPreference = "SilentlyContinue"
PS >$VerbosePreference = "Continue"
PS >Get-DirectorySize
VERBOSE: Getting size
VERBOSE: Got size: 46581
Directory size: 46,581 bytes
PS >$VerbosePreference = "SilentlyContinue"
```

Discussion

Most scripts that you write will output richly structured data, such as the actual count of bytes in a directory. That way, other scripts can use the output of that script as a building block for their functionality.

When you do want to provide output specifically to the user, use the Write-Host, Write-Debug, and Write-Verbose cmdlets.

However, be aware that this type of output bypasses normal file redirection, and is therefore difficult for the user to capture. In the case of the Write-Host cmdlet, use it only when your script already generates other structured data that the user would want to capture in a file or variable.

Most script authors eventually run into the problem illustrated by Example 12-3 when their script tries to output formatted data to the user.

Example 12-3. An error message caused by formatting statements

```
PS >## Get the list of items in a directory, sorted by length
PS >function Get-ChildItemSortedByLength($path = (Get-Location))
>> {
>>     Get-ChildItem $path | Format-Table | Sort Length
>> }
```

Example 12-3. An error message caused by formatting statements (continued)

```
>>
PS >Get-ChildItemSortedByLength
out-lineoutput : Object of type "Microsoft.PowerShell.Commands.Internal.Fo
rmat.FormatEntryData" is not legal or not in the correct sequence. This is
likely caused by a user-specified "format-*" command which is conflicting
with the default formatting.
```

This happens because the Format-* cmdlets actually generate formatting information for the Out-Host cmdlet to consume. The Out-Host cmdlet (which PowerShell adds automatically to the end of your pipelines) then uses this information to generate formatted output. To resolve this problem, always ensure that formatting commands are the last commands in your pipeline, as shown in Example 12-4.

Example 12-4. A function that does not generate formatting errors

```
PS >## Get the list of items in a directory, sorted by length
PS >function Get-ChildItemSortedByLength($path = (Get-Location))
>> {
>>     ## Problematic version
>>     ## Get-ChildItem $path | Format-Table | Sort Length
>>
>>     ## Fixed version
>>     Get-ChildItem $path | Sort Length | Format-Table
>> }
>>
PS >Get-ChildItemSortedByLength

(...)

Mode           LastWriteTime     Length Name
----           -------------     ------ ----
-a---      3/11/2007   3:21 PM       59 LibraryProperties.ps1
-a---       3/6/2007  10:27 AM      150 Get-Tomorrow.ps1
-d---       3/4/2007   3:10 PM      194 ConvertFrom-FahrenheitWithout
                                        Function.ps1
-a---       3/4/2007   4:40 PM      257 LibraryTemperature.ps1
-a---       3/4/2007   4:57 PM      281 ConvertFrom-FahrenheitWithLib
                                        rary.ps1
-a---       3/4/2007   3:14 PM      337 ConvertFrom-FahrenheitWithFunc
                                        tion.ps1

(...)
```

When it comes to producing output for the user, a common reason is to provide progress messages. PowerShell actually supports this in a much richer way, through its Write-Progress cmdlet. For more information about the Write-Progress cmdlet, see the following section Recipe 12.5, "Provide Progress Updates on Long-Running Tasks."

See Also

- Recipe 12.5, "Provide Progress Updates on Long-Running Tasks"

12.5   Provide Progress Updates on Long-Running Tasks

Problem

You want to display status information to the user for long-running tasks.

Solution

To provide status updates, use the `Write-Progress` cmdlet as shown in Example 12-5.

Example 12-5. Using the Write-Progress cmdlet to display status updates

```
$activity = "A long-running operation"

$status = "Initializing"
## Initialize the long-running operation
for($counter = 0; $counter -lt 100; $counter++)
{
    $currentOperation = "Initializing item $counter"
    Write-Progress $activity $status -PercentComplete $counter `
                -CurrentOperation $currentOperation
    Start-Sleep -m 20
}

$status = "Running"
## Initialize the long-running operation
for($counter = 0; $counter -lt 100; $counter++)
{
    $currentOperation = "Running task $counter"
    Write-Progress $activity $status -PercentComplete $counter `
                -CurrentOperation $currentOperation
    Start-Sleep -m 20
}
```

Discussion

The `Write-Progress` cmdlet provides a way for you to provide structured status information to the users of your script for long-running operations (see Figure 12-1).

Like the other detailed information channels (`Write-Debug`, `Write-Verbose`, and the other `Write-*` cmdlets), PowerShell lets users control how much of this information they see.

For more information about the `Write-Progress` cmdlet, type **Get-Help Write-Progress**.

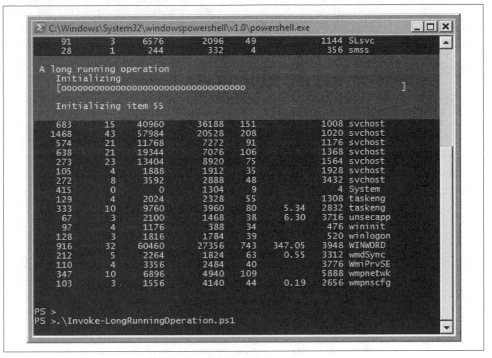

Figure 12-1. Example output from a long-running operation

12.6 Write Culture-Aware Scripts

Problem

You want to ensure that your script works well on computers from around the world.

Solution

To write culture-aware scripts, keep the following guidelines in mind as you develop your scripts:

- Create dates, times, and numbers using PowerShell's language primitives.
- Compare strings using PowerShell's built-in operators.
- Avoid treating user input as a collection of characters.
- Use Parse() methods to convert user input to dates, times, and numbers.

Discussion

Writing culture-aware programs has long been isolated to the world of professional software developers. It's not that users of simple programs and scripts can't benefit from culture awareness though. It has just frequently been too difficult for non-professional programmers to follow the best practices. PowerShell makes this much easier than traditional programming languages however.

As your script travels between different cultures, several things change.

Date, time, and number formats

Most cultures have unique date, time, and number formats. To ensure that your script works in all cultures, PowerShell first ensures that its language primitives remain consistent no matter where your script runs. Even if your script runs on a machine in France (which uses a comma for its decimal separator), you can always rely on the statement $myDouble = 3.5 to create a number halfway between three and four. Likewise, you can always count on the statement $christmas = [DateTime] "12/25/2007" to create a date that represents Christmas in 2007—even in cultures that write dates in the order of day, month, year.

Culturally aware programs always display dates, times, and numbers using the preferences of that culture. This doesn't break scripts as they travel between cultures and is an important aspect of writing culture-aware scripts. PowerShell handles this for you, as it uses the current culture's preferences whenever it displays data.

 If your script asks the user for a date, time, or number, make sure that you respect the format of the user's culture's when you do so. To convert user input to a specific type of data, use that type's Parse() method.

```
$userInput = Read-Host "Please enter a date"
$enteredDate = [DateTime]::Parse($userInput)
```

So, to ensure that your script remains culture-aware with respect to dates, times, and number formats, simply use PowerShell's language primitives when you define them in your script. When you read them from the user, use Parse() methods when you convert them from strings.

Complexity of user input and file content

English is a rare language in that its alphabet is so simple. This leads to all kinds of programming tricks that treat user input and file content as arrays of bytes or simple plain-text (ASCII) characters. In most international languages, these tricks fail. In fact, many international symbols take up two characters' worth of data in the string that contains them.

PowerShell uses the standard Unicode format for all string-based operations: reading input from the user, displaying output to the user, sending data through the pipeline, and working with files.

Although PowerShell fully supports Unicode, the `powershell.exe` command-line host does not output some characters correctly, due to limitations in the Windows console system. Graphical PowerShell hosts (such as the several third-party PowerShell IDEs) are not affected by these limitations however.

If you use PowerShell's standard features when working with user input, you do not have to worry about its complexity. If you want to work with individual characters or words in the input, though, you will need to take special precautions. The `System.Globalization.StringInfo` class lets you do this in a culturally aware way. For more information about working with the `StringInfo` class, see *http://msdn2.microsoft.com/en-us/library/7h9tk6x8(vs.71).aspx*.

So, to ensure that your script remains culturally aware with respect to user input, simply use PowerShell's support for string operations whenever possible.

Capitalization rules

A common requirement in scripts is to compare user input against some predefined text (such as a menu selection). You normally want this comparison to be case insensitive, so that "*QUIT*" and "*qUiT*" mean the same thing.

The most common way to accomplish this is to convert the user input to uppercase or lowercase:

```
### $text comes from the user, and contains the value "quit"
if($text.ToUpper() -eq "QUIT") { ... }
```

Unfortunately, explicitly changing the capitalization of strings fails in subtle ways when run in different cultures, as many cultures have different capitalization and comparison rules. For example, the Turkish language includes two types of the letter "I": one with a dot, and one without. The uppercase version of the lowercase letter "i" corresponds to the version of the capital "I" with a dot, not the capital "I" used in QUIT. That example causes the above string comparison to fail on a Turkish system.

To compare some input against a hard-coded string in a case-insensitive manner, the better solution is to use PowerShell's –eq operator without changing any of the casing yourself. The –eq operator is case-insensitive and culture-neutral by default:

```
PS >$text1 = "Hello"
PS >$text2 = "HELLO"
PS >$text1 -eq $text2
True
```

So, to ensure that your script remains culturally aware with respect to capitalization rules, simply use PowerShell's case-insensitive comparison operators whenever possible.

Sorting rules

Sorting rules frequently change between cultures. For example, compare English and Danish with the script given in Recipe 12.7, "Program: Invoke a Script Block with Alternate Culture Settings:"

```
PS >Use-Culture en-US { "Apple","Æble" | Sort-Object }
Æble
Apple
PS >Use-Culture da-DK { "Apple","Æble" | Sort-Object }
Apple
Æble
```

To ensure that your script remains culturally aware with respect to sorting rules, assume that output is sorted correctly after you sort it—but don't depend on the actual order of sorted output.

Other guidelines

For other resources on these factors for writing culturally aware programs, see *http://msdn2.microsoft.com/en-us/library/h6270d0z(vs.71).aspx* and *http://www.microsoft.com/globaldev/getwr/steps/wrguide.mspx*.

See Also

- Recipe 12.7, "Program: Invoke a Script Block with Alternate Culture Settings"

12.7 Program: Invoke a Script Block with Alternate Culture Settings

Given PowerShell's diverse user community, scripts that you share will often be run on a system set to a language other than English. To ensure that your script runs properly in other languages, it is helpful to give it a test run in that culture. Example 12-6 lets you run the script block you provide in a culture of your choosing.

Example 12-6. Use-Culture.ps1

```
##############################################################################
##
## Use-Culture.ps1
##
## Invoke a scriptblock under the given culture
##
## ie:
##
## PS >Use-Culture fr-FR { [DateTime]::Parse("25/12/2007") }
##
## mardi 25 décembre 2007 00:00:00##
##
##############################################################################
```

Example 12-6. Use-Culture.ps1 (continued)

```
param(
    [System.Globalization.CultureInfo] $culture =
        $(throw "Please specify a culture"),
    [ScriptBlock] $script = $(throw "Please specify a scriptblock")
    )

## A helper function to set the current culture
function Set-Culture([System.Globalization.CultureInfo] $culture)
{
    [System.Threading.Thread]::CurrentThread.CurrentUICulture = $culture
    [System.Threading.Thread]::CurrentThread.CurrentCulture = $culture
}

## Remember the original culture information
$oldCulture = [System.Threading.Thread]::CurrentThread.CurrentUICulture

## Restore the original culture information if
## the user's script encounters errors.
trap { Set-Culture $oldCulture }

## Set the current culture to the user's provided
## culture.
Set-Culture $culture

## Invoke the user's scriptblock
& $script

## Restore the original culture information.
Set-Culture $oldCulture
```

For more information about running scripts, see Recipe 1.1, "Run Programs, Scripts, and Existing Tools."

See Also

- Recipe 1.1, "Run Programs, Scripts, and Existing Tools"

12.8   Access Features of the Host's User Interface

Problem

You want to interact with features in the user interface of the hosting application, but PowerShell doesn't directly provide cmdlets for them.

Solution

To access features of the host's user interface, use the $host.UI.RawUI variable:

```
$host.UI.RawUI.WindowTitle = (Get-Location)
```

Discussion

PowerShell itself consists of two main components. The first is an engine that interprets commands, executes pipelines, and performs other similar actions. The second is the hosting application—the way that users interact with the PowerShell engine.

The default shell, PowerShell.exe, is a user interface based on the traditional Windows console. Other applications exist that host PowerShell in a graphical user interface. In fact, PowerShell makes it relatively simple for developers to build their own hosting applications, or even to embed the PowerShell engine features into their own application.

You (and your scripts) can always depend on the functionality available through the $host.UI variable, as that functionality remains the same for all hosts. Example 12-7 shows the features available to you in all hosts.

Example 12-7. Functionality available through the $host.UI property

```
PS >$host.UI | Get-Member | Select Name,MemberType | Format-Table -Auto

Name                       MemberType
----                       ----------
(...)
Prompt                       Method
PromptForChoice              Method
PromptForCredential          Method
ReadLine                     Method
ReadLineAsSecureString       Method
Write                        Method
WriteDebugLine               Method
WriteErrorLine               Method
WriteLine                    Method
WriteProgress                Method
WriteVerboseLine             Method
WriteWarningLine             Method
RawUI                      Property
```

If you (or your scripts) want to interact with portions of the user interface specific to the current host, PowerShell provides that access through the $host.UI.RawUI variable. Example 12-8 shows the features available to you in the PowerShell console host.

Example 12-8. Functionality available through the default console host

```
PS >$host.UI.RawUI | Get-Member |
>>      Select Name,MemberType | Format-Table -Auto
>>

Name                       MemberType
----                       ----------
(...)
FlushInputBuffer             Method
GetBufferContents            Method
```

```
GetHashCode              Method
GetType                  Method
LengthInBufferCells      Method
NewBufferCellArray       Method
ReadKey                  Method
ScrollBufferContents     Method
SetBufferContents        Method
BackgroundColor          Property
BufferSize               Property
CursorPosition           Property
CursorSize               Property
ForegroundColor          Property
KeyAvailable             Property
MaxPhysicalWindowSize    Property
MaxWindowSize            Property
WindowPosition           Property
WindowSize               Property
WindowTitle              Property
```

If you rely on the host-specific features from $host.UI.RawUI, be aware that your script will require modifications (perhaps major) before it will run properly on other hosts.

12.9   Program: Add a Graphical User Interface to Your Script

While the techniques provided in the rest of this chapter are usually all you need, it is sometimes helpful to provide a graphical user interface to interact with the user.

Since PowerShell fully supports traditional executables, simple programs can usually fill this need. If creating a simple program in an environment such as Visual Studio is inconvenient, you can often use PowerShell to create these applications directly.

Example 12-9 demonstrates the techniques you can use to develop a Windows Forms application using PowerShell scripting alone.

Example 12-9. Select-GraphicalFilteredObject.ps1

```
##############################################################################
##
## Select-GraphicalFilteredObject.ps1
##
## Display a Windows Form to help the user select a list of items piped in.
## Any selected items get passed along the pipeline.
##
## ie:
##
## PS >dir | Select-GraphicalFilteredObject
##
```

Example 12-9. Select-GraphicalFilteredObject.ps1 (continued)

```
##    Directory: Microsoft.PowerShell.Core\FileSystem::C:\
##
##
## Mode                LastWriteTime       Length Name
## ----                -------------       ------ ----
## d----          10/7/2006    4:30 PM            Documents and Settings
## d----          3/18/2007    7:56 PM            Windows
##
###############################################################################

$objectArray = @($input)

## Ensure that they've piped information into the script
if($objectArray.Count -eq 0)
{
    Write-Error "This script requires pipeline input."
    return
}

## Load the Windows Forms assembly
[void] [Reflection.Assembly]::LoadWithPartialName("System.Windows.Forms")

## Create the main form
$form = New-Object Windows.Forms.Form
$form.Size = New-Object Drawing.Size @(600,600)

## Create the listbox to hold the items from the pipeline
$listbox = New-Object Windows.Forms.CheckedListBox
$listbox.CheckOnClick = $true
$listbox.Dock = "Fill"
$form.Text = "Select the list of objects you wish to pass down the pipeline"
$listBox.Items.AddRange($objectArray)

## Create the button panel to hold the OK and Cancel buttons
$buttonPanel = New-Object Windows.Forms.Panel
$buttonPanel.Size = New-Object Drawing.Size @(600,30)
$buttonPanel.Dock = "Bottom"

## Create the Cancel button, which will anchor to the bottom right
$cancelButton = New-Object Windows.Forms.Button
$cancelButton.Text = "Cancel"
$cancelButton.DialogResult = "Cancel"
$cancelButton.Top = $buttonPanel.Height - $cancelButton.Height - 5
$cancelButton.Left = $buttonPanel.Width - $cancelButton.Width - 10
$cancelButton.Anchor = "Right"

## Create the OK button, which will anchor to the left of Cancel
$okButton = New-Object Windows.Forms.Button
$okButton.Text = "Ok"
$okButton.DialogResult = "Ok"
$okButton.Top = $cancelButton.Top
$okButton.Left = $cancelButton.Left - $okButton.Width - 5
$okButton.Anchor = "Right"
```

Example 12-9. Select-GraphicalFilteredObject.ps1 (continued)

```
## Add the buttons to the button panel
$buttonPanel.Controls.Add($okButton)
$buttonPanel.Controls.Add($cancelButton)

## Add the button panel and list box to the form, and also set
## the actions for the buttons
$form.Controls.Add($listBox)
$form.Controls.Add($buttonPanel)
$form.AcceptButton = $okButton
$form.CancelButton = $cancelButton
$form.Add_Shown( { $form.Activate() } )

## Show the form, and wait for the response
$result = $form.ShowDialog()

## If they pressed OK (or Enter,) go through all the
## checked items and send the corresponding object down the pipeline
if($result -eq "OK")
{
    foreach($index in $listBox.CheckedIndices)
    {
        $objectArray[$index]
    }
}
```

For more information about running scripts, see Recipe 1.1, "Run Programs, Scripts, and Existing Tools."

See Also

- Recipe 1.1, "Run Programs, Scripts, and Existing Tools"

CHAPTER 13
Tracing and Error Management

13.0 Introduction

What if it doesn't all go according to plan? This is the core question behind error management in any system and plays a large part in writing PowerShell scripts as well.

While it is a core concern in many systems, PowerShell's support for error management provides several unique features designed to make your job easier: the primary benefit being a distinction between terminating and nonterminating errors.

When running a complex script or scenario, the last thing you want is for your world to come crashing down because a script can't open one of the 1,000 files it is operating on. Although it should make you aware of the failure, the script should still continue to the next file. That is an example of a nonterminating error. But what if the script runs out of disk space while running a backup? That should absolutely be an error that causes the script to exit—also known as a terminating error.

Given this helpful distinction, PowerShell provides several features that allow you to manage errors generated by scripts and programs, and also allows you to generate them yourself.

13.1 View the Errors Generated by a Command

Problem

You want to view the errors generated in the current session.

Solution

To access the list of errors generated so far, use the $error variable, as shown by Example 13-1.

Example 13-1. Viewing errors contained in the $error variable

```
PS >1/0
Attempted to divide by zero.
At line:1 char:3
+ 1/0 <<<<
PS >$error[0] | Format-List -Force


ErrorRecord    : Attempted to divide by zero.
StackTrace     :     at System.Management.Automation.Parser.ExpressionNode.A
                     (...)
Message        : Attempted to divide by zero.
Data           : {}
InnerException : System.DivideByZeroException: Attempted to divide by zero.
                     at System.Management.Automation.ParserOps.polyDiv(Execu
                 val, Object rval)
TargetSite     : System.Collections.ObjectModel.Collection`1[System.Managem
                 ctions.IEnumerable)
HelpLink       :
Source         : System.Management.Automation
```

Discussion

The PowerShell $error variable always holds the list of errors generated so far in the current shell session. This list includes both terminating and nonterminating errors.

By default, PowerShell displays error records in a customized view. If you want to view an error in a table or list (through the Format-Table or Format-List cmdlets), you must also specify the –Force option to override this customized view.

If you want to display errors in a more compact manner, PowerShell supports an additional view called CategoryView that you set through the $errorView preference variable:

```
PS >Get-ChildItem IDoNotExist
Get-ChildItem : Cannot find path 'C:\IDoNotExist' because it does not exist.
At line:1 char:4
+ Get-ChildItem <<<< IDoNotExist
PS >$errorView = "CategoryView"
PS >Get-ChildItem IDoNotExist
ObjectNotFound: (C:\IDoNotExist:String) [Get-ChildItem], ItemNotFoundExcep
tion
```

To clear the list of errors, call the Clear() method on the $error list:

```
PS >$error.Count
2
PS >$error.Clear()
PS >$error.Count
0
```

For more information about PowerShell's preference variables, see Appendix C, *PowerShell Automatic Variables*. If you want to determine only the success or failure of the last command, see Recipe 1.10, "Determine the Status of the Last Command."

See Also

- Recipe 1.10, "Determine the Status of the Last Command"
- Appendix C, *PowerShell Automatic Variables*

13.2   Handle Warnings, Errors, and Terminating Errors

Problem

You want to handle warnings, errors, and terminating errors generated by scripts or other tools that you call.

Solution

To control how your script responds to warning messages, set the $warningPreference variable. In this example, to ignore them:

```
$warningPreference = "SilentlyContinue"
```

To control how your script responds to nonterminating errors, set the $errorActionPreference variable. In this example, to ignore them:

```
$errorActionPreference = "SilentlyContinue"
```

To control how your script responds to terminating errors, use the trap statement. In this example, to output a message and continue with the script:

```
trap [DivideByZeroException] { "Don't divide by zero!"; continue }
```

Discussion

PowerShell defines several preference variables that help you control how your script reacts to warnings, errors, and terminating errors. As an example of these error management techniques, consider the following script:

```
##############################################################################
##
## Get-WarningsAndErrors.ps1
##
## Demonstrates the functionality of the Write-Warning, Write-Error, and throw
## statements
##
##############################################################################

Write-Warning "Warning: About to generate an error"
Write-Error "Error: You are running this script"
throw "Could not complete operation."
```

For more information about running scripts, see Recipe 1.1, "Run Programs, Scripts, and Existing Tools."

You can now see how a script might manage those separate types of errors:

```
PS >$warningPreference = "Continue"
PS >Get-WarningsAndErrors.ps1
WARNING: Warning: About to generate an error
.. Get-WarningsAndErrors.ps1 : Error: You are
 running this script
At line:1 char:27
+ Get-WarningsAndErrors.ps1 <<<<
Could not complete operation.
At .. Get-WarningsAndErrors.ps1:12 char:6
+ throw  <<<< "Could not complete operation."
```

Once you modify the warning preference, the original warning message gets suppressed:

```
PS >$warningPreference = "SilentlyContinue"
PS >Get-WarningsAndErrors.ps1
.. Get-WarningsAndErrors.ps1 : Error: You are
 running this script
At line:1 char:27
+ Get-WarningsAndErrors.ps1 <<<<
Could not complete operation.
At .. Get-WarningsAndErrors.ps1:12 char:6
+ throw  <<<< "Could not complete operation."
```

When you modify the error preference, you suppress errors and exceptions, as well:

```
PS >$errorActionPreference = "SilentlyContinue"
PS >Get-WarningsAndErrors.ps1
PS >
```

An addition to the $errorActionPreference variable, all cmdlets allow you to specify your preference during an individual call:

```
PS >$errorActionPreference = "Continue"
PS >Get-ChildItem IDoNotExist
Get-ChildItem : Cannot find path '...\IDoNotExist' because it does not exist.
At line:1 char:14
+ Get-ChildItem  <<<< IDoNotExist
PS >Get-ChildItem IDoNotExist -ErrorAction SilentlyContinue
PS >
```

If you reset the error preference back to Continue, you can see the impact of a trap statement. The message from the Write-Error call makes it through, but the exception does not:

```
PS >$errorActionPreference = "Continue"
PS >trap { "Caught an error"; continue }; Get-WarningsAndErrors
.. Get-WarningsAndErrors.ps1 : Error: You are
 running this script
At line:1 char:61
+ trap { "Caught an error"; continue }; Get-WarningsAndErrors <<<<
Caught an error
```

For more information about error management in PowerShell, see "Managing Errors" in Appendix A. For more detailed information about the valid settings of these preference variables, see Appendix C, *PowerShell Automatic Variables*.

See Also

- Recipe 1.1, "Run Programs, Scripts, and Existing Tools"
- "Managing Errors" in Appendix A
- Appendix C, *PowerShell Automatic Variables*

13.3 Output Warnings, Errors, and Terminating Errors

Problem

You want your script to notify its caller of a warning, error, or terminating error.

```
##############################################################################
##
## Get-WarningsAndErrors.ps1
##
## Demonstrates the functionality of the Write-Warning, Write-Error, and throw
## statements
##
##############################################################################

Write-Warning "Warning: About to generate an error"
Write-Error "Error: You are running this script"
throw "Could not complete operation."
```

Solution

To write warnings and errors, use the Write-Warning and Write-Error cmdlets, respectively. Use the throw statement to generate a terminating error.

Discussion

When you need to notify the caller of your script about an unusual condition, the Write-Warning, Write-Error, and throw statements are the way to do it. If your user should consider the message as more of a warning, use the Write-Warning cmdlet. If your script encounters an error (but can reasonably continue past that error), use the Write-Error cmdlet. If the error is fatal and your script simply cannot continue, use a throw statement.

For information on how to handle these errors when thrown by other scripts, see Recipe 13.2, "Handle Warnings, Errors, and Terminating Errors." For more information about error management in PowerShell, see "Managing Errors" in Appendix A. For more information about running scripts, see Recipe 1.1, "Run Programs, Scripts, and Existing Tools."

See Also

- Recipe 1.1, "Run Programs, Scripts, and Existing Tools"
- Recipe 13.2, "Handle Warnings, Errors, and Terminating Errors"
- "Managing Errors" in Appendix A

13.4 Debug a Script

Problem

You want to diagnose failures or unexpected behavior in a script interactively.

Solution

To generate debugging statements from your script, Use the `Write-Debug` cmdlet. If you want to step through a region carefully, surround it with `Set-PsDebug -Step` calls. To explore the environment at a specific point of execution, add a line that calls `$host.EnterNestedPrompt()`.

Discussion

By default, PowerShell allows you to assign data to variables you haven't yet created (thereby creating those variables). It also allows you to retrieve data from variables that don't exist—which usually happens by accident and almost always causes bugs. To help save you from getting stung by this problem, PowerShell provides a *strict* mode that generates an error if you attempt to access a nonexisting variable. Example 13-2 demonstrates this mode.

Example 13-2. PowerShell operating in strict mode

```
PS >$testVariable = "Hello"
PS >$tsetVariable += " World"
PS >$testVariable
Hello
PS >Remove-Item Variable:\tsetvariable
PS >Set-PsDebug -Strict
PS >$testVariable = "Hello"
PS >$tsetVariable += " World"
The variable $tsetVariable cannot be retrieved because it has not been set
 yet.
At line:1 char:14
+ $tsetVariable  <<<< += " World"
```

For the sake of your script debugging health and sanity, strict mode should be one of the first additions you make to your PowerShell profile.

When it comes to interactive debugging (as opposed to bug prevention), PowerShell supports several of the most useful debugging features that you might be accustomed to: tracing (through the Set-PsDebug –Trace statement), stepping (through the Set-PsDebug –Step statement), and environment inspection (through the $host.EnterNestedPrompt() call).

As a demonstration of these techniques, consider Example 13-3.

Example 13-3. A complex script that interacts with PowerShell's debugging features

```
##############################################################################
##
## Invoke-ComplexScript.ps1
##
## Demonstrates the functionality of PowerShell's debugging support.
##
##############################################################################

Write-Host "Calculating lots of complex information"

$runningTotal = 0
$runningTotal += [Math]::Pow(5 * 5 + 10, 2)

Write-Debug "Current value: $runningTotal"

Set-PsDebug -Trace 1
$dirCount = @(Get-ChildItem $env:WINDIR).Count

Set-PsDebug -Trace 2
$runningTotal -= 10
$runningTotal /= 2

Set-PsDebug -Step
$runningTotal *= 3
$runningTotal /= 2

$host.EnterNestedPrompt()

Set-PsDebug -off
```

For more information about running scripts, see Recipe 1.1, "Run Programs, Scripts, and Existing Tools."

As you try to determine why this script isn't working as you expect, a debugging session might look like Example 13-4.

Example 13-4. Debugging a complex script

```
PS >$debugPreference = "Continue"
PS >Invoke-ComplexScript.ps1
Calculating lots of complex information
DEBUG: Current value: 1225
```

Example 13-4. Debugging a complex script (continued)

```
DEBUG:    17+ $dirCount = @(Get-ChildItem $env:WINDIR).Count
DEBUG:    17+ $dirCount = @(Get-ChildItem $env:WINDIR).Count
DEBUG:    19+ Set-PsDebug -Trace 2
DEBUG:    20+ $runningTotal -= 10
DEBUG:      ! SET $runningTotal = '1215'.
DEBUG:    21+ $runningTotal /= 2
DEBUG:      ! SET $runningTotal = '607.5'.
DEBUG:    23+ Set-PsDebug -Step

Continue with this operation?
  24+ $runningTotal *= 3
[Y] Yes  [A] Yes to All  [N] No  [L] No to All  [S] Suspend  [?] Help
(default is "Y"):y
DEBUG:    24+ $runningTotal *= 3
DEBUG:      ! SET $runningTotal = '1822.5'.

Continue with this operation?
  25+ $runningTotal /= 2
[Y] Yes  [A] Yes to All  [N] No  [L] No to All  [S] Suspend  [?] Help
(default is "Y"):y
DEBUG:    25+ $runningTotal /= 2
DEBUG:      ! SET $runningTotal = '911.25'.

Continue with this operation?
  27+ $host.EnterNestedPrompt()
[Y] Yes  [A] Yes to All  [N] No  [L] No to All  [S] Suspend  [?] Help
(default is "Y"):y
DEBUG:    27+ $host.EnterNestedPrompt()
DEBUG:      ! CALL method 'System.Void EnterNestedPrompt()'
PS >$dirCount
296
PS >$dirCount + $runningTotal
1207.25
PS >exit

Continue with this operation?
  29+ Set-PsDebug -off
[Y] Yes  [A] Yes to All  [N] No  [L] No to All  [S] Suspend  [?] Help
(default is "Y"):y
DEBUG:    29+ Set-PsDebug -off
```

While not built into a graphical user interface, PowerShell's interactive debugging features are bound to help you diagnose and resolve problems quickly.

For more information about the Set-PsDebug cmdlet, type **Get-Help Set-PsDebug**.

See Also

- Recipe 1.1, "Run Programs, Scripts, and Existing Tools"

13.5   Collect Detailed Traces of a Script or Command

Problem

You want to access detailed debugging or diagnostic information for the execution of a script or command.

Solution

To trace a script as it executes, use the -Trace parameter of the Set-PsDebug cmdlet.

To view detailed trace output for the PowerShell engine and its cmdlets, use the Trace-Command cmdlet.

Discussion

The Set-PsDebug cmdlet lets you configure the amount of debugging detail that PowerShell provides during the execution of a script. By setting the -Trace parameter, PowerShell lets you see the lines of script as PowerShell executes them. For more information about the Set-PsDebug cmdlet, see Recipe 13.4, "Debug a Script."

When you want to investigate issues in the way that your code interacts with PowerShell, or with PowerShell commands, use the Trace-Command cmdlet. The Trace-Command cmdlet provides a huge amount of detail, intended mainly for in-depth problem analysis.

For example, to gain some insight into why PowerShell can't seem to find your script:

```
Trace-Command CommandDiscovery -PsHost { ScriptInTheCurrentDirectory.ps1 }
```

The Trace-Command cmdlet takes a *trace source* (for example, *CommandDiscovery*), a destination (usually –PsHost or –File), and a script block to trace. The output of this command shows that PowerShell never actually searches the current directory for your script, so you need to be explicit: .\ScriptInTheCurrentDirectory.ps1.

For more information about the Trace-Command cmdlet, type **Get-Help Trace-Command**. To learn what trace sources are available, see the command Get-TraceSource.

See Also

- Recipe 13.4, "Debug a Script"

13.6   Program: Analyze a Script's Performance Profile

When you write scripts that heavily interact with the user, you may sometimes feel that your script could benefit from better performance.

When tackling performance problems, the first rule is to measure the problem. Unless you can guide your optimization efforts with hard performance data, you are almost certainly directing your efforts to the wrong spots. Random cute performance improvements will quickly turn your code into an unreadable mess, often with no appreciable performance gain! Low-level optimization has its place, but it should always be guided by hard data that supports it.

The way to obtain hard performance data is from a profiler. PowerShell doesn't ship with a script profiler, but Example 13-5 uses PowerShell features to implement one.

Example 13-5. Get-ScriptPerformanceProfile.ps1

```
##############################################################################
##
## Get-ScriptPerformanceProfile.ps1
##
## Computes the performance characteristics of a script, based on the transcript
## of it running at trace level 1.
##
## To profile a script:
##      1) Turn on script tracing in the window that will run the script:
##          Set-PsDebug -trace 1
##      2) Turn on the transcript for the window that will run the script:
##          Start-Transcript
##          (Note the filename that PowerShell provides as the logging destination.)
##      3) Type in the script name, but don't actually start it.
##      4) Open another PowerShell window, and navigate to the directory holding
##          this script.  Type in 'Get-ScriptPerformanceProfile <transcript>',
##          replacing <transcript> with the path given in step 2.  Don't
##          press <Enter> yet.
##      5) Switch to the profiled script window, and start the script.
##          Switch to the window containing this script, and press <Enter>
##      6) Wait until your profiled script exits, or has run long enough to be
##          representative of its work.  To be statistically accurate, your script
##          should run for at least ten seconds.
##      7) Switch to the window running this script, and press a key.
##      8) Switch to the window holding your profiled script, and type:
##          Stop-Transcript
##      9) Delete the transcript.
##
## Note: You can profile regions of code (ie: functions) rather than just lines
## by placing the following call at the start of the region:
##          write-debug "ENTER <region_name>"
## and the following call and the end of the region:
##          write-debug "EXIT"
## This is implemented to account exclusively for the time spent in that
## region, and does not include time spent in regions contained within the
## region.  For example, if FunctionA calls FunctionB, and you've surrounded
## each by region markers, the statistics for FunctionA will not include the
## statistics for FunctionB.
##
##############################################################################
```

Example 13-5. Get-ScriptPerformanceProfile.ps1 (continued)

```
param($logFilePath = $(throw "Please specify a path to the transcript log file."))

function Main
{
    ## Run the actual profiling of the script.  $uniqueLines gets
    ## the mapping of line number to actual script content.
    ## $samples gets a hashtable mapping line number to the number of times
    ## we observed the script running that line.
    $uniqueLines = @{}
    $samples = GetSamples $uniqueLines

    "Breakdown by line:"
    "--------------------------"

    ## Create a new hash table that flips the $samples hashtable --
    ## one that maps the number of times sampled to the line sampled.
    ## Also, figure out how many samples we got altogether.
    $counts = @{}
    $totalSamples = 0;
    foreach($item in $samples.Keys)
    {
        $counts[$samples[$item]] = $item
        $totalSamples += $samples[$item]
    }

    ## Go through the flipped hashtable, in descending order of number of
    ## samples.  As we do so, output the number of samples as a percentage of
    ## the total samples.  This gives us the percentage of the time our script
    ## spent executing that line.
    foreach($count in ($counts.Keys | Sort-Object -Descending))
    {
        $line = $counts[$count]
        $percentage = "{0:#0}" -f ($count * 100 / $totalSamples)
        "{0,3}%: Line {1,4} -{2}" -f $percentage,$line,
            $uniqueLines[$line]
    }

    ## Go through the transcript log to figure out which lines are part of any
    ## marked regions.  This returns a hashtable that maps region names to
    ## the lines they contain.
    ""
    "Breakdown by marked regions:"
    "----------------------------"
    $functionMembers = GenerateFunctionMembers

    ## For each region name, cycle through the lines in the region.  As we
    ## cycle through the lines, sum up the time spent on those lines and output
    ## the total.
    foreach($key in $functionMembers.Keys)
    {
        $totalTime = 0
        foreach($line in $functionMembers[$key])
```

Example 13-5. Get-ScriptPerformanceProfile.ps1 (continued)

```
        {
            $totalTime += ($samples[$line] * 100 / $totalSamples)
        }

        $percentage = "{0:#0}" -f $totalTime
        "{0,3}%: {1}" -f $percentage,$key
    }
}

## Run the actual profiling of the script.  $uniqueLines gets
## the mapping of line number to actual script content.
## Return a hashtable mapping line number to the number of times
## we observed the script running that line.
function GetSamples($uniqueLines)
{
    ## Open the log file.  We use the .Net file I/O, so that we keep monitoring
    ## just the end of the file.  Otherwise, we would make our timing inaccurate
    ## as we scan the entire length of the file every time.
    $logStream = [System.IO.File]::Open($logFilePath, "Open", "Read", "ReadWrite")
    $logReader = New-Object System.IO.StreamReader $logStream

    $random = New-Object Random
    $samples = @{}

    $lastCounted = $null

    ## Gather statistics until the user presses a key.
    while(-not $host.UI.RawUI.KeyAvailable)
    {
        ## We sleep a slightly random amount of time.  If we sleep a constant
        ## amount of time, we run the very real risk of improperly sampling
        ## scripts that exhibit periodic behaviour.
        $sleepTime = [int] ($random.NextDouble() * 100.0)
        Start-Sleep -Milliseconds $sleepTime

        ## Get any content produced by the transcript since our last poll.
        ## From that poll, extract the last DEBUG statement (which is the last
        ## line executed.)
        $rest = $logReader.ReadToEnd()
        $lastEntryIndex = $rest.LastIndexOf("DEBUG: ")

        ## If we didn't get a new line, then the script is still working on the
        ## last line that we captured.
        if($lastEntryIndex -lt 0)
        {
            if($lastCounted) { $samples[$lastCounted] ++ }
            continue;
        }

        ## Extract the debug line.
        $lastEntryFinish = $rest.IndexOf("\n", $lastEntryIndex)
        if($lastEntryFinish -eq -1) { $lastEntryFinish = $rest.length }
```

Example 13-5. Get-ScriptPerformanceProfile.ps1 (continued)

```
    $scriptLine = $rest.Substring(
        $lastEntryIndex, ($lastEntryFinish -
    $lastEntryIndex)).Trim()
    if($scriptLine -match 'DEBUG:[ \t]*([0-9]*)\+(.*)')
    {
        ## Pull out the line number from the line
        $last = $matches[1]

        $lastCounted = $last
        $samples[$last] ++

        ## Pull out the actual script line that matches the line number
        $uniqueLines[$last] = $matches[2]
    }

    ## Discard anything that's buffered during this poll, and start waiting
    ## again
    $logReader.DiscardBufferedData()
    }

    ## Clean up
    $logStream.Close()
    $logReader.Close()

    $samples
}

## Go through the transcript log to figure out which lines are part of any
## marked regions.  This returns a hashtable that maps region names to
## the lines they contain.
function GenerateFunctionMembers
{
    ## Create a stack that represents the callstack.  That way, if a marked
    ## region contains another marked region, we attribute the statistics
    ## appropriately.
    $callstack = New-Object System.Collections.Stack
    $currentFunction = "Unmarked"
    $callstack.Push($currentFunction)

    $functionMembers = @{}

    ## Go through each line in the transcript file, from the beginning
    foreach($line in (Get-Content $logFilePath))
    {
        ## Check if we're entering a monitor block
        ## If so, store that we're in that function, and push it onto
        ## the callstack.
        if($line -match 'write-debug "ENTER (.*)"')
        {
            $currentFunction = $matches[1]
            $callstack.Push($currentFunction)
        }
```

Example 13-5. Get-ScriptPerformanceProfile.ps1 (continued)

```
    ## Check if we're exiting a monitor block
    ## If so, clear the "current function" from the callstack,
    ## and store the new "current function" onto the callstack.
    elseif($line -match 'write-debug "EXIT"')
    {
        [void] $callstack.Pop()
        $currentFunction = $callstack.Peek()
    }
    ## Otherwise, this is just a line with some code.
    ## Add the line number as a member of the "current function"
    else
    {
        if($line -match 'DEBUG:[ \t]*([0-9]*)\+')
        {
            ## Create the arraylist if it's not initialized
            if(-not $functionMembers[$currentFunction])
            {
                $functionMembers[$currentFunction] =
                    New-Object System.Collections.ArrayList
            }

            ## Add the current line to the ArrayList
            if(-not $functionMembers[$currentFunction].Contains($matches[1]))
            {
                [void] $functionMembers[$currentFunction].Add($matches[1])
            }
        }
    }
    }
    }

    $functionMembers
}

. Main
```

For more information about running scripts, see Recipe 1.1, "Run Programs, Scripts, and Existing Tools."

See Also

- Recipe 1.1, "Run Programs, Scripts, and Existing Tools"

CHAPTER 14
Environmental Awareness

14.0   Introduction

While many of your scripts will be designed to work in isolation, you will often find it helpful to give your script information about its execution environment: its name, current working directory, environment variables, common system paths, and more.

PowerShell offers several ways to get at this information—from its cmdlets, to built-in variables, to features that it offers from the .NET Framework.

14.1   View and Modify Environment Variables

Problem

You want to interact with your system's environment variables.

Solution

To interact with environment variables, access them in almost the same way that you access regular PowerShell variables. The only difference is that you place env: between the ($) dollar sign and the variable name:

```
PS >$env:Username
Lee
```

You can modify environment variables this way, too. For example, to temporarily add the current directory to the path:

```
PS >Invoke-DemonstrationScript
The term 'Invoke-DemonstrationScript' is not recognized as a cmdlet, funct
ion, operable program, or script file. Verify the term and try again.
At line:1 char:26
+ Invoke-DemonstrationScript <<<<
PS >$env:PATH = $env:PATH + ";."
PS >Invoke-DemonstrationScript.ps1
The script ran!
```

Discussion

In batch files, environment variables are the primary way to store temporary information, or to transfer information between batch files. PowerShell variables and script parameters are more effective ways to solve those problems, but environment variables continue to provide a useful way to access common system settings, such as the system's path, temporary directory, domain name, username, and more.

PowerShell surfaces environment variables through its *environment provider*—a container that lets you work with environment variables much like you would work with items in the filesystem or registry providers. By default, PowerShell defines an env: (much like the c: or d:) that provides access to this information:

```
PS >dir env:

Name                    Value
----                    -----
Path                    c:\progra~1\ruby\bin;C:\WINDOWS\system32;C:\
TEMP                    C:\DOCUME~1\Lee\LOCALS~1\Temp
SESSIONNAME             Console
PATHEXT                 .COM;.EXE;.BAT;.CMD;.VBS;.VBE;.JS;.JSE;.WSF;
(...)
```

Since it is a regular PowerShell drive, the full way to get the value of an environment variable looks like this:

```
PS >Get-Content Env:\Username
Lee
```

When it comes to environment variables, though, that is a syntax you will almost never need to use, because of PowerShell's support for the *Get-Content and Set-Content variable syntax*, which shortens that to:

```
PS >$env:Username
Lee
```

This syntax works for all drives but is used most commonly to access environment variables. For more information about this syntax, see "Recipe 14.2, "Access Information About Your Command's Invocation."

Some environment variables actually get their values from a combination of two places: the machinewide settings and the current-user settings. If you want to access environment variable values specifically configured at the machine or user level, use the [Environment]::GetEnvironmentVariable() method. For example, if you've defined a tools directory in your path, you might see:

```
PS >[Environment]::GetEnvironmentVariable("Path", "User")
d:\lee\tools
```

To set these machine or user-specific environment variables permanently, use the [Environment]::SetEnvironmentVariable() method:

```
[Environment]::SetEnvironmentVariable(<name>, <value>, <target>)
```

The *Target* parameter defines where this variable should be stored: User for the current user, and Machine for all users on the machine. For example, to permanently add your Tools directory to your path:

```
PS >$oldPersonalPath = [Environment]::GetEnvironmentVariable("Path", "User")
PS >$oldPersonalPath += ";d:\tools"
PS >[Environment]::SetEnvironmentVariable("Path", $oldPersonalPath, "User")
```

For more information about the Get-Content and Set-Content variable syntax, see "Variables" in Chapter 3. For more information about the environment provider, type **Get-Help About_Environment**.

See Also

- "Variables" in Chapter 3, *Variables and Objects*
- Recipe 14.2, "Access Information About Your Command's Invocation"

14.2 Access Information About Your Command's Invocation

Problem

You want to learn about how the user invoked your script, function, or script block.

Solution

To access information about how the user invoked your command, use the $myInvocation variable:

```
"You invoked this script by typing: " + $myInvocation.Line
```

Discussion

The $myInvocation variable provides a great deal of information about the current script, function, or script block—and the context in which it was invoked:

MyCommand
: Information about the command (script, function, or script block) itself.

ScriptLineNumber
: The line number in the script that called this command.

ScriptName
: When in a function or script block, the name of the script that called this command.

Line
: The verbatim text used in the line of script (or command line) that called this command.

InvocationName
   The name that the user supplied to invoke this command. This will be different
   from the information given by MyCommand if the user has defined an alias for the
   command.

PipelineLength
   The number of commands in the pipeline that invoked this command.

PipelinePosition
   The position of this command in the pipeline that invoked this command.

One important point about working with the $myInvocation variable is that it
changes depending on the type of command from which you call it. If you access this
information from a function, it provides information specific to that function—not
the script from which it was called. Since scripts, functions, and script blocks are
fairly unique, information in the $myInvocation.MyCommand variable changes slightly
between the different command types.

Scripts

Definition *and* Path
   The full path to the currently running script

Name
   The name of the currently running script

CommandType
   Always ExternalScript

Functions

Definition *and* ScriptBlock
   The source code of the currently running function

Options
   The options (None, ReadOnly, Constant, Private, AllScope) that apply to the currently running function

Name
   The name of the currently running function

CommandType
   Always Function

Script blocks

Definition *and* ScriptBlock
   The source code of the currently running script block

```
Name
    Empty
CommandType
    Always Script
```

14.3   Program: Investigate the InvocationInfo Variable

When experimenting with the information available through the $myInvocation variable, it is helpful to see how this information changes between scripts, functions, and script blocks. For a useful deep dive into the resources provided by the $myInvocation variable, review the output of Example 14-1.

Example 14-1. Get-InvocationInfo.ps1

```
##############################################################################
##
## Get-InvocationInfo.ps1
##
## Display the information provided by the $myInvocation variable
##
##############################################################################
param([switch] $preventExpansion)

## Define a helper function, so that we can see how $myInvocation changes
## when it is called, and when it is dot-sourced
function HelperFunction
{
    "    MyInvocation from function:"
    "-"*50
    $myInvocation

    "    Command from function:"
    "-"*50
    $myInvocation.MyCommand
}

## Define a script block, so that we can see how $myInvocation changes
## when it is called, and when it is dot-sourced
$myScriptBlock = {
    "    MyInvocation from script block:"
    "-"*50
    $myInvocation

    "    Command from script block:"
    "-"*50
    $myInvocation.MyCommand
}

## Define a helper alias
Set-Alias gii Get-InvocationInfo
```

Example 14-1. Get-InvocationInfo.ps1 (continued)

```
## Illustrate how $myInvocation.Line returns the entire line that the
## user typed.
"You invoked this script by typing: " + $myInvocation.Line

## Show the information that $myInvocation returns from a script
"MyInvocation from script:"
"-"*50
$myInvocation

"Command from script:"
"-"*50
$myInvocation.MyCommand

## If we were called with the -PreventExpansion switch, don't go
## any further
if($preventExpansion)
{
    return
}

## Show the information that $myInvocation returns from a function
"Calling HelperFunction"
"-"*50
HelperFunction

## Show the information that $myInvocation returns from a dot-sourced
## function
"Dot-Sourcing HelperFunction"
"-"*50
. HelperFunction

## Show the information that $myInvocation returns from an aliased script
"Calling aliased script"
"-"*50
gii -PreventExpansion

## Show the information that $myInvocation returns from a script block
"Calling script block"
"-"*50
& $myScriptBlock

## Show the information that $myInvocation returns from a dot-sourced
## script block
"Dot-Sourcing script block"
"-"*50
. $myScriptBlock

## Show the information that $myInvocation returns from an aliased script
"Calling aliased script"
"-"*50
gii -PreventExpansion
```

For more information about running scripts, see Recipe 1.1, "Run Programs, Scripts, and Existing Tools."

See Also

- Recipe 1.1, "Run Programs, Scripts, and Existing Tools"

14.4 Find Your Script's Name

Problem

You want to know the name of the currently running script.

Solution

To determine the full path and filename of the currently executing script, use this function:

```
function Get-ScriptName
{
    $myInvocation.ScriptName
}
```

To determine the name that the user actually typed to invoke your script (for example, in a "Usage" message), use the $myInvocation.InvocationName variable.

Discussion

By placing the $myInvocation.ScriptName statement in a function, we drastically simplify the logic it takes to determine the name of the currently running script. If you don't want to use a function, you can invoke a script block directly, which also simplifies the logic required to determine the current script's name:

```
$scriptName = & { $myInvocation.ScriptName }
```

Although this is a fairly complex way to get access to the current script's name, the alternative is a bit more error-prone. If you are in the body of a script, you can directly get the name of the current script by typing:

```
$myInvocation.Path
```

If you are in a function or script block, though, you must use:

```
$myInvocation.ScriptName
```

Working with the $myInvocation.InvocationName variable is sometimes tricky, as it returns the script name when called directly in the script, but not when called from a function in that script. If you need this information from a function, pass it to the function as a parameter.

For more information about working with the $myInvocation variable, see Recipe 14.2, "Access Information About Your Command's Invocation."

See Also

- Recipe 14.2, "Access Information About Your Command's Invocation"

14.5   Find Your Script's Location

Problem

You want to know the location of the currently running script.

Solution

To determine the location of the currently executing script, use this function:

```
function Get-ScriptPath
{
    Split-Path $myInvocation.ScriptName
}
```

Discussion

Once we know the full path to a script, the Split-Path cmdlet makes it easy to determine its location. Its sibling, the Join-Path cmdlet, makes it easy to form new paths from their components as well.

By accessing the $myInvocation.ScriptName variable in a function, we drastically simplify the logic it takes to determine the location of the currently running script. For a discussion about alternatives to using a function for this purpose, see Recipe 14.4, "Find Your Script's Name."

For more information about working with the $myInvocation variable, see Recipe 14.2, "Access Information About Your Command's Invocation."

For more information about the Join-Path cmdlet, see Recipe 14.9, "Safely Build File Paths Out of Their Components."

See Also

- Recipe 14.2, "Access Information About Your Command's Invocation"
- Recipe 14.4, "Find Your Script's Name"
- Recipe 14.9, "Safely Build File Paths Out of Their Components"

14.6   Find the Location of Common System Paths

Problem

You want to know the location of common system paths and special folders, such as My Documents and Program Files.

Solution

To determine the location of common system paths and special folders, use the [Environment]::GetFolderPath() method:

```
PS >[Environment]::GetFolderPath("System")
C:\WINDOWS\system32
```

For paths not supported by this method (such as All Users Start Menu), use the WScript.Shell COM object:

```
$shell = New-Object -Com WScript.Shell
$allStartMenu = $shell.SpecialFolders.Item("AllUsersStartMenu")
```

Discussion

The [Environment]::GetFolderPath() method lets you access the many common locations used in Windows. To use it, provide the short name for the location (such as System or Personal). Since you probably don't have all these short names memorized, one way to see all these values is to use the [Enum]::GetValues() method, as shown in Example 14-2.

Example 14-2. Folders supported by the [Environment]::GetFolderPath() method

```
PS >[Enum]::GetValues([Environment+SpecialFolder])
Desktop
Programs
Personal
Favorites
Startup
Recent
SendTo
StartMenu
MyMusic
DesktopDirectory
MyComputer
Templates
ApplicationData
LocalApplicationData
InternetCache
Cookies
History
CommonApplicationData
```

Example 14-2. Folders supported by the [Environment]::GetFolderPath() method (continued)

```
System
ProgramFiles
MyPictures
CommonProgramFiles
```

Since this is such a common task for all enumerated constants, though, PowerShell actually provides the possible values in the error message if it is unable to convert your input:

```
PS >[Environment]::GetFolderPath("aouaoue")
Cannot convert argument "0", with value: "aouaoue", for "GetFolderPath" to
type "System.Environment+SpecialFolder": "Cannot convert value "aouaoue"
to type "System.Environment+SpecialFolder" due to invalid enumeration values.
Specify one of the following enumeration values and try again. The possible
enumeration values are "Desktop, Programs, Personal, MyDocuments, Favorites,
Startup, Recent, SendTo, StartMenu, MyMusic, DesktopDirectory, MyComputer,
Templates, ApplicationData, LocalApplicationData, InternetCache,
Cookies, History, CommonApplicationData, System, ProgramFiles, MyPictures,
CommonProgramFiles"."
At line:1 char:29
+ [Environment]::GetFolderPath( <<<< "aouaoue")
```

Although this method provides access to the most-used common system paths, it does not provide access to all of them. For the paths that the [Environment]:: GetFolderPath() method does not support, use the WScript.Shell COM object. The WScript.Shell COM object supports the following paths: AllUsersDesktop, AllUsersStartMenu, AllUsersPrograms, AllUsersStartup, Desktop, Favorites, Fonts, MyDocuments, NetHood, PrintHood, Programs, Recent, SendTo, StartMenu, Startup, and Templates.

It would be nice if you could use either the [Environment]::GetFolderPath() method *or* the WScript.Shell COM object, but each of them supports a significant number of paths that the other does not, as Example 14-3 illustrates.

Example 14-3. Differences between folders supported by [Environment]::GetFolderPath() and the Wscript.Shell COM object

```
PS >$shell = New-Object -Com WScript.Shell
PS >$shellPaths = $shell.SpecialFolders | Sort-Object
PS >
PS >$netFolders = [Enum]::GetValues([Environment+SpecialFolder])
PS >$netPaths = $netFolders |
>>     Foreach-Object { [Environment]::GetFolderPath($_) } | Sort-Object
>>
PS >## See the shell-only paths
PS >Compare-Object $shellPaths $netPaths |
>>     Where-Object { $_.SideIndicator -eq "<=" }
>>
```

Example 14-3. Differences between folders supported by [Environment]::GetFolderPath() and the
Wscript.Shell COM object (continued)

```
InputObject                                                SideIndicator
-----------                                                -------------
C:\Documents and Settings\All Users\Desktop                <=
C:\Documents and Settings\All Users\Start Menu             <=
C:\Documents and Settings\All Users\Start Menu\Programs    <=
C:\Documents and Settings\All Users\Start Menu\Programs\... <=
C:\Documents and Settings\Lee\NetHood                      <=
C:\Documents and Settings\Lee\PrintHood                    <=
C:\Windows\Fonts                                           <=


PS >## See the .NET-only paths
PS >Compare-Object $shellPaths $netPaths |
>>      Where-Object { $_.SideIndicator -eq "=>" }
>>

InputObject                                                SideIndicator
-----------                                                -------------
                                                           =>
C:\Documents and Settings\All Users\Application Data       =>
C:\Documents and Settings\Lee\Cookies                     =>
C:\Documents and Settings\Lee\Local Settings\Application... =>
C:\Documents and Settings\Lee\Local Settings\History      =>
C:\Documents and Settings\Lee\Local Settings\Temporary I... =>
C:\Program Files                                          =>
C:\Program Files\Common Files                             =>
C:\WINDOWS\system32                                       =>
d:\lee                                                    =>
D:\Lee\My Music                                           =>
D:\Lee\My Pictures                                        =>
```

For more information about working with classes from the .NET Framework, see
Recipe 3.4, "Work with .NET Objects."

See Also

- Recipe 3.4, "Work with .NET Objects"

14.7   Program: Search the Windows Start Menu

When working at the command line, you might want to launch a program that is
normally found only on your Start menu. While you could certainly click through
the Start menu to find it, you could also search the Start menu with a script, as
shown in Example 14-4.

Example 14-4. Search-StartMenu.ps1

```
##############################################################################
##
## Search-StartMenu.ps1
##
## Search the Start Menu for items that match the provided text. This script
## searches both the name (as displayed on the Start Menu itself,) and the
## destination of the link.
##
## ie:
##
##  PS >Search-StartMenu "Character Map" | Invoke-Item
##  PS >Search-StartMenu "network" | Select-FilteredObject | Invoke-Item
##
##############################################################################

param(
    $pattern = $(throw "Please specify a string to search for.")
    )

## Get the locations of the start menu paths
$myStartMenu = [Environment]::GetFolderPath("StartMenu")
$shell = New-Object -Com WScript.Shell
$allStartMenu = $shell.SpecialFolders.Item("AllUsersStartMenu")

## Escape their search term, so that any regular expression
## characters don't affect the search
$escapedMatch = [Regex]::Escape($pattern)

## Search for text in the link name
dir $myStartMenu *.lnk -rec | ? { $_.Name -match "$escapedMatch" }
dir $allStartMenu *.lnk -rec | ? { $_.Name -match "$escapedMatch" }

## Search for text in the link destination
dir $myStartMenu *.lnk -rec |
    Where-Object { $_ | Select-String "\\[^\\]*$escapedMatch\." -Quiet }
dir $allStartMenu *.lnk -rec |
    Where-Object { $_ | Select-String "\\[^\\]*$escapedMatch\." -Quiet }
```

For more information about running scripts, see Recipe 1.1, "Run Programs, Scripts, and Existing Tools."

See Also

- Recipe 1.1, "Run Programs, Scripts, and Existing Tools"

14.8   Get the Current Location

Problem

You want to determine the current location.

Solution

To determine the current location, use the Get-Location cmdlet:

```
PS >Get-Location

Path
----
C:\temp
PS >$currentLocation = (Get-Location).Path
PS >$currentLocation
C:\temp
```

Discussion

One problem that sometimes impacts scripts that work with the .NET Framework is that PowerShell's concept of "current location" isn't always the same as the *PowerShell.exe* process's "current directory." Take, for example:

```
PS >Get-Location

Path
----
C:\temp


PS >Get-Process | Export-CliXml processes.xml
PS >$reader = New-Object Xml.XmlTextReader processes.xml
PS >$reader.BaseURI
file:///C:/Documents and Settings/Lee/processes.xml
```

PowerShell keeps these concepts separate because it supports multiple pipelines of execution. The processwide current directory affects the entire process, so you would risk corrupting the environment of all background tasks as you navigate around the shell if that changed the process's current directory.

When you use filenames in most .NET methods, the best practice is to use fully qualified pathnames. The Resolve-Path cmdlet makes this easy:

```
PS >Get-Location

Path
----
C:\temp
```

```
PS >Get-Process | Export-CliXml processes.xml
PS >$reader = New-Object Xml.XmlTextReader (Resolve-Path processes.xml)
PS >$reader.BaseURI
file:///C:/temp/processes.xml
```

If you want to access a path that doesn't already exist, use the Join-Path in combination with the Get-Location cmdlet:

```
PS >Join-Path (Get-Location) newfile.txt
C:\temp\newfile.txt
```

For more information about the Join-Path cmdlet, see the following section Recipe 14.9, "Safely Build File Paths Out of Their Components."

See Also

- Recipe 14.9, "Safely Build File Paths Out of Their Components"

14.9 Safely Build File Paths Out of Their Components

Problem

You want to build a new path out of a combination of subpaths.

Solution

To join elements of a path together, use the Join-Path cmdlet:

```
PS >Join-Path (Get-Location) newfile.txt
C:\temp\newfile.txt
```

Discussion

The usual way to create new paths is by combining strings for each component, placing a path separator between them:

```
PS >"$(Get-Location)\newfile.txt"
C:\temp\newfile.txt
```

Unfortunately, this approach suffers from a handful of problems:

- What if the directory returned by Get-Location already has a slash at the end?
- What if the path contains forward slashes instead of backslashes?
- What if we are talking about registry paths instead of filesystem paths?

Fortunately, the Join-Path cmdlet resolves these issues and more.

For more information about the Join-Path cmdlet, type **Get-Help Join-Path**.

14.10   Interact with PowerShell's Global Environment

Problem

You want to store information in the PowerShell environment so that other scripts have access to it.

Solution

To make a variable available to the entire PowerShell session, use a $GLOBAL: prefix when you store information in that variable:

```
## Create the web service cache, if it doesn't already exist
if(-not (Test-Path Variable:\Lee.Holmes.WebServiceCache))
{
    ${GLOBAL:Lee.Holmes.WebServiceCache} = @{}
}
```

If the main purpose of your script is to provide permanent functions and variables for its caller, treat that script as a library and have the caller dot-source the script:

```
PS >. LibraryDirectory
PS >Get-DirectorySize
Directory size: 53,420 bytes
```

Discussion

The primary guidance when it comes to storing information in the session's global environment to avoid it when possible. Scripts that store information in the global scope are prone to breaking other scripts and prone to being broken by other scripts.

It is a common practice in batch file programming, but script parameters and return values usually provide a much cleaner alternative.

If you do find yourself needing to write variables to the global scope, make sure that you create them with a name unique enough to prevent collisions with other scripts, as illustrated in the solution. Good options for naming prefixes are the script name, author's name, or company name.

For more information about setting variables at the global scope (and others), see Recipe 3.3, "Control Access and Scope of Variables and Other Items." For more information about dot-sourcing scripts to create libraries, see also Recipe 10.5, "Place Common Functions in a Library."

See Also

- Recipe 3.3, "Control Access and Scope of Variables and Other Items"
- Recipe 10.5, "Place Common Functions in a Library"

## CHAPTER 15

Extend the Reach of Windows PowerShell

15.0 Introduction

The PowerShell environment is phenomenally comprehensive. It provides a great surface of cmdlets to help you manage your system, a great scripting language to let you automate those tasks, and direct access to all the utilities and tools you already know.

The cmdlets, scripting language, and preexisting tools are just part of what makes PowerShell so comprehensive, however. In addition to these features, PowerShell provides access to a handful of technologies that drastically increase its capabilities: the .NET Framework, Windows Management Instrumentation (WMI), COM automation objects, native Windows API calls, and more.

Not only does PowerShell give you access to these technologies, but it also gives you access to them in a consistent way. The techniques you use to interact with properties and methods of PowerShell objects are the same techniques that you use to interact with properties and methods of .NET objects. In turn, those are the same techniques that you use to work with WMI and COM objects, too.

Working with these techniques and technologies provides another huge benefit— knowledge that easily transfers to working in .NET programming languages such as C#.

15.1 Access Windows Management Instrumentation Data

Problem

You want to work with data and functionality provided by the WMI facilities in Windows.

Solution

To retrieve all instances of a WMI class, use the Get-WmiObject cmdlet:

```
Get-WmiObject -ComputerName Computer -Class Win32_Bios
```

To retrieve specific instances of a WMI class, using a WMI filter, supply an argument to the -Filter parameter of the Get-WmiObject cmdlet:

```
Get-WmiObject Win32_Service -Filter "StartMode = 'Auto'"
```

To retrieve instances of a WMI class using WMI's WQL language, use the [WmiSearcher] type shortcut:

```
$query = [WmiSearcher] "SELECT * FROM Win32_Service WHERE StartMode = 'Auto'"
$query.Get()
```

To retrieve a specific instance of a WMI class using a WMI filter, use the [Wmi] type shortcut:

```
[Wmi] 'Win32_Service.Name="winmgmt"'
```

To retrieve a property of a WMI instance, access that property as you would access a .NET property:

```
$service = [Wmi] 'Win32_Service.Name="winmgmt"'
$service.StartMode
```

To invoke a method on a WMI instance, invoke that method as you would invoke a .NET method:

```
$service = [Wmi] 'Win32_Service.Name="winmgmt"'
$service.ChangeStartMode("Manual")
$service.ChangeStartMode("Automatic")
```

To invoke a method on a WMI class, use the [WmiClass] type shortcut to access that WMI class. Then, invoke that method as you would invoke a .NET method:

```
$class = [WmiClass] "Win32_Process"
$class.Create("Notepad")
```

Discussion

Working with WMI has long been a staple of managing Windows systems—especially systems that are part of corporate domains or enterprises. WMI supports a huge amount of Windows management tasks, albeit not in a very user-friendly way.

Traditionally, administrators required either VBScript or the WMIC command-line tool to access and manage these systems through WMI. While powerful and useful, these techniques still provided plenty of opportunities for improvement. VBScript lacks support for an ad hoc investigative approach, and WMIC fails to provide (or take advantage of) knowledge that applies to anything outside WMIC.

In comparison, PowerShell lets you work with WMI just like you work with the rest of the shell. WMI instances provide methods and properties, and you work with them the same way you work with methods and properties of other objects in PowerShell.

Not only does PowerShell make working with WMI instances and classes easy once you have them, but it also provides a clean way to access them in the first place. For most tasks, you need only to use the simple [Wmi], [WmiClass], or [WmiSearcher] syntax as shown in the solution.

Along with WMI's huge scope, though, comes a related problem: finding the WMI class that accomplishes your task. To assist you in learning what WMI classes are available, Appendix F *WMI Reference* provides a helpful listing of the most common ones. For a script that helps you search for WMI classes by name, description, property name, or property description, see Recipe 15.3, "Program: Search for WMI Classes."

Some advanced WMI tasks require that you enable your security privileges or adjust the packet privacy settings used in your request. The syntax given by the solution does not directly support these tasks, but PowerShell still supports these options by providing access to the underlying objects that represent your WMI query. For more information about working with these underlying objects, see Recipe 15.4, "Use .NET to Perform Advanced WMI Tasks."

When you want to access a specific WMI instance with the [Wmi] accelerator, you might at first struggle to determine what properties WMI lets you search on. These properties are called key properties on the class. For a script that lists these key properties, see the following section Recipe 15.2, "Program: Determine Properties Available to WMI Filters."

For more information about the Get-WmiObject cmdlet, type **Get-Help Get-WmiObject**.

See Also

- Recipe 15.2, "Program: Determine Properties Available to WMI Filters"
- Recipe 15.3, "Program: Search for WMI Classes"
- Recipe 15.4, "Use .NET to Perform Advanced WMI Tasks"
- Appendix F *WMI Reference*

15.2 Program: Determine Properties Available to WMI Filters

When you want to access a specific WMI instance with PowerShell's [Wmi] type shortcut, you might at first struggle to determine what properties WMI lets you search on. These properties are called key properties on the class. Example 15-1 gets all the properties you may use in a WMI filter for a given class.

Example 15-1. Get-WmiClassKeyProperty.ps1

```
##############################################################################
##
## Get-WmiClassKeyProperty.ps1
##
## Get all of the properties that you may use in a WMI filter for a given class.
##
## ie:
##
##  PS >Get-WmiClassKeyProperty Win32_Process
##
##############################################################################

param( [WmiClass] $wmiClass )

## WMI classes have properties
foreach($currentProperty in $wmiClass.PsBase.Properties)
{
    ## WMI properties have qualifiers to explain more about them
    foreach($qualifier in $currentProperty.Qualifiers)
    {
        ## If it has a 'Key' qualifier, then you may use it in a filter
        if($qualifier.Name -eq "Key")
        {
            $currentProperty.Name
        }
    }
}
```

For more information about running scripts, see Recipe 1.1, "Run Programs, Scripts, and Existing Tools."

See Also

- Recipe 1.1, "Run Programs, Scripts, and Existing Tools"

15.3   Program: Search for WMI Classes

Along with WMI's huge scope comes a related problem: finding the WMI class that accomplishes your task. To help you learn what WMI classes are available, Appendix F *WMI Reference* provides a helpful listing of the most common ones. If you want to dig a little deeper, though, Example 15-2 lets you search for WMI classes by name, description, property name, or property description.

Example 15-2. Search-WmiNamespace.ps1

```
##############################################################################
##
## Search-WmiNamespace.ps1
##
```

Example 15-2. Search-WmiNamespace.ps1 (continued)

```
## Search the WMI classes installed on the system for the provided match text.
##
## ie:
##
##  PS >Search-WmiNamespace Registry
##  PS >Search-WmiNamespace Process ClassName,PropertyName
##  PS >Search-WmiNamespace CPU -Detailed
##
###########################################################################

param(
    [string] $pattern = $(throw "Please specify a search pattern."),
    [switch] $detailed,
    [switch] $full,

    ## Supports any or all of the following match options:
    ## ClassName, ClassDescription, PropertyName, PropertyDescription
    [string[]] $matchOptions = ("ClassName","ClassDescription")
)

## Helper function to create a new object that represents
## a Wmi match from this script
function New-WmiMatch
{
    param( $matchType, $className, $propertyName, $line )

    $wmiMatch = New-Object PsObject
    $wmiMatch | Add-Member NoteProperty MatchType $matchType
    $wmiMatch | Add-Member NoteProperty ClassName $className
    $wmiMatch | Add-Member NoteProperty PropertyName $propertyName
    $wmiMatch | Add-Member NoteProperty Line $line

    $wmiMatch
}

## If they've specified the -detailed or -full options, update
## the match options to provide them an appropriate amount of detail
if($detailed)
{
    $matchOptions = "ClassName","ClassDescription","PropertyName"
}

if($full)
{
    $matchOptions =
        "ClassName","ClassDescription","PropertyName","PropertyDescription"
}

## Verify that they specified only valid match options
foreach($matchOption in $matchOptions)
{
    $fullMatchOptions =
```

Example 15-2. Search-WmiNamespace.ps1 (continued)

```
        "ClassName","ClassDescription","PropertyName","PropertyDescription"

    if($fullMatchOptions -notcontains $matchOption)
    {
        $error = "Cannot convert value {0} to a match option. " +
                "Specify one of the following values and try again. " +
                "The possible values are ""{1}""."
        $ofs = ", "
        throw ($error -f $matchOption, ([string] $fullMatchOptions))
    }
}


## Go through all of the available classes on the computer
foreach($class in Get-WmiObject -List)
{
    ## Provide explicit get options, so that we get back descriptions
    ## as well
    $managementOptions = New-Object System.Management.ObjectGetOptions
    $managementOptions.UseAmendedQualifiers = $true
    $managementClass =
        New-Object Management.ManagementClass $class.Name,$managementOptions

    ## If they want us to match on class names, check if their text
    ## matches the class name
    if($matchOptions -contains "ClassName")
    {
        if($managementClass.Name -match $pattern)
        {
            New-WmiMatch "ClassName" `
                $managementClass.Name $null $managementClass.__PATH
        }
    }

    ## If they want us to match on class descriptions, check if their text
    ## matches the class description
    if($matchOptions -contains "ClassDescription")
    {
        $description =
            $managementClass.PsBase.Qualifiers |
                foreach { if($_.Name -eq "Description") { $_.Value } }
        if($description -match $pattern)
        {
            New-WmiMatch "ClassDescription" `
                $managementClass.Name $null $description
        }
    }

    ## Go through the properties of the class
    foreach($property in $managementClass.PsBase.Properties)
    {
```

Example 15-2. Search-WmiNamespace.ps1 (continued)

```
        ## If they want us to match on property names, check if their text
        ## matches the property name
        if($matchOptions -contains "PropertyName")
        {
            if($property.Name -match $pattern)
            {
                New-WmiMatch "PropertyName" `
                    $managementClass.Name $property.Name $property.Name
            }
        }

        ## If they want us to match on property descriptions, check if
        ## their text matches the property name
        if($matchOptions -contains "PropertyDescription")
        {
            $propertyDescription =
                $property.Qualifiers |
                    foreach { if($_.Name -eq "Description") { $_.Value } }
            if($propertyDescription -match $pattern)
            {
                New-WmiMatch "PropertyDescription" `
                    $managementClass.Name $property.Name $propertyDescription
            }
        }
    }
}
}
```

For more information about running scripts, see Recipe 1.1, "Run Programs, Scripts, and Existing Tools.

See Also

- Recipe 1.1, "Run Programs, Scripts, and Existing Tools"
- Appendix F *WMI Reference*

15.4 Use .NET to Perform Advanced WMI Tasks

Problem

You want to work with advanced features of WMI, but PowerShell's access (through the [Wmi], [WmiClass], and [WmiSearcher] accelerators) does not directly support them.

Solution

To interact with advanced features through their .NET interface, use the PsBase property of the resulting objects.

Advanced instance features

To get WMI instances related to a given instance, call the GetRelated() method:

```
$instance = [Wmi] 'Win32_Service.Name="winmgmt"'
$instance.PsBase.GetRelated()
```

To enable security privileges for a command that requires them (such as changing the system time), set the EnablePrivileges property to $true:

```
$system = Get-WmiObject Win32_OperatingSystem
$system.PsBase.Scope.Options.EnablePrivileges = $true
$system.SetDateTime($class.ConvertFromDateTime("01/01/2007"))
```

Advanced class features

To retrieve the WMI properties and qualifiers of a class, access the PsBase. Properties property:

```
$class = [WmiClass] "Win32_Service"
$class.PsBase.Properties
```

Advanced query feature

To configure connection options, such as Packet Privacy and Authentication, set the options on the Scope property:

```
$credential = Get-Credential
$query = [WmiSearcher] "SELECT * FROM IISWebServerSetting"
$query.Scope.Path = "\\REMOTE_COMPUTER\Root\MicrosoftIISV2"
$query.Scope.Options.Username = $credential.Username
$query.Scope.Options.Password = $credential.GetNetworkCredential().Password
$query.Scope.Options.Authentication = "PacketPrivacy"
$query.get() | Select-Object AnonymousUserName
```

Discussion

The [Wmi], [WmiClass], and [WmiSearcher] type shortcuts return instances of .NET System.Management.ManagementObject, System.Management.ManagementClass, and System.Management.ManagementObjectSearcher classes, respectively.

As might be expected, the .NET Framework provides comprehensive support for WMI queries, with PowerShell providing an easier-to-use interface to that support. If you need to step outside the support offered directly by PowerShell, these classes in the .NET Framework provide an advanced outlet.

For more information about working with classes from the .NET Framework, see Recipe 3.4, "Work with .NET Objects."

See Also

- Recipe 3.4, "Work with .NET Objects"

15.5 Convert a VBScript WMI Script to PowerShell

Problem

You want to perform a WMI task in PowerShell, but can find only VBScript examples that demonstrate the solution to the problem.

Solution

To accomplish the task of a script that retrieves data from a computer, use the Get-WmiObject cmdlet:

```
foreach($printer in Get-WmiObject -Computer COMPUTER Win32_Printer)
{
    ## Work with the properties
    $printer.Name
}
```

To accomplish the task of a script that calls methods on an instance, use the [Wmi] or [WmiSearcher] accelerators to retrieve the instances, and then call methods on the instances like you would call any other PowerShell method:

```
$service = [Wmi] 'Win32_Service.Name="winmgmt"'
$service.ChangeStartMode("Manual")
$service.ChangeStartMode("Automatic")
```

To accomplish the task of a script that calls methods on a class, use the [WmiClass] accelerator to retrieve the class, and then call methods on the class like you would call any other PowerShell method:

```
$class = [WmiClass] "Win32_Process"
$class.Create("Notepad")
```

Discussion

For many years, VBScript has been the preferred language that administrators use to access WMI data. Because of that, the vast majority of scripts available in books and on the Internet come written in VBScript.

These scripts usually take one of three forms: retrieving data and accessing properties, calling methods of an instance, and calling methods of a class.

 Although most WMI scripts on the Internet accomplish unique tasks, PowerShell supports many of the traditional WMI tasks natively. If you want to translate a WMI example to PowerShell, first check that there aren't any PowerShell cmdlets that might accomplish the task directly.

Retrieving data

One of the most common uses of WMI is for data collection and system inventory tasks. A typical VBScript that retrieves data looks like Example 15-3.

Example 15-3. Retrieving printer information from WMI using VBScript

```
strComputer = "."
Set objWMIService = GetObject("winmgmts:" _
    & "{impersonationLevel=impersonate}!\\" & strComputer & "\root\cimv2")

Set colInstalledPrinters =  objWMIService.ExecQuery _
    ("Select * from Win32_Printer")

For Each objPrinter in colInstalledPrinters
    Wscript.Echo "Name: " & objPrinter.Name
    Wscript.Echo "Location: " & objPrinter.Location
    Wscript.Echo "Default: " & objPrinter.Default
Next
```

The first three lines prepare a WMI connection to a given computer and namespace. The next two lines of code prepare a WMI query that requests all instances of a class. The For Each block loops over all the instances, and the *objPrinter.Property* statements interact with properties on those instances.

In PowerShell, the Get-WmiObject cmdlet takes care of most of that, by retrieving all instances of a class from the computer and namespace that you specify. The first five lines of code then become:

```
$installedPrinters = Get-WmiObject Win32_Printer
```

If you need to specify a different computer, namespace, or query restriction, the Get-WmiObject cmdlets supports those through optional parameters. If you need to specify advanced connection options (such as authentication levels), see Recipe 15.4, "Use .NET to Perform Advanced WMI Tasks."

In PowerShell, the For Each block becomes:

```
foreach($printer in $installedPrinters)
{
    $printer.Name
    $printer.Location
    $printer.Default
}
```

Notice that we spend the bulk of the PowerShell conversion of this script showing how to access properties. If you don't actually need to work with the properties (and only want to display them for reporting purposes), PowerShell's formatting commands simplify that even further:

```
Get-WmiObject Win32_Printer | Format-List Name,Location,Default
```

For more information about working with the Get-WmiObject cmdlet, see Recipe 15.1, "Access Windows Management Instrumentation Data."

Calling methods on an instance

Although data retrieval scripts form the bulk of WMI management examples, another common task is to call methods of an instance that invoke actions.

For example, Example 15-4 changes the startup type of a service.

Example 15-4. Changing the startup type of a service from WMI using VBScript

```
strComputer = "."
Set objWMIService = GetObject("winmgmts:" _
    & "{impersonationLevel=impersonate}!\\" & strComputer & "\root\cimv2")

Set colServiceList = objWMIService.ExecQuery _
    ("Select * from Win32_Service where StartMode = 'Manual'")

For Each objService in colServiceList
    errReturnCode = objService.ChangeStartMode("Disabled")
Next
```

The first three lines prepare a WMI connection to a given computer and namespace. The next two lines of code prepare a WMI query that requests all instances of a class and adds an additional filter (StartMode = 'Manual') to the query. The For Each block loops over all the instances, and the *objService.Change(...)* statement calls the Change() method on the service.

In PowerShell, the Get-WmiObject cmdlet takes care of most of the setup, by retrieving all instances of a class from the computer and namespace that you specify. The first five lines of code then become:

```
$services = Get-WmiObject Win32_Service -Filter "StartMode = 'Manual'"
```

If you need to specify a different computer or namespace, the Get-WmiObject cmdlets supports those through optional parameters. If you need to specify advanced connection options (such as authentication levels), see Recipe 15.4, "Use .NET to Perform Advanced WMI Tasks."

In PowerShell, the For Each block becomes:

```
foreach($service in $services)
{
    $service.ChangeStartMode("Disabled")
}
```

For more information about working with the Get-WmiObject cmdlet, see Recipe 15.1, "Access Windows Management Instrumentation Data."

Calling methods on a class

Although less common than calling methods on an instance, it is sometimes helpful to call methods on a WMI class. PowerShell makes this work almost exactly like calling methods on an instance.

For example, a script that creates a process on a remote computer looks like this:

```
strComputer = "COMPUTER"
Set objWMIService = GetObject _
    ("winmgmts:\\" & strComputer & "\root\cimv2:Win32_Process")

objWMIService.Create("notepad.exe")
```

The first three lines prepare a WMI connection to a given computer and namespace. The final line calls the Create() method on the class.

In PowerShell, the [WmiClass] accelerator lets you easily access WMI classes. The first three lines of code then become:

```
$processClass = [WmiClass] "\\COMPUTER\Root\Cimv2:Win32_Process"
```

If you need to specify advanced connection options (such as authentication levels), see Recipe 15.4, "Use .NET to Perform Advanced WMI Tasks."

In PowerShell, calling the method on the class is nearly identical:

```
$processClass.Create("notepad.exe")
```

For more information about working with the [WmiClass] accelerator, see Recipe 15.1, "Access Windows Management Instrumentation Data."

See Also

- Recipe 15.1, "Access Windows Management Instrumentation Data"
- Recipe 15.4, "Use .NET to Perform Advanced WMI Tasks"

15.6 Automate Programs Using COM Scripting Interfaces

Problem

You want to automate a program or system task through its COM automation interface.

Solution

To instantiate and work with COM objects, use the New-Object cmdlet's –ComObject parameter.

```
$shell = New-Object -ComObject "Shell.Application"
$shell.Windows() | Format-Table LocationName,LocationUrl
```

Discussion

Like WMI, COM automation interfaces have long been a standard tool for scripting and system administration. When an application exposes management or automation tasks, COM objects are the second most common interface (right after custom command-line tools).

PowerShell exposes COM objects like it exposes most other management objects in the system. Once you have access to a COM object, you work with its properties and methods in the same way that you work with methods and properties of other objects in PowerShell.

In addition to automation tasks, many COM objects exist entirely to improve the scripting experience in languages such as VBScript. One example of this is working with files, or sorting an array.

One thing to remember when working with these COM objects is that PowerShell often provides better alternatives to them! In many cases, PowerShell's cmdlets, scripting language, or access to the .NET Framework provide the same or similar functionality to a COM object that you might be used to.

For more information about working with COM objects, see Recipe 3.8, "Use a COM Object. For a list of the most useful COM objects, see Appendix E *Selected .NET Classes and Their Uses*.

See Also

- Recipe 3.8, "Use a COM Object"
- Appendix E *Selected .NET Classes and Their Uses*

15.7 Program: Query a SQL Data Source

It is often helpful to perform ad hoc queries and commands against a data source such as a SQL server, Access database, or even an Excel spreadsheet. This is especially true when you want to take data from one system and put it in another, or when you want to bring the data into your PowerShell environment for detailed interactive manipulation or processing.

Although you can directly access each of these data sources in PowerShell (through its support of the .NET Framework), each data source requires a unique and hard to remember syntax. Example 15-5 makes working with these SQL-based data sources both consistent and powerful.

Example 15-5. Invoke-SqlCommand.ps1

```
###############################################################################
##
## Invoke-SqlCommand.ps1
##
## Return the results of a SQL query or operation
##
## ie:
##
##     ## Use Windows authentication
##     Invoke-SqlCommand.ps1 -Sql "SELECT TOP 10 * FROM Orders"
##
##     ## Use SQL Authentication
##     $cred = Get-Credential
##     Invoke-SqlCommand.ps1 -Sql "SELECT TOP 10 * FROM Orders" -Cred $cred
##
##     ## Perform an update
##     $server = "MYSERVER"
##     $database = "Master"
##     $sql = "UPDATE Orders SET EmployeeID = 6 WHERE OrderID = 10248"
##     Invoke-SqlCommand $server $database $sql
##
##     $sql = "EXEC SalesByCategory 'Beverages'"
##     Invoke-SqlCommand -Sql $sql
##
##     ## Access an access database
##     Invoke-SqlCommand (Resolve-Path access_test.mdb) -Sql "SELECT * from Users"
##
##     ## Access an excel file
##     Invoke-SqlCommand (Resolve-Path xls_test.xls) -Sql 'SELECT * from [Sheet1$]'
##
###############################################################################

param(
    [string] $dataSource = ".\SQLEXPRESS",
    [string] $database = "Northwind",
    [string] $sqlCommand = $(throw "Please specify a query."),
    [System.Management.Automation.PsCredential] $credential
  )


## Prepare the authentication information. By default, we pick
## Windows authentication
$authentication = "Integrated Security=SSPI;"

## If the user supplies a credential, then they want SQL
## authentication
if($credential)
{
    $plainCred = $credential.GetNetworkCredential()
    $authentication =
        ("uid={0};pwd={1};" -f $plainCred.Username,$plainCred.Password)
}
```

Example 15-5. Invoke-SqlCommand.ps1 (continued)

```
## Prepare the connection string out of the information they
## provide
$connectionString = "Provider=sqloledb; " +
                    "Data Source=$dataSource; " +
                    "Initial Catalog=$database; " +
                    "$authentication; "

## If they specify an Access database or Excel file as the connection
## source, modify the connection string to connect to that data source
if($dataSource -match '\.xls$|\.mdb$')
{
    $connectionString = "Provider=Microsoft.Jet.OLEDB.4.0; Data Source=$dataSource; "

    if($dataSource -match '\.xls$')
    {
        $connectionString += 'Extended Properties="Excel 8.0;"; '

        ## Generate an error if they didn't specify the sheet name properly
        if($sqlCommand -notmatch '\[.+\$\]')
        {
            $error = 'Sheet names should be surrounded by square brackets, and ' +
                     'have a dollar sign at the end: [Sheet1$]'
            Write-Error $error
            return
        }
    }
}

## Connect to the data source and open it
$connection = New-Object System.Data.OleDb.OleDbConnection $connectionString
$command = New-Object System.Data.OleDb.OleDbCommand $sqlCommand,$connection
$connection.Open()

## Fetch the results, and close the connection
$adapter = New-Object System.Data.OleDb.OleDbDataAdapter $command
$dataset = New-Object System.Data.DataSet
[void] $adapter.Fill($dataSet)
$connection.Close()

## Return all of the rows from their query
$dataSet.Tables | Select-Object -Expand Rows
```

For more information about running scripts, see Recipe 1.1, "Run Programs, Scripts, and Existing Tools."

See Also

- Recipe 1.1, "Run Programs, Scripts, and Existing Tools"

15.8 Access Windows Performance Counters

Problem

You want to access system performance counter information from PowerShell.

Solution

To retrieve information about a specific performance counter, use the System.Diagnostics.PerformanceCounter class from the .NET Framework, as shown in Example 15-6.

Example 15-6. Accessing performance counter data through the System.Diagnostics. PeformanceCounter class

```
PS >$arguments = "System","System Up Time"
PS >$counter = New-Object System.Diagnostics.PerformanceCounter $arguments
PS >
PS >[void] $counter.NextValue()
PS >New-Object TimeSpan 0,0,0,$counter.NextValue()


Days               : 0
Hours              : 18
Minutes            : 51
Seconds            : 17
Milliseconds       : 0
Ticks              : 678770000000
TotalDays          : 0.785613425925926
TotalHours         : 18.8547222222222
TotalMinutes       : 1131.28333333333
TotalSeconds       : 67877
TotalMilliseconds  : 67877000
```

Alternatively, WMI's Win32_Perf* set of classes support many of the most common performance counters:

```
Get-WmiObject Win32_PerfFormattedData_Tcpip_NetworkInterface
```

Discussion

The System.Diagnostics.PerformanceCounter class from the .NET Framework provides access to the different performance counters you might want to access on a Windows system. Example 15-6 illustrates working with a performance counter from a specific category. In addition, the constructor for the PerformanceCounter class also lets you specify instance names, and even a machine name for the performance counter you want to retrieve.

The first time you access a performance counter, the NextValue() method returns 0. At that point, the system begins to sample the performance information and returns a current value the next time you call the NextValue() method.

For more information about working with classes from the .NET Framework, see Recipe 3.4, "Work with .NET Objects."

See Also

- Recipe 3.4, "Work with .NET Objects"

15.9   Program: Invoke Native Windows API Calls

There are times when neither PowerShell's cmdlets nor scripting language directly support a feature you need. In most of those situations, PowerShell's direct support for the .NET Framework provides another avenue to let you accomplish your task. In some cases, though, even the .NET Framework does not support a feature you need to resolve a problem, and the only way to resolve your problem is to access the core Windows APIs.

For complex API calls (ones that take highly structured data), the solution is to write a PowerShell cmdlet that uses the P/Invoke (*Platform Invoke*) support in the .NET Framework. The P/Invoke support in the .NET Framework lets you access core Windows APIs directly.

Although it is possible to determine these P/Invoke definitions yourself, it is usually easiest to build on the work of others. If you want to know how to call a specific Windows API from a .NET language, the *http://pinvoke.net* web site is the best place to start.

If the API you need to access is straightforward (one that takes and returns only simple data types), however, Example 15-7 lets you call these Windows APIs directly from PowerShell.

For an example of this script in action, see Recipe 17.18, "Program: Create a Filesystem Hard Link."

Example 15-7. Invoke-WindowsApi.ps1

```
##############################################################################
##
## Invoke-WindowsApi.ps1
##
## Invoke a native Windows API call that takes and returns simple data types.
##
## ie:
##
## ## Prepare the parameter types and parameters for the
## CreateHardLink function
## $parameterTypes = [string], [string], [IntPtr]
## $parameters = [string] $filename, [string] $existingFilename, [IntPtr]::Zero
##
```

Example 15-7. Invoke-WindowsApi.ps1 (continued)

```
## ## Call the CreateHardLink method in the Kernel32 DLL
## $result = Invoke-WindowsApi "kernel32" ([bool]) "CreateHardLink" `
##      $parameterTypes $parameters
##
##############################################################################
param(
    [string] $dllName,
    [Type] $returnType,
    [string] $methodName,
    [Type[]] $parameterTypes,
    [Object[]] $parameters
    )

## Begin to build the dynamic assembly
$domain = [AppDomain]::CurrentDomain
$name = New-Object Reflection.AssemblyName 'PInvokeAssembly'
$assembly = $domain.DefineDynamicAssembly($name, 'Run')
$module = $assembly.DefineDynamicModule('PInvokeModule')
$type = $module.DefineType('PInvokeType', "Public,BeforeFieldInit")

## Go through all of the parameters passed to us.  As we do this,
## we clone the user's inputs into another array that we will use for
## the P/Invoke call.
$inputParameters = @()
$refParameters = @()

for($counter = 1; $counter -le $parameterTypes.Length; $counter++)
{
    ## If an item is a PSReference, then the user
    ## wants an [out] parameter.
    if($parameterTypes[$counter - 1] -eq [Ref])
    {
        ## Remember which parameters are used for [Out] parameters
        $refParameters += $counter

        ## On the cloned array, we replace the PSReference type with the
        ## .Net reference type that represents the value of the PSReference,
        ## and the value with the value held by the PSReference.
        $parameterTypes[$counter - 1] =
            $parameters[$counter - 1].Value.GetType().MakeByRefType()
        $inputParameters += $parameters[$counter - 1].Value
    }
    else
    {
        ## Otherwise, just add their actual parameter to the
        ## input array.
        $inputParameters += $parameters[$counter - 1]
    }
}

## Define the actual P/Invoke method, adding the [Out]
## attribute for any parameters that were originally [Ref]
```

Example 15-7. Invoke-WindowsApi.ps1 (continued)

```
## parameters.
$method = $type.DefineMethod($methodName, 'Public,HideBySig,Static,PinvokeImpl',
   $returnType, $parameterTypes)
foreach($refParameter in $refParameters)
{
   [void] $method.DefineParameter($refParameter, "Out", $null)
}

## Apply the P/Invoke constructor
$ctor = [Runtime.InteropServices.DllImportAttribute].GetConstructor([string])
$attr = New-Object Reflection.Emit.CustomAttributeBuilder $ctor, $dllName
$method.SetCustomAttribute($attr)

## Create the temporary type, and invoke the method.
$realType = $type.CreateType()

$realType.InvokeMember($methodName, 'Public,Static,InvokeMethod', $null, $null,
    $inputParameters)

## Finally, go through all of the reference parameters, and update the
## values of the PSReference objects that the user passed in.
foreach($refParameter in $refParameters)
{
   $parameters[$refParameter - 1].Value = $inputParameters[$refParameter - 1]
}
```

For more information about running scripts, see Recipe 1.1, "Run Programs, Scripts, and Existing Tools."

See Also

- Recipe 1.1, "Run Programs, Scripts, and Existing Tools"
- Recipe 17.18, "Program: Create a Filesystem Hard Link"

15.10   Program: Add Inline C# to Your PowerShell Script

One of the natural languages to explore after learning PowerShell is C#. It uses many of the same programming techniques as PowerShell and uses the same classes and methods in the .NET Framework as PowerShell does, too. In addition, C# sometimes offers language features or performance benefits not available through PowerShell.

Rather than having to move to C# completely for these situations, Example 15-8 lets you write and invoke C# directly in your script.

Example 15-8. Invoke-Inline.ps1

```
###############################################################################
## Invoke-Inline.ps1
## Library support for inline C#
##
## Usage
##  1) Define just the body of a C# method, and store it in a string.  "Here
##     strings" work great for this.  The code can be simple:
##
##     $codeToRun = "Console.WriteLine(Math.Sqrt(337));"
##
##     or more complex:
##
##     $codeToRun = @"
##         string firstArg = (string) ((System.Collections.ArrayList) arg)[0];
##         int secondArg = (int) ((System.Collections.ArrayList) arg)[1];
##
##         Console.WriteLine("Hello {0} {1}", firstArg, secondArg );
##
##         returnValue = secondArg * 3;
##     "@
##
##  2) (Optionally) Pack any arguments to your function into a single object.
##     This single object should be strongly-typed, so that PowerShell does
##     not treat it as a PsObject.
##     An ArrayList works great for multiple elements.  If you have only one
##     argument, you can pass it directly.
##
##     [System.Collections.ArrayList] $arguments =
##         New-Object System.Collections.ArrayList
##     [void] $arguments.Add("World")
##     [void] $arguments.Add(337)
##
##  3) Invoke the inline code, optionally retrieving the return value.  You can
##     set the return value in your inline code by assigning it to the
##     "returnValue" variable as shown above.
##
##     $result = Invoke-Inline $codeToRun $arguments
##
##
##     If your code is simple enough, you can even do this entirely inline:
##
##     Invoke-Inline "Console.WriteLine(Math.Pow(337,2));"
##
###############################################################################
param(
    [string] $code = $(throw "Please specify the code to invoke"),
    [object] $arg,
    [string[]] $reference = @()
    )

## Stores a cache of generated inline objects.  If this library is dot-sourced
## from a script, these objects go away when the script exits.
```

Example 15-8. Invoke-Inline.ps1 (continued)

```
if(-not (Test-Path Variable:\Lee.Holmes.inlineCache))
{
    ${GLOBAL:Lee.Holmes.inlineCache} = @{}
}

## The main function to execute inline C#.
## Pass the argument to the function as a strongly-typed variable.  They will
## be available from C# code as the Object variable, "arg".
## Any values assigned to the "returnValue" object by the C# code will be
## returned to the caller as a return value.

function main
{
    ## See if the code has already been compiled and cached
    $cachedObject = ${Lee.Holmes.inlineCache}[$code]

    ## The code has not been compiled or cached
    if($cachedObject -eq $null)
    {
        $codeToCompile =
@"
    using System;

    public class InlineRunner
    {
        public Object Invoke(Object arg)
        {
            Object returnValue = null;

            $code

            return returnValue;
        }
    }
"@

        ## Obtains an ICodeCompiler from a CodeDomProvider class.
        $provider = New-Object Microsoft.CSharp.CSharpCodeProvider

        ## Get the location for System.Management.Automation DLL
        $dllName = [PsObject].Assembly.Location

        ## Configure the compiler parameters
        $compilerParameters = New-Object System.CodeDom.Compiler.CompilerParameters

        $assemblies = @("System.dll", $dllName)
        $compilerParameters.ReferencedAssemblies.AddRange($assemblies)
        $compilerParameters.ReferencedAssemblies.AddRange($reference)
        $compilerParameters.IncludeDebugInformation = $true
        $compilerParameters.GenerateInMemory = $true

        ## Invokes compilation.
```

Example 15-8. Invoke-Inline.ps1 (continued)

```
    $compilerResults =
        $provider.CompileAssemblyFromSource($compilerParameters, $codeToCompile)

    ## Write any errors if generated.
    if($compilerResults.Errors.Count -gt 0)
    {
        $errorLines = "`n$codeToCompile"
        foreach($error in $compilerResults.Errors)
        {
            $errorLines += "`n`t" + $error.Line + ":`t" + $error.ErrorText
        }
        Write-Error $errorLines
    }
    ## There were no errors.  Store the resulting object in the object "
    ## cache.
    else
    {
        ${Lee.Holmes.inlineCache}[$code] =
            $compilerResults.CompiledAssembly.CreateInstance("InlineRunner")
    }

    $cachedObject = ${Lee.Holmes.inlineCache}[$code]
}

## Finally invoke the C# code
if($cachedObject -ne $null)
{
    return $cachedObject.Invoke($arg)
}
}

. Main
```

For more information about running scripts, see Recipe 1.1, "Run Programs, Scripts, and Existing Tools."

See Also

- Recipe 1.1, "Run Programs, Scripts, and Existing Tools"

15.11 Access a .NET SDK Library

Problem

You want to access the functionality exposed by a .NET DLL, but that DLL is packaged as part of a developer-oriented Software Development Kit (SDK).

Solution

To create objects contained in a DLL, use the [System.Reflection.Assembly]::
LoadFile() method to load the DLL, and the New-Object cmdlet to create objects
contained in it. Example 15-9 illustrates this technique.

Example 15-9. Interacting with classes from the SharpZipLib SDK DLL

```
[Reflection.Assembly]::LoadFile("d:\bin\ICSharpCode.SharpZipLib.dll")
$namespace = "ICSharpCode.SharpZipLib.Zip.{0}"

$zipName = Join-Path (Get-Location) "PowerShell_TDG_Scripts.zip"
$zipFile = New-Object ($namespace -f "ZipOutputStream") ([IO.File]::Create($zipName))

foreach($file in dir *.ps1)
{
   $zipEntry = New-Object ($namespace -f "ZipEntry") $file.Name
   $zipFile.PutNextEntry($zipEntry)
}

$zipFile.Close()
```

Discussion

While C# and VB.Net developers are usually the consumers of SDKs created for the
.NET Framework, PowerShell lets you access the SDK features just as easily. To do
this, use the [Reflection.Assembly]::LoadFile() method to load the SDK assembly,
and then work with the classes from that assembly as you would work with other
classes in the .NET Framework.

> Although PowerShell lets you access developer-oriented SDKs easily, it
> can't change the fact that these SDKs are developer-oriented. SDKs
> and programming interfaces are rarely designed with the administra-
> tor in mind, so be prepared to work with programming models that
> require multiple steps to accomplish your task.

One thing you will notice when working with classes from an SDK is that it quickly
becomes tiresome to specify their fully qualified type names. For example, zip-related
classes from the SharpZipLib all start with ICSharpCode.SharpZipLib.Zip. This is
called the *namespace* of that class. Most programming languages solve this problem
with a using statement that lets you specify a list of namespaces for that language to
search when you type a plain class name such as ZipEntry. PowerShell lacks a using
statement, but the solution demonstrates one of several ways to get the benefits of
one.

For more information on how to manage these long class names, see Recipe 3.7,
"Reduce Typing for Long Class Names."

Prepackaged SDKs aren't the only DLLs you can load this way, either. An SDK library is simply a DLL that somebody wrote, compiled, packaged, and released. If you are comfortable with any of the .NET languages, you can also create your own DLL, compile it, and use it exactly the same way.

Take, for example, the simple math library given in Example 15-10. It provides a static Sum method and an instance Product method.

Example 15-10. A simple C# math library

```csharp
namespace MyMathLib
{
  public class Methods
  {
    public Methods()
    {
    }

    public static int Sum(int a, int b)
    {
      return a + b;
    }

    public int Product(int a, int b)
    {
      return a * b;
    }
  }
}
```

Example 15-11 demonstrates everything required to get that working in your PowerShell system.

Example 15-11. Compiling, loading, and using a simple C# library

```
PS >notepad MyMathLib.cs
<add the above code to MyMathLib.cs>

PS >Set-Alias csc $env:WINDIR\Microsoft.NET\Framework\v2.0.50727\csc.exe
PS >csc /target:library MyMathLib.cs

Microsoft (R) Visual C# 2005 Compiler version 8.00.50727.42
for Microsoft (R) Windows (R) 2005 Framework version 2.0.50727
Copyright (C) Microsoft Corporation 2001-2005. All rights reserved.

PS >[Reflection.Assembly]::LoadFile("c:\temp\MyMathLib.dll")

GAC     Version        Location
---     -------        --------
False   v2.0.50727     c:\temp\MyMathLib.dll

PS >[MyMathLib.Methods]::Sum(10, 2)
12
```

Example 15-11. Compiling, loading, and using a simple C# library (continued)

```
PS >$mathInstance = New-Object MyMathLib.Methods
PS >$mathInstance.Product(10, 2)
20
```

For more information about working with classes from the .NET Framework, see Recipe 3.5, "Create an Instance of a .NET Object."

See Also

- Recipe 3.5, "Create an Instance of a .NET Object"
- Recipe 3.7, "Reduce Typing for Long Class Names"

15.12 Create Your Own PowerShell Cmdlet

Problem

You want to write your own PowerShell cmdlet.

Discussion

As mentioned previously in "Structured Commands (Cmdlets)" in *A Guided Tour of Windows PowerShell*, PowerShell cmdlets offer several significant advantages over traditional executable programs. From the user's perspective, cmdlets are incredibly consistent—and their support for strongly typed objects as input makes them powerful. From the cmdlet author's perspective, cmdlets are incredibly easy to write when compared to the amount of power they provide. Creating and exposing a new command-line parameter is as easy as creating a new public property on a class. Supporting a rich pipeline model is as easy as placing your implementation logic into one of three standard method overrides.

While a full discussion on how to implement a cmdlet is outside the scope of this book, the following steps illustrate the process behind implementing a simple cmdlet.

For more information on how to write a PowerShell cmdlet, see the MSDN topic, "How to Create a Windows PowerShell Cmdlet," available at *http://msdn2.microsoft. com/en-us/library/ms714598.aspx*.

Step 1: Download the Windows SDK

The Windows SDK contains samples, tools, reference assemblies, templates, documentation, and other information used when developing PowerShell cmdlets. It is available by searching for "Microsoft Windows SDK" on *http://download.microsoft. com* and downloading the latest Windows Vista SDK.

Step 2: Create a file to hold the cmdlet and snapin source code

Create a file called InvokeTemplateCmdletCommand.cs with the content from Example 15-12 and save it on your hard drive.

Example 15-12. InvokeTemplateCmdletCommand.cs

```
using System;
using System.ComponentModel;
using System.Management.Automation;

/*
To build and install:

1)
Set-Alias csc $env:WINDIR\Microsoft.NET\Framework\v2.0.50727\csc.exe

2)
Set-Alias installutil `
    $env:WINDIR\Microsoft.NET\Framework\v2.0.50727\installutil.exe
3)
$ref = [PsObject].Assembly.Location
csc /out:TemplateSnapin.dll /t:library InvokeTemplateCmdletCommand.cs /r:$ref

4)
installutil TemplateSnapin.dll

5)
Add-PSSnapin TemplateSnapin

To run:

PS >Invoke-TemplateCmdlet

To uninstall:

installutil /u TemplateSnapin.dll

*/

namespace Template.Commands
{
    [Cmdlet("Invoke", "TemplateCmdlet")]
    public class InvokeTemplateCmdletCommand : Cmdlet
    {
        [Parameter(Mandatory=true, Position=0, ValueFromPipeline=true)]
        public string Text
        {
            get
            {
                return text;
            }
```

Example 15-12. InvokeTemplateCmdletCommand.cs (continued)

```
        set
        {
            text = value;
        }
    }
    private string text;

    protected override void BeginProcessing()
    {
        WriteObject("Processing Started");
    }

    protected override void ProcessRecord()
    {
        WriteObject("Processing " + text);
    }

    protected override void EndProcessing()
    {
        WriteObject("Processing Complete.");
    }
}

[RunInstaller(true)]
public class TemplateSnapin : PSSnapIn
{
    public TemplateSnapin()
        : base()
    {
    }

    ///<summary>The snapin name which is used for registration</summary>
    public override string Name
    {
        get
        {
            return "TemplateSnapin";
        }
    }
    /// <summary>Gets vendor of the snapin.</summary>
    public override string Vendor
    {
        get
        {
            return "Template Vendor";
        }
    }
    /// <summary>Gets description of the snapin. </summary>
    public override string Description
```

Example 15-12. InvokeTemplateCmdletCommand.cs (continued)

```
      {
          get
          {
              return "This is a snapin that provides a template cmdlet.";
          }
      }
   }
}
```

Step 3: Compile the snapin

A PowerShell cmdlet is a simple .NET class. The DLL that contains the compiled cmdlet is called a *snapin*.

```
Set-Alias csc $env:WINDIR\Microsoft.NET\Framework\v2.0.50727\csc.exe
$ref = [PsObject].Assembly.Location
csc /out:TemplateSnapin.dll /t:library InvokeTemplateCmdletCommand.cs /r:$ref
```

Step 4: Install and register the snapin

Once you have compiled the snapin, the next step is to register it. Registering a snapin gives PowerShell the information it needs to let you use it. This command requires administrative permissions.

```
Set-Alias installutil `
    $env:WINDIR\Microsoft.NET\Framework\v2.0.50727\installutil.exe
installutil TemplateSnapin.dll
```

Step 5: Add the snapin to your session

Although step 4 registered the snapin, PowerShell doesn't add the commands to your active session until you call the Add-PsSnapin cmdlet.

```
Add-PsSnapin TemplateSnapin
```

Step 6: Use the snapin

Once you've added the snapin to your session, you can call commands from that snapin as though you would call any other cmdlet.

```
PS >"Hello World" | Invoke-TemplateCmdlet
Processing Started
Processing Hello World
Processing Complete.
```

15.13 Add PowerShell Scripting to Your Own Program

Problem

You want to provide your users with an easy way to automate your program, but don't want to write a scripting language on your own.

Discussion

One of the fascinating aspects of PowerShell is how easily it lets you add many of its capabilities to your own program. This is because PowerShell is, at its core, a powerful engine that any application can use. The PowerShell console application is in fact just a text-based interface to this engine.

While a full discussion of the PowerShell hosting model is outside the scope of this book, the following example illustrates the techniques behind exposing features of your application for your users to script.

To frame Example 15-13, imagine an email application that lets you run rules when it receives an email. While you will want to design a standard interface that allows users to create simple rules, you will also want to provide a way for users to write incredibly complex rules. Rather than design a scripting language yourself, you can simply use PowerShell's scripting language. In the following example, we provide user-written scripts with a variable called $message that represents the current message and then runs their commands.

```
PS >Get-Content VerifyCategoryRule.ps1
if($message.Body -match "book")
{
    [Console]::WriteLine("This is a message about the book.")
}
else
{
    [Console]::WriteLine("This is an unknown message.")
}
PS >.\RulesWizardExample.exe (Resolve-Path VerifyCategoryRule.ps1)
This is a message about the book.
```

For more information on how to host PowerShell in your own application, see the MSDN topic, "How to Create a Windows PowerShell Hosting Application," available at *http://msdn2.microsoft.com/en-us/library/ms714661.aspx*.

Step 1: Download the Windows SDK

The Windows SDK contains samples, tools, reference assemblies, templates, documentation, and other information used when developing PowerShell cmdlets. It is available by searching for "Microsoft Windows SDK" on *http://download.microsoft.com*.

Step 2: Create a file to hold the hosting source code

Create a file called RulesWizardExample.cs with the content from Example 15-13, and save it on your hard drive.

Example 15-13. RulesWizardExample.cs

```
using System;
using System.Management.Automation;
using System.Management.Automation.Runspaces;

namespace Template
{
    // Define a simple class that represents a mail message
    public class MailMessage
    {
        public MailMessage(string to, string from, string body)
        {
            this.To = to;
            this.From = from;
            this.Body = body;
        }

        public String To;
        public String From;
        public String Body;
    }

    public class RulesWizardExample
    {
        public static void Main(string[] args)
        {
            // Ensure that they've provided some script text
            if(args.Length == 0)
            {
                Console.WriteLine("Usage:");
                Console.WriteLine(" RulesWizardExample <script text>");
                return;
            }

            // Create an example message to pass to our rules wizard
            MailMessage mailMessage =
                    new MailMessage(
                        "guide_feedback@LeeHolmes.com",
                        "guide_reader@example.com",
                        "This is a message about your book.");

            // Create a runspace, which is the environment for
            // running commands
            Runspace runspace = RunspaceFactory.CreateRunspace();
            runspace.Open();

            // Create a variable, called "$message" in the Runspace, and populate
            // it with a reference to the current message in our application.
```

Example 15-13. RulesWizardExample.cs (continued)

```
            // Pipeline commands can interact with this object like any other
            // .Net object.
            runspace.SessionStateProxy.SetVariable("message", mailMessage);

            // Create a pipeline, and populate it with the script given in the
            // first command line argument.
            Pipeline pipeline = runspace.CreatePipeline(args[0]);

            // Invoke (execute) the pipeline, and close the runspace.
            pipeline.Invoke();
            runspace.Close();
        }
    }
}
```

Step 3: Compile and run the example

Although the example itself provides very little functionality, it demonstrates the core concepts behind adding PowerShell scripting to your own program.

```
Set-Alias csc $env:WINDIR\Microsoft.NET\Framework\v2.0.50727\csc.exe
$dll = [PsObject].Assembly.Location
Csc RulesWizardExample.cs /reference:$dll
RulesWizardExample.exe <script commands to run>
```

For example,

```
PS >.\RulesWizardExample.exe '[Console]::WriteLine($message.From)'
guide_reader@example.com
```

See Also

- "Structured Commands (Cmdlets)" in *A Guided Tour of Windows PowerShell*

CHAPTER 16
Security and Script Signing

16.0   Introduction

Security plays two important roles in PowerShell. The first role is the security of PowerShell itself: scripting languages have long been a vehicle of email-based malware on Windows, so PowerShell's security features have been carefully designed to thwart this danger. The second role is the set of security-related tasks you are likely to encounter when working with your computer: script signing, certificates, and credentials, just to name a few.

When it comes to talking about security in the scripting and command-line world, a great deal of folklore and superstition clouds the picture. One of the most common misconceptions is that that scripting languages and command-line shells somehow lets users bypass the security protections of the Windows graphical user interface.

The Windows security model (as with any security model that actually provides security) protects resources—not the way you get to them. That is because programs that you run, in effect, *are* you. If you can do it, so can a program. If a program can do it, then you can do it without having to use that program. For example, consider the act of changing critical data in the Windows Registry. If you use the Windows Registry Editor graphical user interface, it provides an error message when you attempt to perform an operation that you do not have permission for, as shown in Figure 16-1.

The Registry Editor provides this error message because it is *unable* to delete that key, not because it wanted to prevent you from doing it. Windows itself protects the registry keys, not the programs you use to access them.

Likewise, PowerShell provides an error message when you attempt to perform an operation that you do not have permission for. Not because PowerShell contains

Figure 16-1. Error message from the Windows Registry Editor

extra security checks for that operation, but because it is also simply unable to perform the operation:

```
PS >New-Item "HKLM:\Software\Microsoft\Windows\CurrentVersion\Run\New"
New-Item : Requested registry access is not allowed.
At line:1 char:9
+ New-Item  <<<< "HKLM:\Software\Microsoft\Windows\CurrentVersion\Run\New"
```

While perhaps clear after explanation, this misunderstanding often gets used as a reason to prevent users from running command shells or scripting languages altogether.

16.1   Enable Scripting Through an Execution Policy

Problem

PowerShell provides an error message when you try to run a script:

```
PS>.\Test.ps1
File C:\temp\test.ps1 cannot be loaded because the execution of scripts is disa
bled on this system. Please see "get-help about_signing" for more details.
At line:1 char:10
+ .\Test.ps1 <<<<
```

Solution

To prevent this error message, use the Set-ExecutionPolicy cmdlet to change the PowerShell execution policy to one of the policies that allow scripts to run:

```
Set-ExecutionPolicy RemoteSigned
```

Discussion

As normally configured, PowerShell operates strictly as an interactive shell. By disabling the execution of scripts by default, PowerShell prevents malicious PowerShell scripts from affecting users who have PowerShell installed, but who may never have used (or even heard of!) PowerShell.

You (as a reader of this book) are not part of that target audience, however, so you will want to configure PowerShell to run under one of the following four execution policies:

Restricted
> PowerShell operates as an interactive shell only. Attempting to run a script generates an error message. This is PowerShell's default execution policy.

AllSigned
> PowerShell only runs scripts that contain a digital signature. When you attempt to run a script signed by a publisher that PowerShell hasn't seen before, Power-Shell asks whether you trust that publisher to run scripts on your system.

RemoteSigned *(recommended)*
> PowerShell runs most scripts without prompting, but requires that scripts that originate from the Internet contain a digital signature. As in AllSigned mode, PowerShell asks whether you trust that publisher to run scripts on your system when you run a script signed by a publisher it hasn't seen before. PowerShell considers a script to have come from the Internet when it has been downloaded to your computer by a popular communications programs such as Internet Explorer, Outlook, or Messenger.

Unrestricted
> PowerShell does not require a digital signature on any script, but (like Windows Explorer) warns you when a script originates from the Internet.

Run the Set-ExecutionPolicy cmdlet as an administrator to configure the system's execution policy. If you want to configure your execution policy on Windows Vista, right-click the Windows PowerShell link for the option to launch PowerShell as Administrator.

 Just because a script is signed, it does not mean that the script is safe! The signature on a script gives you a way to verify who the script came from, but not that you can trust its author to run commands on your system. You need to make that decision for yourself, which is why PowerShell asks you.

Alternatively, you may directly modify the registry key that PowerShell uses to store its execution policy. This is the ExecutionPolicy property under the registry path HKLM\SOFTWARE\Microsoft\PowerShell\1\ShellIds\Microsoft.PowerShell.

In an enterprise setting, PowerShell also lets you override this local preference through Group Policy. For more information about PowerShell's Group Policy support, see Recipe 16.4, "Manage PowerShell Security in an Enterprise."

When using an execution policy that detects Internet-based scripts, you may want to stop PowerShell from treating those scripts as remote. To do that, right-click on the file from Windows Explorer, select Properties, and then click Unblock.

In an enterprise setting, PowerShell sometimes warns of the dangers of Internet-based scripts even if they are located only on a network share. If unblocking the file does not resolve the issue, your machine has likely been configured to restrict access to network shares. This is common with Internet Explorer's *Enhanced Security Configuration* mode. To prevent this message, add the path of the network share to Internet Explorer's Intranet or Trusted Sites zone. For more information on managing Internet Explorer's zone mappings, see Recipe 18.6, "Add a Site to an Internet Explorer Security Zone."

For more information about script signing in PowerShell, type **Get-Help about_ signing**. For more information about the Set-ExecutionPolicy cmdlet, type **Get-Help Set-ExecutionPolicy**.

See Also

- Recipe 16.4, "Manage PowerShell Security in an Enterprise"
- Recipe 18.6, "Add a Site to an Internet Explorer Security Zone"

16.2 Sign a PowerShell Script or Formatting File

Problem

You want to sign a PowerShell script so that it may be run on systems that have their execution policy set to require signed scripts.

Solution

To sign the script with your standard code-signing certificate, use the Set-AuthenticodeSignature cmdlet:

```
$cert = @(Get-ChildItem cert:\CurrentUser\My -CodeSigning)[0]
Set-AuthenticodeSignature file.ps1 $cert
```

Alternatively, you may also use other traditional applications (such as signtool.exe) to sign PowerShell *.ps1* and *.ps1xml* files.

Discussion

Signing a script or formatting file provides you and your customers with two primary benefits: publisher identification and file integrity. When you sign a script or formatting file, PowerShell appends your digital signature to the end of that file. This signature verifies that the file came from you and also ensures that nobody can tamper with the content in the file without detection. If you try to load a file that has been tampered with, PowerShell provides the following error message:

```
File C:\temp\test.ps1 cannot be loaded. The contents of file C:\temp\test.ps1
may have been tampered because the hash of the file does not match the hash
stored in the digital signature. The script will not execute on the system. Please
see "get-help about_signing" for more details..
At line:1 char:10
+ .\test.ps1 <<<<
```

When it comes to the signing of scripts and formatting files, PowerShell participates in the standard Windows Authenticode infrastructure. Because of that, techniques you may already know for signing files and working with their signatures continue to work with PowerShell scripts and formatting files. While the Set-AuthenticodeSignature cmdlet is primarily designed to support scripts and formatting files, it also supports DLLs and other standard Windows executable file types.

To sign a file, the Set-AuthenticodeSignature cmdlet requires that you provide it with a valid code-signing certificate. Most certification authorities provide Authenticode code-signing certificates for a fee. By using an Authenticode code-signing certificate from a reputable certification authority (such as VeriSign or Thawte), you can be sure that all users will be able to verify the signature on your script. Some online services offer extremely cheap code-signing certificates, but be aware that many machines may be unable to verify the digital signatures created by those certificates.

> You can still gain many of the benefits of code signing on your own computers by generating your own code-signing certificate. While other computers will not be able to recognize the signature, it still provides tamper-protection on your own computer. For more information about this approach, see the following section Recipe 16.3, "Program: Create a Self-Signed Certificate."

The –TimeStampServer parameter lets you sign your script or formatting file in a way that makes the signature on your script or formatting file valid even after your code-signing certificate expires.

For more information about the Set-AuthenticodeSignature cmdlet, type **Get-Help Set-AuthenticodeSignature**.

See Also

* Recipe 16.3, "Program: Create a Self-Signed Certificate"

16.3   Program: Create a Self-Signed Certificate

Discussion

It is possible to benefit from the tamper-protection features of signed scripts without having to pay for an official code-signing certificate. You do this by creating a *self-signed* certificate. Scripts signed with a self-signed certificate will not be recognized as valid on other computers, but still lets you sign scripts on your own computer.

When Example 16-1 runs, it prompts you for a password. Windows uses this password to prevent malicious programs from automatically signing files on your behalf.

Example 16-1. New-SelfSignedCertificate.ps1

```
##############################################################################
##
## New-SelfSignedCertificate.ps1
##
## Generate a new self-signed certificate. The certificate generated by these
## commands allow you to sign scripts on your own computer for protection
## from tampering. Files signed with this signature are not valid on other
## computers.
##
## ie:
##
##   PS >New-SelfSignedCertificate.ps1
##
##############################################################################

if(-not (Get-Command makecert.exe -ErrorAction SilentlyContinue))
{
    $errorMessage = "Could not find makecert.exe. " +
        "This tool is available as part of Visual Studio, or the Windows SDK."

    Write-Error $errorMessage
    return
}

$keyPath = Join-Path ([IO.Path]::GetTempPath()) "root.pvk"

## Generate the local certification authority
makecert -n "CN=PowerShell Local Certificate Root" -a sha1 `
    -eku 1.3.6.1.5.5.7.3.3 -r -sv $keyPath root.cer `
    -ss Root -sr localMachine

## Use the local certification authority to generate a self-signed
## certificate
makecert -pe -n "CN=PowerShell User" -ss MY -a sha1 `
    -eku 1.3.6.1.5.5.7.3.3 -iv $keyPath -ic root.cer

## Remove the private key from the filesystem.
Remove-Item $keyPath
```

Example 16-1. New-SelfSignedCertificate.ps1 (continued)

```
## Retrieve the certificate
Get-ChildItem cert:\currentuser\my -codesign |
    Where-Object { $_.Subject -match "PowerShell User" }
```

For more information about running scripts, see Recipe 1.1, "Run Programs, Scripts, and Existing Tools."

See Also

- Recipe 1.1, "Run Programs, Scripts, and Existing Tools"

16.4 Manage PowerShell Security in an Enterprise

Problem

You want to control PowerShell's security features in an enterprise setting.

Solution

To manage PowerShell's security features enterprisewide:

- Apply PowerShell's Group Policy templates to control PowerShell's execution policy through Group Policy.
- Deploy Microsoft Certificate Services to automatically generate Authenticode code-signing certificates for domain accounts.
- Apply software restriction policies to prevent PowerShell from trusting specific script publishers.

Discussion

Apply PowerShell's Group Policy templates

The administrative templates for Windows PowerShell let you override the machine's local execution policy preference at both the machine and per-user level. To obtain the PowerShell administrative templates, visit *http://www.microsoft.com/downloads* and search for "Administrative templates for Windows PowerShell."

> Although Group Policy settings override local preferences, Power-Shell's execution policy should not be considered a security measure that protects the system from the user. It is a security measure that helps prevent untrusted scripts from running on the system. As mentioned in the introduction, PowerShell is only a vehicle that allows users to do what they already have the Windows permissions to do.

Once you install the administrative templates for Windows PowerShell, launch the Group Policy Object Editor MMC snapin. Right-click Administrative Templates and then select Add/Remove Administrative Templates. You will find the administrative template in the installation location you chose when you installed the administrative templates for Windows PowerShell. Once added, the Group Policy Editor MMC snapin provides PowerShell as option under its Administrative Templates node, as shown in Figure 16-2.

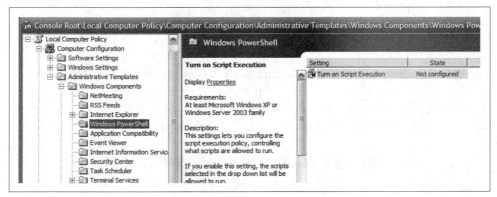

Figure 16-2. PowerShell Group Policy configuration

The default state is Not Configured. In this state, PowerShell takes its execution policy from the machine's local preference (as described in Recipe 16.1, "Enable Scripting Through an Execution Policy"). If you change the state to one of the Enabled options (or Disabled), PowerShell uses this configuration instead of the machine's local preference.

 PowerShell respects these Group Policy settings no matter what. This includes settings that the machine's administrator may consider to *reduce* security—such as an Unrestricted group policy overriding an AllSigned local preference.

Per-user Group Policy settings override the machine's local preference, while per-machine Group Policy settings override per-user settings.

Deploy Microsoft Certificate services

Although outside the scope of this book, Microsoft Certificate Services lets you automatically deploy code-signing certificates to any or all domain users. This provides a significant benefit, as it helps protect users from accidental or malicious script tampering.

For an introduction to this topic, visit *http://technet.microsoft.com* and search for "Enterprise Design for Certificate Services." For more information about script signing, see Recipe 16.2, "Sign a PowerShell Script or Formatting File."

Apply software restriction policies

While not common, you may sometimes want to prevent PowerShell from running scripts signed by specific publishers. If the script would normally be subject to signature verification (for example, it is a remote script, or PowerShell's execution policy is set to AllSigned), PowerShell lets you configure this through certificate rules in the computer's software restriction policies.

 PowerShell does not support software restriction policy path rules.

To configure these certificate rules, launch the Local Security Policy MMC snapin listed in the Administrative Tools group of the Start menu. Expand the Software Restriction Policies node, right-click Additional Rules, and then select New Certificate Rule, as shown in Figure 16-3.

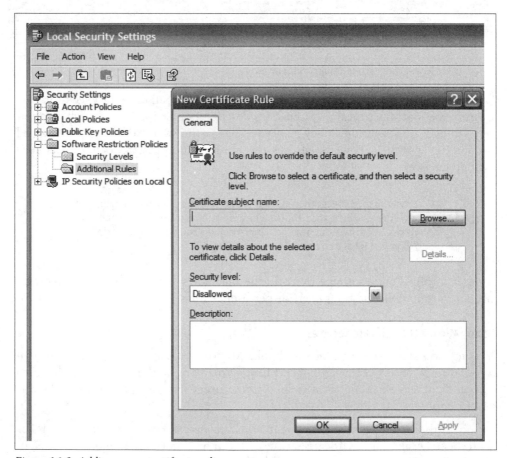

Figure 16-3. Adding a new certificate rule

Browse to the certificate that represents the publisher you want to block, and then click OK to block that publisher.

You can also create certificate policy that allows only certificates from a centrally administered whitelist. To do this, select either *Allow only all administrators to manage Trusted Publishers* or *Allow only enterprise administrators to manage Trusted Publishers* from the Trusted Publishers Management dialog.

See Also

- Recipe 16.1, "Enable Scripting Through an Execution Policy"
- Recipe 16.2, "Sign a PowerShell Script or Formatting File"

16.5 Verify the Digital Signature of a PowerShell Script

Problem

You want to verify the digital signature of a PowerShell script or formatting file.

Solution

To validate the signature of a script or formatting file, use the Get-AuthenticodeSignature cmdlet.

```
PS >Get-AuthenticodeSignature .\test.ps1


    Directory: C:\temp


SignerCertificate                          Status        Path
-----------------                          ------        ----
FD48FAA9281A657DBD089B5A008FAFE61D3B32FD   Valid         test.ps1
```

Discussion

The Get-AuthenticodeSignature cmdlet gets the Authenticode signature from a file. This can be a PowerShell script or formatting file, but the cmdlet also supports DLLs and other Windows standard executable file types.

By default, PowerShell displays the signature in a format that summarizes the certificate and its status. For more information about the signature, use the Format-List cmdlet, as shown in Example 16-2.

Example 16-2. PowerShell displaying detailed information about an Authenticode signature

```
PS >Get-AuthenticodeSignature .\test.ps1 | Format-List
```

```
SignerCertificate       : [Subject]
                            CN=PowerShell User

                          [Issuer]
                            CN=PowerShell Local Certificate Root

                          [Serial Number]
                            454D75B8A18FBDB445D8FCEC4942085C

                          [Not Before]
                            4/22/2007 12:32:37 AM

                          [Not After]
                            12/31/2039 3:59:59 PM

                          [Thumbprint]
                            FD48FAA9281A657DBD089B5A008FAFE61D3B32FD

TimeStamperCertificate :
Status                  : Valid
StatusMessage           : Signature verified.
Path                    : C:\temp\test.ps1
```

For more information about the Get-AuthenticodeSignature cmdlet, type **Get-Help
Get-AuthenticodeSignature**.

16.6   Securely Handle Sensitive Information

Problem

You want to request sensitive information from the user, but want to do this as
securely as possible.

Solution

To securely handle sensitive information, store it in a SecureString whenever possible. The Read-Host cmdlet (with the –AsSecureString parameter) lets you prompt the
user for (and handle) sensitive information by returning the user's response as a
SecureString:

```
PS >$secureInput = Read-Host -AsSecureString "Enter your private key"
Enter your private key: ******************
PS >$secureInput
System.Security.SecureString
```

Discussion

When you use any string in the .NET Framework (and therefore PowerShell), it retains that string so that it can efficiently reuse it later. Unlike most .NET data, unused strings persist even after you finish using them. When this data is in memory, there is always the chance that it could get captured in a crash dump, or swapped to disk in a paging operation. Because some data (such as passwords and other confidential information) may be sensitive, the .NET Framework includes the SecureString class—a container for text data that the framework encrypts when it stores it in memory. Code that needs to interact with the plain-text data inside a SecureString does so as securely as possible.

When a cmdlet author asks you for sensitive data (for example, an encryption key), the best practice is to designate that parameter as a SecureString to help keep your information confidential. You can provide the parameter with a SecureString variable as input, or the host prompts you for the SecureString if you do not provide one. PowerShell also supports two cmdlets (ConvertTo-SecureString and ConvertFrom-SecureString) that allow you to securely persist this data to disk. For more information about securely storing information on disk, see Recipe 16.9, "Securely Store Credentials on Disk."

 Credentials are a common source of sensitive information. See Recipe 16.7, "Securely Request Usernames and Passwords," for information on how to securely manage credentials in PowerShell.

By default, the SecureString cmdlets use Windows' *data protection API* when they convert your SecureString to and from its text representation. The key it uses to encrypt your data is based on your Windows logon credentials, so only you can decrypt the data that you've encrypted. If you want the exported data to work on another system or separate user account, you can use the cmdlet options that let you provide an explicit key. PowerShell treats this sensitive data as an opaque blob—and so should you.

However, there are many instances when you may want to automatically provide the SecureString input to a cmdlet rather than have the host prompt you for it. In these situations, the ideal solution is to use the ConvertTo-SecureString cmdlet to import a previously exported SecureString from disk. This retains the confidentiality of your data and still lets you automate the input.

If the data is highly dynamic (for example, coming from a CSV), then the ConvertTo-SecureString cmdlet supports an –AsPlainText parameter:

```
$secureString = ConvertTo-SecureString "Kinda Secret" -AsPlainText –Force
```

Since you've already provided plain-text input in this case, placing this data in a SecureString no longer provides a security benefit. To prevent a false sense of security, the cmdlet requires the -Force parameter to convert plain-text data into a SecureString.

Once you have data in a SecureString, you may want to access its plain-text representation. PowerShell doest't provide a direct way to do this, as that defeats the purpose of a SecureString. If you still want to convert a SecureString to plain text, you have two options:

1. Use the GetNetworkCredential() method of the PsCredential class

```
$secureString = Read-Host -AsSecureString
$temporaryCredential = New-Object `
    System.Management.Automation.PsCredential "TempUser",$secureString
$unsecureString = $temporaryCredential.GetNetworkCredential().Password
```

2. Use the .NET Framework's Marshal class

```
$secureString = Read-Host -AsSecureString
$unsecureString = [Runtime.InteropServices.Marshal]::PtrToStringAuto(
    [Runtime.InteropServices.Marshal]::SecureStringToBSTR($secureString))
```

See Also

- Recipe 16.7, "Securely Request Usernames and Passwords"
- Recipe 16.9, "Securely Store Credentials on Disk"

16.7 Securely Request Usernames and Passwords

Problem

Your script requires that users provide it with a username and password, but you want to do this as securely as possible.

Solution

To request a credential from the user, use the Get-Credential cmdlet:

```
$credential = Get-Credential
```

Discussion

The Get-Credential cmdlet reads credentials from the user as securely as possible and ensures that the user's password remains highly protected the entire time. For an example of using the Get-Credential cmdlet effectively in a script, see the following section, Recipe 16.8, "Program: Start a Process As Another User."

Once you have the username and password, you can pass that information around to any other command that accepts a PowerShell credential object without worrying about disclosing sensitive information. If a command doesn't accept a PowerShell credential object (but does support a SecureString for its sensitive information), the resulting PsCredential object provides a Username property that returns the username in the credential and a Password property that returns a SecureString containing the user's password.

Unfortunately, not everything that requires credentials can accept either a Power-Shell credential or SecureString. If you need to provide a credential to one of these commands or API calls, the PsCredential object provides a GetNetworkCredential() method to convert the PowerShell credential to a less secure NetworkCredential object. Once you've converted the credential to a NetworkCredential, the UserName and Password properties provide unencrypted access to the username and password from the original credential. Many network-related classes in the .NET Framework support the NetworkCredential class directly.

 The NetworkCredential class is less secure than the PsCredential class because it stores the user's password in plain text. For more information about the security implications of storing sensitive information in plain text, see Recipe 16.6, "Securely Handle Sensitive Information."

If a frequently run script requires credentials, you might consider caching those credentials in memory to improve the usability of that script. For example, in the region of the script that calls the Get-Credential cmdlet, you can instead use the techniques shown by Example 16-3.

Example 16-3. Caching credentials in memory to improve usability

```
$credential = $null
if(Test-Path Variable:\Lee.Holmes.CommonScript.CachedCredential)
{
    $credential = ${GLOBAL:Lee.Holmes.CommonScript.CachedCredential}
}

${GLOBAL:Lee.Holmes.CommonScript.CachedCredential} =
   Get-Credential $credential

$credential = ${GLOBAL:Lee.Holmes.CommonScript.CachedCredential}
```

The script prompts the user for their credentials the first time they call it but uses the cached credentials for subsequent calls.

For more information about the Get-Credential cmdlet, type **Get-Help Get-Credential**.

See Also

- Recipe 16.6, "Securely Handle Sensitive Information"
- Recipe 16.8, "Program: Start a Process As Another User"

16.8   Program: Start a Process As Another User

Discussion

If your script requires user credentials, you will want to store those credentials in a PowerShell PsCredential object. This lets you securely store those credentials, or pass them to other commands that accept PowerShell credentials. When you write a script that accepts credentials, consider letting the user to supply either a username or a preexisting credential. Example 16-4 demonstrates a useful approach that allows that. As the framework for this demonstration, the script lets you start a process as another user.

Example 16-4. Start-ProcessAsUser.ps1

```
##############################################################################
##
## Start-ProcessAsUser.ps1
##
## Launch a process under alternate credentials, providing functionality
## similar to runas.exe.
##
## ie:
##
##  PS >$file = Join-Path ([Environment]::GetFolderPath("System")) certmgr.msc
##  PS >Start-ProcessAsUser Administrator mmc $file
##
##
##
##############################################################################

param(
  $credential = (Get-Credential),
  [string] $process = $(throw "Please specify a process to start."),
  [string] $arguments = ""
  )

## Create a real credential if they supplied a username
if($credential -is "String")
{
    $credential = Get-Credential $credential
}

## Exit if they canceled out of the credential dialog
if(-not ($credential -is "System.Management.Automation.PsCredential"))
{
    return
}

## Prepare the startup information (including username and password)
$startInfo = New-Object Diagnostics.ProcessStartInfo
$startInfo.Filename = $process
```

Example 16-4. Start-ProcessAsUser.ps1 (continued)

```
$startInfo.Arguments = $arguments

## If we're launching as ourselves, set the "runas" verb
if(($credential.Username -eq "$ENV:Username") -or
   ($credential.Username -eq "\$ENV:Username"))
{
    $startInfo.Verb = "runas"
}
else
{
    $startInfo.UserName = $credential.Username
    $startInfo.Password = $credential.Password
    $startInfo.UseShellExecute = $false
}

## Start the process
[Diagnostics.Process]::Start($startInfo)
```

For more information about running scripts, see Recipe 1.1, "Run Programs, Scripts, and Existing Tools."

See Also

- Recipe 1.1, "Run Programs, Scripts, and Existing Tools"

16.9   Securely Store Credentials on Disk

Problem

Your script performs an operation that requires credentials, but you don't want it to require user interaction when it runs.

Solution

To securely store the credential's password to disk so that your script can load it automatically, use the ConvertFrom-SecureString and ConvertTo-SecureString cmdlets.

Save the credential's password to disk

The first step for storing a password on disk is usually a manual one. Given a credential that you've stored in the $credential variable, you can safely export its password to *password.txt* using the following command:

```
PS >$credential.Password | ConvertFrom-SecureString |
    Set-Content c:\temp\password.txt
```

Recreate the credential from the password stored on disk

In the script that you want to run automatically, add the following commands:

```
$password = Get-Content c:\temp\password.txt | ConvertTo-SecureString
$credential = New-Object System.Management.Automation.PsCredential `
    "CachedUser",$password
```

These commands create a new credential object (for the *CachedUser* user) and store that object in the $credential variable.

Discussion

When reading the solution, you might at first be wary of storing a password on disk. While it is natural (and prudent) to be cautious of littering your hard drive with sensitive information, the ConvertFrom-SecureString cmdlet encrypts this data using Windows' standard *Data Protection API*. This ensures that only your user account can properly decrypt its contents.

While keeping a password secure is an important security feature, you may sometimes want to store a password (or other sensitive information) on disk so that other accounts have access to it anyway. This is often the case with scripts run by service accounts or scripts designed to be transferred between computers. The ConvertFrom-SecureString and ConvertTo-SecureString cmdlets support this by letting you to specify an encryption key.

 When used with a hardcoded encryption key, this technique no longer acts as a security measure. If a user can access to the content of your automated script, they have access to the encryption key. If the user has access to the encryption key, they have access to the data you were trying to protect.

Although the solution stores the password in a specific named file, it is more common to store the file in a more generic location—such as the directory that contains the script, or the directory that contains your profile.

To load *password.txt* from the same location as your profile, use the following command:

```
$passwordFile = Join-Path (Split-Path $profile) password.txt
$password = Get-Content $passwordFile | ConvertTo-SecureString
```

To learn how to load it from the same location as your script, see Recipe 14.5, "Find Your Script's Location."

For more information about the ConvertTo-SecureString and ConvertFrom-SecureString cmdlets, type **Get-Help ConvertTo-SecureString** or **Get-Help ConvertFrom-SecureString**.

See Also

- Recipe 14.5, "Find Your Script's Location"

16.10 Access User and Machine Certificates

Problem

You want to retrieve information about certificates for the current user or local machine.

Solution

To browse and retrieve certificates on the local machine, use PowerShell's certificate drive. This drive is created by the certificate provider, as shown in Example 16-5.

Example 16-5. Exploring certificates in the certificate provider

```
PS >Set-Location cert:\CurrentUser\
PS >$cert = Get-ChildItem -Rec -CodeSign
PS >$cert | Format-List


Subject      : CN=PowerShell User
Issuer       : CN=PowerShell Local Certificate Root
Thumbprint   : FD48FAA9281A657DBD089B5A008FAFE61D3B32FD
FriendlyName :
NotBefore    : 4/22/2007 12:32:37 AM
NotAfter     : 12/31/2039 3:59:59 PM
Extensions   : {System.Security.Cryptography.Oid, System.Security.Cryptogr
               aphy.Oid}
```

Discussion

The certificate drive provides a useful way to navigate and view certificates for the current user or local machine. For example, if your execution policy requires the use of digital signatures, the following command tells you which publishers are trusted to run scripts on your system:

```
Get-ChildItem cert:\CurrentUser\TrustedPublisher
```

The certificate provider is probably most commonly used to select a code-signing certificate for the Set-AuthenticodeSignature cmdlet. The following command selects the "best" code signing certificate—that being the one that expires last:

```
$certificates = Get-ChildItem Cert:\CurrentUser\My -CodeSign
$signingCert = @($certificates | Sort -Desc NotAfter)[0]
```

In this -CodeSign parameter lets you search for certificates in the certificate store that support code signing. To search for certificates used for other purposes, see Recipe 16.11, "Program: Search the Certificate Store."

Although the certificate provider is useful for browsing and retrieving information from the computer's certificate stores, it does not lets you add or remove items from these locations. If you want to manage certificates in the certificate store, the System.Security.Cryptography.X509Certificates.X509Store class (and other related classes from the System.Security.Cryptography.X509Certificates namespace) from the .NET Framework support that functionality.

For more information about the certificate provider, type **Get-Help Certificate**.

For more information about working with classes from the .NET Framework, see Recipe 3.4, "Work with .NET Objects."

See Also

- Recipe 3.4, "Work with .NET Objects"
- Recipe 16.11, "Program: Search the Certificate Store"

16.11   Program: Search the Certificate Store

Discussion

One useful feature of the certificate provider is that it provides a –CodeSign parameter that lets you search for certificates in the certificate store that support code signing. Code signing certificates are not the only kind of certificates, however; other frequently used certificate types are Encrypting File System, Client Authentication, and more.

Example 16-6 lets you search the certificate provider for certificates that support a given Enhanced Key Usage (EKU).

Example 16-6. Search-CertificateStore.ps1

```
##############################################################################
##
## Search-CertificateStore.ps1
##
## Search the certificate provider for certificates that match the specified
## Enhanced Key Usage (EKU.)
##
## ie:
##
##   PS >Search-CertificateStore "Encrypting File System"
##
##############################################################################

param(
  $ekuName = $(throw "Please specify the friendly name of an " +
                     "Enhanced Key Usage (such as 'Code Signing'")
  )
```

Example 16-6. Search-CertificateStore.ps1 (continued)

```
## Go through every certificate in the current user's "My" store
foreach($cert in Get-ChildItem cert:\CurrentUser\My)
{
    ## For each of those, go through its extensions
    foreach($extension in $cert.Extensions)
    {
        ## For each extension, go through its Enhanced Key Usages
        foreach($certEku in $extension.EnhancedKeyUsages)
        {
            ## If the friendly name matches, output that certificate
            if($certEku.FriendlyName -eq $ekuName)
            {
                $cert
            }
        }
    }
}
```

For more information about running scripts, see Recipe 1.1, "Run Programs, Scripts, and Existing Tools."

See Also

* Recipe 1.1, "Run Programs, Scripts, and Existing Tools"

Administrator Tasks

## CHAPTER 17

Files and Directories

17.0 Introduction

One of the most common tasks when administering a system is working with its files and directories. This is true when you administer the computer at the command line, and it is true when you write scripts to administer it automatically.

Fortunately, PowerShell makes scripting files and directories as easy as working at the command line—a point that many seasoned programmers and scripters often miss. A perfect example of this comes when you wrestle with limited disk space and need to find the files taking up the most space.

A typical programmer might approach this task by writing functions to scan a specific directory of a system. For each file, they check whether the file is big enough to care about. If so, they add it to a list. For each directory in the original directory, the programmer repeats this process (until there are no more directories to process).

As the saying goes, though, "you can write C in any programming language." The habits and preconceptions you bring to a language often directly influence how open you are to advances in that language.

Being an administrative shell, PowerShell directly supports tasks such as visiting all the files in a subdirectory or moving a file from one directory to another. That complicated programmer-oriented script turns into a one-liner:

```
Get-ChildItem -Recurse | Sort-Object -Descending Length | Select -First 10
```

Before diving into your favorite programmer's toolkit, check to see what PowerShell supports in that area. In many cases, it can handle it without requiring your programmer's bag of tricks.

17.1 Find All Files Modified Before a Certain Date

Problem

You want to find all files last modified before a certain date.

Solution

To find all files modified before a certain date, use the Get-ChildItem cmdlet to list the files in a directory, and then use the Where-Object cmdlet to compare the LastWriteTime property to the date you are interested in. For example, to find all files created before this year:

```
Get-ChildItem -Recurse | Where-Object { $_.LastWriteTime -lt "01/01/2007" }
```

Discussion

A common reason to compare files against a certain date is to find recently modified (or not recently modified) files. This looks almost the same as the example given by the solution, but your script can't know the exact date to compare against.

In this case, the AddDays() method in the .NET Framework's DateTime class gives you a way to perform some simple calendar arithmetic. If you have a DateTime object, you can add or subtract time from it to represent a different date altogether. For example, to find all files modified in the last 30 days:

```
$compareDate = (Get-Date).AddDays(-30)
Get-ChildItem -Recurse | Where-Object { $_.LastWriteTime -ge $compareDate }
```

Similarly, to find all files more than 30 days old:

```
$compareDate = (Get-Date).AddDays(-30)
Get-ChildItem -Recurse | Where-Object { $_.LastWriteTime -lt $compareDate }
```

In this example, the Get-Date cmdlet returns an object that represents the current date and time. You call the AddDays() method to subtract 30 days from that time, which stores the date representing "30 days ago" in the $compareDate variable. Next, you compare that date against the LastWriteTime property of each file that the Get-ChildItem cmdlet returns.

The DateTime class is the administrator's favorite calendar!

```
PS >[DateTime]::IsLeapYear(2008)
True
PS >$daysTillSummer = [DateTime] "06/21/2008" - (Get-Date)
PS >$daysTillSummer.Days
283
```

For more information about the Get-ChildItem cmdlet, type **Get-Help Get-ChildItem**. For more information about the Where-Object cmdlet, see Recipe 2.1, "Filter Items in a List or Command Output."

See Also

- Recipe 2.1, "Filter Items in a List or Command Output"

17.2   Clear or Remove a File

Problem

You want to clear the content of a file, or remove that file altogether.

Solution

To clear the content from a file, use the Clear-Content cmdlet. Use the Remove-Item cmdlet to remove that file altogether, as shown by Example 17-1.

Example 17-1. Clearing content from and removing a file

```
PS >Get-Content test.txt
Hello World
PS >Clear-Content test.txt
PS >Get-Content test.txt
PS >Get-Item test.txt


    Directory: Microsoft.PowerShell.Core\FileSystem::C:\temp


Mode                LastWriteTime     Length Name
----                -------------     ------ ----
-a---         4/23/2007   8:05 PM          0 test.txt


PS >Remove-Item test.txt
PS >Get-Item test.txt
Get-Item : Cannot find path 'C:\temp\test.txt' because it does not exist.
At line:1 char:9
+ Get-Item  <<<< test.txt
```

Discussion

The (aptly named) Clear-Content and Remove-Item cmdlets clear the content from an item and remove an item, respectively. Although the solution demonstrates this only for files in the filesystem, they in fact apply to any PowerShell providers that support the concepts of "content" and "items." Examples of other drives that support these content and item concepts are the Function:, Alias:, and Variable:. The HKLM:,

HKCU:, and Env: drives do not support the concept of content, but do let you remove items with the Remove-Item cmdlet.

The Remove-Item cmdlet has a handful of standard aliases: ri, rm, rmdir, del, erase, and rd.

For more information about the Remove-Item or Clear-Content cmdlets, type **Get-Help Remove-Item** or **Get-Help Clear-Content**.

17.3   Manage and Change the Attributes of a File

Problem

You want to update the ReadOnly, Hidden, or System attributes of a file.

Solution

Most of the time, you will want to use the familiar *attrib.exe* program to change the attributes of a file:

```
attrib +r test.txt
attrib -s test.txt
```

To set only the ReadOnly attribute, you can optionally set the IsReadOnly property on the file:

```
$file = Get-Item test.txt
$file.IsReadOnly = $true
```

To apply a specific set of attributes, use the Attributes property on the file:

```
$file = Get-Item test.txt
$file.Attributes = "ReadOnlyNotContentIndexed"
```

Directory listings show the attributes on a file, but you can also access the Mode or Attributes property directly:

```
PS >$file.Attributes = "ReadOnly","System","NotContentIndexed"
PS >$file.Mode
--r-s
PS >$file.Attributes
ReadOnly, System, NotContentIndexed
```

Discussion

When the Get-Item or Get-ChildItem cmdlets retrieve a file, the resulting file has an Attributes property. This property doesn't offer much in addition to the regular *attrib.exe* program, although it does make it easier to set the attributes to a specific state.

Be aware that setting the Hidden attribute on a file removes it from most default views. If you want to retrieve it after hiding it, most commands require a -Force parameter. Similarly, setting the ReadOnly attribute on a file causes most write operations on that file to fail unless you call that command with the -Force parameter.

If you want to add an attribute to a file using the Attributes property (rather than *attrib.exe* for some reason), this is how you would do that:

```
$file = Get-Item test.txt
$readOnly = [IO.FileAttributes] "ReadOnly"
$file.Attributes = $file.Attributes -bor $readOnly
```

For more information about working with classes from the .NET Framework, see Recipe 3.4, "Work with .NET Objects."

See Also

- Recipe 3.4, "Work with .NET Objects"

17.4   Get the Files in a Directory

Problem

You want to get or list the files in a directory.

Solution

To retrieve the list of files in a directory, use the Get-ChildItem cmdlet. To get a specific item, use the Get-Item cmdlet:

- To list all items in the current directory, use the Get-ChildItem cmdlet:

  ```
  Get-ChildItem
  ```

- To list all items that match a wildcard, supply a wildcard to the Get-ChildItem cmdlet:

  ```
  Get-ChildItem *.txt
  ```

- To list all files that match a wildcard in the current directory (and all its children), use the -Include and -Recurse parameters of the Get-ChildItem cmdlet:

  ```
  Get-ChildItem -Include *.txt -Recurse
  ```

- To list all directories in the current directory, use the Where-Object cmdlet to test the PsIsContainer property:

  ```
  Get-ChildItem | Where { $_.PsIsContainer }
  ```

- To get information about a specific item, use the Get-Item cmdlet:

  ```
  Get-Item test.txt
  ```

Discussion

Although most commonly used on the filesystem, the Get-ChildItem and Get-Item cmdlets in fact work against any items in any of the PowerShell drives. In addition to A: through Z: (the standard file system drives), they also work on Alias:, Cert:, Env:, Function:, HKLM:, HKCU:, and Variable:.

 One example lists files that match a wildcard in a directory and all its children. That example works on any PowerShell provider. However, PowerShell can retrieve your results more quickly if you use a provider-specific filter, as described in the following section, Recipe 17.5, "Find Files That Match a Pattern."

The solution demonstrates some simple wildcard scenarios that the Get-ChildItem cmdlet supports, but PowerShell in fact enables several more advanced scenarios. For more information about these scenarios, see the following section, Recipe 17.5, "Find Files That Match a Pattern."

In the filesystem, these cmdlets return objects from the .NET Framework that represent files and directories—instances of the System.IO.FileInfo and System.IO.DirectoryInfo classes, respectively. Each provides a great deal of useful information: attributes, modification times, full name, and more. Although the default directory listing exposes a lot of information, PowerShell provides even more. For more information about working with classes from the .NET Framework, see Recipe 3.4, "Work with .NET Objects."

See Also

- Recipe 3.4, "Work with .NET Objects"
- Recipe 17.5, "Find Files That Match a Pattern"

17.5   Find Files That Match a Pattern

Problem

You want to get a list of files that match a specific pattern.

Solution

Use the Get-ChildItem cmdlet for both simple and advanced wildcard support:

- To find all items in the current directory that match a PowerShell wildcard, supply that wildcard to the Get-ChildItem cmdlet:

  ```
  Get-ChildItem *.txt
  ```

- To find all items in the current directory that match a *provider-specific* filter, supply that filter to the –Filter parameter:

  ```
  Get-ChildItem -Filter *~2*
  ```
- To find all items in the current directory that do not match a PowerShell wildcard, supply that wildcard to the –Exclude parameter:

  ```
  Get-ChildItem -Exclude *.txt
  ```
- To find all items in subdirectories that match a PowerShell wildcard, use the –Include and –Recurse parameters:

  ```
  Get-ChildItem -Include *.txt -Recurse
  ```
- To find all items in subdirectories that match a *provider-specific* filter, use the –Filter and –Recurse parameters:

  ```
  Get-ChildItem -Filter *.txt -Recurse
  ```
- To find all items in subdirectories that do not match a PowerShell wildcard, use the –Exclude and –Recurse parameters:

  ```
  Get-ChildItem -Exclude *.txt -Recurse
  ```

Use the Where-Object cmdlet for advanced regular expression support:

- To find all items with a filename that matches a regular expression, use the Where-Object cmdlet to compare the Name property to the regular expression:

  ```
  Get-ChildItem | Where-Object { $_.Name -match '^KB[0-9]+\.log$' }
  ```
- To find all items with a directory name that matches a regular expression, use the Where-Object cmdlet to compare the DirectoryName property to the regular expression:

  ```
  Get-ChildItem -Recurse | Where-Object { $_.DirectoryName -match 'Release' }
  ```
- To find all items with a directory name or filename that matches a regular expression, use the Where-Object cmdlet to compare the FullName property to the regular expression:

  ```
  Get-ChildItem -Recurse | Where-Object { $_.FullName -match 'temp' }
  ```

Discussion

The Get-ChildItem cmdlet supports wildcarding through three parameters:

Path

> The -Path parameter is the first (and default) parameter. While you can enter simple paths such as ., C:\ or D:\Documents, you can also supply paths that include wildcards—such as *, *.txt, [a-z]???.log, or even C:\win**.N[a-f]?\ F*\v2*\csc.exe.

Include/Exclude

> The –Include and –Exclude parameters act as a filter on wildcarding that happens on the -Path parameter. If you specify the –Recurse parameter, the –Include and –Exclude wildcards apply to all items returned.

The most common mistake with the -Include parameter comes when you use it against a path with no wildcards. For example, this doesn't seem to produce the expected results:

```
Get-ChildItem $env:WINDIR -Include *.log
```

That command produces no results, as you have not supplied an item wildcard to the path. Instead, the correct command is:

```
Get-ChildItem $env:WINDIR\* -Include *.log
```

Filter

The -Filter parameter lets you filter results based on the *provider-specific* filtering language of the provider from which you retrieve items. Since Power-Shell's wildcarding support closely mimics filesystem wildcards, and most people use the -Filter parameter only on the filesystem, this seems like a redundant (and equivalent) parameter. A SQL provider, however, would use SQL syntax in its -Filter parameter. Likewise, an Active Directory provider would use LDAP paths in its -Filter parameter.

Although it may not be obvious, the filesystem provider's filtering language is not exactly the same as the PowerShell wildcard syntax. For example, the -Filter parameter matches against the short filenames, too:

```
PS >Get-ChildItem | Select-Object Name

Name
----
A Long File Name With Spaces Also.txt
A Long File Name With Spaces.txt


PS >Get-ChildItem *1* | Select-Object Name
PS >Get-ChildItem -Filter *1* | Select-Object Name

Name
----
A Long File Name With Spaces.txt
```

On the other hand, PowerShell's wildcard syntax supports far more than the filesystem's native filtering language. For more information about the PowerShell's wildcard syntax, type **Get-Help About_WildCard**.

When you want to perform filtering even more advanced than what PowerShell's wildcarding syntax offers, the Where-Object cmdlet provides infinite possibilities. For example, to exclude certain directories from a search:

```
Get-ChildItem -Rec | Where-Object { $_.DirectoryName -notmatch "Debug" }
```

or, to list all directories:

```
Get-ChildItem | Where-Object { $_.PsIsContainer }
```

Since the syntax of the `Where-Object` cmdlet can sometimes be burdensome for simple queries, the `Compare-Property` script provided in Recipe 2.2, "Program: Simplify Most Where-Object Filters" provides an attractive alternative:

```
Get-ChildItem -Rec | Compare-Property DirectoryName notmatch Debug
```

For a filter that is difficult (or impossible) to specify programmatically, the `Select-FilteredObject` script provided by Recipe 2.3, "Program: Interactively Filter Lists of Objects" lets you interactively filter the output.

Because of PowerShell's pipeline model, an advanced file set generated by `Get-ChildItem` automatically turns into an advanced file set for other cmdlets to operate on:

```
PS >Get-ChildItem -Rec | Where-Object { $_.Length -gt 20mb } |
>> Sort-Object -Descending Length | Select-FilteredObject |
>> Remove-Item -WhatIf
>>
What if: Performing operation "Remove File" on Target "C:\temp\backup092300
.zip".
What if: Performing operation "Remove File" on Target "C:\temp\sp-tricking_
iT2.zip".
What if: Performing operation "Remove File" on Target "C:\temp\slime.mov".
What if: Performing operation "Remove File" on Target "C:\temp\hello-world.
mov".
```

For more information about the `Get-ChildItem` cmdlet, type **Get-Help Get-ChildItem**.

For more information about the `Where-Object` cmdlet, type **Get-Help Where-Object**.

See Also

- Recipe 2.2, "Program: Simplify Most Where-Object Filters"
- Recipe 2.3, "Program: Interactively Filter Lists of Objects"

17.6 Manage Files That Include Special Characters

Problem

You want to use a cmdlet that supports wildcarding but provide a filename that includes wildcard characters.

Solution

To prevent PowerShell from treating those characters as wildcard characters, use the cmdlet's –LiteralPath (or similarly named) parameter if it defines one:

```
Get-ChildItem -LiteralPath '[My File].txt'
```

Discussion

One consequence of PowerShell's advanced wildcard support is that the square brackets used to specify character ranges sometimes conflict with actual filenames. Consider the following example:

```
PS >Get-ChildItem | Select-Object Name

Name
----
[My File].txt


PS >Get-ChildItem '[My File].txt' | Select-Object Name
PS >Get-ChildItem -LiteralPath '[My File].txt' | Select-Object Name

Name
----
[My File].txt
```

The first command clearly demonstrates that we have a file called *[My File].txt*. When we try to retrieve it (passing its name to the Get-ChildItem cmdlet), we see no results. Since square brackets are wildcard characters in PowerShell (like * and ?), the text we provided turns into a search expression rather than a filename.

The –LiteralPath parameter (or a similarly named parameter in other cmdlets) tells PowerShell that the filename is named exactly—not a wildcard search term.

In addition to wildcard matching, filenames may sometimes run afoul of another topic—PowerShell escape sequences. For example, the back-tick character (`) in PowerShell means the start of an escape sequence, such as `t (tab), `n (newline), or `a (alarm). To prevent PowerShell from interpreting a back-tick as an escape sequence, surround that string in single quotes instead of double quotes.

For more information about the Get-ChildItem cmdlet, type **Get-Help Get-ChildItem**.

For more information about PowerShell's special characters, type **Get-Help About_ Special_Characters**.

17.7 Program: Get Disk Usage Information

Discussion

When disk space starts running low, you'll naturally want to find out where to focus your cleanup efforts. Sometimes, you may tackle this by looking for large directories (including the directories in them), but other times, you may solve this by looking for directories that are large simply from the files they contain.

Example 17-2 collects both types of data. It also demonstrates an effective use of *calculated properties*. Like the Add-Member cmdlet, calculated properties let you add properties to output objects by specifying the expression that generates their data.

For more information about the calculated properties and the Add-Member cmdlet, see Recipe 3.11, "Add Custom Methods and Properties to Objects."

Example 17-2. Get-DiskUsage.ps1

```
##############################################################################
##
## Get-DiskUsage.ps1
##
## Retrieve information about disk usage in the current directory and all
## subdirectories. If you specify the -IncludeSubdirectories flag, this
## script accounts for the size of subdirectories in the size of a directory.
##
## ie:
##
##   PS >Get-DiskUsage
##   PS >Get-DiskUsage -IncludeSubdirectories
##
##############################################################################

param(
  [switch] $includeSubdirectories
  )

## If they specify the -IncludeSubdirectories flag, then we want to account
## for all subdirectories in the size of each directory
if($includeSubdirectories)
{
    Get-ChildItem | Where-Object { $_.PsIsContainer } |
        Select-Object Name,
            @{ Name="Size";
            Expression={ ($_ | Get-ChildItem -Recurse |
                Measure-Object -Sum Length).Sum + 0 } }
}
## Otherwise, we just find all directories below the current directory,
## and determine their size
else
{
    Get-ChildItem -Recurse | Where-Object { $_.PsIsContainer } |
        Select-Object FullName,
            @{ Name="Size";
            Expression={ ($_ | Get-ChildItem |
                Measure-Object -Sum Length).Sum + 0 } }
}
```

For more information about running scripts, see Recipe 1.1, "Run Programs, Scripts, and Existing Tools."

See Also

- Recipe 1.1, "Run Programs, Scripts, and Existing Tools"
- Recipe 3.11, "Add Custom Methods and Properties to Objects"

17.8   Determine the Current Location

Problem

You want to determine the current location from a script or command.

Solution

To retrieve the current location, use the `Get-Location` cmdlet. The `Get-Location` cmdlet provides the `Drive` and `Path` as two common properties:

```
$currentLocation = (Get-Location).Path
```

As a short-form for `(Get-Location).Path`, use the `$pwd` automatic variable.

Discussion

The `Get-Location` cmdlet returns information about the current location. From the information it returns, you can access the current drive, provider, and path.

This current location affects PowerShell commands and programs that you launch from PowerShell. It does not apply when you interact with the .NET Framework, however. If you need to call a .NET method that interacts with the filesystem, always be sure to provide fully qualified paths:

```
[System.Reflection.Assembly]::LoadFile("d:\documents\path_to_library.dll")
```

If you are sure that the file exists, the `Resolve-Path` cmdlet lets you translate a relative path to an absolute path:

```
$filePath = (Resolve-Path library.dll).Path
```

If the file does not exist, use the `Join-Path` cmdlet in combination with the `Get-Location` cmdlet to specify the file:

```
$filePath = Join-Path (Get-Location) library.dll
```

Another alternative that combines the functionality of both approaches is a bit more advanced but also lets you specify relative locations. It comes from methods in the PowerShell `$executionContext` variable, which provides functionality normally used by cmdlet and provider authors:

```
$executionContext.SessionState.Path.`
    GetUnresolvedProviderPathFromPSPath("..\library.dll")
```

For more information about the `Get-Location` cmdlet, type **Get-Help Get-Location**.

17.9 Monitor a File for Changes

Problem

You want to monitor the end of a file for new content.

Solution

To monitor the end of a file for new content, use the -Wait parameter of the Get-Content cmdlet.

```
Get-Content log.txt -Wait
```

Discussion

The -Wait parameter on the Get-Content cmdlet acts much like the traditional Unix tail command with the -follow parameter. If you provide the -Wait parameter, the Get-Content cmdlet reads the content of the file but doesn't exit. When a program appends new content to the end of the file, the Get-Content cmdlet returns that content and continues to wait.

> Unlike the Unix tail command, the Get-Content cmdlet does not support a feature to let you start reading from the end of a file. If you need to monitor the end of an extremely large file, a specialized file monitoring utility is a valid option.

For more information about the Get-Content cmdlet, type **Get-Help Get-Content**. For more information about the -Wait parameter, type **Get-Help FileSystem**.

17.10 Program: Get the MD5 or SHA1 Hash of a File

Discussion

File hashes provide a useful way to check for damage or modification to a file. A digital hash acts like the fingerprint of a file and detects even minor modifications. If the content of a file changes, then so does its hash. Many online download services provide the hash of a file on that file's download page so that you can determine whether the transfer somehow corrupts the file (see Figure 17-1).

↑ Top of page
_____

Additional Information
To verify that your download of the ISO file for the Windows SDK is not corrupt, here is some verification information:
AutoCRC: 0x3DFD5327
Size: 1.15 GB (1,245,220,864 bytes)
MD5 hash: c2ee660c326940d4ea78e7b6e48afb98
SHA-1 hash: 573f966ed120aeda74755283fb6112f1094327dc

Figure 17-1. File hashes as a verification mechanism

There are three common ways to generate the hash of a file: MD5, SHA1, SHA256. The two most common are MD5, followed by SHA1. While popular, these hash types can be trusted to detect only accidental file modification. They can be fooled if somebody wants to tamper with the file without changing its hash. The SHA256 algorithm can be used to protect against even intentional file tampering.

Example 17-3 lets you determine the hash of a file (or of multiple files if provided by the pipeline).

Example 17-3. Get-FileHash.ps1

```
##############################################################################
##
## Get-FileHash.ps1
##
## Get the hash of an input file.
##
## ie:
##
##   PS >Get-FileHash myFile.txt
##   PS >dir | Get-FileHash
##   PS >Get-FileHash myFile.txt -Hash SHA1
##
##############################################################################

param(
  $path,
  $hashAlgorithm = "MD5"
  )

## Create the hash object that calculates the hash of our file. If they
## provide an invalid hash algorithm, provide an error message.
if($hashAlgorithm -eq "MD5")
{
    $hasher = [System.Security.Cryptography.MD5]::Create()
}
elseif($hashAlgorithm -eq "SHA1")
{
    $hasher = [System.Security.Cryptography.SHA1]::Create()
}
elseif($hashAlgorithm -eq "SHA256")
{
    $hasher = [System.Security.Cryptography.SHA256]::Create()
}
else
{
    $errorMessage = "Hash algorithm $hashAlgorithm is not valid. Valid " +
        "algorithms are MD5, SHA1, and SHA256."
    Write-Error $errorMessage
    return
}
```

Example 17-3. Get-FileHash.ps1 (continued)

```
## Create an array to hold the list of files
$files = @()

## If they specified the file name as a parameter, add that to the list
## of files to process
if($path)
{
    $files += $path
}
## Otherwise, take the files that they piped in to the script.
## For each input file, put its full name into the file list
else
{
    $files += @($input | Foreach-Object { $_.FullName })
}

## Go through each of the items in the list of input files
foreach($file in $files)
{
    ## Convert it to a fully-qualified path
    $filename = (Resolve-Path $file -ErrorAction SilentlyContinue).Path

    ## If the path does not exist (or is not a file,) just continue
    if((-not $filename) -or (-not (Test-Path $filename -Type Leaf)))
    {
        continue
    }

    ## Use the ComputeHash method from the hash object to calculate
    ## the hash
    $inputStream = New-Object IO.StreamReader $filename
    $hashBytes = $hasher.ComputeHash($inputStream.BaseStream)
    $inputStream.Close()

    ## Convert the result to hexadecimal
    $builder = New-Object System.Text.StringBuilder
    $hashBytes | Foreach-Object { [void] $builder.Append($_.ToString("X2")) }

    ## Return a custom object with the important details from the
    ## hashing
    $output - New-Object PsObject
    $output | Add-Member NoteProperty Path ([IO.Path]::GetFileName($file))
    $output | Add-Member NoteProperty HashAlgorithm $hashAlgorithm
    $output | Add-Member NoteProperty HashValue ([string] $builder.ToString())
    $output
}
```

For more information about running scripts, see Recipe 1.1, "Run Programs, Scripts, and Existing Tools."

See Also

- Recipe 1.1, "Run Programs, Scripts, and Existing Tools"

17.11 Create a Directory

Problem

You want to create a directory, or file folder.

Solution

To create a directory, use the `md` or `mkdir` function:

```
PS >md NewDirectory


    Directory: Microsoft.PowerShell.Core\FileSystem::C:\temp


Mode                LastWriteTime     Length Name
----                -------------     ------ ----
d----         4/29/2007   7:31 PM            NewDirectory
```

Discussion

The `md` and `mkdir` functions are simple wrappers around the more sophisticated `New-Item` cmdlet. As you might guess, the `New-Item` cmdlet creates an item at the location you provide. The `New-Item` cmdlet doesn't work only against the filesystem, however. Any providers that support the concept of items automatically support this cmdlet as well.

For more information about the `New-Item` cmdlet, type **Get-Help New-Item**.

17.12 Remove a File or Directory

Problem

You want to remove a file or directory.

Solution

To remove a file or directory, use the `Remove-Item` cmdlet:

```
PS >Test-Path NewDirectory
True
PS >Remove-Item NewDirectory
PS >Test-Path NewDirectory
False
```

Discussion

The `Remove-Item` cmdlet removes an item from the location you provide. The `Remove-Item` cmdlet doesn't work only against the filesystem, however. Any providers that support the concept of items automatically support this cmdlet as well.

 The `Remove-Item` cmdlet lets you specify multiple files through its `Path`, `Include`, `Exclude`, and `Filter` parameters. For information on how to use these parameters effectively, see Recipe 17.5, "Find Files That Match a Pattern," earlier in this chapter.

If the item is a container (for example, a directory), PowerShell warns you that your action will also remove anything inside that container. You can provide the –Recurse flag if you want to prevent this message.

For more information about the `Remove-Item` cmdlet, type **Get-Help Remove-Item**.

See Also

- Recipe 17.5, "Find Files That Match a Pattern"

17.13 Rename a File or Directory

Problem

You want to rename a file or directory.

Solution

To rename an item in a provider, use the `Rename-Item` cmdlet:

```
PS > Rename-Item example.txt example2.txt
```

Discussion

The `Rename-Item` cmdlet changes the name of an item. While that may seem like pointing out the obvious, a common mistake is:

```
PS >Rename-Item c:\temp\example.txt c:\temp\example2.txt
Rename-Item : Cannot rename because the target specified is not a path.
At line:1 char:12
+ Rename-Item  <<<< c:\temp\example.txt c:\temp\example2.txt
```

In this situation, PowerShell provides a (not very helpful) error message because we specified a path for the new item, rather than just its name.

One thing that some shells allow you to do is rename multiple files at the same time. In those shells, the command looks like this:

```
ren *.gif *.jpg
```

PowerShell does not support this syntax, but provides even more power through its -replace operator. As a simple example, we can emulate the preceding command:

```
Get-ChildItem *.gif | Rename-Item -NewName { $_.Name -replace '.gif$','.jpg' }
```

This syntax provides an immense amount of power. Consider removing underscores from filenames and replacing them with spaces:

```
Get-ChildItem *_* | Rename-Item -NewName { $_.Name -replace '_',' ' }
```

or restructuring files in a directory with the naming convention of *Report_Project_Quarter.txt*:

```
PS >Get-ChildItem | Select Name

Name
----
Report_Project1_Q3.txt
Report_Project1_Q4.txt
Report_Project2_Q1.txt
```

You might want to change that to *Quarter_Project*.txt with an advanced replacement pattern:

```
PS >Get-ChildItem |
>>     Rename-Item -NewName { $_.Name -replace '.*_(.*)_(.*)\.txt','$2_$1.txt' }
>>
PS >Get-ChildItem | Select Name

Name
----
Q1_Project2.txt
Q3_Project1.txt
Q4_Project1.txt
```

For more information about the -replace operator, see Recipe 5.8, "Replace Text in a String."

Like the other *-Item cmdlets, the Rename-Item doesn't work only against the filesystem. Any providers that support the concept of items automatically support this cmdlet as well. For more information about the Rename-Item cmdlet, type **Get-Help Rename-Item**.

See Also

- Recipe 5.8, "Replace Text in a String"

17.14 Move a File or Directory

Problem

You want to move a file or directory.

Solution

To move a file or directory, use the Move-Item cmdlet:

```
PS >Move-Item example.txt c:\temp\example2.txt
```

Discussion

The Move-Item cmdlet moves an item from one location to another. Like the other *-Item cmdlets, the Move-Item doesn't work only against the filesystem. Any providers that support the concept of items automatically support this cmdlet as well.

 The Move-Item cmdlet lets you specify multiple files through its Path, Include, Exclude, and Filter parameters. For information on how to use these parameters effectively, see Recipe 17.5, "Find Files That Match a Pattern."

Although the Move-Item cmdlet works in every provider, you cannot move items between providers. For more information about the Move-Item cmdlet, type **Get-Help Move-Item**.

See Also

- Recipe 17.5, "Find Files That Match a Pattern"

17.15 Get the ACL of a File or Directory

Problem

You want to retrieve the ACL of a file or directory.

Solution

To retrieve the ACL of a file, use the Get-Acl cmdlet:

```
PS >Get-Acl example.txt


    Directory: Microsoft.PowerShell.Core\FileSystem::C:\temp


Path                  Owner                Access
----                  -----                ------
example.txt           LEE-DESK\Lee         BUILTIN\Administrator...
```

Discussion

The Get-Acl cmdlet retrieves the security descriptor of an item. This cmdlet doesn't work only against the filesystem, however. Any provider (for example, the Registry provider) that supports the concept of security descriptors also supports the Get-Acl cmdlet.

The Get-Acl cmdlet returns an object that represents the security descriptor of the item and is specific to the provider that contains the item. In the filesystem, this returns a .NET System.Security.AccessControl.FileSecurity object that you can explore for further information. For example, Example 17-4 searches a directory for possible ACL misconfigurations by ensuring that each file contains an Administrators, Full Control ACL.

Example 17-4. Get-AclMisconfiguration.ps1

```
##############################################################################
##
## Get-AclMisconfiguration.ps1
##
## Demonstration of functionality exposed by the Get-Acl cmdlet. This script
## goes through all access rules in all files in the current directory, and
## ensures that the Administrator group has full control of that file.
##
##############################################################################

## Get all files in the current directory
foreach($file in Get-ChildItem)
{
    ## Retrieve the ACL from the current file
    $acl = Get-Acl $file
    if(-not $acl)
    {
        continue
    }

    $foundAdministratorAcl = $false

    ## Go through each access rule in that ACL
    foreach($accessRule in $acl.Access)
    {
        ## If we find the Administrator, Full Control access rule,
        ## then set the $foundAdministratorAcl variable
        if(($accessRule.IdentityReference -like "*Administrator*") -and
          ($accessRule.FileSystemRights -eq "FullControl"))
        {
            $foundAdministratorAcl = $true
        }
    }

    ## If we didn't find the administrator ACL, output a message
    if(-not $foundAdministratorAcl)
```

Example 17-4. Get-AclMisconfiguration.ps1 (continued)

```
    {
        "Found possible ACL Misconfiguration: $file"
    }
}
```

For more information about the Get-Acl command, type **Get-Help Get-Acl**. For more information about working with classes from the .NET Framework, see Recipe 3.4, "Work with .NET Objects." For more information about running scripts, see Recipe 1.1, "Run Programs, Scripts, and Existing Tools."

See Also

- Recipe 1.1, "Run Programs, Scripts, and Existing Tools"
- Recipe 3.4, "Work with .NET Objects"

17.16 Set the ACL of a File or Directory

Problem

You want to change the ACL of a file or directory.

Solution

To change the ACL of a file, use the Set-Acl cmdlet. This example prevents the Guest account from accessing a file:

```
$acl = Get-Acl example.txt
$arguments = "LEE-DESK\Guest","FullControl","Deny"
$accessRule =
    New-Object System.Security.AccessControl.FileSystemAccessRule $arguments
$acl.SetAccessRule($accessRule)
$acl | Set-Acl example.txt
```

Discussion

The Set-Acl cmdlet sets the security descriptor of an item. This cmdlet doesn't work only against the filesystem, however. Any provider (for example, the Registry provider) that supports the concept of security descriptors also supports the Set-Acl cmdlet.

The Set-Acl cmdlet requires that you provide it with an ACL to apply to the item. While it is possible to construct the ACL from scratch, it is usually easiest to retrieve it from the item beforehand (as demonstrated in the solution). To retrieve the ACL, use the Get-Acl cmdlet. Once you've modified the access control rules on the ACL, simply pipe them to the Set-Acl cmdlet to make them permanent.

In the solution, the $arguments list that we provide to the FileSystemAccessRule constructor explicitly sets a Deny rule on the Guest account of the LEE-DESK computer for FullControl permission. For more information about working with classes (such as the FileSystemAccessRule class) from the .NET Framework, see Recipe 3.4, "Work with .NET Objects."

Although the Set-Acl command is powerful, you may already be familiar with command-line tools that offer similar functionality (such as cacls.exe). Although these tools generally do not work on the registry (or other providers that support PowerShell security descriptors), you can of course continue to use these tools from PowerShell.

For more information about the Set-Acl cmdlet, type **Get-Help Set-Acl**. For more information about the Get-Acl cmdlet, see Recipe 17.15, "Get the ACL of a File or Directory."

See Also

- Recipe 3.4, "Work with .NET Objects"
- Recipe 17.15, "Get the ACL of a File or Directory"

17.17 Program: Add Extended File Properties to Files

Discussion

The Explorer shell provides useful information about a file when you click on its Properties dialog. It includes the authoring information, image information, music information, and more (see Figure 17-2).

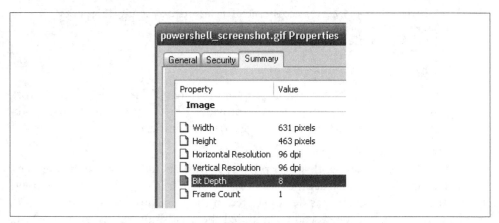

Figure 17-2. Extended file properties in Windows Explorer

PowerShell doesn't expose this information by default, but it is possible to obtain these properties from the Shell.Application COM object. Example 17-5 does just that—and adds this extended information as properties to the files returned by the Get-ChildItem cmdlet.

Example 17-5. Add-ExtendedFileProperties.ps1

```
##############################################################################
##
## Add-ExtendedFileProperties.ps1
##
## Add the extended file properties normally shown in Explorer's
## "File Properties" tab.
##
## ie:
##
##   PS >Get-ChildItem | Add-ExtendedFileProperties.ps1 |
##           Format-Table Name,"Bit Rate"
##
##############################################################################

begin
{
    ## Create the Shell.Application COM object that provides this
    ## functionality
    $shellObject = New-Object -Com Shell.Application

    ## Store the property names and identifiers for all of the shell
    ## properties
    $itemProperties = @{
        1 = "Size"; 2 = "Type"; 3 = "Date Modified";
        4 = "Date Created"; 5 = "Date Accessed";
        7 = "Status"; 8 = "Owner";
        9 = "Author"; 10 = "Title"; 11 = "Subject";
        12 = "Category"; 13 = "Pages"; 14 = "Comments";
        15 = "Copyright"; 16 = "Artist"; 17 = "Album Title";
        19 = "Track Number"; 20 = "Genre"; 21 = "Duration";
        22 = "Bit Rate"; 23 = "Protected"; 24 = "Camera Model";
        25 = "Date Picture Taken"; 26 = "Dimensions";
        30 = "Company"; 31 = "Description"; 32 = "File Version";
        33 = "Product Name"; 34 = "Product Version" }
}

process
{
    ## Get the file from the input pipeline. If it is just a filename
    ## (rather than a real file,) piping it to the Get-Item cmdlet will
    ## get the file it represents.
    $fileItem = $_ | Get-Item

    ## Don't process directories
    if($fileItem.PsIsContainer)
    {
```

Example 17-5. Add-ExtendedFileProperties.ps1 (continued)

```
    $fileItem
    return
}

## Extract the file name and directory name
$directoryName = $fileItem.DirectoryName
$filename = $fileItem.Name

## Create the folder object and shell item from the COM object
$folderObject = $shellObject.NameSpace($directoryName)
$item = $folderObject.ParseName($filename)

## Now, go through each property and add its information as a
## property to the file we are about to return
foreach($itemProperty in $itemProperties.Keys)
{
    $fileItem | Add-Member NoteProperty $itemProperties[$itemProperty] `
        $folderObject.GetDetailsOf($item, $itemProperty)
}

## Finally, return the file with the extra shell information
    $fileItem
}
```

For more information about running scripts, see Recipe 1.1, "Run Programs, Scripts, and Existing Tools."

See Also

- Recipe 1.1, "Run Programs, Scripts, and Existing Tools"

17.18 Program: Create a Filesystem Hard Link

Discussion

It is sometimes useful to refer to the same file by two different names or locations. You can't solve this problem by copying the item, because modifications to one file do not automatically affect the other.

The solution to this is called a *hard link*, an item of a new name that points to the data of another file. The Windows operating system supports hard links, but only Windows Vista includes a utility that lets you create them.

Example 17-6 lets you create hard links without needing to install additional tools. It uses (and requires) the *Invoke-WindowsApi.ps1* script provided in Recipe 15.9, "Program: Invoke Native Windows API Calls."

Example 17-6. New-FilesystemHardLink.ps1

```
##############################################################################
##
## New-FileSystemHardLink.ps1
##
## Create a new hard link, which allows you to create a new name by which you
## can access an existing file. Windows only deletes the actual file once
## you delete all hard links that point to it.
##
## ie:
##
## PS >"Hello" > test.txt
## PS >dir test* | select name
##
## Name
## ----
## test.txt
##
## PS >New-FilesystemHardLink.ps1 test2.txt test.txt
## PS >type test2.txt
## Hello
## PS >dir test* | select name
##
## Name
## ----
## test.txt
## test2.txt
##
##############################################################################

param(
    ## The new filename you want to create
    [string] $filename,

    ## The existing file that you want the new name to point to
    [string] $existingFilename
    )

## Ensure that the provided names are absolute paths
$filename = $executionContext.SessionState.Path.`
    GetUnresolvedProviderPathFromPSPath($filename)
$existingFilename = Resolve-Path $existingFilename

## Prepare the parameter types and parameters for the CreateHardLink function
$parameterTypes = [string], [string], [IntPtr]
$parameters = [string] $filename, [string] $existingFilename, [IntPtr]::Zero

## Call the CreateHardLink method in the Kernel32 DLL
$currentDirectory = Split-Path $myInvocation.MyCommand.Path
$invokeWindowsApiCommand = Join-Path $currentDirectory Invoke-WindowsApi.ps1
$result = & $invokeWindowsApiCommand "kernel32" `
    ([bool]) "CreateHardLink" $parameterTypes $parameters
```

Example 17-6. New-FilesystemHardLink.ps1 (continued)

```
## Provide an error message if the call fails
if(-not $result)
{
    $message = "Could not create hard link of $filename to " +
        "existing file $existingFilename"
    Write-Error $message
}
```

For more information about running scripts, see Recipe 1.1, "Run Programs, Scripts, and Existing Tools."

See Also

- Recipe 1.1, "Run Programs, Scripts, and Existing Tools"
- Recipe 15.9, "Program: Invoke Native Windows API Calls"

17.19 Program: Create a ZIP Archive

Discussion

When transporting or archiving files, it is useful to store those files in an archive. ZIP archives are the most common type of archive, so it would be useful to have a script to help manage them.

For many purposes, traditional command-line ZIP archive utilities may fulfill your needs. If they do not support the level of detail or interaction that you need for administrative tasks, a more programmatic alternative is attractive.

Example 17-7 lets you create ZIP archives simply by piping files into them. It requires that you have the SharpZipLib installed, which you can obtain from *http://www.icsharpcode.net/OpenSource/SharpZipLib/*.

Example 17-7. New-ZipFile.ps1

```
##############################################################################
##
## New-ZipFile.ps1
##
## Create a Zip file from any files piped in. Requires that
## you have the SharpZipLib installed, which is available from
## http://www.icsharpcode.net/OpenSource/SharpZipLib/
##
## ie:
##
##  PS >dir *.ps1 | New-ZipFile scripts.zip d:\bin\ICSharpCode.SharpZipLib.dll
##  PS >"readme.txt" | New-ZipFile docs.zip d:\bin\ICSharpCode.SharpZipLib.dll
##
##############################################################################
```

Example 17-7. New-ZipFile.ps1 (continued)

```
param(
  $zipName = $(throw "Please specify the name of the file to create."),
  $libPath = $(throw "Please specify the path to ICSharpCode.SharpZipLib.dll.")
  )

## Load the Zip library
[void] [Reflection.Assembly]::LoadFile($libPath)
$namespace = "ICSharpCode.SharpZipLib.Zip.{0}"

## Create the Zip File
$zipName =
    $executionContext.SessionState.Path.GetUnresolvedProviderPathFromPSPath($zipName)
$zipFile = New-Object ($namespace -f "ZipOutputStream") ([IO.File]::Create($zipName))
$zipFullName = (Resolve-Path $zipName).Path

[byte[]] $buffer = New-Object byte[] 4096

## Go through each file in the input, adding it to the Zip file
## specified
foreach($file in $input)
{
    ## Skip the current file if it is the zip file itself
    if($file.FullName -eq $zipFullName)
    {
        continue
    }

    ## Convert the path to a relative path, if it is under the current location
    $replacePath = [Regex]::Escape( (Get-Location).Path + "\" )
    $zipName = ([string] $file) -replace $replacePath,""

    ## Create the zip entry, and add it to the file
    $zipEntry = New-Object ($namespace -f "ZipEntry") $zipName
    $zipFile.PutNextEntry($zipEntry)

    $fileStream = [IO.File]::OpenRead($file.FullName)
    [ICSharpCode.SharpZipLib.Core.StreamUtils]::Copy($fileStream, $zipFile, $buffer)
    $fileStream.Close()
}

## Close the file
$zipFile.Close()
```

For more information about running scripts, see Recipe 1.1, "Run Programs, Scripts, and Existing Tools."

See Also

- Recipe 1.1, "Run Programs, Scripts, and Existing Tools"

CHAPTER 18

The Windows Registry

18.0 Introduction

As the configuration store for the vast majority of applications, the registry plays a central role in system administration. It is also generally hard to manage.

While command-line tools (such as *reg.exe*) exist to help you work with the registry, their interfaces are usually inconsistent and confusing. While the Registry Editor graphical user interface is easy to use, it does not support scripted administration.

PowerShell tackles this problem by exposing the Windows Registry as a navigation provider—a data source that you navigate and manage in exactly the same way that you work with the filesystem.

18.1 Navigate the Registry

Problem

You want to navigate and explore the Windows Registry.

Solution

Use the Set-Location just as you would navigate the filesystem to navigate the registry:

```
PS >Set-Location HKCU:
PS >Set-Location \Software\Microsoft\Windows\CurrentVersion\Run
PS >Get-Location

Path
----
HKCU:\Software\Microsoft\Windows\CurrentVersion\Run
```

Discussion

PowerShell lets you navigate the Windows Registry in exactly the same way that you navigate the filesystem, certificate drives, and other navigation-based providers. Like these other providers, the registry provider supports the Set-Location cmdlet (with the standard aliases of sl, cd, and chdir), Push-Location (with the standard alias pushd), Pop-Location (with the standard alias popd), and more.

For information about how to change registry keys once you get to a registry location, see Recipe 18.3, "Modify or Remove a Registry Key Value." For more information about the registry provider, type **Get-Help Registry**.

See Also

- Recipe 18.3, "Modify or Remove a Registry Key Value"

18.2   View a Registry Key

Problem

You want to view the value of a specific registry key.

Solution

To retrieve the value(s) of a registry key, use the Get-ItemProperty cmdlet, as shown in Example 18-1.

Example 18-1. Retrieving properties of a registry key

```
PS >Set-Location HKCU:
PS >Set-Location \Software\Microsoft\Windows\CurrentVersion\Run
PS >Get-ItemProperty .


PSPath                : Microsoft.PowerShell.Core\Registry::HKEY_CURRENT_U
                        SER\Software\Microsoft\Windows\CurrentVersion\Run
PSParentPath          : Microsoft.PowerShell.Core\Registry::HKEY_CURRENT_U
                        SER\Software\Microsoft\Windows\CurrentVersion
PSChildName           : Run
PSDrive               : HKCU
PSProvider            : Microsoft.PowerShell.Core\Registry
FolderShare           : "C:\Program Files\FolderShare\FolderShare.exe" /ba
                        ckground
TaskSwitchXP          : d:\lee\tools\TaskSwitchXP.exe
ctfmon.exe            : C:\WINDOWS\system32\ctfmon.exe
Ditto                 : C:\Program Files\Ditto\Ditto.exe
QuickTime Task        : "C:\Program Files\QuickTime Alternative\qttask.exe
                        " -atboottime
H/PC Connection Agent : "C:\Program Files\Microsoft ActiveSync\wcescomm.exe"
```

Discussion

In the registry provider, PowerShell treats registry keys as items and key values as properties of those items. To get the properties of an item, use the `Get-ItemProperty` cmdlet. The `Get-ItemProperty` cmdlet has the standard alias, gp.

Example 18-1 lists all property values associated with that specific key. To retrieve the value of a specific item, access it as though you would access a property on a .NET object, or anywhere else in PowerShell:

```
PS >$item = Get-ItemProperty .
PS >$item.TaskSwitchXp
d:\lee\tools\TaskSwitchXP.exe
```

If you want to do this all at once, the command looks like:

```
PS >$runKey = "HKCU:\Software\Microsoft\Windows\CurrentVersion\Run"
PS >(Get-ItemProperty $runKey).TaskSwitchXp
d:\lee\tools\TaskSwitchXP.exe
```

For more information about the `Get-ItemProperty` cmdlet, type **Get-Help Get-ItemProperty**. For more information about the registry provider, type **Get-Help Registry**.

18.3   Modify or Remove a Registry Key Value

Problem

You want to modify or remove a property of a specific registry key.

Solution

To set the value of a registry key, use the `Set-ItemProperty` cmdlet:

```
PS >(Get-ItemProperty .).MyProgram
c:\temp\MyProgram.exe
PS >Set-ItemProperty . MyProgram d:\Lee\tools\MyProgram.exe
PS >(Get-ItemProperty .).MyProgram
d:\Lee\tools\MyProgram.exe
```

To remove the value of a registry key, use the `Remove-ItemProperty` cmdlet:

```
PS >Remove-ItemProperty . MyProgram
PS >(Get-ItemProperty .).MyProgram
```

Discussion

In the registry provider, PowerShell treats registry keys as items and key values as properties of those items. To change the value of a key property, use the `Set-ItemProperty` cmdlet. The `Set-ItemProperty` cmdlet has the standard alias, sp. To remove a key property altogether, use the `Remove-ItemProperty` cmdlet.

As always, use caution when changing information in the registry. Deleting or changing the wrong item can easily render your system unbootable.

For more information about the Get-ItemProperty cmdlet, type **Get-Help Get-ItemProperty**. For information about the Set-ItemProperty and Remove-ItemProperty cmdlets, type **Get-Help Set-ItemProperty** or **Get-Help Remove-ItemProperty**, respectively. For more information about the registry provider, type **Get-Help Registry**.

18.4   Create a Registry Key Value

Problem

You want to add a new key value to an existing registry key.

Solution

To add a value to a registry key, use the New-ItemProperty cmdlet. Example 18-2 adds *MyProgram.exe* to the list of programs that start when the current user logs in.

Example 18-2. Creating new properties on a registry key

```
PS >New-ItemProperty . -Name MyProgram -Value c:\temp\MyProgram.exe


PSPath       : Microsoft.PowerShell.Core\Registry::HKEY_CURRENT_USER\Softw
               are\Microsoft\Windows\CurrentVersion\Run
PSParentPath : Microsoft.PowerShell.Core\Registry::HKEY_CURRENT_USER\Softw
               are\Microsoft\Windows\CurrentVersion
PSChildName  : Run
PSDrive      : HKCU
PSProvider   : Microsoft.PowerShell.Core\Registry
MyProgram    : c:\temp\MyProgram.exe



PS >Get-ItemProperty .


PSPath              : Microsoft.PowerShell.Core\Registry::HKEY_CURRENT_U
                      SER\Software\Microsoft\Windows\CurrentVersion\Run
PSParentPath        : Microsoft.PowerShell.Core\Registry::HKEY_CURRENT_U
                      SER\Software\Microsoft\Windows\CurrentVersion
PSChildName         : Run
PSDrive             : HKCU
PSProvider          : Microsoft.PowerShell.Core\Registry
FolderShare         : "C:\Program Files\FolderShare\FolderShare.exe" /ba
                      ckground
TaskSwitchXP        : d:\lee\tools\TaskSwitchXP.exe
```

Example 18-2. Creating new properties on a registry key (continued)

```
ctfmon.exe             : C:\WINDOWS\system32\ctfmon.exe
Ditto                  : C:\Program Files\Ditto\Ditto.exe
QuickTime Task         : "C:\Program Files\QuickTime Alternative\qttask.exe
                         " -atboottime
H/PC Connection Agent : "C:\Program Files\Microsoft ActiveSync\wcescomm.ex
                         e"
MyProgram              : c:\temp\MyProgram.exe
```

Discussion

In the registry provider, PowerShell treats registry keys as items and key values as properties of those items. To create a key property, use the New-ItemProperty cmdlet.

For more information about the New-ItemProperty cmdlet, type **Get-Help New-ItemProperty**. For more information about the registry provider, type **Get-Help Registry**.

18.5   Remove a Registry Key

Problem

You want to remove a registry key and all its properties.

Solution

To remove a registry key, use the Remove-Item cmdlet:

```
PS >dir


    Hive: Microsoft.PowerShell.Core\Registry::HKEY_CURRENT_USER\Software\
Microsoft\Windows\CurrentVersion\Run

SKC  VC Name                        Property
---  -- ----                        --------
  0   0 Spyware                      {}


PS >Remove-Item Spyware
```

Discussion

As mentioned in Recipe 18.4, "Create a Registry Key Value," the registry provider lets you remove items and containers with the Remove-Item cmdlet. The Remove-Item cmdlet has the standard aliases rm, rmdir, del, erase, and rd.

As always, use caution when changing information in the registry. Deleting or changing the wrong item can easily render your system unbootable.

As in the filesystem, the `Remove-Item` cmdlet lets you specify multiple files through its `Path`, `Include`, `Exclude`, and `Filter` parameters. For information on how to use these parameters effectively, see Recipe 17.5, "Find Files That Match a Pattern."

For more information about the `Remove-Item` cmdlet, type **`Get-Help Remove-Item`**. For more information about the registry provider, type **`Get-Help Registry`**.

See Also

- Recipe 17.5, "Find Files That Match a Pattern"
- Recipe 18.4, "Create a Registry Key Value"

18.6   Add a Site to an Internet Explorer Security Zone

Problem

You want to add a site to a specific Internet Explorer security zone.

Solution

To create the registry keys and properties required to add a site to a specific security zone, use the `New-Item` and `New-ItemProperty` cmdlets. Example 18-3 adds *www. example.com* to the list of sites trusted by Internet Explorer.

Example 18-3. Adding www.example.com to the list of trusted sites in Internet Explorer

```
Set-Location "HKCU:\Software\Microsoft\Windows\CurrentVersion\Internet Settings"
Set-Location ZoneMap\Domains
New-Item example.com
Set-Location example.com
New-Item www
Set-Location www
New-ItemProperty . -Name http -Value 2 -Type DWORD
```

Discussion

One task that requires modifying data in the registry is working with Internet Explorer to add and remove sites from its different security zones.

Internet Explorer stores its zone mapping information in the registry at *HKCU:\ Software\Microsoft\Windows\CurrentVersion\Internet   Settings\ZoneMap\Domains*. Below that key, Explorer stores the domain name (such as `leeholmes.com`) with the hostname (such as www) as a subkey of that one (see Figure 18-1). In the host key, Explorer stores a property (such as http) with a DWORD value that corresponds to the zone identifier.

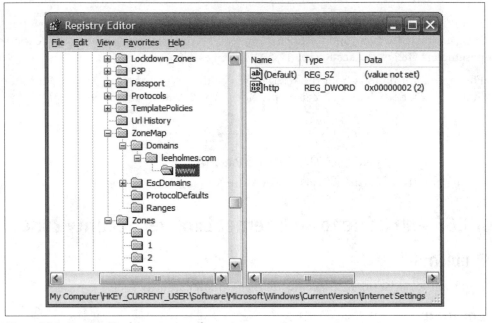

Figure 18-1. Internet Explorer zone configuration

The Internet Explorer zone identifiers are:

0. My Computer
1. Local intranet
2. Trusted sites
3. Internet
4. Restricted sites

When Internet Explorer is configured in its Enhanced Security Configuration mode, you must also update entries under the EscDomains key.

 Once a machine has enabled Internet Explorer's Enhanced Security Configuration, those settings persist even after removing Enhanced Security Configuration. The following commands allow your machine to trust UNC paths again:

```
Set-Location "HKCU:\Software\Microsoft\Windows\"
Set-Location "CurrentVersion"

Set-Location "Internet Settings"

Set-ItemProperty ZoneMap UNCAsIntranet -Type DWORD 1

Set-ItemProperty ZoneMap IntranetName -Type DWORD 1
```

To remove the zone mapping for a specific domain, use the `Remove-Item` cmdlet:

```
PS >Get-ChildItem


    Hive: Microsoft.PowerShell.Core\Registry::HKEY_CURRENT_USER\Software\Mi
crosoft\Windows\CurrentVersion\Internet Settings\ZoneMap\Domains

SKC  VC Name                          Property
---  -- ----                          --------
  1   0 example.com                   {}


PS >Remove-Item -Recurse example.com
PS >Get-ChildItem
PS >
```

For more information about using the Internet Explorer registry entries to configure security zones, see the Microsoft KB article "Description of Internet Explorer Security Zones Registry Entries" at *http://support.microsoft.com/kb/182569*. For more information about managing Internet Explorer's Enhanced Security Configuration, search for it on *http://technet.microsoft.com*.

For more information about modifying data in the registry, see Recipe 18.3, "Modify or Remove a Registry Key Value."

See Also

- Recipe 18.3, "Modify or Remove a Registry Key Value"

18.7   Modify Internet Explorer Settings

Problem

You want to modify Internet Explorer's configuration options.

Solution

To modify the Internet Explorer configuration registry keys, use the `Set-ItemProperty` cmdlet. For example, to update the proxy:

```
Set-Location "HKCU:\Software\Microsoft\Windows\CurrentVersion\Internet Settings"
Set-ItemProperty . -Name ProxyServer -Value http://proxy.example.com
Set-ItemProperty . -Name ProxyEnable -Value 1
```

Discussion

Internet Explorer stores its main configuration information as properties on the registry key `HKCU:\Software\Microsoft\Windows\CurrentVersion\Internet Settings`. To change these properties, use the `Set-ItemProperty` cmdlet as demonstrated in the solution.

Another common set of properties to tweak are the configuration parameters that define a security zone. An example of this is to prevent scripts from running in the Restricted Sites zone. For each zone, Internet Explorer stores this information as properties of the registry key `HKCU:\Software\Microsoft\Windows\CurrentVersion\Internet Settings\Zones\<Zone>`, where *<Zone>* represents the zone identifier (0, 1, 2, 3, or 4) to manage.

The Internet Explorer zone identifiers are:

0. My Computer
1. Local intranet
2. Trusted sites
3. Internet
4. Restricted sites

The names of the properties in this key are not designed for human consumption, as they carry illuminating titles such as 1A04 and 1809. While not well-named, you can still script them.

For more information about using the Internet Explorer registry settings to configure security zones, see the Microsoft KB article "Description of Internet Explorer Security Zones Registry Entries" at *http://support.microsoft.com/kb/182569*.

For more information about modifying data in the registry, see Recipe 18.3, "Modify or Remove a Registry Key Value."

See Also

- Recipe 18.3, "Modify or Remove a Registry Key Value"

18.8   Program: Search the Windows Registry

Discussion

While the Windows Registry Editor is useful for searching the registry, it sometimes may not provide the power you need. For example, the registry editor does not support searches with wildcards or regular expressions.

In the filesystem, we have the `Select-String` cmdlet to search files for content. PowerShell does not have that for other stores, but we can write a script to do it. The key here is to think of registry key values like you think of content in a file:

- Directories have items; items have content.
- Registry keys have properties; properties have values.

Example 18-4 goes through all registry keys (and their values) for a search term and returns information about the match.

Example 18-4. Search-Registry.ps1

```
###############################################################################
##
## Search-Registry.ps1
##
## Search the registry for keys or properties that match a specific value.
##
## ie:
##
##   PS >Set-Location HKCU:\Software\Microsoft\
##   PS >Search-Registry Run
##
###############################################################################

param([string] $searchText = $(throw "Please specify text to search for."))

## Helper function to create a new object that represents
## a registry match from this script
function New-RegistryMatch
{
    param( $matchType, $keyName, $propertyName, $line )

    $registryMatch = New-Object PsObject
    $registryMatch | Add-Member NoteProperty MatchType $matchType
    $registryMatch | Add-Member NoteProperty KeyName $keyName
    $registryMatch | Add-Member NoteProperty PropertyName $propertyName
    $registryMatch | Add-Member NoteProperty Line $line


    $registryMatch
}

## Go through each item in the registry
foreach($item in Get-ChildItem -Recurse -ErrorAction SilentlyContinue)
{
    ## Check if the key name matches
    if($item.Name  match $searchText)
    {
        New-RegistryMatch "Key" $item.Name $null $item.Name
    }

    ## Check if a key property matches
    foreach($property in (Get-ItemProperty $item.PsPath).PsObject.Properties)
    {
        ## Skip the property if it was one PowerShell added
        if(($property.Name -eq "PSPath") -or ($property.Name -eq "PSChildName"))
        {
            continue
        }

        ## Search the text of the property
        $propertyText = "$($property.Name)=$($property.Value)"
        if($propertyText -match $searchText)
        {
```

Example 18-4. Search-Registry.ps1 (continued)

```
        New-RegistryMatch "Property" $item.Name $property.Name $propertyText
    }
  }
}
```

For more information about running scripts, see also Recipe 1.1, "Run Programs, Scripts, and Existing Tools."

See Also

* Recipe 1.1, "Run Programs, Scripts, and Existing Tools"

18.9   Get the ACL of a Registry Key

Problem

You want to retrieve the ACL of a registry key.

Solution

To retrieve the ACL of a registry key, use the Get-Acl cmdlet:

```
PS >Get-Acl HKLM:\Software

Path                    Owner                Access
----                    -----                ------
Microsoft.PowerShell.... BUILTIN\Administrators  CREATOR OWNER Allow  ...
```

Discussion

As mentioned in Recipe 17.15, "Get the ACL of a File or Directory," the Get-Acl cmdlet retrieves the security descriptor of an item. This cmdlet doesn't only work against the registry, however. Any provider (for example, the filesystem provider) that supports the concept of security descriptors also supports the Get-Acl cmdlet.

The Get-Acl cmdlet returns an object that represents the security descriptor of the item and is specific to the provider that contains the item. In the registry provider, this returns a .NET System.Security.AccessControl.RegistrySecurity object that you can explore for further information. For an example of a script that works with ACLs, see Recipe 17.15, "Get the ACL of a File or Directory."

For more information about the Get-Acl command, type **Get-Help Get-Acl**. For more information about working with classes from the .NET Framework, see Recipe 3.4, "Work with .NET Objects."

See Also

- Recipe 3.4, "Work with .NET Objects"
- Recipe 17.15, "Get the ACL of a File or Directory"

18.10 Set the ACL of a Registry Key

Problem

You want to change the ACL of a registry key.

Solution

To set the ACL on a registry key, use the Set-Acl cmdlet. This example grants an account write access to a registry key under HKLM:\Software. This is especially useful for programs that write to administrator-only regions of the registry, which prevents them from running under a nonadministrator account.

```
cd HKLM:\Software\MyProgram
$acl = Get-Acl .
$arguments = "LEE-DESK\Lee","FullControl","Allow"
$accessRule = New-Object System.Security.AccessControl.RegistryAccessRule $arguments
$acl.SetAccessRule($accessRule)
$acl | Set-Acl .
```

Discussion

As mentioned in Recipe 17.16, "Set the ACL of a File or Directory," the Set-Acl cmdlet sets the security descriptor of an item. This cmdlet doesn't only work against the registry, however. Any provider (for example, the filesystem provider) that supports the concept of security descriptors also supports the Set-Acl cmdlet.

The Set-Acl cmdlet requires that you provide it with an ACL to apply to the item. While it is possible to construct the ACL from scratch, it is usually easiest to retrieve it from the item beforehand (as demonstrated in the solution). To retrieve the ACL, use the Get-Acl cmdlet. Once you've modified the access control rules on the ACL, simply pipe them to the Set-Acl cmdlet to make them permanent.

In the solution, the $arguments list that we provide to the RegistryAccessRule constructor explicitly sets an Allow rule on the Lee account of the LEE-DESK computer for FullControl permission. For more information about working with classes (such as the RegistryAccessRule class) from the .NET Framework, see Recipe 3.4, "Work with .NET Objects."

Although the Set-Acl command is powerful, you may already be familiar with command-line tools that offer similar functionality (such as *SubInAcl.exe*). You can of course continue to use these tools from PowerShell.

For more information about the Set-Acl cmdlet, type **Get-Help Set-Acl**. For more information about the Get-Acl cmdlet, see Recipe 18.9, "Get the ACL of a Registry Key."

See Also

- Recipe 3.4, "Work with .NET Objects"
- Recipe 17.16, "Set the ACL of a File or Directory"
- Recipe 18.9, "Get the ACL of a Registry Key"

18.11 Work with the Registry of a Remote Computer

Problem

You want to work with the registry keys and values of a remote computer.

Solution

To work with the registry of a remote computer, use the scripts provided in this chapter: Get-RemoteRegistryChildItem, Get-RemoteRegistryProperty, and Set-RemoteRegistryProperty. These scripts require that the remote computer has the remote registry service enabled and running. Example 18-5 updates the PowerShell execution policy of a remote machine.

Example 18-5. Setting the PowerShell execution policy of a remote machine

```
PS >$registryPath = "HKLM:\Software\Microsoft\PowerShell\1"
PS >Get-RemoteRegistryChildItem LEE-DESK $registryPath

SKC  VC Name                     Property
---  -- ----                     --------
  0   1 1033                     {Install}
  0   5 PowerShellEngine         {ApplicationBase, ConsoleHostAss...
  2   0 PowerShellSnapIns        {}
  1   0 ShellIds                 {}


PS >Get-RemoteRegistryChildItem LEE-DESK $registryPath\ShellIds

SKC  VC Name                     Property
---  -- ----                     --------
  0   2 Microsoft.PowerShell     {Path, ExecutionPolicy}


PS >
PS >$registryPath = "HKLM:\Software\Microsoft\PowerShell\1\" +
>>     "ShellIds\Microsoft.PowerShell"
>>
```

Example 18-5. Setting the PowerShell execution policy of a remote machine (continued)

```
PS >Get-RemoteRegistryKeyProperty LEE-DESK $registryPath ExecutionPolicy

ExecutionPolicy
---------------
Unrestricted


PS >Set-RemoteRegistryKeyProperty LEE-DESK $registryPath `
>>      "ExecutionPolicy" "RemoteSigned"
>>
PS >Get-RemoteRegistryKeyProperty LEE-DESK $registryPath ExecutionPolicy

ExecutionPolicy
---------------
RemoteSigned
```

Discussion

Although this specific task is perhaps better solved through PowerShell's Group Policy support, it demonstrates a useful scenario that includes both remote registry exploration and modification.

For more information about the `Get-RemoteRegistryChildItem`, `Get-RemoteRegistryProperty`, and `Set-RemoteRegistryProperty` scripts, see Recipe 18.12, "Program: Get Registry Items from Remote Machines," Recipe 18.13, "Program: Get Properties of Remote Registry Keys," and Recipe 18.14, "Program: Set Properties of Remote Registry Keys."

See Also

- Recipe 18.12, "Program: Get Registry Items from Remote Machines"
- Recipe 18.13, "Program: Get Properties of Remote Registry Keys"
- Recipe 18.14, "Program: Set Properties of Remote Registry Keys"

18.12 Program: Get Registry Items from Remote Machines

Discussion

Although PowerShell does not directly let you access and manipulate the registry of a remote computer, it still supports this by working with the .NET Framework. The functionality exposed by the .NET Framework is a bit more developer-oriented than we want, so we can instead use a script to make it easier to work with.

Example 18-6 lets you list child items in a remote registry key, much like you do on the local computer. In order for this script to succeed, the target computer must have the remote registry service enabled and running.

Example 18-6. Get-RemoteRegistryChildItem.ps1

```
##############################################################################
##
## Get-RemoteRegistryChildItem.ps1
##
## Get the list of subkeys below a given key.
##
## ie:
##
##  PS >Get-RemoteRegistryChildItem LEE-DESK HKLM:\Software
##
##############################################################################

param(
  $computer = $(throw "Please specify a computer name."),
  $path = $(throw "Please specify a registry path")
  )

## Validate and extract out the registry key
if($path -match "^HKLM:\\(.*)")
{
    $baseKey = [Microsoft.Win32.RegistryKey]::OpenRemoteBaseKey(
        "LocalMachine", $computer)
}
elseif($path -match "^HKCU:\\(.*)")
{
    $baseKey = [Microsoft.Win32.RegistryKey]::OpenRemoteBaseKey
        ("CurrentUser", $computer)
}
else
{
    Write-Error ("Please specify a fully-qualified registry path " +
        "(i.e.: HKLM:\Software) of the registry key to open.")
    return
}

## Open the key
$key = $baseKey.OpenSubKey($matches[1])

## Retrieve all of its children
foreach($subkeyName in $key.GetSubKeyNames())
{
    ## Open the subkey
    $subkey = $key.OpenSubKey($subkeyName)

    ## Add information so that PowerShell displays this key like regular
    ## registry key
    $returnObject = [PsObject] $subKey
```

Example 18-6. Get-RemoteRegistryChildItem.ps1 (continued)

```
    $returnObject | Add-Member NoteProperty PsChildName $subkeyName
    $returnObject | Add-Member NoteProperty Property $subkey.GetValueNames()

    ## Output the key
    $returnObject

    ## Close the child key
    $subkey.Close()
}

## Close the key and base keys
$key.Close()
$baseKey.Close()
```

For more information about running scripts, see Recipe 1.1, "Run Programs, Scripts, and Existing Tools."

See Also

- Recipe 1.1, "Run Programs, Scripts, and Existing Tools"

18.13 Program: Get Properties of Remote Registry Keys

Discussion

Although PowerShell does not directly let you access and manipulate the registry of a remote computer, it still supports this by working with the .NET Framework. The functionality exposed by the .NET Framework is a bit more developer-oriented than we want, so we can instead use a script to make it easier to work with.

Example 18-7 lets you get the properties (or a specific property) from a given remote registry key. In order for this script to succeed, the target computer must have the remote registry service enabled and running.

Example 18-7. Get-RemoteRegistryKeyProperty.ps1

```
##############################################################################
##
## Get-RemoteRegistryKeyProperty.ps1
##
## Get the value of a remote registry key property
##
## ie:
##
##   PS >$registryPath =
##       "HKLM:\software\Microsoft\PowerShell\1\ShellIds\Microsoft.PowerShell"
##   PS >Get-RemoteRegistryKeyProperty LEE-DESK $registryPath "ExecutionPolicy"
##
```

Example 18-7. Get-RemoteRegistryKeyProperty.ps1 (continued)

```
############################################################################

param(
  $computer = $(throw "Please specify a computer name."),
  $path = $(throw "Please specify a registry path"),
  $property = "*"
  )

## Validate and extract out the registry key
if($path -match "^HKLM:\\(.*)")
{
    $baseKey = [Microsoft.Win32.RegistryKey]::OpenRemoteBaseKey(
        "LocalMachine", $computer)
}
elseif($path -match "^HKCU:\\(.*)")
{
    $baseKey = [Microsoft.Win32.RegistryKey]::OpenRemoteBaseKey(
        "CurrentUser", $computer)
}
else
{
    Write-Error ("Please specify a fully-qualified registry path " +
        "(i.e.: HKLM:\Software) of the registry key to open.")
    return
}

## Open the key
$key = $baseKey.OpenSubKey($matches[1])
$returnObject = New-Object PsObject

## Go through each of the properties in the key
foreach($keyProperty in $key.GetValueNames())
{
    ## If the property matches the search term, add it as a
    ## property to the output
    if($keyProperty -like $property)
    {
        $returnObject |
            Add-Member NoteProperty $keyProperty $key.GetValue($keyProperty)
    }
}

## Return the resulting object
$returnObject

## Close the key and base keys
$key.Close()
$baseKey.Close()
```

For more information about running scripts, see Recipe 1.1, "Run Programs, Scripts, and Existing Tools."

See Also

- Recipe 1.1, "Run Programs, Scripts, and Existing Tools"

18.14 Program: Set Properties of Remote Registry Keys

Discussion

Although PowerShell does not directly let you access and manipulate the registry of a remote computer, it still supports this by working with the .NET Framework. The functionality exposed by the .NET Framework is a bit more developer-oriented than we want, so we can instead use a script to make it easier to work with.

Example 18-8 lets you set the value of a property on a given remote registry key. In order for this script to succeed, the target computer must have the remote registry service enabled and running.

Example 18-8. Set-RemoteRegistryKeyProperty.ps1

```
##############################################################################
##
## Set-RemoteRegistryKeyProperty.ps1
##
## Set the value of a remote registry key property
##
## ie:
##
##  PS >$registryPath =
##       "HKLM:\software\Microsoft\PowerShell\1\ShellIds\Microsoft.PowerShell"
##  PS >Set-RemoteRegistryKeyProperty LEE-DESK $registryPath `
##       "ExecutionPolicy" "RemoteSigned"
##
##############################################################################

param(
  $computer = $(throw "Please specify a computer name."),
  $path = $(throw "Please specify a registry path"),
  $property = $(throw "Please specify a property name"),
  $propertyValue = $(throw "Please specify a property value")
  )

## Validate and extract out the registry key
if($path -match "^HKLM:\\(.*)")
{
    $baseKey = [Microsoft.Win32.RegistryKey]::OpenRemoteBaseKey
        ("LocalMachine", $computer)
}
elseif($path -match "^HKCU:\\(.*)")
{
    $baseKey = [Microsoft.Win32.RegistryKey]::OpenRemoteBaseKey
        ("CurrentUser", $computer)
}
```

Example 18-8. Set-RemoteRegistryKeyProperty.ps1 (continued)

```
else
{
    Write-Error ("Please specify a fully-qualified registry path " +
        "(i.e.: HKLM:\Software) of the registry key to open.")
    return
}

## Open the key and set its value
$key = $baseKey.OpenSubKey($matches[1], $true)
$key.SetValue($property, $propertyValue)

## Close the key and base keys
$key.Close()
$baseKey.Close()
```

For more information about running scripts, see Recipe 1.1, "Run Programs, Scripts, and Existing Tools."

See Also

- Recipe 1.1, "Run Programs, Scripts, and Existing Tools"

18.15 Discover Registry Settings for Programs

Problem

You want to automate the configuration of a program, but that program does not document its registry configuration settings.

Solution

To discover a registry setting for a program, use Sysinternals' Process Monitor to observe registry access by that program. Process Monitor is available from *http://www.microsoft.com/technet/sysinternals/FileAndDisk/processmonitor.mspx*.

Discussion

In an ideal world, all programs would fully support command-line administration and configuration through PowerShell cmdlets. Many programs do not, however, so the solution is to look through their documentation in the hope that they list the registry keys and properties that control their settings. While many programs document their registry configuration settings, many still do not.

Although these programs may not document their registry settings, you can usually observe their registry access activity to determine the registry paths they use. To illustrate this, we will use the Sysinternals' Process Monitor to discover PowerShell's execution policy configuration keys. Although PowerShell documents these keys *and* makes its automated configuration a breeze, it illustrates the general technique.

Launch and configure Process Monitor

Once you've downloaded Process Monitor, the first step is to filter its output to include only the program you are interested in. By default, Process Monitor logs almost all registry and file activity on the system.

First, launch Process Monitor, and then press Ctrl-E (or click the magnifying glass icon) to temporarily prevent it from capturing any data (see Figure 18-2). Next, press Ctrl-X (or click the white sheet with an eraser icon) to clear the extra information that it captured automatically. Finally, drag the target icon and drop it on top of the application in question. You can press Ctrl-L (or click the funnel icon) to see the filter that Process Monitor now applies to its output.

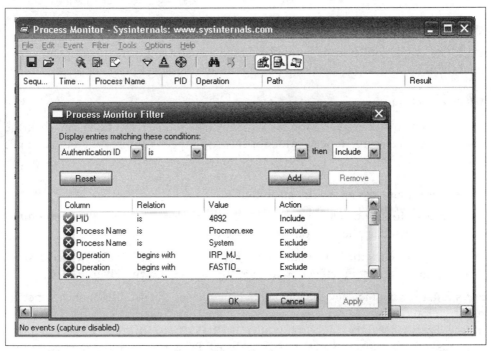

Figure 18-2. Process Monitor ready to capture

Prepare to manually set the configuration option

Next, prepare to manually set the program's configuration option. Usually, this means typing and clicking all the property settings, but just not clicking OK or Apply. For this PowerShell example, type the `Set-ExecutionPolicy` command line, but do not press Enter (see Figure 18-3).

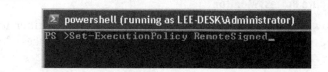

Figure 18-3. Preparing to apply the configuration option

Tell Process Monitor to begin capturing information

Switch to the Process Monitor window, and then press Ctrl-E (or click the magnifying glass icon). Process Monitor now captures all registry access for the program in question.

Manually set the configuration option

Click OK, Apply, or whatever action it takes to actually complete the program's configuration. For the PowerShell example, this means pressing Enter.

Tell Process Monitor to stop capturing information

Switch again to the Process Monitor window, and then press Ctrl-E (or click the magnifying glass icon). Process Monitor now no longer captures the application's activity.

Review the capture logs for registry modification

The Process Monitor window now shows all registry keys that the application interacted with when it applied its configuration setting.

Press Ctrl-F (or click the binoculars icon); then search for RegSetValue. Process Monitor highlights the first modification to a registry key, as shown in Figure 18-4.

Press Enter (or double-click the highlighted row) to see the details about this specific registry modification. In this example, we can see that PowerShell changed the value of the ExecutionPolicy property (under HKLM:\Software\Microsoft\PowerShell\1\ShellIds\Microsoft.PowerShell) to RemoteSigned. Press F3 to see the next entry that corresponds to a registry modification.

Automate these registry writes

Now that you know all registry writes that the application performed when it updated its settings, judgment and experimentation will help you determine which modifications actually represent this setting. Since PowerShell only performed one registry write (to a key that very obviously represents the execution policy), the choice is pretty clear in this example.

Once you've discovered the registry keys, properties, and values that the application uses to store its configuration data, you can use the techniques discussed in Recipe

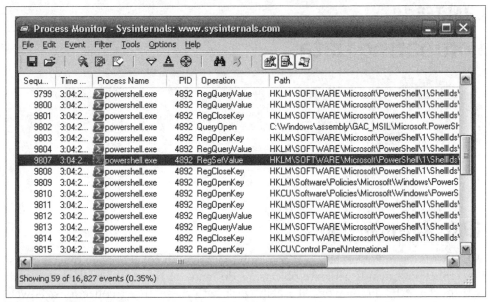

Figure 18-4. Process Monitor's registry access detail

18.3, "Modify or Remove a Registry Key Value" to automate these configuration settings. For example:

```
PS >$key = "HKLM:\Software\Microsoft\PowerShell\1\" +
>>       "ShellIds\Microsoft.PowerShell"
>>
PS >Set-ItemProperty $key ExecutionPolicy AllSigned
PS >Get-ExecutionPolicy
AllSigned
PS >Set-ItemProperty $key ExecutionPolicy RemoteSigned
PS >Get-ExecutionPolicy
RemoteSigned
```

See Also

- Recipe 18.3, "Modify or Remove a Registry Key Value"

CHAPTER 19

Comparing Data

19.0   Introduction

When working in PowerShell, it is common to work with collections of objects. Most PowerShell commands generate objects, as do many of the methods that you work with in the .NET Framework. To help work with these object collections, Power-Shell introduces the `Compare-Object` cmdlet. The `Compare-Object` cmdlet provides functionality similar to well-known `diff` commands, but with an object-oriented flavor.

19.1   Compare the Output of Two Commands

Problem

You want to compare the output of two commands.

Solution

To compare the output of two commands, store the output of each command in variables, and then use the `Compare-Object` cmdlet to compare those variables:

```
PS >notepad
PS >$processes = Get-Process
PS >Stop-Process -ProcessName Notepad
PS >$newProcesses = Get-Process
PS >Compare-Object $processes $newProcesses

InputObject                        SideIndicator
-----------                        -------------
System.Diagnostics.Process (notepad)  <=
```

Discussion

The solution shows how to determine which processes have exited between the two calls to Get-Process. The SideIndicator of `<=` tells us that the process was present in the left collection ($processes) but not in the right ($newProcesses).

For more information about the Compare-Object cmdlet, type **Get-Help Compare-Object**.

19.2   Determine the Differences Between Two Files

Problem

You want to determine the differences between two files.

Solution

To determine simple differences in the content of each file, store their content in variables, and then use the Compare-Object cmdlet to compare those variables:

```
PS >"Hello World" > c:\temp\file1.txt
PS >"Hello World" > c:\temp\file2.txt
PS >"More Information" >> c:\temp\file2.txt
PS >$content1 = Get-Content c:\temp\file1.txt
PS >$content2 = Get-Content c:\temp\file2.txt
PS >Compare-Object $content1 $content2

InputObject                     SideIndicator
-----------                     -------------
More Information                =>
```

Discussion

The primary focus of the Compare-Object cmdlet is to compare two unordered sets of objects. Although those sets of objects can be strings (as in the content of two files), the output of Compare-Object when run against files is usually counterintuitive due to the content losing its order.

When comparing large files (or files where the order of comparison matters), you can still use traditional file comparison tools such as diff.exe or the WinDiff application that comes with both the Windows Support Tools and Visual Studio.

For more information about the Compare-Object cmdlet, type **Get-Help Compare-Object**.

19.3 Verify Integrity of File Sets

Problem

You want to determine whether any files have been modified or damaged in a set of files.

Solution

To verify the integrity of file sets, use the `Get-FileHash` script provided in Recipe 17.10, "Program: Get the MD5 or SHA1 Hash of a File" to generate the signatures of those files in question. Do the same for the files on a known good system. Finally, use the `Compare-Object` cmdlet to compare those two sets.

Discussion

To generate the information from the files in question, use a command like:

```
dir C:\Windows\System32\WindowsPowerShell\v1.0 | Get-FileHash |
    Export-CliXml c:\temp\PowerShellHashes.clixml
```

This command gets the hash values of the files from *C:\Windows\System32\WindowsPowerShell\v1.0*, and uses the `Export-CliXml` cmdlet to store that data in a file.

Transport this file to a system with files in a known good state, and then import the data from that file.

```
$otherHashes = Import-CliXml c:\temp\PowerShellHashes.clixml
```

 You can also map a network drive to the files in question and skip the export, transport, and import steps altogether:

```
net use x: \\lee-desk\c$\Windows\System32\WindowsPowerShell\
v1.0

$otherHashes = dir x: | Get-FileHash
```

Generate the information from the files you know are in a good state:

```
$knownHashes = dir C:\Windows\System32\WindowsPowerShell\v1.0 |
    Get-FileHash
```

Finally, use the `Compare-Object` cmdlet to detect any differences:

```
Compare-Object $otherHashes $knownHashes -Property Path,HashValue
```

If there are any differences, the `Compare-Object` cmdlet displays them in a list, as shown in Example 19-1.

Example 19-1. The Compare-Object cmdlet showing differences between two files

```
PS >Compare-Object $otherHashes $knownHashes -Property Path,HashValue

Path                    HashValue               SideIndicator
```

Example 19-1. The Compare-Object cmdlet showing differences between two files (continued)

```
----                      ---------                    -------------
system.management.aut... 247F291CCDA8E669FF9FA... =>
system.management.aut... 5A68BC5819E29B8E3648F... <=


PS >Compare-Object $otherHashes $knownHashes -Property Path,HashValue |
>>     Select-Object Path
>>

Path
----
system.management.automation.dll-help.xml
system.management.automation.dll-help.xml
```

For more information about the Compare-Object cmdlet, type **Get-Help Compare-Object**. For more information about the Export-CliXml and Import-CliXml cmdlets, type **Get-Help Export-CliXml and Get-Help Import-CliXml**, respectively.

See Also

- Recipe 17.10, "Program: Get the MD5 or SHA1 Hash of a File"

CHAPTER 20
Event Logs

20.0 Introduction

Event logs form the core of most monitoring and diagnosis on Windows. To support this activity, PowerShell offers the Get-EventLog cmdlet to let you query and work with event log data on a system. In addition to PowerShell's built-in Get-EventLog cmdlet, its support for the .NET Framework means that you can access event logs on remote computers, add entries to event logs, and even create and delete event logs.

20.1 List All Event Logs

Problem

You want to determine which event logs exist on a system.

Solution

To list event logs on a system, use the –List parameter of the Get-EventLog cmdlet:

```
PS >Get-EventLog -List

  Max(K) Retain OverflowAction        Entries Name
  ------ ------ --------------        ------- ----
     512      0 OverwriteAsNeeded       2,157 ADAM (Test)
     512      7 OverwriteOlder          2,090 Application
     512      7 OverwriteOlder              0 Internet Explorer
   8,192     45 OverwriteOlder              0 Media Center
     512      7 OverwriteOlder              0 ScriptEvents
     512      7 OverwriteOlder          2,368 System
  15,360      0 OverwriteAsNeeded           0 Windows PowerShell
```

Discussion

The -List parameter of the Get-EventLog cmdlet generates a list of the event logs registered on the system. Like the output of nearly all PowerShell commands, these event logs are fully featured .NET objects—in this case, objects of the .NET System.Diagnostics.EventLog type. For information on how to use these objects to write entries to an event log, see Recipe 20.8, "Write to an Event Log."

 Although the heading of the Get-EventLog output shows a table heading called Name, the actual property you need to use in Where-Object (and similar commands) is Log.

For more information about the Get-EventLog cmdlet, type **Get-Help Get-EventLog**.

See Also

- Recipe 20.8, "Write to an Event Log"

20.2   Get the Newest Entries from an Event Log

Problem

You want to retrieve the most recent entries from an event log.

Solution

To retrieve the most recent entries from an event log, use the -Newest parameter of the Get-EventLog cmdlet, as shown in Example 20-1.

Example 20-1. Retrieving the 10 newest entries from the System event log

```
PS >Get-EventLog System -Newest 10 | Format-Table Index,Source,Message -A

Index Source                  Message
----- ------                  -------
 2922 Service Control Manager The Background Intelligent Transfer Servi...
 2921 Service Control Manager The Background Intelligent Transfer Servi...
 2920 Service Control Manager The Logical Disk Manager Administrative S...
 2919 Service Control Manager The Logical Disk Manager Administrative S...
 2918 Service Control Manager The Logical Disk Manager Administrative S...
 2917 TermServDevices         Driver Microsoft XPS Document Writer requ...
 2916 Print                   Printer Microsoft Office Document Image W...
 2915 Print                   Printer Microsoft Office Document Image W...
 2914 Print                   Printer Microsoft Office Document Image W...
 2913 TermServDevices         Driver Microsoft Shared Fax Driver requir...
```

Discussion

The –Newest parameter of the Get-EventLog cmdlet retrieves the most recent entries from an event log that you specify. To list the event logs available on the system, see Recipe 20.1, "List All Event Logs."

For more information about the Get-EventLog cmdlet, type **Get-Help Get-EventLog**.

See Also

- Recipe 20.1, "List All Event Logs"

20.3   Find Event Log Entries with Specific Text

Problem

You want to retrieve all event log entries that contain a given term.

Solution

To find specific event log entries, use the Get-EventLog cmdlet to retrieve the items, and then pipe them to the Where-Object cmdlet to filter them, as shown in Example 20-2.

Example 20-2. Searching the event log for entries that mention the term "disk"

```
PS >Get-EventLog System | Where-Object { $_.Message -match "disk" }
```

Index	Time		Type	Source	EventID	Message
2920	May 06	09:18	Info	Service Control M...	7036	The Logical Disk...
2919	May 06	09:17	Info	Service Control M...	7036	The Logical Disk...
2918	May 06	09:17	Info	Service Control M...	7035	The Logical Disk...
2884	May 06	00:28	Erro	sr	1	The System Resto...
2333	Apr 03	00:16	Erro	Disk	11	The driver detec...
2332	Apr 03	00:16	Erro	Disk	11	The driver detec...
2131	Mar 27	13:59	Info	Service Control M...	7036	The Logical Disk...
2127	Mar 27	12:48	Info	Service Control M...	7036	The Logical Disk...
2126	Mar 27	12:48	Info	Service Control M...	7035	The Logical Disk...
2123	Mar 27	12:31	Info	Service Control M...	7036	The Logical Disk...
2122	Mar 27	12:29	Info	Service Control M...	7036	The Logical Disk...
2121	Mar 27	12:29	Info	Service Control M...	7035	The Logical Disk...

Discussion

Since the Get-EventLog cmdlet retrieves rich objects that represent event log entries, you can pipe them to the Where-Object cmdlet for equally rich filtering.

By default, PowerShell's default table formatting displays a summary of event log entries. If you are searching the event log message, however, you are probably interested in seeing more details about the message itself. In this case, use the Format-List cmdlet to format these entries in a more detailed list view. Example 20-3 shows this view.

Example 20-3. A detailed list view of an event log entry

```
PS >Get-EventLog System | Where-Object { $_.Message -match "disk" } |
>>     Format-List
>>


Index              : 2920
EntryType          : Information
EventID            : 7036
Message            : The Logical Disk Manager Administrative Service servi
                     ce entered the stopped state.
Category           : (0)
CategoryNumber     : 0
ReplacementStrings : {Logical Disk Manager Administrative Service, stopped
                     }
Source             : Service Control Manager
TimeGenerated      : 5/6/2007 9:18:25 AM
TimeWritten        : 5/6/2007 9:18:25 AM
UserName           :

Index              : 2919
(...)
```

For more information about the Get-EventLog cmdlet, type **Get-Help Get-EventLog**. For more information about filtering command output, see Recipe 2.1, "Filter Items in a List or Command Output."

See Also

- Recipe 2.1, "Filter Items in a List or Command Output"

20.4   Retrieve a Specific Event Log Entry

Problem

You want to retrieve a specific event log entry.

Solution

To retrieve a specific event log entry, use the Get-EventLog cmdlet to retrieve the entries in the event log, and then pipe them to the Where-Object cmdlet to filter them to the one you are looking for.

```
PS >Get-EventLog System | Where-Object { $_.Index -eq 2920 }

Index Time          Type Source              EventID Message
----- ----          ---- ------              ------- -------
 2920 May 06 09:18  Info Service Control M...    7036 The Logical Disk...
```

Discussion

If you've listed the items in an event log or searched it for entries that have a message with specific text, you often want to get more details about a specific event log entry.

Since the `Get-EventLog` cmdlet retrieves rich objects that represent event log entries, you can pipe them to the `Where-Object` cmdlet for equally rich filtering.

By default, PowerShell's default table formatting displays a summary of event log entries. If you are retrieving a specific entry, however, you are probably interested in seeing more details about the entry. In this case, use the `Format-List` cmdlet to format these entries in a more detailed list view, as shown in Example 20-4.

Example 20-4. A detailed list view of an event log entry

```
PS > Get-EventLog System | Where-Object { $_.Index -eq 2920 } |
>>      Format-List
>>


Index              : 2920
EntryType          : Information
EventID            : 7036
Message            : The Logical Disk Manager Administrative Service servi
                     ce entered the stopped state.
Category           : (0)
CategoryNumber     : 0
ReplacementStrings : {Logical Disk Manager Administrative Service, stopped
                     }
Source             : Service Control Manager
TimeGenerated      : 5/6/2007 9:18:25 AM
TimeWritten        : 5/6/2007 9:18:25 AM
UserName           :

Index              : 2919
(...)
```

For more information about the `Get-EventLog` cmdlet, type **Get-Help Get-EventLog**. For more information about filtering command output, see Recipe 2.1, "Filter Items in a List or Command Output."

See Also

- Recipe 2.1, "Filter Items in a List or Command Output"

20.5   Find Event Log Entries by Their Frequency

Problem

You want to find the event log entries that occur most frequently.

Solution

To find event log entries by frequency, use the Get-EventLog cmdlet to retrieve the entries in the event log, and then pipe them to the Group-Object cmdlet to group them by their message.

```
PS >Get-EventLog System | Group-Object Message

Count Name                    Group
----- ----                    -----
   23 The Background Intelli... {LEE-DESK, LEE-DESK, LEE-DESK, LEE-DESK...
   23 The Background Intelli... {LEE-DESK, LEE-DESK, LEE-DESK, LEE-DESK...
    3 The Logical Disk Manag... {LEE-DESK, LEE-DESK, LEE-DESK}
    3 The Logical Disk Manag... {LEE-DESK, LEE-DESK, LEE-DESK}
    3 The Logical Disk Manag... {LEE-DESK, LEE-DESK, LEE-DESK}
  161 Driver Microsoft XPS D... {LEE-DESK, LEE-DESK, LEE-DESK, LEE-DESK...
(...)
```

Discussion

The Group-Object cmdlet is a useful way to determine which events occur most frequently on your system. It also provides a useful way to summarize the information in the event log.

If you want to learn more information about the items in a specific group, use the Where-Object cmdlet. Since we used the Message property in the Group-Object cmdlet, we need to filter on Message in the Where-Object cmdlet. For example, to learn more about the entries relating to the Microsoft XPS Driver (from the scenario in the solution):

```
PS >Get-EventLog System |
>>    Where-Object { $_.Message -like "Driver Microsoft XPS*" }
>>

Index Time          Type Source              EventID Message
----- ----          ---- ------              ------- -------
 2917 May 06 09:13  Erro TermServDevices        1111 Driver Microsoft...
 2883 May 05 10:40  Erro TermServDevices        1111 Driver Microsoft...
 2877 May 05 08:10  Erro TermServDevices        1111 Driver Microsoft...
(...)
```

If grouping by message doesn't provide useful information, you can group by any other property—such as source:

```
PS >Get-EventLog Application | Group-Object Source

Count Name                      Group
----- ----                      -----
    4 Application               {LEE-DESK, LEE-DESK, LEE-DESK, LEE-DESK}
  191 Media Center Scheduler    {LEE-DESK, LEE-DESK, LEE-DESK, LEE-DESK...
 1082 MSSQL$SQLEXPRESS          {LEE-DESK, LEE-DESK, LEE-DESK, LEE-DESK...
(...)
```

If you've listed the items in an event log or searched it for entries that have a message with specific text, you often want to get more details about a specific event log entry.

By default, PowerShell's default table formatting displays a summary of event log entries. If you are retrieving a specific entry, however, you are probably interested in seeing more details about the entry. In this case, use the Format-List cmdlet to format these entries in a more detailed list view, as shown in Example 20-5.

Example 20-5. A detailed list view of an event log entry

```
PS >Get-EventLog System | Where-Object { $_.Index -eq 2917 } |
>>     Format-List
>>


Index              : 2917
EntryType          : Error
EventID            : 1111
Message            : Driver Microsoft XPS Document Writer required for pri
                     nter Microsoft XPS Document Writer is unknown. Contac
                     t the administrator to install the driver before you
                     log in again.
Category           : (0)
CategoryNumber     : 0
ReplacementStrings : {Microsoft XPS Document Writer, Microsoft XPS Documen
                     t Writer}
Source             : TermServDevices
TimeGenerated      : 5/6/2007 9:13:31 AM
TimeWritten        : 5/6/2007 9:13:31 AM
UserName           :
```

For more information about the Get-EventLog cmdlet, type **Get-Help Get-EventLog**. For more information about filtering command output, see Recipe 2.1, "Filter Items in a List or Command Output." For more information about the Group-Object cmdlet, type **Get-Help Group-Object**.

See Also

- Recipe 2.1, "Filter Items in a List or Command Output"

20.6 Back Up an Event Log

Problem

You want to store the information in an event log in a file for storage or later review.

Solution

To store event log entries in a file, use the Get-EventLog cmdlet to retrieve the entries in the event log, and then pipe them to the Export-CliXml cmdlet to store them in a file.

```
Get-EventLog System | Export-CliXml c:\temp\SystemLogBackup.clixml
```

Discussion

Once you've exported the events from an event log, you can archive them, or use the Import-CliXml cmdlet to review them on any machine that has PowerShell installed:

```
PS >$archivedLogs = Import-CliXml c:\temp\SystemLogBackup.clixml
PS >$archivedLogs | Group Source

Count Name                     Group
----- ----                     -----
  856 Service Control Manager  {LEE-DESK, LEE-DESK, LEE-DESK, LEE-DESK...
  640 TermServDevices          {LEE-DESK, LEE-DESK, LEE-DESK, LEE-DESK...
   91 Print                    {LEE-DESK, LEE-DESK, LEE-DESK, LEE-DESK...
  100 WMPNetworkSvc            {LEE-DESK, LEE-DESK, LEE-DESK, LEE-DESK...
  12] Tcpip                    {LEE-DESK, LEE-DESK, LEE-DESK, LEE-DESK...
(...)
```

For more information about the Get-EventLog cmdlet, type **Get-Help Get-EventLog**. For more information about the Export-CliXml and Import-CliXml cmdlets, type **Get-Help Export-CliXml** and **Get-Help Import-CliXml**, respectively.

20.7 Create or Remove an Event Log

Problem

You want to create or remove an event log.

Solution

To create an event log, use the [System.Diagnostics.EventLog]:: CreateEventSource() method from the .NET Framework:

```
$newLog =
    New-Object Diagnostics.EventSourceCreationData
    "PowerShellCookbook","ScriptEvents"

[Diagnostics.EventLog]::CreateEventSource($newLog)
```

To delete an event log, use the [System.Diagnostics.EventLog]::Delete() method from the .NET Framework:

```
[Diagnostics.EventLog]::Delete("ScriptEvents")
```

Discussion

The [System.Diagnostics.EventLog]::CreateEventSource() method from the .NET Framework registers a new event source (PowerShellCookbook in the solution) to write entries to an event log (ScriptEvents in the solution). If the event log does not exist, the CreateEventSource() method creates the event log.

The [System.Diagnostics.EventLog]::Delete() method from the .NET Framework deletes the event log altogether, along with any event sources associated with it. To delete only a specific event source, use the [System.Diagnostics.EventLog]::DeleteEventSource() method from the .NET Framework.

 Be careful when deleting event logs, as it is difficult to recreate all the event sources if you delete the wrong log by accident.

For more information about working with classes from the .NET Framework, see Recipe 3.4, "Work with .NET Objects."

See Also

- Recipe 3.4, "Work with .NET Objects"

20.8   Write to an Event Log

Problem

You want to add an entry to an event log.

Solution

To write to an event log, use the -List parameter on the Get-EventLog cmdlet to retrieve the proper event log. Then, set its source to a registered event log source and call its WriteEntry() method:

```
PS >$log = Get-EventLog -List | Where-Object { $_.Log -eq "ScriptEvents" }
PS >$log.Source = "PowerShellCookbook"
PS >$log.WriteEntry("This is a message from my script.")
PS >
PS >Get-EventLog ScriptEvents -Newest 1 | Select Source,Message

Source                          Message
------                          -------

PowerShellCookbook                 This is a message from my script.
```

Discussion

As the solution mentions, you must set the event log's Source property to a registered event log source before you can write information to the log. If you have not already registered an event log source on the system, see Recipe 20.7, "Create or Remove an Event Log."

For more information about working with classes from the .NET Framework, see Recipe 3.4, "Work with .NET Objects."

See Also

- Recipe 3.4, "Work with .NET Objects"
- Recipe 20.7, "Create or Remove an Event Log"

20.9   Access Event Logs of a Remote Machine

Problem

You want to access event log entries from a remote machine.

Solution

To access event logs on a remote machine, create a new System.Diagnostics.EventLog class with the log name and computer name. Then access its Entries property:

```
PS >$log = New-Object Diagnostics.EventLog "System","LEE-DESK"
PS >$log.Entries | Group-Object Source

Count Name                       Group
----- ----                       -----
   91 Print                      {LEE-DESK, LEE-DESK, LEE-DESK, LEE-DESK...
  640 TermServDevices            {LEE-DESK, LEE-DESK, LEE-DESK, LEE-DESK...
  148 W32Time                    {LEE-DESK, LEE-DESK, LEE-DESK, LEE-DESK...
  100 WMPNetworkSvc              {LEE-DESK, LEE-DESK, LEE-DESK, LEE-DESK...
  856 Service Control Manager    {LEE-DESK, LEE-DESK, LEE-DESK, LEE-DESK...
  123 Tcpip                      {LEE-DESK, LEE-DESK, LEE-DESK, LEE-DESK...
(...)
```

Discussion

The solution demonstrates one way to get access to event logs on a remote machine. In addition to retrieving the event log entries, the System.Diagnostics.EventLog class also lets you perform other operations on remote computers, such as creating event logs, removing event logs, writing event log entries, and more.

The System.Diagnostics.EventLog class supports this through additional parameters to the methods that manage event logs. For example, to get the event logs from a remote machine:

```
[Diagnostics.EventLog]::GetEventLogs("LEE-DESK")
```

To create an event log or event source on a remote machine:

```
$newLog =
    New-Object Diagnostics.EventSourceCreationData
"PowerShellCookbook","ScriptEvents"
$newLog.MachineName = "LEE-DESK"
[Diagnostics.EventLog]::CreateEventSource($newLog)
```

To write entries to an event log on a remote machine:

```
$log = New-Object Diagnostics.EventLog "ScriptEvents","LEE-DESK"
$log.Source = "PowerShellCookbook"
$log.WriteEntry("Test event from a remote machine.")
```

For information about how to get event logs, see Recipe 20.1, "List All Event Logs;" for more information about how to create or delete event logs, see Recipe 20.7, "Create or Remove an Event Log;" and for more information about how to write event log entries, see Recipe 20.8, "Write to an Event Log."

For more information about working with classes from the .NET Framework, see Recipe 3.4, "Work with .NET Objects."

See Also

- Recipe 3.4, "Work with .NET Objects"
- Recipe 20.1, "List All Event Logs"
- Recipe 20.7, "Create or Remove an Event Log"
- Recipe 20.8, "Write to an Event Log"

## CHAPTER 21

Processes

21.0 Introduction

Working with system processes is a natural aspect of system administration. It is also the source of most of the regular expression magic and kung fu that makes system administrators proud. After all, who wouldn't boast about this Unix one-liner to stop all processes using more than 100 MB of memory:

```
ps -el | awk '{ if ( $6 > (1024*100)) { print $3 } }' | grep -v PID | xargs kill
```

While helpful, it also demonstrates the inherently fragile nature of pure text processing. For this command to succeed, it must:

* Depend on the ps command to display memory usage in column 6.
* Depend on column 6 of the ps command's output to represent the memory usage in kilobytes.
* Depend on column 3 of the ps command's output to represent the process id.
* Remove the header column from the ps command's output.

Since PowerShell's Get-Process cmdlet returns information as highly structured .NET objects, fragile text parsing becomes a thing of the past:

```
Get-Process | Where-Object { $_.WorkingSet -gt 100mb } | Stop-Process -WhatIf
```

If brevity is important, PowerShell defines aliases to make most commands easier to type:

```
gps | ? { $_.WS -gt 100mb } | kill -WhatIf
```

21.1 List Currently Running Processes

Problem

You want to see which processes are running on the system.

Solution

To retrieve the list of currently running processes, use the Get-Process cmdlet:

```
PS >Get-Process

Handles  NPM(K)    PM(K)      WS(K) VM(M)   CPU(s)     Id ProcessName
-------  ------    -----      ----- -----   ------     -- -----------
    274       6     1328       3940    33             1084 alg
     85       4     3816       6656    57     5.67    3460 AutoHotkey
     50       2     2292       1980    14   384.25    1560 BrmfRsmg
     71       3     2520       4680    35     0.42    2592 cmd
    946       7     3676       6204    32              848 csrss
     84       4      732       2248    22             3144 csrss
     68       4      936       3364    30     0.38    3904 ctfmon
    243       7     3648       9324    48     2.02    2892 Ditto
(...)
```

Discussion

The Get-Process cmdlet retrieves information about all processes running on the system. Because these are rich .NET objects (of the type System.Diagnostics.Process), advanced filters and operations are easier than ever before.

For example, to find all processes using more than 100 MB of memory:

```
PS >Get-Process | Where-Object { $_.WorkingSet -gt 100mb }

Handles  NPM(K)    PM(K)      WS(K) VM(M)   CPU(s)     Id ProcessName
-------  ------    -----      ----- -----   ------     -- -----------
   1458      29    83468     105824   273   323.80   3992 BigBloatedApp
```

To group processes by company:

```
PS >Get-Process | Group-Object Company

Count Name                     Group
----- ----                     -----
   39                          {alg, csrss, csrss, dllhost...}
    4                          {AutoHotkey, Ditto, gnuserv, mafwTray}
    1 Brother Industries, Ltd. {BrmfRsmg}
   19 Microsoft Corporation    {cmd, ctfmon, EXCEL, explorer...}
    1 Free Software Foundation  {emacs}
    1 Microsoft (R) Corporation {FwcMgmt}
(...)
```

Or perhaps to sort by start time (with the most recent first):

```
PS >Get-Process | Sort -Descending StartTime | Select-Object -First 10

Handles  NPM(K)    PM(K)      WS(K) VM(M)   CPU(s)     Id ProcessName
-------  ------    -----      ----- -----   ------     -- -----------
   1810      39    53616      33964   193   318.02   1452 iTunes
    675       6    41472      50180   146    49.36    296 powershell
   1240      35    48220      58860   316   167.58   4012 OUTLOOK
```

305	8	5736	2460	105	21.22	3384	WindowsSearch...
464	7	29704	30920	153	6.00	3680	powershell
1458	29	83468	105824	273	324.22	3992	iexplore
478	6	24620	23688	143	17.83	3548	powershell
222	8	8532	19084	144	20.69	3924	EXCEL
14	2	396	1600	15	0.06	2900	logon.scr
544	18	21336	50216	294	180.72	2660	WINWORD

These advanced tasks become incredibly simple due to the rich amount of information that PowerShell returns for each process. For more information about the Get-Process cmdlet, type **Get-Help Get-Process**. For more information about filtering, grouping, and sorting in PowerShell commands, see Recipe 2.1, "Filter Items in a List or Command Output."

For more information about working with classes from the .NET Framework, see Recipe 3.4, "Work with .NET Objects."

See Also

- Recipe 2.1, "Filter Items in a List or Command Output"
- Recipe 3.4, "Work with .NET Objects"

21.2 Launch a Process

Problem

You want to launch a new process on the system, but also want to configure its startup environment.

Solution

To launch a new process, use the [System.Diagnostics.Process]::Start() method. To control its startup environment, supply it with a System.Diagnostics. ProcessStartInfo object that you prepare, as shown in Example 21-1.

Example 21-1. Configuring the startup environment of a new process

```
$credential = Get-Credential

## Prepare the startup information (including username and password)
$startInfo = New-Object Diagnostics.ProcessStartInfo
$startInfo.UserName = $credential.Username
$startInfo.Password = $credential.Password
$startInfo.Filename = "powershell"

## Start the process
$startInfo.UseShellExecute = $false
[Diagnostics.Process]::Start($startInfo)
```

Discussion

Normally, launching a process in PowerShell is as simple as typing the program name:

```
PS >notepad c:\temp\test.txt
```

However, you may sometimes need detailed control over the process details, such as its credentials, startup directory, environment variables, and more. In those situations, use the [System.Diagnostics.Process]::Start() method to provide that functionality.

> The following function acts like the *cmd.exe* start command and like the Start | Run dialog in Windows:
>
> ```
> PS >function start { [Diagnostics.Process]::Start($args) }
> PS >start www.msn.com
> ```

For more information about launching programs from PowerShell, see Recipe 1.1, "Run Programs, Scripts, and Existing Tools." For more information about working with classes from the .NET Framework, see Recipe 3.4, "Work with .NET Objects."

See Also

- Recipe 1.1, "Run Programs, Scripts, and Existing Tools"
- Recipe 3.4, "Work with .NET Objects"

21.3   Stop a Process

Problem

You want to stop (or kill) a process on the system.

Solution

To stop a process, use the Stop-Process cmdlet, as shown in Example 21-2.

Example 21-2. Stopping a process using the Stop-Process cmdlet

```
PS >notepad
PS >Get-Process Notepad

Handles  NPM(K)    PM(K)     WS(K) VM(M)   CPU(s)     Id ProcessName
-------  ------    -----     ----- -----   ------     -- -----------
     42       3     1276      3916    32     0.09   3520 notepad


PS >Stop-Process  -ProcessName notepad
PS >Get-Process Notepad
```

Example 21-2. Stopping a process using the Stop-Process cmdlet (continued)

```
Get-Process : Cannot find a process with the name 'Notepad'. Verify the
process name and call the cmdlet again.
At line:1 char:12
+ Get-Process  <<<< Notepad
```

Discussion

While the parameters of the Stop-Process cmdlet are useful in their own right, Power-Shell's pipeline model lets you be even more precise. The Stop-Process cmdlet stops any processes that you pipeline into it, so an advanced process set generated by Get-Process automatically turns into an advanced process set for the Stop-Process cmdlet to operate on:

```
PS >Get-Process | Where-Object { $_.WorkingSet -lt 10mb } |
>>     Sort-Object -Descending Name | Stop-Process -WhatIf
>>
What if: Performing operation "Stop-Process" on Target "svchost (1368)".
What if: Performing operation "Stop-Process" on Target "sqlwriter (1772)".
What if: Performing operation "Stop-Process" on Target "qttask (3672)".
What if: Performing operation "Stop-Process" on Target "Ditto (2892)".
What if: Performing operation "Stop-Process" on Target "ctfmon (3904)".
What if: Performing operation "Stop-Process" on Target "csrss (848)".
What if: Performing operation "Stop-Process" on Target "BrmfRsmg (1560)".
What if: Performing operation "Stop-Process" on Target "AutoHotkey (3460)".
What if: Performing operation "Stop Process" on Target "alg (1084)".
```

 Notice that this example uses the -WhatIf flag on the Stop-Process cmdlet. This flag lets you see what would happen if you were to run the command but doesn't actually perform the action.

For more information about the Stop-Process cmdlet, type **Get-Help Stop-Process**. For more information about the Where-Object cmdlet, type **Get-Help Where-Object**.

21.4 Program: Invoke a PowerShell Expression on a Remote Machine

Example 21-4 lets you start processes and invoke PowerShell expressions on remote machines. It uses PsExec (from *http://www.microsoft.com/technet/sysinternals/utilities/psexec.mspx*) to support the actual remote command execution.

This script offers more power than just remote command execution, however. As Example 21-3 demonstrates, it leverages PowerShell's capability to import and export strongly structured data, so you can work with the command output using many of the same techniques you use to work with command output on the local system. Example 21-3 demonstrates this power by filtering command output on the remote system but sorting it on the local system.

Example 21-3. Invoking a PowerShell expression on a remote machine

```
PS >$command = { Get-Process | Where-Object { $_.Handles -gt 1000 } }
PS >Invoke-RemoteExpression \\LEE-DESK $command | Sort Handles

Handles  NPM(K)    PM(K)    WS(K) VM(M)   CPU(s)    Id ProcessName
-------  ------    -----    ----- -----   ------    -- -----------
   1025       8     3780     3772    32   134.42   848 csrss
   1306      37    50364    64160   322   409.23  4012 OUTLOOK
   1813      39    54764    36360   321   340.45  1452 iTunes
   2316     273    29168    41164   218   134.09  1244 svchost
```

Since this strongly structured data comes from objects on another system, PowerShell does not regenerate the functionality of those objects (except in rare cases). For more information about importing and exporting structured data, see Recipe 8.4, "Easily Import and Export Your Structured Data."

Example 21-4. Invoke-RemoteExpression.ps1

```
##############################################################################
##
## Invoke-RemoteExpression.ps1
##
## Invoke a PowerShell expression on a remote machine. Requires PsExec from
## http://www.microsoft.com/technet/sysinternals/utilities/psexec.mspx
##
## ie:
##
##  PS >Invoke-RemoteExpression \\LEE-DESK { Get-Process }
##  PS >(Invoke-RemoteExpression \\LEE-DESK { Get-Date }).AddDays(1)
##  PS >Invoke-RemoteExpression \\LEE-DESK { Get-Process } | Sort Handles
##
##############################################################################

param(
  $computer = "\\$ENV:ComputerName",
  [ScriptBlock] $expression = $(throw "Please specify an expression to invoke."),
  [switch] $noProfile
  )

## Prepare the command line for PsExec. We use the XML output encoding so
## that PowerShell can convert the output back into structured objects.
$commandLine = "echo . | powershell -Output XML "

if($noProfile)
{
    $commandLine += "-NoProfile "
}

## Convert the command into an encoded command for PowerShell
$commandBytes = [System.Text.Encoding]::Unicode.GetBytes($expression)
$encodedCommand = [Convert]::ToBase64String($commandBytes)
$commandLine += "-EncodedCommand $encodedCommand"
```

Example 21-4. Invoke-RemoteExpression.ps1 (continued)

```
## Collect the output and error output
$errorOutput = [IO.Path]::GetTempFileName()
$output = psexec /acceptEula $computer cmd /c $commandLine 2>$errorOutput

## Check for any errors
$errorContent = Get-Content $errorOutput
Remove-Item $errorOutput
if($errorContent -match "Access is denied")
{
    $OFS = "`n"
    $errorMessage = "Could not execute remote expression. "
    $errorMessage += "Ensure that your account has administrative " +
        "privileges on the target machine.`n"
    $errorMessage += ($errorContent -match "psexec.exe :")

    Write-Error $errorMessage
}

## Return the output to the user
$output
```

For more information about running scripts, see Recipe 1.1, "Run Programs, Scripts, and Existing Tools."

See Also

- Recipe 1.1, "Run Programs, Scripts, and Existing Tools"
- Recipe 8.4, "Easily Import and Export Your Structured Data"

CHAPTER 22
System Services

22.0 Introduction

As the support mechanism for many administrative tasks on Windows, managing and working with system services naturally fits into the administrator's toolbox.

PowerShell offers a handful of cmdlets to help make working with system services easier: from listing services, to life cycle management, and even to service installation.

22.1 List All Running Services

Problem

You want to see which services are running on the system.

Solution

To list all running services, use the Get-Service cmdlet:

```
PS >Get-Service

Status   Name          DisplayName
------   ----          -----------
Running  ADAM_Test     Test
Stopped  Alerter       Alerter
Running  ALG           Application Layer Gateway Service
Stopped  AppMgmt       Application Management
Stopped  aspnet_state  ASP.NET State Service
Running  AudioSrv      Windows Audio
Running  BITS          Background Intelligent Transfer Ser...
Running  Browser       Computer Browser
(...)
```

Discussion

The Get-Service cmdlet retrieves information about all services running on the system. Because these are rich .NET objects (of the type System.ServiceProcess. ServiceController), you can apply advanced filters and operations to make managing services straightforward.

For example, to find all running services:

```
PS >Get-Service | Where-Object { $_.Status -eq "Running" }

Status   Name           DisplayName
------   ----           -----------
Running  ADAM_Test      Test
Running  ALG            Application Layer Gateway Service
Running  AudioSrv       Windows Audio
Running  BITS           Background Intelligent Transfer Ser...
Running  Browser        Computer Browser
Running  COMSysApp      COM+ System Application
Running  CryptSvc       Cryptographic Services
```

Or, to sort services by the number of services that depend on them:

```
PS >Get-Service | Sort-Object -Descending { $_.DependentServices.Count }

Status   Name              DisplayName
------   ----              -----------
Running  RpcSs             Remote Procedure Call (RPC)
Running  PlugPlay          Plug and Play
Running  lanmanworkstation Workstation
Running  SSDPSRV           SSDP Discovery Service
Running  TapiSrv           Telephony
(...)
```

Since PowerShell returns full-fidelity .NET objects that represent system services, these tasks and more become incredibly simple due to the rich amount of information that PowerShell returns for each service. For more information about the Get-Service cmdlet, type **Get-Help Get-Service**. For more information about filtering, grouping, and sorting in PowerShell commands, see Recipe 2.1, "Filter Items in a List or Command Output."

> The Get-Service cmdlet displays most (but not all) information about running services. For additional information (such as the service's startup mode), use the Get-WmiObject cmdlet:
> ```
> $service = Get-WmiObject Win32_Service |
>     Where-Object { $_.Name -eq "AudioSrv" }
> $service.StartMode
> ```

For more information about working with classes from the .NET Framework, see Recipe 3.4, "Work with .NET Objects." For more information about working with the Get-WmiObject cmdlet, see Recipe 15.1, "Access Windows Management Instrumentation Data."

See Also

- Recipe 2.1, "Filter Items in a List or Command Output"
- Recipe 3.4, "Work with .NET Objects"
- Recipe 15.1, "Access Windows Management Instrumentation Data"

22.2   Manage a Running Service

Problem

You want to manage a running service.

Solution

To stop a service, use the Stop-Service cmdlet:

```
PS >Stop-Service AudioSrv -WhatIf
What if: Performing operation "Stop-Service" on Target "Windows Audio (Audi
oSrv)".
```

Likewise, use the Suspend-Service, Restart-Service, and Resume-Service cmdlets to suspend, restart, and resume services, respectively.

For other tasks (such as setting the startup mode), use the Get-WmiObject cmdlet:

```
$service = Get-WmiObject Win32_Service |
    Where-Object { $_.Name -eq "AudioSrv" }
$service.ChangeStartMode("Manual")
$service.ChangeStartMode("Automatic")
```

Discussion

The Stop-Service cmdlet lets you stop a service either by name or display name.

 Notice that the solution uses the -WhatIf flag on the Stop-Service cmdlet. This parameter lets you see what would happen if you were to run the command but doesn't actually perform the action.

For more information about the Stop-Service cmdlet, type **Get-Help Stop-Service**. If you want to suspend, restart, or resume a service, see the Suspend-Service, Restart-Service, and Resume-Service cmdlets, respectively.

For more information about working with the Get-WmiObject cmdlet, see Recipe 15.1, "Access Windows Management Instrumentation Data."

See Also

*   Recipe 15.1, "Access Windows Management Instrumentation Data"

22.3   Access Services on a Remote Machine

Problem

You want to list or manage services on a remote machine.

Solution

To retrieve the services from a remote machine, use the `[System.ServiceProcess.ServiceController]::GetServices()` method from the .NET Framework.

```
PS >[void] ([Reflection.Assembly]::LoadWithPartialName("System.ServiceProcess"))
PS >[System.ServiceProcess.ServiceController]::GetServices("LEE-DESK")

Status    Name           DisplayName
------    ----           -----------
Running   ADAM_Test      Test
Stopped   Alerter        Alerter
Running   ALG            Application Layer Gateway Service
Stopped   AppMgmt        Application Management
Stopped   aspnet_state   ASP.NET State Service
Running   AudioSrv       Windows Audio
Running   BITS           Background Intelligent Transfer Ser...
Running   Browser        Computer Browser
Stopped   CiSvc          Indexing Service
```

To control one, use the `Where-Object` cmdlet to retrieve that one specifically and then call the methods on the object that manage it:

```
[void] ([Reflection.Assembly]::LoadWithPartialName("System.ServiceProcess"))
$service -
   [System.ServiceProcess.ServiceController]::GetServices("LEE-DESK") |
   Where-Object { $_.Name -eq "Themes" }

$service.Stop()
$service.WaitForStatus("Stopped")
Start-Sleep 2
$service.Start()
```

Discussion

If you have administrator privileges on a remote machine, the [System.
ServiceProcess.ServiceController]::GetServices() method from the .NET Framework lets you control services on that machine.

 When doing this, note that both of the examples from the solution
require that you first load the assembly that contains the .NET classes
that manage services. The *-Service cmdlets load this DLL automatically.

For more information about working with classes from the .NET Framework, see
Recipe 3.4, "Work with .NET Objects."

See Also

- Recipe 3.4, "Work with .NET Objects"

## CHAPTER 23

Active Directory

23.0 Introduction

By far, the one thing that makes system administration on the Windows platform most unique is its interaction with Active Directory. As the centralized authorization, authentication, and information store for Windows networks, Active Directory automation forms the core of many enterprise administration tasks.

While PowerShell doesn't include either Active Directory cmdlets or an Active Directory provider, its access through the .NET Framework provides support for the broad range of Active Directory administration.

23.1 Test Active Directory Scripts on a Local Installation

Problem

You want to test your Active Directory scripts against a local installation.

Solution

To test your scripts against a local system, install Active Directory Application Mode (ADAM) and its sample configuration.

Discussion

To test your scripts against a local installation, you'll need to install ADAM, and then create a test instance.

Install ADAM

To install ADAM, the first step is to download it. Microsoft provides ADAM free of charge from the Download Center. You can obtain it by searching for "Active Directory Application Mode" at *http://download.microsoft.com*.

Once you've downloaded it, run the setup program to install ADAM. Figure 23.1 shows the ADAM setup wizard.

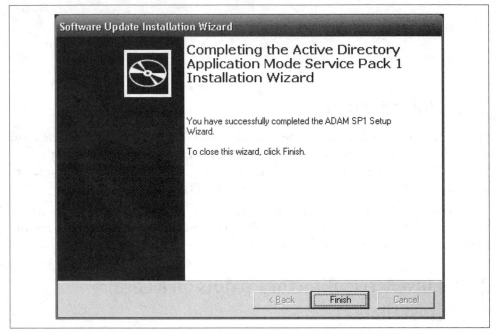

Figure 23-1. ADAM's post-installation screen

Create a test instance

From the ADAM menu in the Windows Start menu, select Create an ADAM instance. In the Setup Options page that appears next, select *A unique instance*. In the Instance Name page, type **Test** as an instance name. Accept the default ports, and then select Yes, create an application directory partition on the next page. As the partition name, type **DC=Fabrikam,DC=COM**, as shown in Figure 23-2.

In the next pages, accept the default file locations, service accounts, and administrators.

When the setup wizard gives you the option to import LDIF files, import all available files except for *MS-AZMan.LDF*. Click Next on this page and the confirmation page to complete the instance setup.

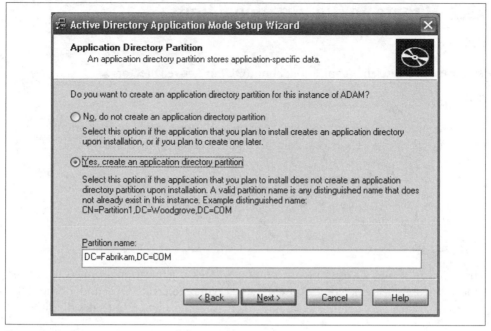

Figure 23-2. Creating a partition of a test ADAM instance

Open a PowerShell window, and test your new instance:

```
PS >[adsi] "LDAP://localhost:389/dc=Fabrikam,dc=COM"

distinguishedName
-----------------
{DC=Fabrikam,DC=COM}
```

The [adsi] tag is a *type shortcut*, like several other type shortcuts in PowerShell. The [adsi] type shortcut provides a quick way to create and work with directory entries through *Active Directory Service Interfaces*.

Although scripts that act against an ADAM test environment are almost identical to those that operate directly against Active Directory, there are a few minor differences. ADAM scripts specify the host and port in their binding string (that is, localhost:389/), whereas Active Directory scripts do not.

For more information about type shortcuts in PowerShell, see "Working with the .NET Framework" in Appendix A.

See Also

* "Working with the .NET Framework" in Appendix A

23.2   Create an Organizational Unit

Problem

You want to create an organizational unit (OU) in Active Directory.

Solution

To create an organizational unit in a container, use the [adsi] type shortcut to bind to a part of the Active Directory, and then call the Create() method.

```
$domain = [adsi] "LDAP://localhost:389/dc=Fabrikam,dc=COM"
$salesOrg = $domain.Create("OrganizationalUnit", "OU=Sales")
$salesOrg.Put("Description", "Sales Headquarters, SF")
$salesOrg.Put("wwwHomePage", "http://fabrikam.com/sales")
$salesOrg.SetInfo()
```

Discussion

The solution shows an example of creating a Sales organizational unit (OU) at the root of the organization. You can use the same syntax to create OUs under other OUs as well. Example 23-1 demonstrates how to create an East and West sales division.

Example 23-1. Creating East and West sales divisions

```
$sales = [adsi] "LDAP://localhost:389/ou=Sales,dc=Fabrikam,dc=COM"

$east = $sales.Create("OrganizationalUnit", "OU=East")
$east.Put("wwwHomePage", "http://fabrikam.com/sales/east")
$east.SetInfo()

$west = $sales.Create("OrganizationalUnit", "OU=West")
$west.Put("wwwHomePage", "http://fabrikam.com/sales/west")
$west.SetInfo()
```

To see that these OUs have been created, see Recipe 23.5, "Get the Children of an Active Directory Container."

See Also

- Recipe 23.5, "Get the Children of an Active Directory Container"

23.3   Get the Properties of an Organizational Unit

Problem

You want to get and list the properties of a specific OU.

Solution

To list the properties of an OU, use the [adsi] type shortcut to bind to the OU in Active Directory, and then pass the OU to the Format-List cmdlet:

```
$organizationalUnit =
  [adsi] "LDAP://localhost:389/ou=West,ou=Sales,dc=Fabrikam,dc=COM"

$organizationalUnit | Format-List *
```

Discussion

The solution retrieves the Sales West OU. By default, the Format-List cmdlet shows only the distinguished name of the group, so we type **Format-List** * to display all properties.

If you know which property you want the value of, you can specify it by name:

```
PS >$organizationalUnit.wWWHomePage
http://fabrikam.com/sales/west
```

Unlike OUs, some types of Active Directory objects don't let you retrieve their properties by name this way. Instead, you must call the Get() method to retrieve specific properties:

```
PS >$organizationalUnit.Get("name")
West
```

23.4 Modify Properties of an Organizational Unit

Problem

You want to modify properties of a specific OU.

Solution

To modify the properties of an OU, use the [adsi] type shortcut to bind to the OU in Active Directory, and then call the Put() method. Finally, call the SetInfo() method to apply the changes.

```
$organizationalUnit =
  [adsi] "LDAP://localhost:389/ou=West,ou=Sales,dc=Fabrikam,dc=COM"

$organizationalUnit.Put("Description", "Sales West Organization")
$organizationalUnit.SetInfo()
```

Discussion

The solution retrieves the Sales West OU. It then sets the description to Sales West Organization, and then applies those changes to Active Directory.

23.5   Get the Children of an Active Directory Container

Problem

You want to list all the children of an Active Directory container.

Solution

To list the items in a container, use the [adsi] type shortcut to bind to the OU in Active Directory, and then access the PsBase.Children property of that container:

```
$sales =
  [adsi] "LDAP://localhost:389/ou=Sales,dc=Fabrikam,dc=COM"
$sales.PsBase.Children
```

Discussion

The solution lists all the children of the Sales OU. This is the level of information you typically get from selecting a node in the ADSIEdit MMC snapin. If you want to filter this information to include only users, other organizational units, or more complex queries, see Recipe 23.8, "Search for a User Account."

See Also

- Recipe 23.8, "Search for a User Account"

23.6   Create a User Account

Problem

You want to create a user account in a specific OU.

Solution

To create a user in a container, use the [adsi] type shortcut to bind to the OU in Active Directory, and then call the Create() method:

```
$salesWest =
  [adsi] "LDAP://localhost:389/ou=West,ou=Sales,dc=Fabrikam,dc=COM"

$user = $salesWest.Create("User", "CN=MyerKen")
$user.Put("userPrincipalName", "Ken.Myer@fabrikam.com")
$user.Put("displayName", "Ken Myer")
$user.SetInfo()
```

Discussion

The solution creates a user under the Sales West organizational unit. It sets the userPrincipalName (a unique identifier for the user), as well as the user's display name.

 When you run this script against a real Active Directory deployment (as opposed to an ADAM instance), be sure to update the sAMAccountName property, or you'll get an autogenerated default.

To see that these users have been created, see Recipe 23.5, "Get the Children of an Active Directory Container."

If you need to create users in bulk, see the following section, Recipe 23.7, "Program: Import Users in Bulk to Active Directory."

See Also

- Recipe 23.5, "Get the Children of an Active Directory Container"
- Recipe 23.7, "Program: Import Users in Bulk to Active Directory"

23.7   Program: Import Users in Bulk to Active Directory

When importing several users into Active Directory, it quickly becomes tiresome to do it by hand (or even to script the addition of each user one-by-one). To solve this problem, we can put all our data into a CSV, and then do a bulk import from the information in the CSV.

Example 23-2 supports this in a flexible way. You provide a container to hold the user accounts and a CSV that holds the account information. For each row in the CSV, the script creates a user from the data in that row. The only mandatory column is a CN column to define the common name of the user. Any other columns, if present, represent other Active Directory attributes you want to define for that user.

Example 23-2. Import-ADUser.ps1

```
##############################################################################
##
## Import-AdUser.ps1
##
## Create users in Active Directory from the content of a CSV.
##
## For example:
## $container = "LDAP://localhost:389/ou=West,ou=Sales,dc=Fabrikam,dc=COM"
## Import-ADUser.ps1 $container .\users.csv
##
## In the user CSV, One column must be named "CN" for the user name.
```

Example 23-2. Import-ADUser.ps1 (continued)

```
## All other columns represent properties in Active Directory for that user.
##
## For example:
## CN,userPrincipalName,displayName,manager
## MyerKen,Ken.Myer@fabrikam.com,Ken Myer,
## DoeJane,Jane.Doe@fabrikam.com,Jane Doe,"CN=MyerKen,OU=West,OU=Sales,DC=..."
## SmithRobin,Robin.Smith@fabrikam.com,Robin Smith,"CN=MyerKen,OU=West,OU=..."
##
################################################################################

param(
  $container = $(throw "Please specify a container (such as " +
    "LDAP://localhost:389/ou=West,ou=Sales,dc=Fabrikam,dc=COM)"),
  $csvPath = $(throw "Please specify the path to the users CSV")
  )

## Bind to the container
$userContainer = [adsi] $container

## Ensure that the container was valid
if(-not $userContainer.Name)
{
    Write-Error "Could not connect to $container"
    return
}

## Load the CSV
$users = @(Import-Csv $csvPath)
if($users.Count -eq 0)
{
    return
}

## Go through each user from the CSV
foreach($user in $users)
{
    ## Pull out the name, and create that user
    $username = $user.CN
    $newUser = $userContainer.Create("User", "CN=$username")

    ## Go through each of the properties from the CSV, and set its value
    ## on the user
    foreach($property in $user.PsObject.Properties)
    {
        ## Skip the property if it was the CN property that sets the
        ## user name
        if($property.Name -eq "CN")
        {
            continue
        }

        ## Ensure they specified a value for the property
```

Example 23-2. Import-ADUser.ps1 (continued)

```
        if(-not $property.Value)
        {
            continue
        }

        ## Set the value of the property
        $newUser.Put($property.Name, $property.Value)
    }

    ## Finalize the information in Active Directory
    $newUser.SetInfo()
}
```

For more information about running scripts, see Recipe 1.1, "Run Programs, Scripts, and Existing Tools."

See Also

*   Recipe 1.1, "Run Programs, Scripts, and Existing Tools"

23.8   Search for a User Account

Problem

You want to search for a specific user account, but don't know the user's distinguished name (DN).

Solution

To search for a user in Active Directory, use the [adsi] type shortcut to bind to a container that holds the user account, and then use the System.DirectoryServices. DirectorySearcher class from the .NET Framework to search for the user:

```
$domain = [adsi] "LDAP://localhost:389/dc=Fabrikam,dc=COM"
$searcher = New-Object System.DirectoryServices.DirectorySearcher $domain
$searcher.Filter = '(&(objectClass=User)(displayName=Ken Myer))'

$userResult = $searcher.FindOne()
$user = $userResult.GetDirectoryEntry()
```

Discussion

When you don't know the full DN of a user account, the System.DirectoryServices. DirectorySearcher class from the .NET Framework lets you search for it.

You provide an LDAP filter (in this case, searching for users with the display name of *Ken Myer*), and then call the FindOne() method. The FindOne() method returns the first search result that matches the filter, so we retrieve its actual Active Directory entry. Although the solution searches on the user's display name, you can search on any field in Active Directory—the userPrincipalName and sAMAccountName are two other good choices.

When you do this search, always try to restrict it to the lowest level of the domain possible. If we know that Ken Myer is in the Sales OU, it would be better to bind to that OU instead:

```
$domain = [adsi] "LDAP://localhost:389/ou=Sales,dc=Fabrikam,dc=COM"
```

For more information about the LDAP search filter syntax, search *http://msdn.microsoft.com* for "Search Filter Syntax."

23.9   Get and List the Properties of a User Account

Problem

You want to get and list the properties of a specific user account.

Solution

To list the properties of a user account, use the [adsi] type shortcut to bind to the user in Active Directory, and then pass the user to the Format-List cmdlet:

```
$user =
  [adsi] "LDAP://localhost:389/cn=MyerKen,ou=West,ou=Sales,dc=Fabrikam,dc=COM"

$user | Format-List *
```

Discussion

The solution retrieves the MyerKen user from the Sales West OU. By default, the Format-List cmdlet shows only the distinguished name of the user, so we type **Format-List** * to display all properties.

If you know the property for which you want the value, specify it by name:

```
PS >$user.DirectReports
CN=SmithRobin,OU=West,OU=Sales,DC=Fabrikam,DC=COM
CN=DoeJane,OU=West,OU=Sales,DC=Fabrikam,DC=COM
```

Unlike users, some types of Active Directory objects don't allow you to retrieve their properties by name this way. Instead, you must call the Get() method to retrieve specific properties:

```
PS >$user.Get("userPrincipalName")
Ken.Myer@fabrikam.com
```

23.10 Modify Properties of a User Account

Problem

You want to modify properties of a specific user account.

Solution

To modify a user account, use the [adsi] type shortcut to bind to the user in Active Directory, and then call the Put() method to modify properties. Finally, call the SetInfo() method to apply the changes.

```
$user =
   [adsi] "LDAP://localhost:389/cn=MyerKen,ou=West,ou=Sales,dc=Fabrikam,dc=COM"

$user.Put("Title", "Sr. Exec. Overlord")
$user.SetInfo()
```

Discussion

The solution retrieves the MyerKen user from the Sales West OU. It then sets the user's title to Sr. Exec. Overlord and applies those changes to Active Directory.

23.11 Create a Security or Distribution Group

Problem

You want to create a security or distribution group.

Solution

To create a security or distribution group, use the [adsi] type shortcut to bind to a container in Active Directory, and then call the Create() method:

```
$salesWest =
   [adsi] "LDAP://localhost:389/ou=West,ou=Sales,dc=Fabrikam,dc=COM"
$management = $salesWest.Create("Group", "CN=Management")
$management.SetInfo()
```

Discussion

The solution creates a group named Management in the Sales West OU.

When you run this script against a real Active Directory deployment (as opposed to an ADAM instance), be sure to update the sAMAccountName property, or you'll get an autogenerated default.

When you create a group in Active Directory, it is customary to also set the type of group by defining the groupType attribute on that group. To specify a group type, use the –bor operator to combine group flags and use the resulting value as the groupType property. Example 23-3 defines the group as a global, security-enabled group.

Example 23-3. Creating an Active Directory security group with a custom groupType

```
$ADS_GROUP_TYPE_GLOBAL_GROUP = 0x00000002
$ADS_GROUP_TYPE_DOMAIN_LOCAL_GROUP = 0x00000004
$ADS_GROUP_TYPE_LOCAL_GROUP = 0x00000004
$ADS_GROUP_TYPE_UNIVERSAL_GROUP = 0x00000008
$ADS_GROUP_TYPE_SECURITY_ENABLED = 0x80000000

$salesWest =
  [adsi] "LDAP://localhost:389/ou=West,ou=Sales,dc=Fabrikam,dc=COM"

$groupType = $ADS_GROUP_TYPE_SECURITY_ENABLED -bor
    $ADS_GROUP_TYPE_GLOBAL_GROUP

$management = $salesWest.Create("Group", "CN=Management")
$management.Put("groupType", $groupType)
$management.SetInfo()
```

If you need to create groups in bulk from the data in a CSV, the `Import-ADUser` script given in Recipe 23.7, "Program: Import Users in Bulk to Active Directory" provides an excellent starting point. To make the script create groups instead of users, change this line:

```
$newUser = $userContainer.Create("User", "CN=$username")
```

to this:

```
$newUser = $userContainer.Create("Group", "CN=$username")
```

If you change the script to create groups in bulk, it is helpful to also change the variable names ($user, $users, $username, and $newUser) to correspond to group-related names: $group, $groups, $groupname, and $newgroup.

See Also

- Recipe 23.7, "Program: Import Users in Bulk to Active Directory"

23.12 Search for a Security or Distribution Group

Problem

You want to search for a specific group, but don't know its DN.

Solution

To search for a security or distribution group, use the [adsi] type shortcut to bind to a container that holds the group in Active Directory, and then use the System.DirectoryServices.DirectorySearcher class from the .NET Framework to search for the group:

```
$domain = [adsi] "LDAP://localhost:389/dc=Fabrikam,dc=COM"
$searcher = New-Object System.DirectoryServices.DirectorySearcher $domain
$searcher.Filter = '(&(objectClass=Group)(name=Management))'

$groupResult = $searcher.FindOne()
$group = $groupResult.GetDirectoryEntry()
```

Discussion

When you don't know the full DN of a group, the System.DirectoryServices.DirectorySearcher class from the .NET Framework lets you search for it.

You provide an LDAP filter (in this case, searching for groups with the name of *Management*), and then call the FindOne() method. The FindOne() method returns the first search result that matches the filter, so we retrieve its actual Active Directory entry. Although the solution searches on the group's name, you can search on any field in Active Directory—the mailNickname and sAMAccountName are two other good choices.

When you do this search, always try to restrict it to the lowest level of the domain possible. If we know that the Management group is in the Sales OU, it would be better to bind to that OU instead:

```
$domain = [adsi] "LDAP://localhost:389/ou=Sales,dc=Fabrikam,dc=COM"
```

For more information about the LDAP search filter syntax, search *http://msdn.microsoft.com* for "Search Filter Syntax."

23.13 Get the Properties of a Group

Problem

You want to get and list the properties of a specific security or distribution group.

Solution

To list the properties of a group, use the [adsi] type shortcut to bind to the group in Active Directory, and then pass the group to the Format-List cmdlet:

```
$group =
  [adsi] "LDAP://localhost:389/cn=Management,ou=West,ou=Sales,dc=Fabrikam,dc=COM"

$group | Format-List *
```

Discussion

The solution retrieves the Management group from the Sales West OU. By default, the Format-List cmdlet shows only the DN of the group, so we type **Format-List** * to display all properties.

If you know the property for which you want the value, specify it by name:

```
PS >$group.Member
CN=SmithRobin,OU=West,OU=Sales,DC=Fabrikam,DC=COM
CN=MyerKen,OU=West,OU=Sales,DC=Fabrikam,DC=COM
```

Unlike groups, some types of Active Directory objects don't allow you to retrieve their properties by name this way. Instead, you must call the Get() method to retrieve specific properties:

```
PS >$group.Get("name")
Management
```

23.14 Find the Owner of a Group

Problem

You want to get the owner of a security or distribution group.

Solution

To determine the owner of a group, use the [adsi] type shortcut to bind to the group in Active Directory, and then retrieve the ManagedBy property:

```
$group =
    [adsi] "LDAP://localhost:389/cn=Management,ou=West,ou=Sales,dc=Fabrikam,dc=COM"

$group.ManagedBy
```

Discussion

The solution retrieves the owner of the Management group from the Sales West OU. To do this, it accesses the ManagedBy property of that group. This property exists only when populated by the administrator group, but it is a best practice to do so.

Unlike groups, some types of Active Directory objects don't allow you to retrieve their properties by name this way. Instead, you must call the Get() method to retrieve specific properties:

```
PS >$group.Get("name")
Management
```

23.15 Modify Properties of a Security or Distribution Group

Problem

You want to modify properties of a specific security or distribution group.

Solution

To modify a security or distribution group, use the [adsi] type shortcut to bind to the group in Active Directory, and then call the Put() method to modify properties. Finally, call the SetInfo() method to apply the changes.

```
$group =
  [adsi] "LDAP://localhost:389/cn=Management,ou=West,ou=Sales,dc=Fabrikam,dc=COM"

PS >$group.Put("Description", "Managers in the Sales West Organization")
PS >$group.SetInfo()
```

Discussion

The solution retrieves the Management group from the Sales West OU. It then sets the description to Managers in the Sales West Organization, and then applies those changes to Active Directory.

23.16 Add a User to a Security or Distribution Group

Problem

You want to add a user to a security or distribution group.

Solution

To add a user to a security or distribution group, use the [adsi] type shortcut to bind to the group in Active Directory, and then call the Add() method:

```
$management =
  [adsi] "LDAP://localhost:389/cn=Management,ou=West,ou=Sales,dc=Fabrikam,dc=COM"

$user = "LDAP://localhost:389/cn=MyerKen,ou=West,ou=Sales,dc=Fabrikam,dc=COM"
$management.Add($user)
```

Discussion

The solution adds the MyerKen user to a group named Management in the Sales West OU.

To see whether you have removed the user successfully, see Recipe 23.18, "List a User's Group Membership."

See Also

- Recipe 23.18, "List a User's Group Membership"

23.17 Remove a User from a Security or Distribution Group

Problem

You want to remove a user from a security or distribution group.

Solution

To remove a user from a security or distribution group, use the [adsi] type shortcut to bind to the group in Active Directory, and then call the Remove() method:

```
$management =
  [adsi] "LDAP://localhost:389/cn=Management,ou=West,ou=Sales,dc=Fabrikam,dc=COM"

$user = "LDAP://localhost:389/cn=MyerKen,ou=West,ou=Sales,dc=Fabrikam,dc=COM"
$management.Remove($user)
```

Discussion

The solution removes the MyerKen user from a group named Management in the Sales West OU.

To see whether you have removed the user successfully, see the following section, Recipe 23.18, "List a User's Group Membership."

See Also

- Recipe 23.18, "List a User's Group Membership"

23.18 List a User's Group Membership

Problem

You want to list the groups to which a user belongs.

Solution

To list a user's group membership, use the [adsi] type shortcut to bind to the user in Active Directory, and then access the MemberOf property:

```
$user =
  [adsi] "LDAP://localhost:389/cn=MyerKen,ou=West,ou=Sales,dc=Fabrikam,dc=COM"
$user.MemberOf
```

Discussion

The solution lists all groups in which the MyerKen user is a member. Since Active Directory stores this information as a user property, this is simply a specific case of retrieving information about the user. For more information about retrieving information about a user, see Recipe 23.9, "Get and List the Properties of a User Account."

See Also

- Recipe 23.9, "Get and List the Properties of a User Account"

23.19 List the Members of a Group

Problem

You want to list all the members in a group.

Solution

To list the members of a group, use the [adsi] type shortcut to bind to the group in Active Directory, and then access the Member property:

```
$group =
   [adsi] "LDAP://localhost:389/cn=Management,ou=West,ou=Sales,dc=Fabrikam,dc=COM"
$group.Member
```

Discussion

The solution lists all members of the Management group in the Sales West OU. Since Active Directory stores this information as a property of the group, this is simply a specific case of retrieving information about the group. For more information about retrieving information about a group, see Recipe 23.13, "Get the Properties of a Group."

See Also

- Recipe 23.13, "Get the Properties of a Group"

23.20 List the Users in an Organizational Unit

Problem

You want to list all the users in an OU.

Solution

To list the users in an OU, use the [adsi] type shortcut to bind to the OU in Active Directory. Create a new System.DirectoryServices.DirectorySearcher for that OU, and then set its Filter property to (objectClass=User). Finally, call the searcher's FindAll() method to perform the search.

```
$sales =
  [adsi] "LDAP://localhost:389/ou=Sales,dc=Fabrikam,dc=COM"

$searcher = New-Object System.DirectoryServices.DirectorySearcher $sales
$searcher.Filter = '(objectClass=User)'
$searcher.FindOne()
```

Discussion

The solution lists all users in the Sales OU. It does this through the System.DirectoryServices.DirectorySearcher class from the .NET Framework, which lets you query Active Directory. The Filter property specifies an LDAP filter string.

 By default, a DirectorySearcher searches the given container and all containers below it. Set the SearchScope property to change this behavior. A value of Base searches only the current container, while a value of OneLevel searches only the immediate children.

For more information about working with classes from the .NET Framework, see Recipe 3.4, "Work with .NET Objects."

See Also

- Recipe 3.4, "Work with .NET Objects"

23.21 Search for a Computer Account

Problem

You want to search for a specific computer account, but don't know its DN.

Solution

To search for a computer account, use the [adsi] type shortcut to bind to a container that holds the account in Active Directory, and then use the System.DirectoryServices.DirectorySearcher class from the .NET Framework to search for the account:

```
$domain = [adsi] "LDAP://localhost:389/dc=Fabrikam,dc=COM"
$searcher = New-Object System.DirectoryServices.DirectorySearcher $domain
$searcher.Filter = '(&(objectClass=Computer)(name=kenmyer_laptop))'
```

```
$computerResult = $searcher.FindOne()
$computer = $computerResult.GetDirectoryEntry()
```

Discussion

When you don't know the full DN of a computer account, the System.
DirectoryServices.DirectorySearcher class from the .NET Framework lets you
search for it.

You provide an LDAP filter (in this case, searching for computers with the name of
kenmyer_laptop), and then call the FindOne() method. The FindOne1() method returns
the first search result that matches the filter, so we retrieve its actual Active Directory
entry. Although the solution searches on the computer's name, you can search on any
field in Active Directory—the sAMAccountName and operating system characteristics
(operatingSystem, operatingSystemVersion, operatingSystemServicePack) are other
good choices.

When you do this search, always try to restrict it to the lowest level of the domain
possible. If you know that the computer is in the Sales OU, it would be better to bind
to that OU instead:

```
$domain = [adsi] "LDAP://localhost:389/ou=Sales,dc=Fabrikam,dc=COM"
```

For more information about the LDAP search filter syntax, search *http://msdn.
microsoft.com* for "Search Filter Syntax."

23.22 Get and List the Properties of a Computer Account

Problem

You want to get and list the properties of a specific computer account.

Solution

To list the properties of a computer account, use the [adsi] type shortcut to bind to
the computer in Active Directory, and then pass the computer to the Format-List
cmdlet:

```
$computer =
   [adsi] "LDAP://localhost:389/cn=kenmyer_laptop,ou=West,ou=Sales,dc=Fabrikam,dc=COM"

$computer | Format-List *
```

Discussion

The solution retrieves the kenmyer_laptop computer from the Sales West OU. By
default, the Format-List cmdlet shows only the distinguished name of the computer,
so we type **Format-List** * to display all properties.

If you know the property for which you want the value, specify it by name:

```
PS >$computer.OperatingSystem
Windows Server 2003
```

Unlike users, some types of Active Directory objects don't allow you to retrieve their properties by name this way. Instead, you must call the Get() method to retrieve specific properties:

```
PS >$user.Get("operatingSystem")
Windows Server 2003
```

## CHAPTER 24

Enterprise Computer Management

24.0   Introduction

When working with Windows systems across an enterprise, the question often arises: *"How do I do* <some task> *in PowerShell?"* In an administrator's perfect world, anybody who designs a feature with management implications also supports (via PowerShell cmdlets) the tasks that manage that feature. Many management tasks have been around longer than PowerShell, though, so the answer can sometimes be, *"The same way you did it before PowerShell."*

That's not to say that your life as an administrator doesn't improve with the introduction of PowerShell, however. Pre-PowerShell administration tasks generally fall into one of several models: command line utilities, Windows Management Instrumentation (WMI) interaction, registry manipulation, file manipulation, interaction with COM objects, or interaction with .NET objects.

PowerShell makes it easier to interact with all these task models, and therefore makes it easier to manage functionality that depends on them.

24.1   Program: List Logon or Logoff Scripts for a User

The Group Policy system in Windows stores logon and logoff scripts under the registry keys HKLM:\SOFTWARE\Microsoft\Windows\CurrentVersion\Group Policy\State*<User SID>*\Scripts\Logon and HKLM:\SOFTWARE\Microsoft\Windows\CurrentVersion\Group Policy\State*<User SID>*\Scripts\Logoff. Each key has a subkey for each group policy object that applies. Each of those child keys has another level of keys that correspond to individual scripts that apply to the user.

This can be difficult to investigate when you don't know the SID of the user in question, so Example 24-1 automates the mapping of username to SID, as well as all the registry manipulation tasks required to access this information.

Example 24-1. Get-UserLogonLogoffScript.ps1

```
#################################################################################
##
## Get-UserLogonLogoffScript.ps1
##
## Get the logon or logoff scripts assigned to a specific user
##
## ie:
##
##  PS >Get-UserLogonLogoffScript LEE-DESK\LEE Logon
##
#################################################################################

param(
  $username = $(throw "Please specify a username"),
  $scriptType = $(throw "Please specify the script type")
  )

## Verify that they've specified a correct script type
$scriptOptions = "Logon","Logoff"
if($scriptOptions -notcontains $scriptType)
{
    $error = "Cannot convert value {0} to a script type. " +
             "Specify one of the following values and try again. " +
             "The possible values are ""{1}""."
    $ofs = ", "
    throw ($error -f $scriptType, ([string] $scriptOptions))
}

## Find the SID for the username
$account = New-Object System.Security.Principal.NTAccount $username
$sid =
    $account.Translate([System.Security.Principal.SecurityIdentifier]).Value

## Map that to their group policy scripts
$registryKey = "HKLM:\SOFTWARE\Microsoft\Windows\CurrentVersion\" +
    "Group Policy\State\$sid\Scripts"

## Go through each of the policies in the specified key
foreach($policy in Get-ChildItem $registryKey\$scriptType)
{
    ## For each of the scripts in that policy, get its script name
    ## and parameters
    foreach($script in Get-ChildItem $policy.PsPath)
    {
        Get-ItemProperty $script.PsPath | Select Script,Parameters
    }
}
```

For more information about working with the Windows Registry in PowerShell, see Chapter 18, *The Windows Registry*. For more information about running scripts, see Recipe 1.1, "Run Programs, Scripts, and Existing Tools."

See Also

- Recipe 1.1, "Run Programs, Scripts, and Existing Tools"
- Chapter 18, *The Windows Registry*

24.2 Program: List Startup or Shutdown Scripts for a Machine

The Group Policy system in Windows stores startup and shutdown scripts under the registry keys HKLM:\SOFTWARE\Policies\Microsoft\Windows\System\Scripts\Startup and HKLM:\SOFTWARE\Policies\Microsoft\Windows\System\Scripts\Shutdown. Each key has a subkey for each group policy object that applies. Each of those child keys has another level of keys that correspond to individual scripts that apply to the machine.

Example 24-2 allows you to easily retrieve and access the startup and shutdown scripts for a machine.

Example 24-2. Get-MachineStartupShutdownScript.ps1

```
##############################################################################
##
## Get-MachineStartupShutdownScript.ps1
##
## Get the startup or shutdown scripts assigned to a machine
##
## ie:
##
##   PS >Get-MachineStartupShutdownScript Startup
##
##############################################################################

param(
    $scriptType = $(throw "Please specify the script type")
    )

## Verify that they've specified a correct script type
$scriptOptions = "Startup","Shutdown"
if($scriptOptions -notcontains $scriptType)
{
    $error = "Cannot convert value {0} to a script type. " +
            "Specify one of the following values and try again. " +
            "The possible values are ""{1}""."
    $ofs = ", "
    throw ($error -f $scriptType, ([string] $scriptOptions))
}

## Store the location of the group policy scripts for the machine
$registryKey = "HKLM:\SOFTWARE\Policies\Microsoft\Windows\System\Scripts"
```

Example 24-2. Get-MachineStartupShutdownScript.ps1 (continued)

```
## Go through each of the policies in the specified key
foreach($policy in Get-ChildItem $registryKey\$scriptType)
{
    ## For each of the scripts in that policy, get its script name
    ## and parameters
    foreach($script in Get-ChildItem $policy.PsPath)
    {
        Get-ItemProperty $script.PsPath | Select Script,Parameters
    }
}
```

For more information about working with the Windows Registry in PowerShell, see Chapter 18, *The Windows Registry*. For more information about running scripts, see Recipe 1.1, "Run Programs, Scripts, and Existing Tools."

See Also

- Recipe 1.1, "Run Programs, Scripts, and Existing Tools"
- Chapter 18, *The Windows Registry*

24.3   Enable or Disable the Windows Firewall

Problem

You want to enable or disable the Windows Firewall.

Solution

To manage the Windows Firewall, use the `LocalPolicy.CurrentProfile.FirewallEnabled` property of the `HNetCfg.FwMgr` COM object:

```
PS >$firewall = New-Object -com HNetCfg.FwMgr
PS >$firewall.LocalPolicy.CurrentProfile.FirewallEnabled = $true
PS >$firewall.LocalPolicy.CurrentProfile.FirewallEnabled
True
```

Discussion

The `HNetCfg.FwMgr` COM object provides programmatic access to the Windows Firewall in Windows XP SP2 and later. The `LocalPolicy.CurrentProfile` property provides the majority of its functionality.

For more information about managing the Windows Firewall through its COM API, visit *http://msdn.microsoft.com* and search for "Using Windows Firewall API." The documentation provides examples in VBScript but gives a useful overview of the functionality available.

If you are unfamiliar with the VBScript-specific portions of the documentation, the Microsoft Script Center provides a useful guide to help you convert from VBScript to PowerShell. You can find that document at: *http://www.microsoft.com/technet/ scriptcenter/topics/winpsh/convert/default.mspx*.

For more information about working with COM objects in PowerShell, see Recipe 15.6, "Automate Programs Using COM Scripting Interfaces."

See Also

- Recipe 15.6, "Automate Programs Using COM Scripting Interfaces"

24.4   Open or Close Ports in the Windows Firewall

Problem

You want to open or close ports in the Windows Firewall.

Solution

To open or close ports in the Windows Firewall, use the `LocalPolicy. CurrentProfile.GloballyOpenPorts` collection of the `HNetCfg.FwMgr` COM object.

To add a port, create a `HNetCfg.FWOpenPort` COM object to represent the port, and then add it to the `GloballyOpenPorts` collection:

```
$PROTOCOL_TCP = 6
$firewall = New-Object -com HNetCfg.FwMgr
$port = New-Object -com HNetCfg.FWOpenPort

$port.Name = "Webserver at 8080"
$port.Port = 8080
$port.Protocol = $PROTOCOL_TCP

$firewall.LocalPolicy.CurrentProfile.GloballyOpenPorts.Add($port)
```

To close a port, remove it from the `GloballyOpenPorts` collection:

```
$PROTOCOL_TCP = 6
$firewall.LocalPolicy.CurrentProfile.GloballyOpenPorts.Remove(8080, $PROTOCOL_TCP)
```

Discussion

The `HNetCfg.FwMgr` COM object provides programmatic access to the Windows Firewall in Windows XP SP2 and later. The `LocalPolicy.CurrentProfile` property provides the majority of its functionality.

For more information about managing the Windows Firewall through its COM API, visit *http://msdn.microsoft.com* and search for "Using Windows Firewall API." The documentation provides examples in VBScript but gives a useful overview of the functionality available.

If you are unfamiliar with the VBScript-specific portions of the documentation, the Microsoft Script Center provides a useful guide to help you convert from VBScript to PowerShell. You can find that document at *http://www.microsoft.com/technet/ scriptcenter/topics/winpsh/convert/default.mspx*.

For more information about working with COM objects in PowerShell, see Recipe 15.6, "Automate Programs Using COM Scripting Interfaces."

See Also

- Recipe 15.6, "Automate Programs Using COM Scripting Interfaces"

24.5   Program: List All Installed Software

The best place to find information about currently installed software is actually from the place that stores information about how to uninstall it: the HKLM:\SOFTWARE\ Microsoft\Windows\CurrentVersion\Uninstall registry key.

Each child of that registry key represents a piece of software you can uninstall—traditionally through the Add/Remove Programs entry in the Control Panel. In addition to the DisplayName of the application, other useful properties usually exist (depending on the application). Examples include Publisher, UninstallString, and HelpLink.

To see all the properties available from software installed on your system, type the following:

```
$properties = Get-InstalledSoftware |
    Foreach-Object { $_.PsObject.Properties }

$properties | Select-Object Name | Sort-Object -Unique Name
```

This lists all properties mentioned by at least one installed application (although very few are shared by all installed applications).

To work with this data, though, you first need to retrieve it. Example 24-3 provides a script to list all installed software on the current system, returning all information as properties of PowerShell objects.

Example 24-3. Get-InstalledSoftware.ps1

```
##############################################################################
##
## Get-InstalledSoftware.ps1
##
## List all installed software on the current computer.
##
## ie:
##
```

Example 24-3. Get-InstalledSoftware.ps1 (continued)

```
##  PS >Get-InstalledSoftware PowerShell
##
###########################################################################

param(
  $displayName = ".*"
  )

## Get all the listed software in the Uninstall key
$keys = Get-ChildItem HKLM:\SOFTWARE\Microsoft\Windows\CurrentVersion\Uninstall

## Get all of the properties from those items
$items = $keys | Foreach-Object { Get-ItemProperty $_.PsPath }

## For each of those items, display the DisplayName and Publisher
foreach($item in $items)
{
    if(($item.DisplayName) -and ($item.DisplayName -match $displayName))
    {
        $item
    }
}
```

For more information about working with the Windows Registry in PowerShell, see Chapter 18, *The Windows Registry* For more information about running scripts, see Recipe 1.1, "Run Programs, Scripts, and Existing Tools."

See Also

- Recipe 1.1, "Run Programs, Scripts, and Existing Tools"
- Chapter 18, *The Windows Registry*

24.6   Uninstall an Application

Problem

You want to uninstall a specific software application.

Solution

To uninstall an application, use the Get-InstalledSoftware script provided in Recipe 24.5, "Program: List All Installed Software" to retrieve the command that uninstalls the software. Since the UninstallString uses batch file syntax, use cmd.exe to launch the uninstaller:

```
PS > $software = Get-InstalledSoftware UnwantedProgram
PS > cmd /c $software.UninstallString
```

Alternatively, use the `Win32_Product` WMI class for an unattended installation:

```
$application = Get-WmiObject Win32_Product -filter "Name='UnwantedProgram'"
$application.Uninstall()
```

Discussion

The `UninstallString` provided by applications starts the interactive experience you would see if you were to uninstall the application through the Add/Remove Programs entry in the Control Panel. If you need to remove the software in an unattended manner, you have two options: use the "quiet mode" of the application's uninstaller (for example, the `/quiet` switch to `msiexec.exe`), or use the software removal functionality of the `Win32_Product` WMI class as demonstrated in the solution.

For more information about working with WMI in PowerShell, see Recipe 15.1, "Access Windows Management Instrumentation Data."

See Also

- Recipe 15.1, "Access Windows Management Instrumentation Data"
- Recipe 24.5, "Program: List All Installed Software"

24.7   Manage Scheduled Tasks on a Computer

Problem

You want to schedule a task on a computer.

Solution

To manage scheduled tasks, use the `schtasks.exe` application.

To view the list of scheduled tasks:

```
PS >schtasks

TaskName                              Next Run Time            Status
==================================== ======================== =============
Defrag C                             03:00:00, 5/21/2007
User_Feed_Synchronization-{CA4D6D9C- 18:34:00, 5/20/2007
User_Feed_Synchronization-{CA4D6D9C- 18:34:00, 5/20/2007
```

To schedule a task to defragment C: every day at 3:00 a.m.:

```
schtasks /create /tn "Defrag C" /sc DAILY `
    /st 03:00:00 /tr "defrag c:" /ru Administrator
```

To remove a scheduled task by name:

```
schtasks /delete /tn "Defrag C"
```

Discussion

The example in the solution tells the system to defragment *C:* every day at 3:00 a.m.. It runs this command under the Administrator account, since the defrag.exe command requires administrative privileges. In addition to scheduling tasks on the local computer, the schtasks.exe application also allows you to schedule tasks on remote computers.

On Windows Vista, the schtasks.exe application has been enhanced to support event triggers, conditions, and additional settings.

For more information about the schtasks.exe application, type **schtasks /?**.

24.8   Retrieve Printer Information

Problem

You want to get information about printers on the current system.

Solution

To retrieve information about printers attached to the system, use the Win32_Printer WMI class:

```
PS >Get-WmiObject Win32_Printer | Select-Object Name,PrinterStatus

Name                                              PrinterStatus
----                                              -------------
Microsoft Office Document Image Wr...                         3
Microsoft Office Document Image Wr...                         3
CutePDF Writer                                               3
Brother DCP-1000                                             3
```

To retrieve information about a specific printer, apply a filter based on its name:

```
PS >$device = Get-WmiObject Win32_Printer -Filter "Name='Brother DCP-1000'"
PS >$device | Format-List *


Status                  : Unknown
Name                    : Brother DCP-1000
Attributes              : 588
Availability            :
AvailableJobSheets      :
AveragePagesPerMinute   : 0
Capabilities            : {4, 2, 5}
CapabilityDescriptions  : {Copies, Color, Collate}
Caption                 : Brother DCP-1000
(...)
```

To retrieve specific properties, access as you would access properties on other Power-Shell objects:

```
PS >$device.VerticalResolution
600
PS >$device.HorizontalResolution
600
```

Discussion

The example in the solution uses the Win32_Printer WMI class to retrieve infor-mation about installed printers on the computer. While the Win32_Printer class gives access to most commonly used information, WMI supports several other printer-related classes: Win32_TCPIPPrinterPort, Win32_PrinterDriver, CIM_Printer, Win32_PrinterConfiguration, Win32_PrinterSetting, Win32_PrinterController, Win32_PrinterShare, and Win32_PrinterDriverDll. For more information about working with WMI in PowerShell, see Recipe 15.1, "Access Windows Manage-ment Instrumentation Data."

See Also

- Recipe 15.1, "Access Windows Management Instrumentation Data"

24.9   Retrieve Printer Queue Statistics

Problem

You want to get information about print queues for printers on the current system.

Solution

To retrieve information about printers attached to the system, use the Win32_ PerfFormattedData_Spooler_PrintQueue WMI class:

```
PS >Get-WmiObject Win32_PerfFormattedData_Spooler_PrintQueue |
>>    Select Name,TotalJobsPrinted
>>

Name                                            TotalJobsPrinted
----                                            ----------------
Microsoft Office Document Image Wr...                          0
Microsoft Office Document Image Wr...                          0
CutePDF Writer                                                0
Brother DCP-1000                                              2
_Total                                                       2
```

To retrieve information about a specific printer, apply a filter based on its name, as shown in Example 24-4.

Example 24-4. Retrieving information about a specific printer

```
PS >$queueClass = "Win32_PerfFormattedData_Spooler_PrintQueue"
PS >$filter = "Name='Brother DCP-1000'"
PS >$stats = Get-WmiObject $queueClass  -Filter $filter
PS >$stats | Format-List *
```

```
AddNetworkPrinterCalls       : 129
BytesPrintedPersec           : 0
Caption                      :
Description                  :
EnumerateNetworkPrinterCalls : 0
Frequency_Object             :
Frequency_PerfTime           :
Frequency_Sys100NS           :
JobErrors                    : 0
Jobs                         : 0
JobsSpooling                 : 0
MaxJobsSpooling              : 1
MaxReferences                : 3
Name                         : Brother DCP-1000
NotReadyErrors               : 0
OutofPaperErrors             : 0
References                   : 2
Timestamp_Object             :
Timestamp_PerfTime           :
Timestamp_Sys100NS           :
TotalJobsPrinted             : 2
TotalPagesPrinted            : 0
```

To retrieve specific properties, access as you would access properties on other Power-Shell objects:

```
PS >$stats.TotalJobsPrinted
2
```

Discussion

The Win32_PerfFormattedData_Spooler_PrintQueue WMI class provides access to the various Windows performance counters associated with print queues. Because of this, you can also access them through the .NET Framework, as mentioned in Recipe 15.8, "Access Windows Performance Counters":

```
$printer = "Brother DCP-1000"
$pc = New-Object Diagnostics.PerformanceCounter "Print Queue","Jobs",$printer
$pc.NextValue()
```

For more information about working with WMI in PowerShell, see Recipe 15.1, "Access Windows Management Instrumentation Data."

See Also

- Recipe 15.1, "Access Windows Management Instrumentation Data"
- Recipe 15.8, "Access Windows Performance Counters"

24.10 Manage Printers and Print Queues

Problem

You want to clear pending print jobs from a printer.

Solution

To manage printers attached to the system, use the Win32_Printer WMI class. By default, the WMI class lists all printers:

```
PS >Get-WmiObject Win32_Printer | Select-Object Name,PrinterStatus

Name                                          PrinterStatus
----                                          -------------
Microsoft Office Document Image Wr...                     3
Microsoft Office Document Image Wr...                     3
CutePDF Writer                                           3
Brother DCP-1000                                          3
```

To clear the print queue of a specific printer, apply a filter based on its name and call the CancelAllJobs() method:

```
PS >$device = Get-WmiObject Win32_Printer -Filter "Name='Brother DCP-1000'"
PS >$device.CancelAllJobs()


__GENUS         : 2
__CLASS         : __PARAMETERS
__SUPERCLASS    :
__DYNASTY       : __PARAMETERS
__RELPATH       :
__PROPERTY_COUNT : 1
__DERIVATION    : {}
__SERVER        :
__NAMESPACE     :
__PATH          :
ReturnValue     : 5
```

Discussion

The example in the solution uses the Win32_Printer WMI class to cancel all jobs for a printer. In addition to cancelling all print jobs, the Win32_Printer class supports other tasks:

```
PS >$device | Get-Member -MemberType Method


    TypeName: System.Management.ManagementObject#root\cimv2\Win32_Printer

Name                MemberType Definition
----                ---------- ----------
CancelAllJobs       Method     System.Management.ManagementBaseObject Can...
Pause               Method     System.Management.ManagementBaseObject Pau...
PrintTestPage       Method     System.Management.ManagementBaseObject Pri...
RenamePrinter       Method     System.Management.ManagementBaseObject Ren...
Reset               Method     System.Management.ManagementBaseObject Res...
Resume              Method     System.Management.ManagementBaseObject Res...
SetDefaultPrinter   Method     System.Management.ManagementBaseObject Set...
SetPowerState       Method     System.Management.ManagementBaseObject Set...
```

For more information about working with WMI in PowerShell, see Recipe 15.1, "Access Windows Management Instrumentation Data."

See Also

- Recipe 15.1, "Access Windows Management Instrumentation Data"

24.11 Determine Whether a Hotfix Is Installed

Problem

You want to determine whether a specific hotfix is installed on a system.

Solution

To retrieve a list of hotfixes applied to the system, use the Win32_QuickfixEngineering WMI class:

```
PS >Get-WmiObject Win32_QuickfixEngineering -Filter "HotFixID='KB925228'"


Description         : Windows PowerShell(TM) 1.0
FixComments         :
HotFixID            : KB925228
Install Date        :
InstalledBy         :
InstalledOn         :
Name                :
ServicePackInEffect : SP3
Status              :
```

To determine whether a specific fix is applied, use the Test-HotfixInstallation script provided in Example 24-5:

```
PS >Test-HotfixInstallation KB925228 LEE-DESK
True
PS >Test-HotfixInstallation KB92522228 LEE-DESK
False
```

Discussion

Example 24-5 lets you determine whether a hotfix is installed on a specific system. It uses the Win32_QuickfixEngineering WMI class to retrieve this information.

Example 24-5. Test-HotfixInstallation.ps1

```
##############################################################################
##
## Test-HotfixInstallation.ps1
##
## Determine if a hotfix is installed on a computer
##
## ie:
##
##   PS >Test-HotfixInstallation KB925228 LEE-DESK
##   True
##
##############################################################################

param(
  $hotfix = $(throw "Please specify a hotfix ID"),
  $computer = "."
  )


## Create the WMI query to determine if the hotfix is installed
$filter = "HotFixID='$hotfix'"
$results = Get-WmiObject Win32_QuickfixEngineering `
    -Filter $filter -Computer $computer

## Return the results as a boolean, which tells us if the hotfix is installed
[bool] $results
```

For more information about working with WMI in PowerShell, see Recipe 15.1, "Access Windows Management Instrumentation Data." For more information about running scripts, see Recipe 1.1, "Run Programs, Scripts, and Existing Tools."

See Also

- Recipe 1.1, "Run Programs, Scripts, and Existing Tools"
- Recipe 15.1, "Access Windows Management Instrumentation Data"

24.12 Program: Summarize System Information

WMI provides an immense amount of information about the current system or remote systems. In fact, the msinfo32.exe application traditionally used to gather system information is based largely on WMI.

The script shown in Example 24-6 summarizes the most common information, but WMI provides a great deal more than that. For a list of other commonly used WMI classes, see Appendix F, *WMI Reference*. For more information about working with WMI in PowerShell, see Recipe 15.1, "Access Windows Management Instrumentation Data."

Example 24-6. Get-DetailedSystemInformation.ps1

```
##############################################################################
##
## Get-DetailedSystemInformation.ps1
##
## Get detailed information about a system.
##
## ie:
##
##  PS >Get-DetailedSystemInformation LEE-DESK > output.txt
##
##############################################################################

param(
  $computer = "."
  )

"#"*80
"System Information Summary"
"Generated $(Get-Date)"
"#"*80
""
""


"#"*80
"Computer System Information"
"#"*80
Get-WmiObject Win32_ComputerSystem -Computer $computer | Format-List *

"#"*80
"Operating System Information"
"#"*80
Get-WmiObject Win32_OperatingSystem -Computer $computer | Format-List *

"#"*80
"BIOS Information"
"#"*80
Get-WmiObject Win32_Bios -Computer $computer | Format-List *
```

Example 24-6. Get-DetailedSystemInformation.ps1 (continued)

```
"#"*80
"Memory Information"
"#"*80
Get-WmiObject Win32_PhysicalMemory -Computer $computer | Format-List *

"#"*80
"Physical Disk Information"
"#"*80
Get-WmiObject Win32_DiskDrive -Computer $computer | Format-List *

"#"*80
"Logical Disk Information"
"#"*80
Get-WmiObject Win32_LogicalDisk -Computer $computer | Format-List *
```

For more information about running scripts, see Recipe 1.1, "Run Programs, Scripts, and Existing Tools."

See Also

- Recipe 1.1, "Run Programs, Scripts, and Existing Tools"
- Recipe 15.1, "Access Windows Management Instrumentation Data"
- Appendix F, *WMI Reference*

24.13 Renew a DHCP Lease

Problem

You want to renew the DHCP lease for a connection on a computer.

Solution

To renew DHCP leases, use the `ipconfig` application. To renew the lease on all connections:

```
PS >ipconfig /renew
```

To renew the lease on a specific connection:

```
PS >ipconfig /renew "Wireless Network Connection 4"
```

Discussion

The standard `ipconfig` application works well to manage network configuration options on a local machine. To renew the lease on a remote computer, you have two options.

Use the Win32_NetworkAdapterConfiguration WMI class

To renew the lease on a remote computer, use the Win32_NetworkAdapterConfiguration WMI class. The WMI class requires that you know the description of the network adapter, so first obtain that by reviewing the output of Get-WmiObject Win32_NetworkAdapterConfiguration –Computer <ComputerName>:

```
PS >Get-WmiObject Win32_NetworkAdapterConfiguration –Computer LEE-DESK

(...)
DHCPEnabled       : True
IPAddress         : {192.168.1.100}
DefaultIPGateway  : {192.168.1.1}
DNSDomain         : hsd1.wa.comcast.net.
ServiceName       : USB_RNDIS
Description       : Linksys Wireless-G USB Network Adapter with (...)
Index             : 13
(...)
```

Knowing which adapter you want to renew, call its RenewDHCPLease() method:

```
$description = "Linksys Wireless-G USB"
$adapter = Get-WmiObject Win32_NetworkAdapterConfiguration –Computer LEE-DESK |
    Where-Object { $_.Description –match $description}
$adapter.RenewDHCPLease()
```

Run ipconfig on the remote computer

Another way to renew the DHCP lease on a remote computer is to use the solution offered by Recipe 21.4, "Program: Invoke a PowerShell Expression on a Remote Machine":

```
PS >Invoke-RemoteExpression \\LEE-DESK { ipconfig /renew }
```

For more information about working with WMI in PowerShell, see Recipe 15.1, "Access Windows Management Instrumentation Data."

See Also

- Recipe 15.1, "Access Windows Management Instrumentation Data"
- Recipe 21.4, "Program: Invoke a PowerShell Expression on a Remote Machine"

24.14 Assign a Static IP Address

Problem

You want to assign a static IP address to a computer.

Solution

Use the `Win32_NetworkAdapterConfiguration` WMI class to manage network settings for a computer:

```
$description = "Linksys Wireless-G USB"
$staticIp = "192.168.1.100"
$subnetMask = "255.255.255.0"
$gateway = "192.168.1.1"

$adapter = Get-WmiObject Win32_NetworkAdapterConfiguration -Computer LEE-DESK |
    Where-Object { $_.Description -match $description}
$adapter.EnableStatic($staticIp, $subnetMask)
$adapter.SetGateways($gateway, [UInt16] 1)
```

Discussion

When managing network settings for a computer, the `Win32_NetworkAdapter Configuration` WMI class requires that you know the description of the network adapter. Obtain that by reviewing the output of `Get-WmiObject Win32_ NetworkAdapterConfiguration -Computer <ComputerName>`:

```
PS >Get-WmiObject Win32_NetworkAdapterConfiguration -Computer LEE-DESK

(...)
DHCPEnabled     : True
IPAddress       : {192.168.1.100}
DefaultIPGateway : {192.168.1.1}
DNSDomain       : hsd1.wa.comcast.net.
ServiceName     : USB_RNDIS
Description     : Linksys Wireless-G USB Network Adapter with (...)
Index           : 13
(...)
```

Knowing which adapter you want to renew, you can now call methods on that object as illustrated in the solution. To enable DHCP on an adapter again, use the `EnableDHCP()` method:

```
PS >$adapter.EnableDHCP()
```

For more information about working with WMI in PowerShell, see Recipe 15.1, "Access Windows Management Instrumentation Data."

See Also

- Recipe 15.1, "Access Windows Management Instrumentation Data"

24.15 List All IP Addresses for a Computer

Problem

You want to list all IP addresses for a computer.

Solution

To list IP addresses assigned to a computer, use the `ipconfig` application:

```
PS >ipconfig
```

Discussion

The standard `ipconfig` application works well to manage network configuration options on a local machine. To view IP addresses on a remote computer, you have two options.

Use the Win32_NetworkAdapterConfiguration WMI class

To view IP addresses a remote computer, use the `Win32_NetworkAdapterConfiguration` WMI class. Since that lists all network adapters, use the `Where-Object` cmdlet to restrict the results to those with an IP address assigned to them:

```
PS >Get-WmiObject Win32_NetworkAdapterConfiguration –Computer LEE-DESK |
>>     Where-Object { $_.IpEnabled }
>>


DHCPEnabled      : True
IPAddress        : {192.168.1.100}
DefaultIPGateway : {192.168.1.1}
DNSDomain        : hsd1.wa.comcast.net.
ServiceName      : USB_RNDIS
Description      : Linksys Wireless-G USB Network Adapter with SpeedBooste
                   r v2 - Packet Scheduler Miniport
Index            : 13
```

Run ipconfig on the remote computer

Another way to view the IP addresses of a remote computer is to use the solution offered by Recipe 21.4, "Program: Invoke a PowerShell Expression on a Remote Machine":

```
PS >Invoke-RemoteExpression \\LEE-DESK { ipconfig }
```

For more information about working with WMI in PowerShell, see Recipe 15.1, "Access Windows Management Instrumentation Data."

See Also

- Recipe 15.1, "Access Windows Management Instrumentation Data"
- Recipe 21.4, "Program: Invoke a PowerShell Expression on a Remote Machine"

24.16 List Network Adapter Properties

Problem

You want to retrieve information about network adapters on a computer.

Solution

To retrieve information about network adapters on a computer, use the Win32_NetworkAdapterConfiguration WMI class:

```
Get-WmiObject Win32_NetworkAdapterConfiguration –Computer <ComputerName>
```

To list only those with IP addresses assigned to them, use the Where-Object cmdlet to filter on the IpEnabled property:

```
PS >Get-WmiObject Win32_NetworkAdapterConfiguration –Computer LEE-DESK |
>>     Where-Object { $_.IpEnabled }
>>


DHCPEnabled       : True
IPAddress         : {192.168.1.100}
DefaultIPGateway  : {192.168.1.1}
DNSDomain         : hsd1.wa.comcast.net.
ServiceName       : USB_RNDIS
Description       : Linksys Wireless-G USB Network Adapter with SpeedBooste
                    r v2 - Packet Scheduler Miniport
Index             : 13
```

Discussion

The solution uses the Win32_NetworkAdapterConfiguration WMI class to retrieve information about network adapters on a given system. By default, PowerShell displays only the most important information about the network adapter but provides access to much more.

To see all information available, use the Format-List cmdlet, as shown in Example 24-7.

Example 24-7. Using the Format-List cmdlet to see detailed information about a network adapter

```
PS >$adapter = Get-WmiObject Win32_NetworkAdapterConfiguration |
>>     Where-Object { $_.IpEnabled }
>>
PS >$adapter
```

Example 24-7. Using the Format-List cmdlet to see detailed information about a network adapter

```
DHCPEnabled       : True
IPAddress         : {192.168.1.100}
DefaultIPGateway  : {192.168.1.1}
DNSDomain         : hsd1.wa.comcast.net.
ServiceName       : USB_RNDIS
Description       : Linksys Wireless-G USB Network Adapter with SpeedBooste
                    r v2 - Packet Scheduler Miniport
Index             : 13



PS >$adapter | Format-List *


DHCPLeaseExpires             : 20070521221927.000000-420
Index                        : 13
Description                  : Linksys Wireless-G USB Network Adapter with
                                SpeedBooster v2 - Packet Scheduler Minipor
                               t
DHCPEnabled                  : True
DHCPLeaseObtained            : 20070520221927.000000-420
DHCPServer                   : 192.168.1.1
DNSDomain                    : hsd1.wa.comcast.net.
DNSDomainSuffixSearchOrder   :
DNSEnabledForWINSResolution  : False
DNSHostName                  : Lee-Desk
DNSServerSearchOrder         : {68.87.69.146, 68.87.85.98}
DomainDNSRegistrationEnabled : False
FullDNSRegistrationEnabled   : True
IPAddress                    : {192.168.1.100}
IPConnectionMetric           : 25
IPEnabled                    : True
IPFilterSecurityEnabled      : False
WINSEnableLMHostsLookup      : True
(...)
```

To retrieve specific properties, access as you would access properties on other Power-Shell objects:

```
PS >$adapter.MacAddress
00:12:17:77:B4:EB
```

For more information about working with WMI in PowerShell, see Recipe 15.1, "Access Windows Management Instrumentation Data."

See Also

- Recipe 15.1, "Access Windows Management Instrumentation Data"

CHAPTER 25
Manage an Exchange 2007 Server

25.0   Introduction

Point-and-click management has long been the stereotype of Windows administration. While it has always been possible to manage portions of Windows (or other applications) through the command line, support usually comes as an afterthought. Once all the administration support has been added to the user interface, the developers of an application might quickly cobble together a COM API or command-line tool if you are lucky. If you aren't lucky, they might decide only to publish some registry key settings, or perhaps nothing at all.

This inequality comes almost naturally from implementing a management model as an afterthought: with a fully functional user interface complete, very few application developers deem fully functional scriptable administration to be a high priority.

And then there's Exchange 2007.

In contrast to those who cobble together a management model only after completing the user interface, the Exchange 2007 team wrote their management infrastructure first. In Exchange 2007, it's not only a first-class feature—it's a way of life. Exchange 2007 includes nearly 400 cmdlets to let you manage Exchange systems. Not only is the magnitude stunning, but its breadth and depth is as well. To guarantee full coverage by way of PowerShell cmdlets, the Exchange Management Console user interface builds itself completely on top of PowerShell cmdlets.

Any command that affects the Exchange environment does so through one of the included Exchange Management cmdlets.

The benefit of this model is immense. It doesn't matter whether you are working with users, groups, mailboxes, or anything else in Exchange: you can automate it all.

25.1   Experiment with Exchange Management Shell

Problem

You want to experiment with the features and functionality of the Exchange Management Shell without working on a production system.

Solution

To explore the Exchange Management Shell, use the shell-focused Exchange 2007 Microsoft Virtual Lab.

Discussion

Microsoft recently introduced virtual labs as a core technology to help you experiment with new technologies. Exchange 2007 offers several of these labs. The one that applies to the Exchange Management Shell is called "Exchange Server 2007: Using the Exchange Server 2007 Management Console and Shell Virtual Lab."

To launch this lab, visit the Technet Virtual Labs home page at *http://www.microsoft. com/technet/traincert/virtuallab/default.mspx*. In the Virtual Labs by Product section, click Exchange Server; then select Exchange Server 2007: Using the Exchange Server 2007 Management Console and Shell.

After registering, a virtual lab launches that gives you an environment in which to experiment (see Figure 25-1). Click Start → All Programs → Microsoft Exchange Server 2007 → Exchange Management Shell to launch the Exchange Management Shell.

25.2   Automate Wizard-Guided Tasks

Problem

You want to automate tasks you normally complete through one of the wizards in the Exchange Management Console.

Solution

To automate a wizard-guided task, complete the wizard in the Exchange Management Shell, and then save the script it displays for future reference.

Discussion

Since the Exchange Management Console user interface uses PowerShell cmdlets to accomplish all its actions, every wizard displays the PowerShell script that you could run to accomplish the same task.

Figure 25-1. Exchange Server 2007 virtual lab

Launch the Exchange Management Console, and then click Recipient Configuration → Mailbox. In the Actions pane, click New Mailbox. Select User Mailbox → Existing User → Preeda Ola. Type **preeda** as an alias, and then complete the wizard. The final step provides the PowerShell command that you can use next time, as shown in Figure 25-2.

25.3   Manage Exchange Users

Problem

You want to get and modify information about user domain accounts from the Exchange Management Shell.

Solution

To get and set information about Active Directory users, use the Get-User and Set-User cmdlets, respectively:

```
$user = Get-User *preeda*
$user | Format-List *
```

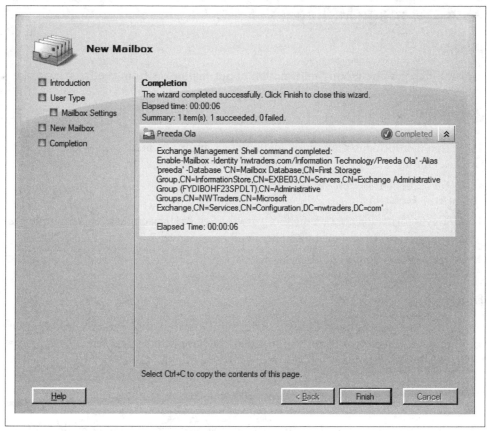

Figure 25-2. Script Wizard in Exchange 2007

To update *Preeda*'s title to Senior Vice President:

```
$user | Set-User -Title "Senior Vice President"
$user.Title
```

Discussion

Active Directory accounts are an integral part of working with Exchange 2007. While you will often want to modify the mailboxes of domain users, Get-User and Set-User lets you work with the user accounts themselves.

For more information about the Get-User cmdlet, type **Get-Help Get-User**. For more information about the Set-User cmdlet, type **Get-Help Set-User**.

25.4 Manage Mailboxes

Problem

You want to get and modify information about mailboxes from the Exchange Management Shell.

Solution

To retrieve information about a mailbox (or multiple mailboxes), use the Get-Mailbox cmdlet:

```
$user = Get-Mailbox *preeda*
$user | Format-List *
```

To modify information about a mailbox, use the Set-Mailbox cmdlet. This example prevents *Preeda* from sending mail when her mailbox goes over 2 GB, and then verifies it:

```
$user | Set-Mailbox –ProhibitSendQuota 2GB
$user | Get-Mailbox
```

Discussion

In addition to the common task of retrieving and modifying mailbox information, another useful mailbox-related command is the Move-Mailbox cmdlet. For example, to move all users from one storage group to another database:

```
Get-Mailbox |
    Where-Object { $_.Database –like "*SMBEX01\First Storage Group" } |
    Move-Mailbox –TargetDatabase "Mailbox Database 3"
```

After a few moments, that command displays the progress of the bulk mailbox move, as shown in Figure 25-3.

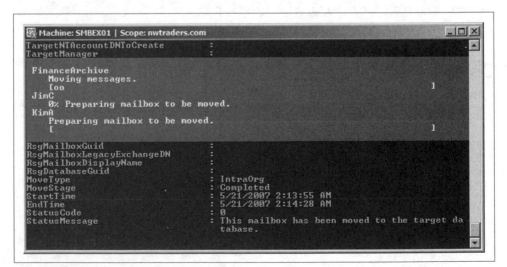

Figure 25-3. The Move-Mailbox cmdlet in action

For more information about the Get-Mailbox cmdlet, type **Get-Help Get-Mailbox**. For more information about the Set-Mailbox cmdlet, type **Get-Help Set-Mailbox**. For more information about the Move-Mailbox cmdlet, type **Get-Help Move-Mailbox**.

25.5   Manage Distribution Groups

Problem

You want to get and modify information about distribution groups from the Exchange Management Shell.

Solution

To retrieve information about a distribution group, or distribution groups, use the Get-DistributionGroup cmdlet:

```
$group = Get-DistributionGroup "Stock Traders"
$group | Format-List *
```

To modify information about a group, use the Set-DistributionGroup cmdlet. This example updates the Stock Traders distribution group to accept messages only from other members of the Stock Traders distribution group:

```
$group | Set-DistributionGroup -AcceptMessagesOnlyFromDLMembers "Stock Traders"
```

To add a user to a distribution group, use the Add-DistributionGroupMember cmdlet:

```
$group | Add-DistributionGroupMember -Member *rreeda*
```

To list members of a distribution group, use the Get-DistributionGroupMember cmdlet:

```
$group | Get-DistributionGroupMember
```

Discussion

For more information about the Get-DistributionGroup cmdlet, type **Get-Help Get-DistributionGroup**. For more information about the Set-DistributionGroup cmdlet, type **Get-Help Set-DistributionGroup**. For more information about the Add-DistributionGroupMember cmdlet, type **Get-Help Add-DistributionGroupMember**. For more information about the Get-DistributionGroupMember cmdlet, type **Get-Help Get-DistributionGroupMember**.

25.6   Manage Transport Rules

Problem

You want to manage transport rules applied to incoming or outgoing mail.

Solution

To create transport rules on the server, use the `New-TransportRule` cmdlet, as shown in Example 25-1.

Example 25-1. Creating a new transport rule

```
$from = Get-TransportRulePredicate FromScope
$from.Scope = "NotInOrganization"

$attachmentSize = Get-TransportRulePredicate AttachmentSizeOver
$attachmentSize.Size = 0

$action = Get-TransportRuleAction ApplyDisclaimer
$action.Text = "Warning: Only open attachments you were already expecting."

New-TransportRule -Name "Attachment Warning" `
    -Conditions $from,$attachmentSize -Action $action -Enabled:$true
```

Discussion

The `New-TransportRule` cmdlet adds transport rules on the server. A *transport rule* is a collection of predicates and actions—conditions and actions that apply to the rule.

In the example given by the solution, we add a rule that warns internal users about the dangers of unexpected attachments received from the outside world. For more information about the `New-TransportRule` cmdlet, type **Get-Help New-TransportRule**.

25.7   Manage Outlook Web Access

Problem

You want to get and modify Outlook Web Access settings from the Exchange Management Shell.

Solution

To retrieve information about an Outlook Web Access virtual directory, use the `Get-OwaVirtualDirectory` cmdlet:

```
$owa = Get-OwaVirtualDirectory "owa (Default Web Site)"
```

To modify information about that virtual directory, use the `Set-OwaVirtualDirectory` cmdlet. This example prevents users from changing their passwords through Outlook Web Access:

```
$owa | Set-OwaVirtualDirectory –ChangePasswordEnabled:$false
```

Discussion

For more information about the Get-OwaVirtualDirectory cmdlet, type **Get-Help Get-OwaVirtualDirectory**. For more information about the Set-OwaVirtualDirectory cmdlet, type **Get-Help Set-OwaVirtualDirectory**.

## CHAPTER 26

Manage an Operations Manager 2007 Server

26.0   Introduction

Like Exchange 2007, System Center Operations Manager 2007 (previously known as Microsoft Operations Manager) broadly adopts PowerShell as a technique for automated management. Operations Manager 2007 takes a dual-pronged approach to this. It includes a set of more than 70 PowerShell cmdlets, as well as a PowerShell provider that lets you scope commands to (and navigate) management groups.

The most common management tasks in Operations Manager 2007 fall largely into one of several categories: managing agents, management packs, rules, tasks, alerts, and maintenance windows.

26.1   Experiment with the Command Shell

Problem

You want to experiment with the features and functionality of the Operations Manager Command Shell without working on a production system.

Solution

To explore the Operations Manager Command Shell, use the Microsoft Forefront and System Center Demonstration Toolkit.

Discussion

Downloadable Virtual PC images and online virtual labs have recently become an incredibly effective means by which you can experiment with new technologies. The Microsoft System Center application suite offers several Virtual PC images for download, one of them tailored to Forefront Security and its interaction with the rest of the System Center family. The Oxford computer in this virtual lab represents a computer running System Center Operations Manager 2007, which provides an excellent avenue for exploration of this new technology.

To download this demonstration toolkit, visit the Microsoft download page at *http://download.microsoft.com*. Then, search for "System Center demonstration toolkit."

After registering, download all the files for the demonstration toolkit and launch the included installer. Once the installation completes, visit the *VMImages* directory in the installation directory and launch the Oxford demo virtual machine.

Once the machine loads, Click Start → All Programs → System Center Operations Manager 2007 → Command Shell to launch the Operations Manager Command Shell, as shown in Figure 26-1.

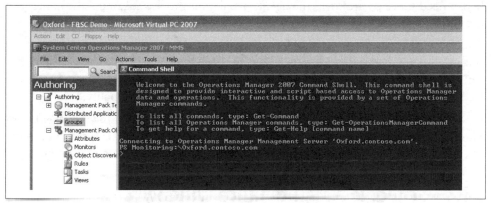

Figure 26-1. System Center Operations Manager Command Shell

26.2   Manage Operations Manager Agents

Problem

You want to manage Operations Manager agents on remote machines.

Solution

To retrieve information about installed agents, use the Get-Agent cmdlet:

```
PS Monitoring:\Oxford.contoso.com
>Get-Agent | Select-Object DisplayName

DisplayName
-----------
Ibiza.contoso.com
Denver.contoso.com
Sydney.contoso.com
```

To remove an agent, use the Uninstall-Agent cmdlet:

```
>Get-Agent | Where-Object { $_.DisplayName -match "Denver" } |
>>     Uninstall-Agent
```

To install an agent on a specific computer, use the `Install-AgentByName` function:

```
PS Monitoring:\Oxford.contoso.com
>Install-AgentByName Oxford.contoso.com
```

Discussion

The `Get-Agent` cmdlet returns a great deal of information about each agent it retrieves. The example in the solution filters this to show only the `DisplayName`, but you may omit the `Select-Object` cmdlet to retrieve all information about that agent.

If you need more control over the agent installation process, examine the content of the `Install-AgentByName` function:

```
PS Monitoring:\Oxford.contoso.com
>Get-Content Function:\Install-AgentByName
```

The function simplifies the most common scenario for installing agents, but the `Install-Agent` cmdlet that supports it provides additional functionality.

For more information about the `Get-Agent` cmdlet, type **Get-Help Get-Agent**. For more information about the `Install-Agent` cmdlet, type **Install-Agent**. For more information about the `Uninstall-Agent` cmdlet, type **Get-Help Uninstall-Agent**.

26.3   Schedule a Maintenance Window

Problem

You want to place a server in maintenance mode to prevent it from generating incorrect alerts.

Solution

To schedule a maintenance window on a computer, use the `New-MaintenanceWindow` cmdlet:

```
$computer = Get-Agent | Where-Object { $_.Name -match "Denver" }
$computer.HostComputer | New-MaintenanceWindow `
    -StartTime (Get-Date) `
    -EndTime   (Get-Date).AddMinutes(5) `
    -Comment "Security updates"
```

To retrieve information about that maintenance window, use the `Get-MaintenanceWindow` cmdlet:

```
>$computer.HostComputer | Get-MaintenanceWindow


MonitoringObjectId : a542ffe8-91a2-84a6-37b0-0555b15513bd
```

```
StartTime           : 5/22/2007 9:27:23 AM
ScheduledEndTime    : 5/22/2007 9:32:23 AM
EndTime             :
Reason              : PlannedOther
Comments            : Security updates
User                : CONTOSO\Administrator
LastModified        : 5/22/2007 9:27:23 AM
ManagementGroup     : MMS
ManagementGroupId   : 846c0974-7fd0-58f2-8020-400f125beb67
```

To stop maintenance mode, use the Set-MaintenanceWindow cmdlet to end the maintenance window immediately:

```
$computer.HostComputer | Set-MaintenanceWindow -EndTime (Get-Date)
```

Discussion

For more information about the New-MaintenanceWindow cmdlet, type **Get-Help New-MaintenanceWindow**. For more information about the Get-MaintenanceWindow cmdlet, type **Get-Help   Get-MaintenanceWindow**. For more information about the Set-MaintenanceWindow cmdlet, type **Get-Help Set-MaintenanceWindow**.

26.4   Get, Install, and Uninstall Management Packs

Problem

You want to automate the deployment or configuration of management packs.

Solution

To retrieve information about installed management packs, use the Get-ManagementPack cmdlet, as shown in Example 26-1.

Example 26-1. Using the Get-ManagementPack cmdlet

```
PS Monitoring:\Oxford.contoso.com
>$mp = Get-ManagementPack | Where-Object { $_.DisplayName -eq "Health Internal Library" }
PS Monitoring:\Oxford.contoso.com
>$mp


Name          : System.Health.Internal
TimeCreated   : 5/22/2007 9:38:40 AM
LastModified  : 5/22/2007 9:38:40 AM
KeyToken      : 31bf3856ad364e35
Version       : 6.0.5000.0
Id            : 9395a1eb-6322-1c8b-71ad-7ab6955c7e11
VersionId     : dfaeece9-437e-7d46-edce-260bd77a8667
References    : {System.Library, System.Health.Library}
Sealed        : True
```

Example 26-1. Using the Get-ManagementPack cmdlet (continued)

```
ContentReadable      : False
FriendlyName         : System Health Internal Library
DisplayName          : Health Internal Library
Description          : System Health Interal Library: This Management Pack (...)
DefaultLanguageCode  : ENU
LockObject           : System.Object
```

Use the `Uninstall-ManagementPack` cmdlet to remove a management pack:

```
$mp = Get-ManagementPack | Where-Object { $_.DisplayName -eq "Management Pack Name" }
$mp | Uninstall-ManagementPack
```

To install a management pack, provide its path to the `Install-ManagementPack` cmdlet:

```
Install-ManagementPack <PathToManagementPack>
```

Discussion

For more information about the `Get-ManagementPack` cmdlet, type **Get-Help Get-ManagementPack**. For more information about the `Install-ManagementPack` cmdlet, type **Get-Help Install-ManagementPack**. For more information about the `Uninstall-ManagementPack` cmdlet, type **Get-Help Uninstall-ManagementPack**.

26.5   Enable or Disable Rules

Problem

You want to enable or disable rules not sealed in a management pack.

Solution

To retrieve a rule, use the `Get-Rule`:

```
$rule = Get-Rule | Where-Object { $_.DisplayName -match "RuleName" }
```

Then, use the `Enable-Rule` or `Disable-Rule` cmdlet to enable or disable that rule, respectively:

```
$rule | Enable-Rule
$rule | Disable-Rule
```

Discussion

For more information about the `Get-Rule` cmdlet, type **Get-Help Get-Rule**. For more information about the `Disable-Rule` cmdlet, type **Get-Help Disable-Rule**. For more information about the `Enable-Rule` cmdlet, type **Get-Help Enable-Rule**.

26.6　List and Start Tasks

Problem

You want to list all the tasks allowed in a monitoring object, and then invoke one.

Solution

To retrieve cmdlets allowed for the current monitoring object, use the Get-Task cmdlet:

```
$task = Get-Task | Where-Object { $_.DisplayName -match "TaskName" }
```

Then use the Start-Task cmdlet to start the task:

```
$task | Start-Task
```

Discussion

The Get-Task cmdlet retrieves tasks specific to the monitoring object that applies to the current path. To change the list of tasks the cmdlet returns, navigate to the directory that represents the monitoring object you want to manage.

For more information about the Get-Task cmdlet, type **Get-Help Get-Task**. For more information about the Start-Task cmdlet, type **Get-Help Start-Task**.

26.7　Manage Alerts

Problem

You want to retrieve and manage alerts in the current monitoring object.

Solution

To retrieve alerts on the current monitoring object, use the Get-Alert cmdlet. To retrieve only active alerts, apply a filter to include only those with a ResolutionState of 0.

```
>Get-Alert | Where-Object { $_.ResolutionState -eq 0 } | Select-Object Description

Description
-----------
The process started at 2:15:56 AM failed to create System.Discovery.Data, no error
The process started at 2:05:23 PM failed to create System.Discovery.Data. Errors
MSExchangeIS service is stopped. This may be caused by missing patch KB 915786.
The computer Ibiza.contoso.com was not pingable.
The computer Sydney.contoso.com was not pingable.
```

To resolve an alert, pipe it to the Resolve-Alert cmdlet. For example, to clean up the alert entries in bulk:

```
Get-Alert | Where-Object { $_.ResolutionState -eq 0 } | Resolve-Alert
```

Discussion

For more information about the Get-Alert cmdlet, type **Get-Help Get-Alert**. For more information about the Resolve-Alert cmdlet, type **Get-Help Resolve-Alert**.

References

PowerShell Language and Environment

Commands and Expressions

PowerShell breaks any line that you enter into its individual units (*tokens*), and then interprets each token in one of two ways: as a command or as an expression. The difference is subtle: expressions support logic and flow control statements (such as if, foreach, and throw) while commands do not.

You will often want to control the way that Windows PowerShell interprets your statements, so Table A-1 lists the options available to you.

Table A-1. Windows PowerShell evaluation controls

Statement	Example	Explanation

Precedence control: ( )	```PS >5 * (1 + 2)```
	```15```
	```PS >(dir).Count```
	```2276```
		Forces the evaluation of a command or expression, similar to the way that parentheses are used to force the order of evaluation in a mathematical expression.

Expression subparse: $( )	```PS >"The answer is (2+2)"```
	```The answer is (2+2)```
	
	```PS >"The answer is $(2+2)"```
	```The answer is 4```
	
	```PS >$value = 10```
	```PS >$result = $(```
	```>> if($value -gt 0) { $true }```
	```> else { $false }```
	```>>)```
	```>>```
	```PS >$result```
	```True```
		Forces the evaluation of a command or expression, similar to the way that parentheses are used to force the order of evaluation in a mathematical expression.
		
		However, a subparse is as powerful as a subprogram, and is required only when it contains logic or flow control statements.
		
		This statement is also used to expand dynamic information inside a string.

Statement	Example	Explanation
List evaluation: @( )	PS >"Hello".Length 5 PS >@("Hello").Length 1 PS >(Get-ChildItem).Count 12 PS >(Get-ChildItem *.txt).Count PS >@(Get-ChildItem *.txt).Count 1	Forces an expression to be evaluated as a list. If it is already a list, it will remain a list. If it is not, PowerShell temporarily treats it as one.

Comments

To create single-line comments, begin a line with the # character. Windows Power-Shell does not support multiline comments, but you can deactivate larger regions of your script by placing them in a *here string*:

```
# This is a regular comment

# Start of the here string
$null = @"
function MyTest
{
    "This should not be considered a function"
}

$myVariable = 10;
"@
# End of the here string

# This is regular script again
```

 See the "Strings" seaction later in this chapter, to learn more about *here strings*.

Variables

Windows PowerShell provides several ways to define and access variables, as summarized in Table A-2.

Table A-2. Windows PowerShell variable syntaxes

Syntax	Meaning
`$simpleVariable = "Value"`	A simple variable name. The variable name must consist of alphanumeric characters. Variable names are not case sensitive.
`${arbitrary!@#@#`{var`}iable} = "Value"`	An arbitrary variable name. The variable name must be surrounded by curly braces, but may contain any characters. Curly braces in the variable name must be escaped with a backtick (` ` `).
`${c:\filename.extension}`	*Variable "Get and Set Content" syntax.* This is similar to the arbitrary variable name syntax. If the name corresponds to a valid PowerShell path, you can get and set the content of the item at that location by reading and writing to the variable.
`[datatype] $variable = "Value"`	Strongly typed variable. Ensures that the variable may contain only data of the type you declare. PowerShell throws an error if it cannot coerce the data to this type when you assign it.
`$SCOPE:variable`	Gets or sets the variable at that specific scope. Valid scope names are `global` (to make a variable available to the entire shell), `script` (to make a variable available only to the current script), `local` (to make a variable available only to the current scope and subscopes), and `private` (to make a variable available only to the current scope). The default scope is the *current* scope: `global` when defined interactively in the shell, `script` when defined outside any functions or script blocks in a script, and `local` elsewhere.
`New-Item Variable:\variable -Value value`	Creates a new variable using the Variable Provider.
`Get-Item Variable:\variable` `Get-Variable variable`	Gets the variable using the Variable Provider or `Get-Variable` cmdlet. This lets you access extra information about the variable, such as its options and description.
`New-Variable variable -Option option -Value value`	Creates a variable using the `New-Variable` cmdlet. This lets you provide extra information about the variable, such as its options and description.

Unlike some languages, PowerShell rounds (not truncates) numbers when it converts them to the [`int`] data type:

```
PS >(3/2)
1.5
PS >[int] (3/2)
2
```

To have PowerShell truncate a number, see Chapter 6, *Calculations and Math*.

Booleans

Boolean (true or false) variables are most commonly initialized to their literal values of $true and $false. When it evaluates variables as part of a Boolean expression (for example, an if statement), though, PowerShell maps them to a suitable Boolean representation, as listed in Table A-3.

Table A-3. Windows PowerShell Boolean interpretations

Result	Boolean representation
$true	True
$false	False
$null	False
Nonzero number	True
Zero	False
Nonempty string	True
Empty string	False
Nonempty array	True
Empty array	False
Hashtable (either empty or not)	True

Strings

Windows PowerShell offers several facilities for working with plain-text data.

Literal and Expanding Strings

To define a literal string (one in which no variable or escape expansion occurs), enclose it in single quotes:

```
$myString = 'hello `t $ENV:SystemRoot'
```

$myString gets the actual value of hello `t $ENV:SystemRoot.

To define an expanding string (one in which variable and escape expansion occurs), enclose it in double quotes:

```
$myString = "hello `t $ENV:SystemRoot"
```

$myString gets a value similar to hello   C:\WINDOWS.

To include a single quote in a single-quoted string, or a double quote in a double-quoted string, you may include two of the quote characters in a row:

```
PS >"Hello ""There""!"
Hello "There"!
PS >'Hello ''There''!'
Hello 'There'!
```

To include a complex expression inside an expanding string, use a subexpression. For example:

```
$prompt = "$(get-location) >"
```

$prompt gets a value similar to c:\temp >.

Accessing the properties of an object requires a subexpression:

```
$output =
    "Current script name is: $($myInvocation.MyCommand.Path)"
```

$output gets a value similar to Current script name is c:\Test-Script.ps1.

Here Strings

To define a *here string* (one that may span multiple lines), place the two characters @" at the beginning, and the two characters "@ on their own line at the end.

For example:

```
$myHereString = @"
This text may span multiple lines, and may
contain "quotes".
"@
```

Here strings may be of either the literal (single quoted) or expanding (double quoted) variety.

Escape Sequences

Windows PowerShell supports escape sequences inside strings, as listed in Table A-4.

Table A-4. Windows PowerShell escape sequences

Sequence	Meaning
`` `0 ``	The *null* character. Often used as a record separator.
`` `a ``	The *alarm* character. Generates a beep when displayed on the console.
`` `b ``	The *backspace* character. The previous character remains in the string but is overwritten when displayed on the console.
`` `f ``	A *form feed*. Creates a page break when printed on most printers.
`` `n ``	A *newline*.
`` `r ``	A *carriage return*. Newlines in PowerShell are indicated entirely by the `` `n `` character, so this is rarely required.
`` `t ``	A *tab*.
`` `v ``	A *vertical tab*.
`' '` (Two single quotes)	A *single quote*, when in a literal string.
`" "` (Two double quotes)	A *double quote*, when in an expanding string.
`` `<any other character> ``	That character, taken literally.

Numbers

PowerShell offers several options for interacting with numbers and numeric data.

Simple Assignment

To define a variable that holds numeric data, simply assign it as you would other variables. PowerShell automatically stores your data in a format that is sufficient to accurately hold it.

```
$myInt = 10
```

$myInt gets the value of 10, as a (32-bit) integer.

```
$myDouble = 3.14
```

$myDouble gets the value of 3.14, as a (53-bit, 9 bits of precision) double.

To explicitly assign a number as a long (64-bit) integer or decimal (96-bit, 96 bits of precision), use the long and decimal suffixes:

```
$myLong = 2147483648L
```

$myLong gets the value of 2147483648, as a long integer.

```
$myDecimal = 0.999D
```

$myDecimal gets the value of 0.999.

PowerShell also supports scientific notation:

```
$myPi = 3141592653e-9
```

$myPi gets the value of 3.141592653.

The data types in PowerShell (integer, long integer, double, and decimal) are built on the .NET data types of the same name.

Administrative Numeric Constants

Since computer administrators rarely get the chance to work with numbers in even powers of ten, PowerShell offers the numeric constants of gb, mb, and kb to represent gigabytes, megabytes, and kilobytes, respectively:

```
PS >$downloadTime = (1gb + 250mb) / 120kb
PS >$downloadTime
10871.4666666667
```

Hexadecimal and Other Number Bases

To directly enter a hexadecimal number, use the hexadecimal prefix 0x:

```
$myErrorCode = 0xFE4A
```

$myErrorCode gets the integer value 65098.

The PowerShell scripting language does not natively support other number bases, but its support for interaction with the .NET Framework enables conversion to and from binary, octal, decimal, and hexadecimal:

```
$myBinary = [Convert]::ToInt32("101101010101", 2)
```

$myBinary gets the integer value of 2901.

```
$myOctal = [Convert]::ToInt32("1234567", 8)
```

$myOctal gets the integer value of 342391.

```
$myHexString = [Convert]::ToString(65098, 16)
```

$myHexString gets the string value of fe4a.

```
$myBinaryString = [Convert]::ToString(12345, 2)
```

$myBinaryString gets the string value of 11000000111001.

 See the "Working with the .NET Framework" section later in this chapter to learn more about using PowerShell to interact with the .NET Framework.

Arrays and Lists

Array Definitions

PowerShell arrays hold lists of data. The @() (*array cast*) syntax tells PowerShell to treat the contents between the parentheses as an array. To create an empty array, type:

```
$myArray = @()
```

To define a nonempty array, use a comma to separate its elements:

```
$mySimpleArray = 1,"Two",3.14
```

Arrays may optionally be only a single element long:

```
$myList = ,"Hello"
```

Or, alternatively (using the array cast syntax),

```
$myList = @("Hello")
```

Elements of an array do not need to be all of the same data type, unless you declare it as a strongly typed array. In the following example, the outer square brackets define a strongly typed variable (as mentioned in the "Variables" section earlier in this chapter), and int[] represents an array of integers:

```
[int[]] $myArray = 1,2,3.14
```

In this mode, PowerShell throws an error if it cannot convert any of the elements in your list to the required data type. In this case, it rounds 3.14 to the integer value of 3.

```
PS >$myArray[2]
3
```

 To ensure that PowerShell treats collections of uncertain length (such as history lists or directory listings) as a list, use the list evaluation syntax @(…) described in the "Commands and Expressions" section earlier in this chapter.

Arrays can also be multidimensional "jagged" arrays —arrays within arrays:

```
$multiDimensional = @(
    (1,2,3,4),
    (5,6,7,8)
)
```

`$multiDimensional[0][1]` returns 2, coming from row 0, column 1.

`$multiDimensional[1][3]` returns 8, coming from row 1, column 3.

To define a multidimensional array that is not jagged, create a multidimensional instance of the .NET type. For integers, that would be an array of System.Int32:

```
$multidimensional = New-Object "Int32[,]" 2,4
$multidimensional[0,1] = 2
$multidimensional[1,3] = 8
```

Array Access

To access a specific element in an array, use the [ ] operator. PowerShell numbers your array elements starting at zero. Using `$myArray = 1,2,3,4,5,6` as an example:

```
$myArray[0]
```

Returns 1, the first element in the array.

```
$myArray[2]
```

Returns 3, the third element in the array.

```
$myArray[-1]
```

Returns 6, the last element of the array.

```
$myArray[-2]
```

Returns 5, the second-to-last element of the array.

You can also access ranges of elements in your array:

```
PS >$myArray[0..2]
1
2
3
```

Returns elements 0 through 2, inclusive.

```
PS >$myArray[-1..2]
6
1
2
3
```

Returns the final element, wraps around, and returns elements 0 through 2, inclusive. PowerShell wraps around because the one number in the range is positive, and the second number in the range is negative.

```
PS >$myArray[-1..-3]
6
5
4
```

Returns the last element of the array through to the third-to-last element in array, in decreasing order. PowerShell does not wrap around (and therefore scans backward in this case) because both numbers in the range share the same sign.

Array Slicing

You can combine several of the above statements at once to extract more complex ranges from an array. Use the + sign to separate array ranges from explicit indexes:

```
$myArray[0,2,4]
```

Returns the elements at indices 0, 2, and 4.

```
$myArray[0,2+4..5]
```

Returns the elements at indices 0, 2, and 4 through 5, inclusive.

```
$myArray[,0+2..3+0,0]
```

Returns the elements at indices 0, 2 through 3 inclusive, 0, and 0 again.

You can use the array slicing syntax to create arrays, as well:

```
$myArray = ,0+2..3+0,0
```

Hashtables (Associative Arrays)

Hashtable Definitions

PowerShell *hashtables* (also called *associative arrays*) let you associate keys with values. To define a hashtable, use the syntax:

```
$myHashtable = @{}
```

You can initialize a hashtable with its key/value pairs when you create it. PowerShell assumes that the keys are strings, but the values may be any data type.

```
$myHashtable = @{ Key1 = "Value1"; "Key 2" = 1,2,3; 3.14 = "Pi" }
```

Hashtable Access

To access or modify a specific element in an associative array, you may use either the array-access or property-access syntax:

```
$myHashtable["Key1"]
```

Returns "Value1".

```
$myHashtable."Key 2"
```

Returns the array 1,2,3.

```
$myHashtable["New Item"] = 5
```

Adds "New Item" to the hashtable.

```
$myHashtable."New Item" = 5
```

Also adds "New Item" to the hashtable.

XML

PowerShell supports XML as a native data type. To create an XML variable, cast a string to the [xml] type:

```
$myXml = [xml] @"
<AddressBook>
    <Person contactType="Personal">
        <Name>Lee</Name>
        <Phone type="home">555-1212</Phone>
        <Phone type="work">555-1213</Phone>
    </Person>
    <Person contactType="Business">
        <Name>Ariel</Name>
        <Phone>555-1234</Phone>
    </Person>
</AddressBook>
"@
```

PowerShell exposes all child nodes and attributes as properties. When it does this, PowerShell automatically groups children that share the same node type:

```
$myXml.AddressBook
```

Returns an object that contains a Person property.

```
$myXml.AddressBook.Person
```

Returns a list of `Person` nodes. Each person node exposes `contactType`, `Name`, and `Phone` as properties.

```
$myXml.AddressBook.Person[0]
```

Returns the first `Person` node.

```
$myXml.AddressBook.Person[0].ContactType
```

Returns `Personal` as the contact type of the first `Person` node.

The XML data type wraps the .NET `XmlDocument` and `XmlElement` classes. Unlike most PowerShell .NET wrappers, this wrapper does not expose the properties from the underlying class, because they may conflict with the dynamic properties that PowerShell adds for node names.

To access properties of the underlying class, use the `PsBase` property. For example:

```
$myXml.PsBase.InnerXml
```

See "Working with the .NET Framework" later in the chapter for more about using PowerShell to interact with the .NET Framework.

Simple Operators

Once you have defined your data, the next step is to work with it.

Arithmetic Operators

The arithmetic operators let you perform mathematical operations on your data, as shown in Table A-5.

The `System.Math` class in the .NET Framework offers many powerful operations in addition to the native operators supported by Power-Shell:

```
PS >[Math]::Pow([Math]::E, [Math]::Pi)
23.1406926327793
```

See "Working with the .NET Framework" later in thie chapter to learn more about using PowerShell to interact with the .NET Framework.

Table A-5. Windows PowerShell arithmetic operators

Operator	Meaning
+	The *addition operator*: `$leftValue + $rightValue` When used with numbers, returns their sum. When used with strings, returns a new string created by appending the second string to the first. When used with arrays, returns a new array created by appending the second array to the first. When used with hashtables, returns a new hashtable created by merging the two hashtables. Since hashtable keys must be unique, PowerShell returns an error if the second hashtable includes any keys already defined in the first hashtable. When used with any other type, PowerShell uses that type's addition operator (`op_Addition`) if it implements one.
-	The *subtraction operator*: `$leftValue - $rightValue` When used with numbers, returns their difference. This operator does not apply to strings. This operator does not apply to arrays. This operator does not apply to hashtables. When used with any other type, PowerShell uses that type's subtraction operator (`op_Subtraction`) if it implements one.
*	The *multiplication operator*: `$leftValue * $rightValue` When used with numbers, returns their product. When used with strings (`"=" * 80`), returns a new string created by appending the string to itself the number of times you specify. When used with arrays (`1..3 * 7`), returns a new array created by appending the array to itself the number of times you specify. This operator does not apply to hashtables. When used with any other type, PowerShell uses that type's multiplication operator (`op_Multiply`) if it implements one.
/	The *division operator*: `$leftValue / $rightValue` When used with numbers, returns their quotient. This operator does not apply to strings. This operator does not apply to arrays. This operator does not apply to hashtables. When used with any other type, PowerShell uses that type's multiplication operator (`op_Division`) if it implements one.

Operator	Meaning
%	The *modulus operator*: `$leftValue % $rightValue` When used with numbers, returns the remainder of their division. This operator does not apply to strings. This operator does not apply to arrays. This operator does not apply to hashtables. When used with any other type, PowerShell uses that type's multiplication operator (`op_Modulus`) if it implements one.

+=
 -=
 *=
 /=
 %=
	Assignment operators:
	
	    `$variable operator= value`
	
	These operators match the simple arithmetic operators (+, -, *, /, and %) but store the result in the variable on the left-hand side of the operator. It is a short-form for
	
	    `$variable = $variable operator value.`

Logical Operators

The logical operators let you compare Boolean values, as shown in Table A-6.

Table A-6. Windows PowerShell logical operators

Operator	Meaning

-and	*Logical AND*:
	
	    `$leftValue -and $rightValue`
	
	Returns `$true` if both left-hand and right-hand arguments evaluate to `$true`. Returns `$false` otherwise.
	
	You can combine several –and operators in the same expression:
	
	    `$value1 -and $value2 -and $value3 …`
	
	PowerShell implements the –and operator as a short-circuit operator, and evaluates arguments only if all arguments preceding it evaluate to `$true`.

-or	*Logical OR*:
	
	    `$leftValue -or $rightValue`
	
	Returns `$true` if the left-hand or right-hand arguments evaluate to `$true`. Returns `$false` otherwise.
	
	You can combine several –or operators in the same expression:
	
	    `$value1 -or $value2 -or $value3 …`
	
	PowerShell implements the –or operator as a short-circuit operator—and evaluates arguments only if all arguments preceding it evaluate to `$false`.

-xor	*Logical Exclusive OR*: `$leftValue -xor $rightValue` Returns `$true` if either the left-hand or right-hand argument evaluates to `$true`, but not if both do. Returns `$false` otherwise.
-not !	*Logical NOT*: `-not $value` Returns `$true` if its (only) right-hand argument evaluates to `$false`. Returns `$false` otherwise.

Binary Operators

The binary operators, listed in Table A-7, let you apply the Boolean logical operators bit by bit to the operator's arguments. When comparing bits, a 1 represents $true, while a 0 represents $false.

Table A-7. Windows PowerShell binary operators

Operator	Meaning

-band	*Binary AND*:
	
	`$leftValue -band $rightValue`
	
	Returns a number where bits are set to 1 if the bits of the left-hand and right-hand arguments at that position are both 1. All other bits are set to 0.
	
	For example:
	
	``PS >$boolean1 = "110110110"
	PS >$boolean2 = "010010010"
	PS >$int1 = [Convert]::ToInt32($boolean1, 2)
	PS >$int2 = [Convert]::ToInt32($boolean2, 2)
	PS >$result = $int1 -band $int2
	PS >[Convert]::ToString($result, 2)```
	
	10010010

-bor	*Binary OR*:
	
	`$leftValue -bor $rightValue`
	
	Returns a number where bits are set to 1 if either of the bits of the left-hand and right-hand arguments at that position is 1. All other bits are set to 0.
	
	For example:
	
	``PS >$boolean1 = "110110110"
	PS >$boolean2 = "010010010"
	PS >$int1 = [Convert]::ToInt32($boolean1, 2)
	PS >$int2 = [Convert]::ToInt32($boolean2, 2)
	PS >$result = $int1 -bor $int2
	PS >[Convert]::ToString($result, 2)```
	
	110110110

-bxor	*Binary Exclusive OR*:
	
	`$leftValue -bxor $rightValue`
	
	Returns a number where bits are set to 1 if either of the bits of the left-hand and right-hand arguments at that position is 1, but not if both are. All other bits are set to 0.
	
	For example:
	
	``PS >$boolean1 = "110110110"
	PS >$boolean2 = "010010010"
	PS >$int1 = [Convert]::ToInt32($boolean1, 2)
	PS >$int2 = [Convert]::ToInt32($boolean2, 2)
	PS >$result = $int1 -bor $int2
	PS >[Convert]::ToString($result, 2)```
	
	100100100

Table A-7. Windows PowerShell binary operators (continued)

Operator	Meaning
-bnot	*Binary NOT*: -bnot $*value* Returns a number where bits are set to 1 if the bit of the right-hand (and only) argument at that position is set to 1. All other bits are set to 0. For example: ``` PS >$boolean1 = "110110110" PS >$int1 = [Convert]::ToInt32($boolean1, 2) PS >$result = -bnot $int1 PS >[Convert]::ToString($result, 2) ``` 11111111111111111111111001001001

Other Operators

PowerShell supports several other simple operators, as listed in Table A-8.

Table A-8. Other Windows PowerShell operators

Operator	Meaning
-replace	The *replace operator*: "*target*" -replace "*pattern*","*replacement*" Returns a new string, where the text in "*target*" that matches the regular expression "*pattern*" has been replaced with the replacement text, "*replacement*". By default, PowerShell performs a case-insensitive comparison. The –ireplace operator makes this case insensitivity explicit, while the –creplace operator performs a case-sensitive comparison. If the regular expression pattern contains named captures or capture groups, the replacement string may reference those as well. For example: ``` PS >"Hello World" -replace "(.*) (.*)",'$2 $1' World Hello ``` If "*target*" represents an array, the –replace operator operates on each element of that array. For more information on the details of regular expressions, see also Appendix B.
-f	The *format operator*: "*Format String*" -f *Values* Returns a string, where the format items in the format string have been replaced with the text equivalent of the values in the value array. For example: ``` PS >"{0:n0}" -f 1000000000 1,000,000,000 ``` The format string for the format operator is exactly the format string supported by the .NET String. Format method. For more details about the syntax of the format string, see also Appendix H.

Table A-8. Other Windows PowerShell operators (continued)

Operator	Meaning
-as	The *type conversion* operator:

```
$value -as [Type]
```

Returns $value cast to the given .NET type. If this conversion is not possible, PowerShell returns $null.

For example:

```
PS >3/2 -as [int]
2
PS >$result = "Hello" -as [int]
PS >$result -eq $null
True
```

Comparison Operators

The PowerShell comparison operators, listed in Table A-9, let you compare expressions against each other. By default, PowerShell's comparison operators are case insensitive. For all operators where case sensitivity applies, the -i prefix makes this case insensitivity explicit, while the -c prefix performs a case-sensitive comparison.

Table A-9. Windows PowerShell comparison operators

Operator	Meaning
-eq	The *equality operator*:

```
$leftValue -eq $rightValue
```

For all primitive types, returns $true if $leftValue and $rightValue are equal.

When used with arrays, returns all elements in $leftValue that are equal to $rightValue.

When used with any other type, PowerShell uses that type's Equals() method if it implements one.

-ne	The *negated equality operator*:

```
$leftValue -ne $rightValue
```

For all primitive types, returns $true if $leftValue and $rightValue are not equal.

When used with arrays, returns all elements in $leftValue that are not equal to $rightValue.

When used with any other type, PowerShell returns the negation of that type's Equals() method if it implements one.

-ge	The *greater-than-or-equal operator*:

```
$leftValue -ge $rightValue
```

For all primitive types, returns $true if $leftValue is greater than or equal to $rightValue.

When used with arrays, returns all elements in $leftValue that are greater than or equal to $rightValue.

When used with any other type, PowerShell returns the result of that object's Compare() method if it implements one. If the method returns a number greater than or equal to zero, the operator returns $true.

Table A-9. Windows PowerShell comparison operators (continued)

Operator	Meaning
-gt	The *greater-than operator*: `$leftValue -gt $rightValue` For all primitive types, returns $true if $*leftValue* is greater than $*rightValue*. When used with arrays, returns all elements in $*leftValue* that are greater than $*rightValue*. When used with any other type, PowerShell returns the result of that object's Compare() method if it implements one. If the method returns a number greater than zero, the operator returns $true.
-lt	The *less-than operator*: `$leftValue -lt $rightValue` For all primitive types, returns $true if $*leftValue* is less than $*rightValue*. When used with arrays, returns all elements in $*leftValue* that are less than $*rightValue*. When used with any other type, PowerShell returns the result of that object's Compare() method if it implements one. If the method returns a number less than zero, the operator returns $true.
-le	The *less-than-or-equal operator*: `$leftValue -le $rightValue` For all primitive types, returns $true if $*leftValue* is less than or equal to $*rightValue*. When used with arrays, returns all elements in $*leftValue* that are less than or equal to $*rightValue*. When used with any other type, PowerShell returns the result of that object's Compare() method if it implements one. If the method returns a number less than or equal to zero, the operator returns $true.

-like	The *like operator*:
	
	`$leftValue -like Pattern`
	
	Evaluates the pattern against the target, returning $true if the simple match is successful.
	
	When used with arrays, returns all elements in $*leftValue* that match *Pattern*.
	
	The -like operator supports the following simple wildcard characters:
	
	? Any single unspecified character
	* Zero or more unspecified characters
	[a-b] Any character in the range of a-b
	[ab] The specified characters a or b
	
	For example:
	
	`PS >"Test" -like "[A-Z]e?[tr]"`
	`True`

-notlike	The *negated like operator*: Returns $true when the -like operator would return $false.

Operator	Meaning
-match	The *match operator*:
	`"Target" -match Regular Expression`
	Evaluates the regular expression against the target, returning `$true` if the match is successful. Once complete, PowerShell places the successful matches in the `$matches` variable.
	When used with arrays, returns all elements in `Target` that match `Regular Expression`.
	The `$matches` variable is a hashtable that maps the individual matches to the text they match. 0 is the entire text of the match, 1 and on contain the text from any unnamed captures in the regular expression, and string values contain the text from any named captures in the regular expression.
	For example:
	``` PS >"Hello World" -match "(.*) (.*)" True PS >$matches[1] Hello ```
	For more information on the details of regular expressions, see also Appendix B.
-notmatch	The *negated match operator:*
	Returns `$true` when the –match operator would return `$false`.
	The –notmatch operator still populates the `$matches` variable with the results of match.
-contains	The *contains operator:*
	`$list -contains $value`
	Returns `$true` if the list specified by `$list` contains the value `$value`. That is, if `$item -eq $value` returns `$true` for at least one item in the list.
-not- contains	The *negated contains operator:*
	Returns `$true` when the –contains operator would return `$false`.
-is	The *type operator:*
	`$leftValue -is [type]`
	Returns `$true` if `$value` is (or extends) the specified .NET type.
-isnot	The *negated type operator:*
	Returns `$true` when the -is operator would return `$false`.

Conditional Statements

Conditional statements in PowerShell let you change the flow of execution in your script.

if, elseif, and else Statements

```
if(condition)
{
    statement block
}
elseif(condition)
```

```
    {
        statement block
    }
    else
    {
        statement block
    }
```

If *condition* evaluates to $true, then PowerShell executes the statement block you provide. Then, it resumes execution at the end of the if / elseif / else statement list. PowerShell requires the enclosing braces around the statement block even if the statement block contains only one statement.

 See "Simple Operators" and "Comparison Operators," earlier in this chapter for a discussion on how PowerShell evaluates expressions as conditions.

If *condition* evaluates to $false, then PowerShell evaluates any following (optional) elseif conditions until one matches. If one matches, PowerShell executes the statement block associated with that condition, then resumes execution at the end of the if / elseif / else statement list.

For example:

```
$textToMatch = Read-Host "Enter some text"
$matchType = Read-Host "Apply Simple or Regex matching?"
$pattern = Read-Host "Match pattern"
if($matchType -eq "Simple")
{
    $textToMatch -like $pattern
}
elseif($matchType -eq "Regex")
{
    $textToMatch -match $pattern
}
else
{
    Write-Host "Match type must be Simple or Regex"
}
```

If none of the conditions evaluate to $true, PowerShell executes the statement block associated with the (optional) else clause, and then resumes execution at the end of the if / elseif / else statement list.

switch Statements

```
switch options expression
{
    comparison value          { statement block }
    -or-
```

```
    { comparison expression }  { statement block }

    (...)
    default                    { statement block }
}
```

or:

```
switch options -file filename
{
    comparison value          { statement block }
    -or-
    { comparison expression }  { statement block }

    (...)
    default                    { statement block }
}
```

When PowerShell evaluates a switch statement, it evaluates *expression* against the statements in the switch body. If *expression* is a list of values, PowerShell evaluates each item against the statements in the switch body. If you specify the –file option, PowerShell treats the lines in the file as though they were a list of items in *expression*.

The *comparison value* statements let you match the current input item against the pattern specified by *comparison value*. By default, PowerShell treats this as a case-insensitive exact match, but the options you provide to the switch statement can change this, as shown in Table A-10.

Table A-10. Options supported by PowerShell switch statements

Option	Meaning
-casesensitive -c	*Case-sensitive match.* With this option active, PowerShell executes the associated statement block only if the current input item exactly matches the value specified by *comparison value*. If the current input object is a string, the match is case-sensitive.
-exact -e	*Exact match.* With this option active, PowerShell executes the associated statement block only if the current input item exactly matches the value specified by *comparison value*. This match is case-insensitive. This is the default mode of operation.
-regex -r	*Regular-expression match.* With this option active, PowerShell executes the associated statement block only if the current input item matches the regular expression specified by *comparison value*. This match is case-insensitive.

Table A-10. Options supported by PowerShell switch statements (continued)

Option	Meaning
-wildcard -w	*Wildcard match.* With this option active, PowerShell executes the associated statement block only if the current input item matches the wildcard specified by `comparison value`. The wildcard match supports the following simple wildcard characters: ? Any single unspecified character * Zero or more unspecified characters [a-b] Any character in the range of a-b [ab] The specified characters a or b This match is case-insensitive.

The { *comparison expression* } statements let you process the current input item, which is stored in the $_ variable, in an arbitrary script block. When it processes a { *comparison expression* } statement, PowerShell executes the associated statement block only if { *comparison expression* } evaluates to $true.

PowerShell executes the statement block associated with the (optional) default statement if no other statements in the switch body match.

When processing a switch statement, PowerShell tries to match the current input object against each statement in the switch body, falling through to the next statement even after one or more have already matched. To have PowerShell exit a switch statement after it processes a match, include a break statement as the last statement in the statement block.

For example:

```
$myPhones = "(555) 555-1212","555-1234"

switch -regex ($myPhones)
{
  { $_.Length -le 8 }  { "Area code was not specified"; break }
  { $_.Length -gt 8 }  { "Area code was specified" }
  "\((555)\).*"        { "In the $($matches[1]) area code" }
}
```

Produces the output:

```
Area code was specified
In the 555 area code
Area code was not specified
```

 See the following section, "Looping Statements," for more information about the break statement.

By default, PowerShell treats this as a case-insensitive exact match, but the options you provide to the switch statement can change this.

Looping Statements

Looping statements in PowerShell let you execute groups of statements multiple times.

for Statement

```
:loop_label for(initialization; condition; increment)
{
    statement block
}
```

When PowerShell executes a for statement, it first executes the expression given by *initialization*. It next evaluates *condition*. If *condition* evaluates to $true, Power-Shell executes the given statement block. It then executes the expression given by *increment*. PowerShell continues to execute the statement block and *increment* statement as long as *condition* evaluates to $true.

For example:

```
for($counter = 0; $counter -lt 10; $counter++)
{
    Write-Host "Processing item $counter"
}
```

The break and continue statements (discussed later in the chapter) can specify the *loop_label* of any enclosing looping statement as their target.

foreach Statement

```
:loop_label foreach(variable in expression)
{
    statement block
}
```

When PowerShell executes a foreach statement, it executes the pipeline given by *expression*—for example, Get-Process | Where-Object { $_.Handles -gt 500 } or 1..10. For each item produced by the expression, it assigns that item to the variable specified by *variable* and then executes the given statement block. For example:

```
$handleSum = 0;
foreach($process in Get-Process |
    Where-Object { $_.Handles -gt 500 })
{
    $handleSum += $process.Handles
}
$handleSum
```

The break and continue statements (discussed later in the chapter) can specify the *loop_label* of any enclosing looping statement as their target.

while Statement

```
:loop_label while(condition)
{
    statement block
}
```

When PowerShell executes a while statement, it first evaluates the expression given by *condition*. If this expression evaluates to $true, PowerShell executes the given statement block. PowerShell continues to execute the statement block as long as *condition* evaluates to $true. For example:

```
$command = "";
while($command -notmatch "quit")
{
    $command = Read-Host "Enter your command"
}
```

The break and continue statements (discussed later in the chapter) can specify the *loop_label* of any enclosing looping statement as their target.

do ... while Statement/do ... until Statement

```
:loop_label do
{
    statement block
} while(condition)
```

or

```
:loop_label do
{
    statement block
} until(condition)
```

When PowerShell executes a do...while or do...until statement, it first executes the given statement block. In a do...while statement, PowerShell continues to execute the statement block as long as *condition* evaluates to $true. In a do...until statement, PowerShell continues to execute the statement as long as *condition* evaluates to $false. For example:

```
$validResponses = "Yes","No"
$response = ""
do
{
    $response = read-host "Yes or No?"
} while($validResponses -notcontains $response)
"Got it."

$response = ""
do
```

```
    {
        $response = read-host "Yes or No?"
    } until($validResponses -contains $response)
    "Got it."
```

The break and continue statements (discussed later in the chapter) can specify the *loop_label* of any enclosing looping statement as their target.

Flow Control Statements

PowerShell supports two statements to help you control flow within loops: break and continue.

break

The break statement halts execution of the current loop. PowerShell then resumes execution at the end of the current looping statement, as though the looping statement had completed naturally. If you specify a label with the break statement—for example, break :outer_loop—PowerShell halts the execution of that loop instead.

For example:

```
    :outer for($counter = 0; $counter -lt 5; $counter++)
    {
        for($counter2 = 0; $counter2 -lt 5; $counter2++)
        {
            if($counter2 -eq 2)
            {
                break :outer
            }

            Write-Host "Processing item $counter,$counter2"
        }
    }
```

Produces the output:

```
    Processing item 0,0
    Processing item 0,1
    Processing item 1,0
    Processing item 1,1
    Processing item 2,0
    Processing item 2,1
    Processing item 3,0
    Processing item 3,1
    Processing item 4,0
    Processing item 4,1
```

continue

The continue statement skips execution of the rest of the current statement block. PowerShell then continues with the next iteration of the current looping statement, as though the statement block had completed naturally. If you specify a label with the continue statement—for example, continue :outer—PowerShell continues with the next iteration of that loop instead.

For example:

```
:outer for($counter = 0; $counter -lt 5; $counter++)
{
    for($counter2 = 0; $counter2 -lt 5; $counter2++)
    {
        if($counter2 -eq 2)
        {
            continue :outer
        }

        Write-Host "Processing item $counter,$counter2"
    }
}
```

Produces the output:

```
Processing item 0,0
Processing item 0,1
Processing item 0,3
Processing item 0,4
Processing item 1,0
Processing item 1,1
Processing item 1,3
Processing item 1,4
Processing item 2,0
Processing item 2,1
Processing item 2,3
Processing item 2,4
Processing item 3,0
Processing item 3,1
Processing item 3,3
Processing item 3,4
Processing item 4,0
Processing item 4,1
Processing item 4,3
Processing item 4,4
```

Working with the .NET Framework

One feature that gives PowerShell its incredible reach into both system administration and application development is its capability to leverage Microsoft's enormous and broad .NET Framework.

Work with the .NET Framework in PowerShell comes mainly by way of one of two tasks: calling methods or accessing properties.

Static Methods

To call a static method on a class, type:

```
[ClassName]::MethodName(parameter list)
```

For example:

```
PS >[System.Diagnostics.Process]::GetProcessById(0)
```

gets the process with the ID of 0 and displays the following output:

```
Handles  NPM(K)    PM(K)      WS(K) VM(M)   CPU(s)     Id ProcessName
-------  ------    -----      ----- -----   ------     -- -----------
      0       0        0         16     0                0 Idle
```

Instance Methods

To call a method on an instance of an object, type:

```
$objectReference.MethodName(parameter list)
```

For example:

```
PS >$process = [System.Diagnostics.Process]::GetProcessById(0)
PS >$process.Refresh()
```

This stores the process with ID of 0 into the $process variable. It then calls the Refresh() instance method on that specific process.

Static Properties

To access a static property on a class, type:

```
[ClassName]::PropertyName
```

or:

```
[ClassName]::PropertyName = value
```

For example, the [System.DateTime] class provides a Now static property that returns the current time:

```
PS >[System.DateTime]::Now
Sunday, July 16, 2006 2:07:20 PM
```

Although rare, some types let you set the value of some static properties.

Instance Properties

To access an instance property on an object, type:

```
$objectReference.PropertyName
```

or:

```
$objectReference.PropertyName = value
```

For example:

```
PS >$today = [System.DateTime]::Now
PS >$today.DayOfWeek
Sunday
```

This stores the current date in the $today variable. It then calls the DayOfWeek instance property on that specific date.

Learning About Types

The two primary avenues for learning about classes and types are the Get-Member cmdlet and the documentation for the .NET Framework.

The Get-Member Cmdlet

To learn what methods and properties a given type supports, pass it through the Get-Member cmdlet, as shown in Table A-11.

Table A-11. Working with the Get-Member cmdlet

Action	Result
[*typename*] | Get-Member –Static	All the static methods and properties of a given type
$*objectReference* | Get-Member –Static	All the static methods and properties provided by the type in $*objectReference*
$*objectReference* | Get-Member	All the instance methods and properties provided by the type in $*objectReference*. If $*objectReference* represents a collection of items, PowerShell returns the instances and properties of the types contained by that collection. To view the instances and properties of a collection itself, use the –InputObject parameter of Get-Member: `Get-Member –InputObject $objectReference`
[*typename*] | Get-Member	All the instance methods and properties of a System.Runtime-Type object that represents this type

.NET framework documentation

Another source of information about the classes in the .NET Framework is the documentation itself, available through the search facilities at *http://msdn.microsoft.com*.

Typical documentation for a class first starts with a general overview, then provides a hyperlink to the members of the class—the list of methods and properties it supports.

 To get to the documentation for the members quickly, search for them more explicitly by adding the term "members" to your MSDN search term:

```
classname members
```

The documentation for the members of a class lists their constructors, methods, properties, and more. It uses an S icon to represent the static methods and properties. Click the member name for more information about that member—including the type of object that the member produces.

Type Shortcuts

When you specify a type name, PowerShell lets you use a short form for some of the most common types, as listed in Table A-12.

Table A-12. PowerShell type shortcuts

Type shortcut	Full classname
[Adsi]	[System.DirectoryServices.DirectoryEntry]
[Hashtable]	[System.Collections.Hashtable]
[PSObject]	[System.Management.Automation.PSObject]
[Ref]	[System.Management.Automation.PSReference]
[Regex]	[System.Text.RegularExpressions.Regex]
[ScriptBlock]	[System.Management.Automation.ScriptBlock]
[Switch]	[System.Management.Automation.SwitchParameter]
[Wmi]	[System.Management.ManagementObject]
[WmiClass]	[System.Management.ManagementClass]
[WmiSearcher]	[System.Management.ManagementObjectSearcher]
[Xml]	[System.Xml.XmlDocument]
[TypeName]	[System.TypeName]

Creating Instances of Types

```
$objectReference = New-Object TypeName parameters
```

Although static methods and properties of a class generate objects, you will often want to create them explicitly yourself. PowerShell's New-Object cmdlet lets you create an instance of the type you specify. The parameter list must match the list of parameters accepted by one of the type's constructors, as documented on MSDN.

For example:

```
$webClient = New-Object Net.WebClient
$webClient.DownloadString("http://search.msn.com")
```

Most common types are available by default. However, many are available only after you load the library (called the *assembly*) that defines them. The MSDN documentation for a class includes the assembly that defines it.

To load an assembly, use the methods provided by the System.Reflection.Assembly class:

```
PS >[Reflection.Assembly]::LoadWithPartialName("System.Web")
```

```
GAC     Version         Location
---     -------         --------
True    v2.0.50727      C:\WINDOWS\assembly\GAC_32\(…)\System.Web.dll


PS >[Web.HttpUtility]::UrlEncode("http://search.msn.com")
http%3a%2f%2fsearch.msn.com
```

 The LoadWithPartialName method is unsuitable for scripts that you want to share with others, or use in a production environment. It loads the most current version of the assembly, which may not be the same as the version you used to develop your script. To load an assembly in the safest way possible, use its fully qualified name with the [Reflection.Assembly]::Load() method.

Interacting with COM Objects

PowerShell lets you access methods and properties on COM objects the same way you would interact with objects from the .NET Framework. To interact with a COM object, use its ProgId with the –ComObject parameter (often shortened to –Com) on New-Object:

```
PS >$shell = New-Object -Com Shell.Application
PS >$shell.Windows() | Select-Object LocationName,LocationUrl
```

For more information about the COM objects most useful to system administrators, see also Appendix G, *Selected COM Objects and Their Uses*.

Extending Types

PowerShell supports two ways to add your own methods and properties to any type: the Add-Member cmdlet and a custom types extension file.

The Add-Member cmdlet

The Add-Member cmdlet lets you dynamically add methods, properties, and more to an object. It supports the extensions shown in Table A-13.

Table A-13. Selected member types supported by the Add-Member cmdlet

Member type	Meaning

AliasProperty	A property defined to alias another property:
	
	```PS >$testObject = [PsObject] "Test"```
	``PS >$testObject
		Add-Member "AliasProperty" Count Length```
		```PS >$testObject.Count```
		```4```

CodeProperty	A property defined by a: System.Reflection.MethodInfo. This method must be public, static, return results (nonvoid), and take one parameter of type PsObject.

Table A-13. Selected member types supported by the Add-Member cmdlet (continued)

Member type	Meaning
NoteProperty	A property defined by the initial value you provide: ```PS >$testObject = [PsObject] "Test" PS >$testObject	Add-Member NoteProperty Reversed tseT PS >$testObject.Reversed tseT```
ScriptProperty	A property defined by the script block you provide. In that script block, $this refers to the current instance: ```PS >$testObject = [PsObject] ("Hi" * 100) PS >$testObject	Add-Member ScriptProperty IsLong { >> $this.Length -gt 100 >> } >> $testObject.IsLong >> True```

PropertySet	A property defined as a shortcut to a set of properties. Used in cmdlets such as Select-Object:
	
	``PS >$testObject = [PsObject] [DateTime]::Now
	PS >$collection = New-Object `
	>> Collections.ObjectModel.Collection``1[System.String]
	>> $collection.Add("Month")
	>> $collection.Add("Year")
	>> $testObject
		Add-Member PropertySet MonthYear $collection
		>> $testObject
			select MonthYear
			>>```
			
			<pre> Year Month
			    ------ -----
			    2007 6</pre>

CodeMethod	A method defined by a: System.Reflection.MethodInfo. This method must be public, static, and take one parameter of type PsObject.
ScriptMethod	A method defined by the script block you provide. In that script block, $this refers to the current instance, and $args refers to the input parameters: ```PS >$testObject = [PsObject] "Hello" PS >$testObject	Add-Member ScriptMethod IsLong { >> $this.Length -gt $args[0] >> } >> $testObject.IsLong(3) >> $testObject.IsLong(100) >> True False```

Custom type extension files

While the Add-Member cmdlet lets you customize individual objects, PowerShell also supports configuration files that let you customize all objects of a given type. For example, you might want to add a Reverse() method to all strings or a HelpUrl property (based on the MSDN *Url Aliases*) to all types.

PowerShell adds several type extensions to the file *types.ps1xml*, in the PowerShell installation directory. This file is useful as a source of examples, but you should not modify it directly. Instead, create a new one and use the `Update-TypeData` cmdlet to load your customizations. The following command loads *Types.custom.ps1xml* from the same directory as your profile:

```
$typesFile = Join-Path (Split-Path $profile) "Types.Custom.Ps1Xml"
Update-TypeData –PrependPath $typesFile
```

For more information about custom type extensions files, see Recipe 3.12, "Add Custom Methods and Properties to Types."

Writing Scripts, Reusing Functionality

When you want to start packaging and reusing your commands, the best place to put them is in scripts and functions. A *script* is a text file that contains a sequence of PowerShell commands. A *function* is also a sequence of PowerShell commands but is usually used within a script to break it into smaller, more easily understood segments.

Writing Scripts

To write a script, write your PowerShell commands in a text editor and save the file with a *.ps1* extension.

Running Scripts

There are two ways to execute a script: by invoking it or by dot-sourcing it.

Invoking

Invoking a script runs the commands inside it. Unless explicitly defined with the `GLOBAL` scope keyword, variables and functions defined in the script do not persist once the script exits.

You invoke a script by using the invoke/call operator (&) with the script name as the parameter:

```
& "C:\Script Directory\Run-Commands.ps1" Parameters
```

You can use either a fully qualified path or a path relative to the current location. If the script is in the current directory, you must explicitly say so:

```
.\Run-Commands.ps1 Parameters
```

If the path contains no spaces, you may omit both the quotes and invoke operator.

Dot-sourcing

Dot-sourcing a script runs the commands inside it. Unlike invoking a script, variables and functions defined in the script *do* persist after the script exits.

You invoke a script by using the dot operator (.) and providing the script name as the parameter:

```
. "C:\Script Directory\Run-Commands.ps1" Parameters
```

You can use either a fully qualified path, or a path relative to the current location. If the script is in the current directory, you must explicitly say so:

```
. .\Run-Commands.ps1 Parameters
```

If the path contains no spaces, you may omit the quotes.

 By default, a security feature in PowerShell called the Execution Policy prevents scripts from running. When you want to enable scripting in PowerShell, you must change this setting. To understand the different execution policies available to you, type Get-Help about_signing. After selecting an execution policy, use the Set-ExecutionPolicy cmdlet to configure it:

```
Set-ExecutionPolicy RemoteSigned
```

Providing Input to Scripts

PowerShell offers several options for processing input to a script.

Argument array

To access the command-line arguments by position, use the argument array that PowerShell places in the $args special variable:

```
$firstArgument = $args[0]
$secondArgument = $args[1]
$argumentCount = $args.Count
```

Formal parameters

```
param([TypeName] $variableName = Default, …)
```

Formal parameters let you benefit from some of the many benefits of PowerShell's consistent command-line parsing engine.

PowerShell exposes your parameter names (for example, $variableName) the same way that it exposes parameters in cmdlets. Users need only to type enough of your parameter name to disambiguate it from the rest of the parameters. If the user does not specify the parameter name, PowerShell attempts to assign the input to your parameters by position.

If you specify a type name for the parameter, PowerShell ensures that the user input is of that type. If you specify a default value, PowerShell uses that value if the user does not provide input for that parameter.

To make a parameter mandatory, define the default value so that it throws an error:

```
param($mandatory = $(throw "This parameter is required."))
```

Pipeline input

To access the data being passed to your script via the pipeline, use the input enumerator that PowerShell places in the $input special variable:

```
foreach($element in $input)
{
    "Input was: $element"
}
```

The $input variable is a .NET enumerator over the pipeline input. Enumerators support streaming scenarios very efficiently but do not let you access arbitrary elements as you would with an array. If you want to process their elements again, you must call the Reset() method on the $input enumerator once you reach the end.

If you need to access the pipeline input in an unstructured way, use the following command to convert the input enumerator to an array:

```
$inputArray = @($input)
```

Cmdlet keywords in scripts

When pipeline input is a core scenario of your script, you may include statement blocks labeled begin, process, and end:

```
param(…)

begin
{
    …
}
process
{
    …
}
end
{
    …
}
```

PowerShell executes the begin statement when it loads your script, the process statement for each item passed down the pipeline, and the end statement after all pipeline input has been processed. In the process statement block, the $_ variable represents the current pipeline object.

When you write a script that includes these keywords, all the commands in your script must be contained within the statement blocks.

$MyInvocation automatic variable

The $MyInvocation automatic variable contains information about the context under which the script was run, including detailed information about the command (*MyCommand*), the script that defines it (*ScriptName*), and more.

Retrieving Output from Scripts

PowerShell provides three primary ways to retrieve output from a script.

Pipeline output

```
any command
```

The return value/output of a script is any data that it generates, but does not capture. If a script contains the commands:

```
"Text Output"
5*5
```

then assigning the output of that script to a variable creates an array with the two values, Text Output and 25.

Return statement

```
return value
```

The statement

```
return $false
```

is simply a short form for pipeline output:

```
$false
return
```

Exit statement

```
exit errorlevel
```

The exit statement returns an error code from the current script or instance of PowerShell. If called in anywhere in a script (inline, in a function, or in a script block,) it exits the script. If called outside of a script, it exits PowerShell. The exit statement sets the $LastExitCode automatic variable to *errorlevel*. In turn, that sets the $? automatic variable to $false if *errorlevel* is not zero.

See also Appendix C, *PowerShell Automatic Variables* for more information about automatic variables.

Functions

```
function SCOPE:name(parameters)
{
    statement block
}
```

or:

```
filter SCOPE:name(parameters)
{
    statement block
}
```

Functions let you package blocks of closely related commands into a single unit that you can access by name.

Valid scope names are `global` (to create a function available to the entire shell), `script` (to create a function available only to the current script), `local` (to create a function available only to the current scope and subscopes), and `private` (to create a function available only to the current scope). The default scope is the `local` scope, which follows the same rules as those of default variable scopes.

The content of a function's statement block follows the same rules as the content of a script. Functions support the `$args` array, formal parameters, the `$input` enumerator, cmdlet keywords, pipeline output, and equivalent return semantics.

> A common mistake is to call a function as you would call a method:
>
> ```
> $result = GetMyResults($item1, $item2)
> ```
>
> PowerShell treats functions as it treats scripts and other commands, so this should instead be:
>
> ```
> $result = GetMyResults $item1 $item2
> ```
>
> The first command passes an array that contains the items `$item1` and `$item2` to the `GetMyResults` function.

A parameter declaration, as an alternative to a `param` statement, follows the same syntax as the formal parameter list, but does not require the `param` keyword.

A filter is simply a function where the statements are treated as though they are contained within a `process` statement block.

Commands in your script can access only functions that have already been defined. This can often make large scripts difficult to understand when the beginning of the script is composed entirely of helper functions. Structuring a script in the following manner often makes it more clear:

```
function Main
{
    (...)
    HelperFunction
    (...)
}

function HelperFunction
{
    (...)
}

. Main
```

As with a script, you may either invoke or dot-source a function.

Script Blocks

```
$objectReference =
{
    statement block
}
```

PowerShell supports script blocks, which act exactly like unnamed functions and scripts. Like both scripts and functions, the content of a script block's statement block follows the same rules as the content of a function or script. Script blocks support the $args array, formal parameters, the $input enumerator, cmdlet keywords, pipeline output, and equivalent return semantics.

As with both scripts and functions, you may either invoke or dot-source a script block. Since a script block does not have a name, you either invoke it directly (& { "Hello" }), or invoke the variable (& $objectReference) that contains it.

Managing Errors

PowerShell supports two classes of errors: *nonterminating* and *terminating*. It collects both types of errors as a list in the $error automatic variable.

Nonterminating Errors

Most errors are *nonterminating errors*, in that they do not halt execution of the current cmdlet, script, function, or pipeline. When a command outputs an error (via PowerShell's error-output facilities), PowerShell writes that error to a stream called the *error output stream*.

You can output a nonterminating error using the `Write-Error` cmdlet (or the `WriteError()` API when writing a cmdlet).

The `$ErrorActionPreference` automatic variable lets you control how PowerShell handles nonterminating errors. It supports the following values, as shown in Table A-14.

Table A-14. ErrorActionPreference automatic variable values

Value	Meaning
SilentlyContinue	Do not display errors.
Stop	Treat nonterminating errors as terminating errors.
Continue	Display errors, but continue execution of the current cmdlet, script, function, or pipeline. This is the default.
Inquire	Display a prompt that asks how PowerShell should treat this error.

Most cmdlets let you configure this explicitly by passing one of the above values to its `ErrorAction` parameter.

Terminating Errors

A *terminating error* halts execution of the current cmdlet, script, function, or pipeline. If a command (such as a cmdlet or .NET method call) generates a structured exception (for example, if you provide a method with parameters outside their valid range), PowerShell exposes this as a terminating error. PowerShell also generates a terminating error if it fails to parse an element of your script, function, or pipeline.

You can generate a terminating error in your script using the `throw` keyword:

```
throw message
```

> In your own scripts and cmdlets, generate terminating errors only when the fundamental intent of the operation is impossible to accomplish. For example, failing to execute a command on a remote server should be considered a nonterminating error, while failing to connect to the remote server altogether should be considered a terminating error.

PowerShell lets you intercept terminating errors if you define a `trap` statement before PowerShell encounters that error:

```
trap [exception type]
{
    statement block
    [continue or break]
}
```

If you specify an exception type, the trap statement applies only to terminating errors of that type.

If specified, the `continue` keyword tells PowerShell to continue processing the rest of your script, function, or pipeline after the point at which it encountered the terminating error.

If specified, the `break` keyword tells PowerShell to halt processing the rest of your script, function, or pipeline after the point at which it encountered the terminating error. Break is the default mode, and applies if you specify neither `break` nor `continue` at all.

Formatting Output

Pipeline | Formatting Command

When objects reach the end of the output pipeline, PowerShell converts them to text to make them suitable for human consumption. PowerShell supports several options to help you control this formatting process, as listed in Table A-15.

Table A-15. PowerShell formatting commands

Formatting command	Result
Format-Table *Properties*	Formats the properties of the input objects as a table, including only the object properties you specify. If you do not specify a property list, PowerShell picks a default set.
	In addition to supplying object properties, you may also provide advanced formatting statements:
| | ```
PS > Get-Process | `
    Format-Table -Auto Name,`
    @{Label="HexId";
      Expression={ "{0:x}" -f $_.Id}
      Width=4
      Align="Right"
    }
``` |
| | The advanced formatting statement is a hashtable with the keys `Label` and `Expression` (or any short form of them). The value of the expression key should be a script block that returns a result for the current object (represented by the `$_` variable). |
| | For more information about the `Format-Table` cmdlet, type `Get-Help Format-Table`. |
```

Formatting command	Result
`Format-List` *Properties*	Formats the properties of the input objects as a list, including only the object properties you specify. If you do not specify a property list, PowerShell picks a default set.
	The `Format-List` cmdlet supports the advanced formatting statements as used by the `Format-Table` cmdlet.
	The `Format-List` cmdlet is the one you will use most often to get a detailed summary of an object's properties.
	The command `Format-List` `*` returns all properties, but does not include those that PowerShell hides by default. The command, `Format-List` `*` `-Force` returns all properties.
	For more information about the `Format-List` cmdlet, type `Get-Help Format-List`.
`Format-Wide` *Property*	Formats the properties of the input objects in an extremely terse summary view. If you do not specify a property, PowerShell picks a default.
	In addition to supplying object properties, you may also provide advanced formatting statements:
| | ```
PS >Get-Process | `
    Format-Wide -Auto `
    @{ Expression={ "{0:x}" -f $_.Id} }
``` |
| | The advanced formatting statement is a hashtable with the key `Expression` (or any short form of it). The value of the expression key should be a script block that returns a result for the current object (represented by the $_ variable). |
| | For more information about the `Format-Wide` cmdlet, type `Get-Help Format-Wide`. |

Custom formatting files

All the formatting defaults in PowerShell (for example, when you do not specify a formatting command, or when you do not specify formatting properties) are driven by the **.Format.Ps1Xml* files in the installation directory in a manner similar to the type extension files mentioned in Recipe 3.12, "Add Custom Methods and Properties to Types."

To create your own formatting customizations, use these files as a source of examples, but do not modify them directly. Instead, create a new file and use the `Update-FormatData` cmdlet to load your customizations. The `Update-FormatData` cmdlet applies your changes to the current instance of PowerShell. If you wish to load them every time you launch PowerShell, call `Update-FormatData` in your profile script. The following command loads *Format.custom.ps1xml* from the same directory as your profile:

```
$formatFile = Join-Path (Split-Path $profile) "Format.Custom.Ps1Xml"
Update-FormatData -PrependPath $typesFile
```
```

Capturing Output

There are several ways to capture the output of commands in PowerShell, as listed in Table A-16.

Table A-16. Capturing output in PowerShell

Command	Result
`$variable = Command`	Stores the objects produced by the PowerShell command into `$variable`.
`$variable = Command	Out-String`	Stores the visual representation of the PowerShell command into `$variable`. This is the PowerShell command after it's been converted to human-readable output.
`$variable = NativeCommand`	Stores the (string) output of the native command into `$variable`. PowerShell stores this as a list of strings—one for each line of output from the native command.
`Command -OutVariable variable`	For most commands, stores the objects produced by the PowerShell command into `$variable`. The parameter `-OutVariable` can also be written `-Ov`.
`Command > File`	Redirects the visual representation of the PowerShell (or standard output of a native command) into `File`, overwriting `File` if it exists. Errors are not captured by this redirection.
`Command >> File`	Redirects the visual representation of the PowerShell (or standard output of a native command) into `File`, appending to `File` if it exists. Errors are not captured by this redirection.
`Command 2> File`	Redirects the errors from the PowerShell or native command into `File`, overwriting `File` if it exists.
`Command 2>> File`	Redirects the errors from the PowerShell or native command into `File`, appending to `File` if it exists.
`Command > File 2>&1`	Redirects both the error and standard output streams of the PowerShell or native command into `File`, overwriting `File` if it exists.
`Command >> File 2>&1`	Redirects both the error and standard output streams of the PowerShell or native command into `File`, appending to `File` if it exists.

Tracing and Debugging

The three facilities for tracing and debugging in PowerShell are the `Set-PsDebug` cmdlet, the `Trace-Command` cmdlet, and verbose cmdlet output.

The Set-PsDebug Cmdlet

The `Set-PsDebug` cmdlet lets you control tracing, stepping, and strict mode in Power-Shell. Table A-17 lists the parameters of the `Set-PsDebug` cmdlet.

Table A-17. Parameters of the Set-PsDebug cmdlet

Parameter	Description
Trace	Sets the amount of tracing detail that PowerShell outputs when running commands.
	A value of 1 outputs all lines as PowerShell evaluates them. A value of 2 outputs all lines as PowerShell evaluates them, along with information about variable assignments, function calls, and scripts. A value of 0 disables tracing.
Step	Enables and disables per-command stepping. When enabled, PowerShell prompts you before it executes a command.
Strict	Enables and disables strict mode. When enabled, PowerShell throws a terminating error if you attempt to reference a variable that you have not yet defined.
Off	Turns off tracing, stepping, and strict mode.

The Trace-Command Cmdlet

```
Trace-Command CommandDiscovery -PsHost { gci c:\ }
```

The Trace-Command cmdlet exposes diagnostic and support information for Power-Shell commands. PowerShell groups its diagnostic information into categories called *trace sources*.

A full list of trace sources is available through the Get-TraceSource cmdlet.

For more information about the Trace-Command cmdlet, type **Get-Help Trace-Command**.

Verbose Cmdlet Output

```
Cmdlet -Verbose
```

PowerShell commands can generate verbose output using the Write-Verbose cmdlet (if written as a script), or the WriteVerbose() API (when written as a cmdlet).

The $VerbosePreference automatic variable lets you control how PowerShell handles verbose output. It supports the values listed in Table A-18.

Table A-18.

Value	Meaning
SilentlyContinue	Do not display verbose output. This is the default.
Stop	Treat verbose output as a terminating error.
Continue	Display verbose output and continue execution of the current cmdlet, script, function, or pipeline.
Inquire	Display a prompt that asks how PowerShell should treat this verbose output.

Most cmdlets let you configure this explicitly by passing one of the values listed in Table A-18 to its Verbose parameter.

Common Customization Points

As useful as it is out of the box, PowerShell offers several avenues for customization and personalization.

Console Settings

The Windows PowerShell user interface offers several features to make your shell experience more efficient.

Adjust your window size

In the System menu (right-click the PowerShell icon at the top left of the console window), select Properties → Layout. The Window Size options let you control the actual window size (how big the window appears on screen), while the Screen Buffer Size options let you control the virtual window size (how much content the window can hold). If the screen buffer size is larger than the actual window size, the console window changes to include scrollbars. Increase the virtual window height to make PowerShell store more output from earlier in your session. If you launch PowerShell from the Start menu, PowerShell launches with some default modifications to the window size.

Make text selection easier

In the System menu, click Options → QuickEdit Mode. QuickEdit mode lets you use the mouse to efficiently copy and paste text into or out of your PowerShell console. If you launch PowerShell from the Start menu, PowerShell launches with QuickEdit mode enabled.

Use hotkeys to operate the shell more efficiently

The Windows PowerShell console supports many hotkeys that help make operating the console more efficient, as shown in Table A-19.

Table A-19. Windows PowerShell hotkeys

Hotkey	Meaning
Windows key + r, and then type `powershell`	Launch Windows PowerShell.
Up arrow	Scan backward through your command history.
Down arrow	Scan forward through your command history.
Page Up	Display the first command in your command history.
Page Down	Display the last command in your command history.
Left arrow	Move cursor one character to the left on your command line.

Table A-19. *Windows PowerShell hotkeys (continued)*

Hotkey	Meaning
Right arrow	Move cursor one character to the right on your command line. If at the end of the line, inserts a character from the text of your last command at that position.
Home	Move the cursor to the beginning of the command line.
End	Move the cursor to the end of the command line.
Control + left arrow	Move the cursor one word to the left on your command line.
Control + right arrow	Move the cursor one word to the right on your command line.
Alt + space, e, l	Scroll through the screen buffer.
Alt + space, e, f	Search for text in the screen buffer.
Alt + space, e, k	Select text to be copied from the screen buffer.
Alt + space, e, p	Paste clipboard contents into the Windows PowerShell console.
Alt + space, c	Close the Windows PowerShell console.
Control + c	Cancel the current operation.
Control + break	Forcefully close the Windows PowerShell window.
Control + home	Deletes characters from the beginning of the current command line up to (but not including) the current cursor position.
Control + end	Deletes characters from (and including) the current cursor position to the end of the current command line.
F1	Move cursor one character to the right on your command line. If at the end of the line, inserts a character from the text of your last command at that position.
F2	Creates a new command line by copying your last command line up to the character that you type.
F3	Complete the command line with content from your last command line, from the current cursor position to the end.
F4	Deletes characters from your cursor position up to (but not including) the character that you type.
F5	Scan backward through your command history.
F7	Interactively select a command from your command history. Use the arrow keys to scroll through the window that appears. Press the Enter key to execute the command, or use the right arrow key to place the text on your command line instead.
F8	Scan backward through your command history, only displaying matches for commands that match the text you've typed so far on the command line.
F9	Invoke a specific numbered command from your command history. The numbers of these commands correspond to the numbers that the command-history selection window (F7) shows.
Alt + F7	Clear the command history list.

While useful in their own right, the hotkeys listed in Table A-19 become even more useful when you map them to shorter or more intuitive keystrokes using a hotkey program such as the free AutoHotkey *http://www.autohotkey.com*.

Profiles

Windows PowerShell automatically runs the four scripts listed in Table A-20 during startup. Each, if present, lets you customize your execution environment. PowerShell runs anything you place in these files as though you had entered it manually at the command line.

Table A-20. Windows PowerShell profiles

Profile purpose	Profile location
Customization of all PowerShell sessions, including PowerShell hosting applications for all users on the system	*InstallationDirectory*\profile.ps1
Customization of *PowerShell.exe* sessions for all users on the system	*InstallationDirectory*\Microsoft. PowerShell_profile.ps1
Customization of all PowerShell sessions, including PowerShell hosting applications	My Documents\WindowsPowerShell\profile.ps1
Typical customization of *PowerShell.exe* sessions	My Documents\WindowsPowerShell\Microsoft. PowerShell_profile.ps1

PowerShell makes editing your profile script simple by defining the automatic variable, $profile.

To create a new profile, type:

```
New-Item -Type file -Force $profile
```

To edit this profile, type:

```
Notepad $profile
```

For more information on writing scripts, see the "Writing Scripts, Reusing Functionality" section earlier in this chapter.

Prompts

To customize your prompt, add a prompt function to your profile. This function returns a string. For example:

```
function Prompt
{
    "PS [$env:COMPUTERNAME] >"
}
```

For more information about customizing your prompt, see also Recipe 1.3, "Customize Your Shell, Profile, and Prompt."

Tab Completion

You may define a TabExpansion function to customize the way that Windows Power-Shell completes properties, variables, parameters, and files when you press the Tab key.

Your TabExpansion function overrides the one that PowerShell defines by default, though, so you may want to use its definition as a starting point:

```
Get-Content function:\TabExpansion
```

As its arguments, this function receives the entire command line as input, as well as the last word of the command line. If the function returns one or more strings, Power-Shell cycles through those strings during tab completion. Otherwise, it uses its built-in logic to tab-complete file names, directory names, cmdlet names, and variable names.

Regular Expression Reference

Regular expressions play an important role in most text parsing and text matching tasks. They form an important underpinning of the –match operator, the switch statement, the Select-String cmdlet, and more. Tables B-1 through B-9 list commonly used regular expressions.

Table B-1. Character classes: Patterns that represent sets of characters

Character class	Matches

.	Any character except for a newline. If the regular expression uses the SingleLine option, it matches any character.
	
	```PS >"T" -match '.'```
	```True```

[*characters*]	Any character in the brackets. For example: [*aeiou*].
	
	```PS >"Test" -match '[Tes]'```
	```True```

[^*characters*]	Any character not in the brackets. For example: [^*aeiou*].
	
	```PS >"Test" -match '[^Tes]'```
	```False```

[*start-end*]	Any character between the characters start and end, inclusive. You may include multiple character ranges between the brackets. For example, [*a-eh-j*].
	
	```PS >"Test" -match '[e-t]'```
	```True```

[^*start-end*]	Any character not between any of the character ranges start through end, inclusive. You may include multiple character ranges between the brackets. For example, [^*a-eh-j*].
	
	```PS >"Test" -match '[^e-t]'```
	```False```

\p{*character class*}	Any character in the Unicode group or block range specified by {*character class*}.
	
	```PS >"+" -match '\p{Sm}'```
	```True```

\P{*character class*}	Any character not in the Unicode group or block range specified by {*character class*}.
	
	```PS >"+" -match '\P{Sm}'```
	```False```

Table B-1. Character classes: Patterns that represent sets of characters (continued)

Character class	Matches
\w	Any word character.
| | ```
PS >"a" -match '\w'
True
``` |
| \W | Any nonword character. |
| | ```
PS >"!" -match '\W'
True
``` |
| \s | Any whitespace character. |
| | ```
PS >"`t" -match '\s'
True
``` |
| \S | Any nonwhitespace character. |
| | ```
PS >" `t" -match '\S'
False
``` |
| \d | Any decimal digit. |
| | ```
PS >"5" -match '\d'
True
``` |
| \D | Any nondecimal digit. |
| | ```
PS >"!" -match '\D'
True
``` |

Table B-2. Quantifiers: Expressions that enforce quantity on the preceding expression

Quantifier	Meaning
<none>	One match.
| | ```
PS >"T" -match 'T'
True
``` |
| * | Zero or more matches, matching as much as possible. |
| | ```
PS >"A" -match 'T*'
True
PS >"TTTTT" -match '^T*$'
True
``` |
| + | One or more matches, matching as much as possible. |
| | ```
PS >"A" -match 'T+'
False
PS >"TTTTT" -match '^T+$'
True
``` |
| ? | Zero or one matches, matching as much as possible. |
| | ```
PS >"TTTTT" -match '^T?$'
False
``` |
| {n} | Exactly n matches. |
| | ```
PS >"TTTTT" -match '^T{5}$'
True
``` |
| {n,} | n or more matches, matching as much as possible. |
| | ```
PS >"TTTTT" -match '^T{4,}$'
True
``` |

Table B-2. Quantifiers: Expressions that enforce quantity on the preceding expression (continued)

Quantifier	Meaning
{n,m}	Between *n* and *m* matches (inclusive), matching as much as possible.
	`PS >"TTTTT" -match '^T{4,6}$'` `True`
*?	Zero or more matches, matching as little as possible.
	`PS >"A" -match '^AT*?$'` `True`
+?	One or more matches, matching as little as possible.
	`PS >"A" -match '^AT+?$'` `False`
??	Zero or one matches, matching as little as possible.
	`PS >"A" -match '^AT??$'` `True`
{n}?	Exactly *n* matches.
	`PS >"TTTTT" -match '^T{5}?$'` `True`
{n,}?	*n* or more matches, matching as little as possible.
	`PS >"TTTTT" -match '^T{4,}?$'` `True`
{n,m}?	Between *n* and *m* matches (inclusive), matching as little as possible.
	`PS >"TTTTT" -match '^T{4,6}?$'` `True`

Table B-3. Grouping constructs: Expressions that let you group characters, patterns, and other expressions

Grouping construct	Description
(*text*)	Captures the text matched inside the parentheses. These captures are named by number (starting at one) based on the order of the opening parenthesis.

	`PS >"Hello" -match '^(.*)llo$'; $matches[1]`
	`True`
	`He`

(?<*name*>)	Captures the text matched inside the parentheses. These captures are named by the name given in *name*.

	`PS >"Hello" -match '^(?<One>.*)llo$'; $matches.One`
	`True`
	`He`

(?<*name1-name2*>)	A balancing group definition. This is an advanced regular expression construct, but lets you match evenly balanced pairs of terms.

Table B-3. Grouping constructs: Expressions that let you group characters, patterns, and other expressions (continued)

Grouping construct	Description
(?:)	Noncapturing group.

```
PS >"A1" -match '((A|B)\d)'; $matches
True

Name                        Value
----                        -----
2                           A
1                           A1
0                           A1

PS >"A1" -match '((?:A|B)\d)'; $matches
True

Name                        Value
----                        -----
1                           A1
0                           A1
```

Grouping construct	Description
(?imnsx-imnsx:)	Applies or disables the given option for this group. Supported options are:

```
i    case-insensitive
m    multiline
n    explicit capture
s    singleline
x    ignore whitespace


PS >"Te`nst" -match '(T e.st)'
False
PS >"Te`nst" -match '(?sx:T e.st)'
True
```

Grouping construct	Description
(?=)	Zero-width positive lookahead assertion. Ensures that the given pattern matches to the right, without actually performing the match.

```
PS >"555-1212" -match '(?=...-)(.*)'; $matches[1]
True
555-1212
```

Grouping construct	Description
(?!)	Zero-width negative lookahead assertion. Ensures that the given pattern does not match to the right, without actually performing the match.

```
PS >"friendly" -match '(?!friendly)friend'
False
```

Grouping construct	Description
(?<=)	Zero-width positive lookbehind assertion. Ensures that the given pattern matches to the left, without actually performing the match.

```
PS >"public int X" -match '^.*(?<=public )int .*$'
True
```

Grouping construct	Description
(?<!)	Zero-width negative lookbehind assertion. Ensures that the given pattern does not match to the left, without actually performing the match.

```
PS >"private int X" -match '^.*(?<!private )int .*$'
False
```

Table B-3. Grouping constructs: Expressions that let you group characters, patterns, and other expressions (continued)

Grouping construct	Description
(?>)	Nonbacktracking subexpression. Matches only if this subexpression can be matched completely. ``` PS >"Hello World" -match '(Hello.*)orld' True PS >"Hello World" -match '(?>Hello.*)orld' False ``` The nonbacktracking version of the subexpression fails to match, as its complete match would be "Hello World".

Table B-4. Atomic zero-width assertions: Patterns that restrict where a match may occur

Assertion	Restriction
^	The match must occur at the beginning of the string (or line, if the Multiline option is in effect). ``` PS >"Test" -match '^est' False ```
$	The match must occur at the end of the string (or line, if the Multiline option is in effect). ``` PS >"Test" -match 'Tes$' False ```
\A	The match must occur at the beginning of the string. ``` PS >"The`nTest" -match '(?m:^Test)' True PS >"The`nTest" -match '(?m:\ATest)' False ```
\Z	The match must occur at the end of the string, or before \n at the end of the string. ``` PS >"The`nTest`n" -match '(?m:The$)' True PS >"The`nTest`n" -match '(?m:The\Z)' False PS >"The`nTest`n" -match 'Test\Z' True ```
\z	The match must occur at the end of the string. ``` PS >"The`nTest`n" -match 'Test\z' False ```
\G	The match must occur where the previous match ended. Used with the System.Text.RegularExpressions.Match.NextMatch() method.
\b	The match must occur on a word boundary—the first or last characters in words separated by nonalphanumeric characters. ``` PS >"Testing" -match 'ing\b' True ```
\B	The match must not occur on a word boundary. ``` PS >"Testing" -match 'ing\B' False ```

Table B-5. Substitution patterns: Patterns used in a regular expression replace operation

Pattern	Substitution

$*number*	The text matched by group number <number>.
	<pre>PS >"Test" -replace "(.*)st",'$1ar'
	Tear</pre>

${*name*}	The text matched by group named <name>.
	<pre>PS >"Test" -replace "(?<pre>.*)st",'${pre}ar'
	Tear</pre>

$$	A literal $.
	<pre>PS >"Test" -replace ".",'$$'
	$$$$</pre>

$&	A copy of the entire match.
	<pre>PS >"Test" -replace "^.*$",'Found: $&'
	Found: Test</pre>

$`	The text of the input string that precedes the match.
	<pre>PS >"Test" -replace "est$",'Te$`'
	TTeT</pre>

$'	The text of the input string that follows the match.
	<pre>PS >"Test" -replace "^Tes",'Res$'''
	Restt</pre>

$+	The last group captured.
	<pre>PS >"Testing" -replace "(.*)ing",'$+ed'
	Tested</pre>

$_	The entire input string.
	<pre>PS >"Testing" -replace "(.*)ing",'String: $ '
	String: Testing</pre>

Table B-6. Alternation constructs: Expressions that allow you to perform either/or logic

Alternation construct	Description

|	Matches any of the terms separated by the vertical bar character.
	<pre>PS >"Test" -match '(B|T)est'
	True</pre>

(?(expression)yes|no)	Matches the yes term if expression matches at this point. Otherwise, matches the no term. The no term is optional.
	<pre>PS >"3.14" -match '(?(\d)3.14|Pi)'
	True
	PS >"Pi" -match '(?(\d)3.14|Pi)'
	True
	PS >"2.71" -match '(?(\d)3.14|Pi)'
	False</pre>

(?(name)yes|no)	Matches the yes term if the capture group named name has a capture at this point. Otherwise, matches the no term. The no term is optional.
	<pre>PS >"123" -match '(?<one>1)?(?(one)23|234)'
	True
	PS >"23" -match '(?<one>1)?(?(one)23|234)'
	False
	PS >"234" -match '(?<one>1)?(?(one)23|234)'
	True</pre>

Table B-7. Backreference constructs: Expressions that refer to a capture group within the expression

Backreference construct	Refers to
number	Group number number in the expression. ``` PS >"|Text|" -match '(.)Text\1' True PS >"|Text+" -match '(.)Text\1' False ```
\k<*name*>	The group named name in the expression. ``` PS >"|Text|" -match '(?<Symbol>.)Text\k<Symbol>' True PS >"|Text+" -match '(?<Symbol>.)Text\k<Symbol>' False ```

Table B-8. Other constructs: Other expressions that modify a regular expression

Construct	Description
(?imnsx-imnsx)	Applies or disables the given option for the rest of this expression. Supported options are: ``` i case-insensitive m multiline n explicit capture s singleline x ignore whitespace ``` ``` PS >"Te`nst" -match '(?sx)T e.st' True ```
(?#)	Inline comment. This terminates at the first closing parenthesis. ``` PS >"Test" -match '(?# Match 'Test')Test' True ```
# [to end of line]	Comment form allowed when the regular expression has the IgnoreWhitespace option enabled. ``` PS >"Test" -match '(?x)Test # Matches Test' True ```

Table B-9. Character escapes: Character sequences that represent another character

Escaped character	Match
<ordinary characters>	Characters other than . $ ^ { [(	) * + ? \ match themselves.
\a	A bell (alarm) \u0007.
\b	A backspace \u0008 if in a [ ] character class. In a regular expression, \b denotes a word boundary (between \w and \W characters) except within a [ ] character class, where \b refers to the backspace character. In a replacement pattern, \b always denotes a backspace.
\t	A tab \u0009.
\r	A carriage return \u000D.
\v	A vertical tab \u000B.
\f	A form feed \u000C.
\n	A new line \u000A.

Table B-9. Character escapes: Character sequences that represent another character (continued)

Escaped character	Match
\e	An escape \u001B.
\ddd	An ASCII character as octal (up to three digits.) Numbers with no leading zero are treated as backreferences if they have only one digit, or if they correspond to a capturing group number.
\xdd	An ASCII character using hexadecimal representation (exactly two digits).
\cC	An ASCII control character; for example, \cC is control-C.
\udddd	A Unicode character using hexadecimal representation (exactly four digits).
\	When followed by a character that is not recognized as an escaped character, matches that character. For example, * is the literal character *.

PowerShell Automatic Variables

PowerShell defines and populates several variables automatically. These variables let you access information about the execution environment, PowerShell preferences, and more.

Table C-1 provides a listing of these automatic variables and their meanings.

Table C-1. Windows PowerShell automatic variables: Variables automatically used and set by Windows PowerShell

Variable	Meaning
$$	Last token of the last line received by the shell.
$?	Success/fail status of the last operation.
$^	First token of the last line received by the shell.
$_	Current pipeline object in a pipelined script block.
$args	Array of parameters passed to the script, function, or script block.
$confirmPreference	Preference that controls the level of impact that operations may have before requesting confirmation. Supports the values none, low, medium, high. A value of none disables confirmation messages.
$consoleFilename	Filename of the PowerShell console file that configured this session, if one was used.
$currentlyExecutingCommand	Currently executing command, when in a suspended prompt.
$debugPreference	Preference that controls how PowerShell should handle debug output written by a script or cmdlet. Supports the values SilentlyContinue, Continue, Inquire, and Stop.
$error	Array that holds the (terminating and nonterminating) errors generated in the shell.
$errorActionPreference	Preference that controls how PowerShell should handle error output written by a script or cmdlet. Supports the values SilentlyContinue, Continue, Inquire, and Stop.
$errorView	Preference that controls how PowerShell should output errors in the shell. Supports the values of Normal and CategoryView (a more succinct and categorical view of the error).

Table C-1. Windows PowerShell automatic variables: Variables automatically used and set by Windows PowerShell (continued)

Variable	Meaning
$executionContext	Means by which scripts can access the APIs typically used by cmdlets and providers.
$false	Variable that represents the Boolean value False.
$foreach	Enumerator within a foreach loop.
$formatEnumerationLimit	Limit on how deep into an object the formatting and output facilities travel before outputting an object.
$home	User's home directory.
$host	Means by which scripts can access the APIs and implementation details of the current host and user interface.
$input	Current input pipeline in a pipelined script block.
$lastExitCode	Exit code of the last command—can be explicitly set by scripts, and is automatically set when calling native executables.
$logEngineHealthEvent	Preference that tells PowerShell to log engine health events, such as errors and exceptions. Supports the values $true and $false.
$logEngineLifecycleEvent	Preference that tells PowerShell to log engine lifecycle events, such as Start and Stop. Supports the values $true and $false.
$logCommandHealthEvent	Preference that tells PowerShell to log command health events, such as errors and exceptions. Supports the values $true and $false.
$logCommandLifecycleEvent	Preference that tells PowerShell to log command lifecycle events such as Start and Stop. Supports the values $true and $false.
$logProviderHealthEvent	Preference that tells PowerShell to log provider health events, such as errors and exceptions. Supports the values $true and $false.
$logProviderLifecycleEvent	Preference that tells PowerShell to log provider lifecycle events, such as Start and Stop. Supports the values $true and $false.
$matches	Results of the last successful regular expression match (through the –match operator.)
$maximumAliasCount	Limit on how many aliases may be defined.
$maximumDriveCount	Limit on how many drives may be defined. Does not include default system drives.
$maximumErrorCount	Limit on how many errors PowerShell retains in the $error collection.
$maximumFunctionCount	Limit on how many functions may be defined.
$maximumHistoryCount	Limit on how many history items are retained.
$maximumVariableCount	Limit on how many variables may be defined.
$myInvocation	Information about the context under which the script, function, or script block was run, including detailed information about the command (MyCommand), the script that defines it (ScriptName).
$nestedPromptLevel	Nesting level of the current prompt. Incremented by operations that enter a nested prompt (such as $host.EnterNestedPrompt()) and decremented by the exit statement.
$null	Variable that represents the concept of Null.
$ofs	Output field separator. Placed between elements when PowerShell outputs a list as a string.

Table C-1. Windows PowerShell automatic variables: Variables automatically used and set by Windows PowerShell (continued)

Variable	Meaning
$outputEncoding	Character encoding used when sending pipeline data to external processes.
$pid	Process ID of the current PowerShell instance.
$profile	Location and filename of the PowerShell profile for this host.
$progressPreference	Preference that controls how PowerShell should handle progress output written by a script or cmdlet. Supports the values SilentlyContinue, Continue, Inquire, and Stop.
$psHome	Installation location of PowerShell.
$pwd	Current working directory.
$shellId	Shell identifier of this host.
$stackTrace	Detailed stack trace information of the last error.
$this	Reference to the current object in ScriptMethods and ScriptProperties.
$transcript	Filename used by the Start-Transcript cmdlet.
$true	Variable that represents the Boolean value True.
$verboseHelpErrors	Preference that tells PowerShell to output detailed error information when parsing malformed help files. Supports the values $true and $false.
$verbosePreference	Preference that controls how PowerShell should handle verbose output written by a script or cmdlet. Supports the values SilentlyContinue, Continue, Inquire, and Stop.
$warningPreference	Preference that controls how PowerShell should handle warning output written by a script or cmdlet. Supports the values SilentlyContinue, Continue, Inquire, and Stop.
$whatifPreference	Preference that controls how PowerShell should handle confirmation requests called by a script or cmdlet. Supports the values SilentlyContinue, Continue, Inquire, and Stop.

Standard PowerShell Verbs

Cmdlets and scripts should be named using a *Verb-Noun* syntax. For example, `Get-ChildItem`. The official guidance is that, with rare exception, cmdlets should use the standard PowerShell verbs. They should avoid any synonyms or concepts that can be mapped to the standard. This allows administrators to quickly understand a set of cmdlets that use a new noun.

Verbs should be phrased in the present tense, and nouns should be singular. Tables D-1 through D-6 list the different categories of standard PowerShell verbs.

Table D-1. Standard Windows PowerShell common verbs

Verb	Meaning	Synonyms
Add	Adds a resource to a container, or attaches an element to another element	Append, Attach, Concatenate, Insert
Clear	Removes all elements from a container	Flush, Erase, Release, Unmark, Unset, Nullify
Copy	Copies a resource to another name or container	Duplicate, Clone, Replicate
Get	Retrieves data	Read, Open, Cat, Type, Dir, Obtain, Dump, Acquire, Examine, Find, Search
Hide	Makes a display not visible	Suppress
Join	Joins a resource	Combine, Unite, Connect, Associate
Lock	Locks a resource	Restrict, Bar
Move	Moves a resource	Transfer, Name, Migrate
New	Creates a new resource	Create, Generate, Build, Make, Allocate
Push	Puts an item onto the top of a stack	Put, Add, Copy
Pop	Removes an item from the top of a stack	Remove, Paste
Remove	Removes a resource from a container	Delete, Kill
Rename	Gives a resource a new name	Ren, Swap
Search	Finds a resource (or summary information about that resource) in a collection; (does not actually retrieve the resource but provides information to be used when retrieving it)	Find, Get, Grep, Select

Table D-1. *Standard Windows PowerShell common verbs (continued)*

Verb	Meaning	Synonyms
Select	Creates a subset of data from a larger data set	Pick, Grep, Filter
Set	Places data	Write, Assign, Configure
Show	Retrieves, formats, and displays information	Display, Report
Split	Separates data into smaller elements	Divide, Chop, Parse
Unlock	Unlocks a resource	Free, Unrestrict
Use	Applies or associates a resource with a context	With, Having

Table D-2. *Standard Windows PowerShell communication verbs*

Verb	Meaning	Synonyms
Connect	Connects a source to a destination	Join, Telnet
Disconnect	Disconnects a source from a destination	Break, Logoff
Read	Acquires information from a nonconnected source	Prompt, Get
Receive	Acquires information from a connected source	Read, Accept, Peek
Send	Writes information to a connected destination	Put, Broadcast, Mail
Write	Writes information to a non-connected destination	Puts, Print

Table D-3. *Standard Windows PowerShell data verbs*

Verb	Meaning	Synonyms
Backup	Backs up data	Save, Burn
Checkpoint	Creates a snapshot of the current state of data, or its configuration	Diff, StartTransaction
Compare	Compares a resource with another resource	Diff, Bc
Convert	Changes from one representation to another, when the cmdlet supports bidirectional conversion, or conversion of many data types	Change, Resize, Resample
ConvertFrom	Converts from one primary input to several supported outputs	Export, Output, Out
ConvertTo	Converts from several supported inputs to one primary output	Import, Input, In
Dismount	Detaches a name entity from a location in a namespace	Dismount, Unlink
Export	Stores the primary input resource into a backing store or interchange format	Extract, Backup
Import	Creates a primary output resource from a backing store or interchange format	Load, Read
Initialize	Prepares a resource for use, and initializes it to a default state	Setup, Renew, Rebuild
Limit	Applies constraints to a resource	Quota, Enforce
Merge	Creates a single data instance from multiple data sets	Combine, Join
Mount	Attach a named entity to a location in a namespace	Attach, Link
Out	Sends data to a terminal location	Print, Format, Send
Publish	Make a resource known or visible to others	Deploy, Release, Install

Table D-3. Standard Windows PowerShell data verbs (continued)

Verb	Meaning	Synonyms
Restore	Restores a resource to a set of conditions that have been pre-defined or set by a checkpoint	Repair, Return, Fix
Unpublish	Removes a resource from public visibility	Uninstall, Revert
Update	Updates or refreshes a resource	Refresh, Renew, Index

Table D-4. Standard Windows PowerShell diagnostic verbs

Verb	Meaning	Synonyms
Debug	Examines a resource, diagnoses operational problems	Attach, Diagnose
Measure	Identifies resources consumed by an operation, or retrieves statistics about a resource	Calculate, Determine, Analyze
Ping	Determines if a resource is active and responsive. In most instances, this should be replaced by the verb, Test	Connect, Debug
Resolve	Maps a shorthand representation to a more complete one	Expand, Determine
Test	Verify the validity or consistency of a resource	Diagnose, Verify, Analyze
Trace	Follow the activities of the resource	Inspect, Dig

Table D-5. Standard Windows PowerShell life cycle verbs

Verb	Meaning	Synonyms
Disable	Configures an item to be unavailable	Halt, Hide
Enable	Configures an item to be available	Allow, Permit
Install	Places a resource in the specified location and optionally initializes it	Setup, Configure
Invoke	Calls or launches an activity that cannot be stopped	Run, Call, Perform
Restart	Stops an operation and starts it again	Recycle, Hup
Resume	Begins an operation after it has been suspended	Continue
Start	Begins an activity	Launch, Initiate
Stop	Discontinues an activity	Halt, End, Discontinue
Suspend	Pauses an operation, but does not discontinue it	Pause, Sleep, Break
Uninstall	Removes a resource from the specified location	Remove, Clear, Clean
Wait	To pause until an expected event occurs	Sleep, Pause, Join

Table D-6. Standard Windows PowerShell security verbs

Verb	Meaning	Synonyms
Block	Restricts access to a resource	Prevent, Limit, Deny
Grant	Grants access to a resource	Allow, Enable
Revoke	Removes access to a resource	Remove, Disable
Unblock	Removes a restriction of access to a resource	Clear, Allow

Selected .NET Classes and Their Uses

Tables E-1 through E-16 provide pointers to types in the .NET Framework that usefully complement the functionality that PowerShell provides. For detailed descriptions and documentation, search *http://msdn.microsoft.com* for the official documentation.

Table E-1. Windows PowerShell

Class	Description
System.Management.Automation.PSObject	Represents a PowerShell object to which you can add notes, properties, and more.

Table E-2. Utility

Class	Description
System.DateTime	Represents an instant in time, typically expressed as a date and time of day.
System.Guid	Represents a globally unique identifier (GUID).
System.Math	Provides constants and static methods for trigonometric, logarithmic, and other common mathematical functions.
System.Random	Represents a pseudorandom number generator, a device that produces a sequence of numbers that meet certain statistical requirements for randomness.
System.Convert	Converts a base data type to another base data type.
System.Environment	Provides information about, and means to manipulate, the current environment and platform.
System.Console	Represents the standard input, output, and error streams for console applications.
System.Text.RegularExpressions.Regex	Represents an immutable regular expression.
System.Diagnostics.Debug	Provides a set of methods and properties that help debug your code.
System.Diagnostics.EventLog	Provides interaction with Windows event logs.

Table E-2. Utility (continued)

Class	Description
System.Diagnostics.Process	Provides access to local and remote processes and enables you to start and stop local system processes.
System.Diagnostics.Stopwatch	Provides a set of methods and properties that you can use to accurately measure elapsed time.
System.Media.SoundPlayer	Controls playback of a sound from a *.wav* file.

Table E-3. Collections and object utilities

Class	Description
System.Array	Provides methods for creating, manipulating, searching, and sorting arrays, thereby serving as the base class for all arrays in the Common Language Runtime.
System.Enum	Provides the base class for enumerations.
System.String	Represents text as a series of Unicode characters.
System.Text.StringBuilder	Represents a mutable string of characters.
System.Collections.Specialized.OrderedDictionary	Represents a collection of key/value pairs that are accessible by the key or index.
System.Collections.ArrayList	Implements the IList interface using an array whose size is dynamically increased as required.

Table E-4. The .NET Framework

Class	Description
System.AppDomain	Represents an application domain, which is an isolated environment where applications execute.
System.Reflection.Assembly	Defines an Assembly, which is a reusable, versionable, and self-describing building block of a common language runtime application.
System.Type	Represents type declarations: class types, Interface types, array types, value types, enumeration types, type parameters, generic type definitions, and open or closed constructed generic types.
System.Threading.Thread	Creates and controls a thread, sets its priority, and gets its status.
System.Runtime.InteropServices.Marshal	Provides a collection of methods for allocating unmanaged memory, copying unmanaged memory blocks, and converting managed to unmanaged types, as well as other miscellaneous methods used when interacting with unmanaged code.
Microsoft.CSharp.CSharpCodeProvider	Provides access to instances of the C# code generator and code compiler.

Table E-5. Registry

Class	Description
`Microsoft.Win32.Registry`	Provides RegistryKey objects that represent the root keys in the Windows registry, and static methods to access key/value pairs.
`Microsoft.Win32.RegistryKey`	Represents a key-level node in the Windows registry.

Table E-6. Input and output

Class	Description
`System.IO.Stream`	Provides a generic view of a sequence of bytes.
`System.IO.BinaryReader`	Reads primitive data types as binary values.
`System.IO.BinaryWriter`	Writes primitive types in binary to a stream.
`System.IO.BufferedStream`	Adds a buffering layer to read and write operations on another stream.
`System.IO.Directory`	Exposes static methods for creating, moving, and enumerating through directories and subdirectories.
`System.IO.FileInfo`	Provides instance methods for the creation, copying, deletion, moving, and opening of files, and aids in the creation of `FileStream` objects.
`System.IO.DirectoryInfo`	Exposes instance methods for creating, moving, and enumerating through directories and subdirectories.
`System.IO.File`	Provides static methods for the creation, copying, deletion, moving, and opening of files, and aids in the creation of `FileStream` objects.
`System.IO.MemoryStream`	Creates a stream whose backing store is memory.
`System.IO.Path`	Performs operations on String instances that contain file or directory path information. These operations are performed in a cross-platform manner.
`System.IO.TextReader`	Represents a reader that can read a sequential series of characters.
`System.IO.StreamReader`	Implements a `TextReader` that reads characters from a byte stream in a particular encoding.
`System.IO.TextWriter`	Represents a writer that can write a sequential series of characters.
`System.IO.StreamWriter`	Implements a `TextWriter` for writing characters to a stream in a particular encoding.
`System.IO.StringReader`	Implements a `TextReader` that reads from a string.
`System.IO.StringWriter`	Implements a `TextWriter` for writing information to a string.
`System.IO.Compression.DeflateStream`	Provides methods and properties used to compress and decompress streams using the Deflate algorithm.
`System.IO.Compression.GZipStream`	Provides methods and properties used to compress and decompress streams using the GZip algorithm.

Table E-6. Input and output (continued)

Class	Description
System.IO.FileSystemWatcher	Listens to the file system change notifications and raises events when a directory, or file in a directory, changes.

Table E-7. Security

Class	Description
System.Security.Principal.WindowsIdentity	Represents a Windows user.
System.Security.Principal.WindowsPrincipal	Allows code to check the Windows group membership of a Windows user.
System.Security.Principal.WellKnownSidType	Defines a set of commonly used security identifiers (SIDs).
System.Security.Principal.WindowsBuiltInRole	Specifies common roles to be used with IsInRole.
System.Security.SecureString	Represents text that should be kept confidential. The text is encrypted for privacy when being used, and deleted from computer memory when no longer needed.
System.Security.Cryptography.TripleDESCryptoServiceProvider	Defines a wrapper object to access the cryptographic service provider (CSP) version of the TripleDES algorithm.
System.Security.Cryptography.PasswordDeriveBytes	Derives a key from a password using an extension of the PBKDF1 algorithm.
System.Security.Cryptography.SHA1	Computes the SHA1 hash for the input data.
System.Security.AccessControl.FileSystemSecurity	Represents the access control and audit security for a file or directory.
System.Security.AccessControl.RegistrySecurity	Represents the Windows access control security for a registry key.

Table E-8. User interface

Class	Description
System.Windows.Forms.Form	Represents a window or dialog box that makes up an application's user interface.
System.Windows.Forms.FlowLayoutPanel	Represents a panel that dynamically lays out its contents.

Table E-9. Image manipulation

Class	Description
System.Drawing.Image	A class that provides functionality for the Bitmap and Metafile classes.
System.Drawing.Bitmap	Encapsulates a GDI+ bitmap, which consists of the pixel data for a graphics image and its attributes. A bitmap is an object used to work with images defined by pixel data.

Table E-10. Networking

Class	Description
System.Uri	Provides an object representation of a uniform resource identifier (URI) and easy access to the parts of the URI.
System.Net.NetworkCredential	Provides credentials for password-based authentication schemes such as basic, digest, Kerberos authentication, and NTLM.
System.Net.Dns	Provides simple domain name resolution functionality.
System.Net.FtpWebRequest	Implements a File Transfer Protocol (FTP) client.
System.Net.HttpWebRequest	Provides an HTTP-specific implementation of the WebRequest class.
System.Net.WebClient	Provides common methods for sending data to and receiving data from a resource identified by a URI.
System.Net.Sockets.TcpClient	Provides client connections for TCP network services.
System.Net.Mail.MailAddress	Represents the address of an electronic mail sender or recipient.
System.Net.Mail.MailMessage	Represents an email message that can be sent using the SmtpClient class.
System.Net.Mail.SmtpClient	Allows applications to send email by using the Simple Mail Transfer Protocol (SMTP).
System.IO.Ports.SerialPort	Represents a serial port resource.
System.Web.HttpUtility	Provides methods for encoding and decoding URLs when processing web requests.

Table E-11. XML

Class	Description
System.Xml.XmlTextWriter	Represents a writer that provides a fast, noncached, forward-only way of generating streams or files containing XML data that conforms to the W3C Extensible Markup Language (XML) 1.0 and the Namespaces in XML recommendations.
System.Xml.XmlDocument	Represents an XML document.

Table E-12. Windows Management Instrumentation (WMI)

Class	Description
System.Management.ManagementObject	Represents a WMI instance.
System.Management.ManagementClass	Represents a management class. A management class is a WMI class such as Win32_LogicalDisk, which can represent a disk drive, and Win32_Process, which represents a process such as an instance of *Notepad.exe*. The members of this class enable you to access WMI data using a specific WMI class path. For more information, see "Win32 Classes" in the Windows Management Instrumentation documentation in the MSDN Library at *http://msdn.microsoft.com/library*.

Table E-12. Windows Management Instrumentation (WMI) (continued)

Class	Description
System.Management.ManagementObjectSearcher	Retrieves a collection of WMI management objects based on a specified query. This class is one of the more commonly used entry points to retrieving management information. For example, it can be used to enumerate all disk drives, network adapters, processes, and many more management objects on a system, or to query for all network connections that are up, services that are paused, and so on. When instantiated, an instance of this class takes as input a WMI query represented in an ObjectQuery or its derivatives, and optionally a ManagementScope representing the WMI namespace to execute the query in. It can also take additional advanced options in an EnumerationOptions. When the Get method on this object is invoked, the ManagementObjectSearcher executes the given query in the specified scope and returns a collection of management objects that match the query in a ManagementObjectCollection.
System.Management.ManagementDateTimeConverter	Provides methods to convert DMTF datetime and time intervals to CLR-compliant DateTime and TimeSpan formats and vice versa.
System.Management.ManagementEventWatcher	Subscribes to temporary event notifications based on a specified event query.

Table E-13. Active Directory

Class	Description
System.DirectoryServices.DirectorySearcher	Performs queries against Active Directory.
System.DirectoryServices.DirectoryEntry	The DirectoryEntry class encapsulates a node or object in the Active Directory hierarchy.

Table E-14. Database

Class	Description
System.Data.DataSet	Represents an in-memory cache of data.
System.Data.DataTable	Represents one table of in-memory data.
System.Data.SqlClient.SqlCommand	Represents a Transact-SQL statement or stored procedure to execute against a SQL Server database.
System.Data.SqlClient.SqlConnection	Represents an open connection to a SQL Server database.
System.Data.SqlClient.SqlDataAdapter	Represents a set of data commands and a database connection that are used to fill the DataSet and update a SQL Server database.
System.Data.Odbc.OdbcCommand	Represents a SQL statement or stored procedure to execute against a data source.

Table E-14. Database (continued)

Class	Description
System.Data.Odbc.OdbcConnection	Represents an open connection to a data source.
System.Data.Odbc.OdbcDataAdapter	Represents a set of data commands and a connection to a data source that are used to fill the DataSet and update the data source.

Table E-15. Message queuing

Class	Description
System.Messaging.MessageQueue	Provides access to a queue on a Message Queuing server.

Table E-16. Transactions

Class	Description
System.Transactions.Transaction	Represents a transaction.

WMI Reference

The Windows Management Instrumentation (WMI) facilities in Windows offer thousands of classes that provide information of interest to administrators. Table F-1 lists the categories and subcategories covered by WMI, and can be used to get a general idea of the scope of WMI classes. Table F-2 provides a selected subset of the most useful WMI classes. For more information about a category, search the official WMI documentation at *http://msdn.microsoft.com*.

Table F-1. WMI class categories and subcategories

Category	Subcategory
Computer System Hardware	Cooling device, input device, mass storage, motherboard, controller and port, networking device, power, printing, telephony, video, and monitor.
Operating System	COM, desktop, drivers, filesystem, job objects, memory and page files, multimedia audio/visual, networking, operating system events, operating system settings, processes, registry, scheduler jobs, security, services, shares, Start menu, storage, users, Windows NT event log, Windows product activation.
WMI Service Management	WMI configuration, WMI management.
General	Installed applications, Performance counter, security descriptor.

Table F-2. Selected WMI Classes

Class	Description
Win32_BaseBoard	Represents a baseboard, which is also known as a motherboard or system board.
Win32_BIOS	Represents the attributes of the computer system's basic input/output services (BIOS) that are installed on a computer.
Win32_BootConfiguration	Represents the boot configuration of a Windows system.
Win32_CDROMDrive	Represents a CD-ROM drive on a Windows computer system. Be aware that the name of the drive does not correspond to the logical drive letter assigned to the device.

Table F-2. Selected WMI Classes (continued)

Class	Description
Win32_ComputerSystem	Represents a computer system in a Windows environment.
Win32_Processor	Represents a device that can interpret a sequence of instructions on a computer running on a Windows operating system. On a multiprocessor computer, one instance of the Win32_Processor class exists for each processor.
Win32_ComputerSystemProduct	Represents a product. This includes software and hardware used on this computer system.
CIM_DataFile	Represents a named collection of data or executable code. Currently, the provider returns files on fixed and mapped logical disks. In the future, only instances of files on local fixed disks will be returned.
Win32_DCOMApplication	Represents the properties of a DCOM application.
Win32_Desktop	Represents the common characteristics of a user's desktop. The properties of this class can be modified by the user to customize the desktop.
Win32_DesktopMonitor	Represents the type of monitor or display device attached to the computer system.
Win32_DeviceMemoryAddress	Represents a device memory address on a Windows system.
Win32_DiskDrive	Represents a physical disk drive as seen by a computer running the Windows operating system. Any interface to a Windows physical disk drive is a descendant (or member) of this class. The features of the disk drive seen through this object correspond to the logical and management characteristics of the drive. In some cases, this may not reflect the actual physical characteristics of the device. Any object based on another logical device would not be a member of this class.
Win32_DiskQuota	Tracks disk space usage for NTFS filesystem volumes. A system administrator (SA) can configure Windows to prevent further disk space use, and log an event when a user exceeds a specified disk space limit. An SA can also log an event when a user exceeds a specified disk space warning level. This class is new in Windows XP.
Win32_DMAChannel	Represents a direct memory access (DMA) channel on a Windows computer system. DMA is a method of moving data from a device to memory (or vice versa) without the help of the microprocessor. The system board uses a DMA controller to handle a fixed number of channels, each of which can be used by one (and only one) device at a time.
Win32_Environment	Represents an environment or system environment setting on a Windows computer system. Querying this class returns environment variables found in: HKLM\System\CurrentControlSet\Control\ Sessionmanager\Environment as well as: HKEY_USERS\<user sid>\Environment
Win32_Directory	Represents a directory entry on a Windows computer system. A *directory* is a type of file that logically groups data files and provides path information for the grouped files. Win32_Directory does not include directories of network drives.

Class	Description
Win32_Group	Represents data about a group account. A group account allows access privileges to be changed for a list of users. Example: Administrators.
Win32_IDEController	Manages the capabilities of an integrated device electronics (IDE) controller device.
Win32_IRQResource	Represents an interrupt request line (IRQ) number on a Windows computer system. An interrupt request is a signal sent to the CPU by a device or program for time-critical events. IRQ can be hardware- or software-based.
Win32_ScheduledJob	Represents a job created with the AT command. The Win32_ScheduledJob class does not represent a job created with the Scheduled Task Wizard from the Control Panel. You cannot change a task created by WMI in the Scheduled Tasks UI.
	Windows 2000 and Windows NT 4.0: You can use the Scheduled Tasks UI to modify the task you originally created with WMI. However, although the task is successfully modified, you can no longer access the task using WMI.
	Each job scheduled against the schedule service is stored persistently (the scheduler can start a job after a reboot), and is executed at the specified time and day of the week or month. If the computer is not active or if the scheduled service is not running at the specified job time, the schedule service runs the specified job on the next day at the specified time.
	Jobs are scheduled according to Universal Coordinated Time (UTC) with bias offset from Greenwich mean time (GMT), which means that a job can be specified using any time zone. The Win32_ScheduledJob class returns the local time with UTC offset when enumerating an object, and converts to local time when creating new jobs. For example, a job specified to run on a computer in Boston at 10:30 P.M. Monday PST time will be scheduled to run locally at 1:30 A.M. Tuesday EST. Note that a client must take into account whether Daylight Savings Time is in operation on the local computer, and if it is, then subtract a bias of 60 minutes from the UTC offset.
Win32_LoadOrderGroup	Represents a group of system services that define execution dependencies. The services must be initiated in the order specified by the Load Order Group, as the services are dependent on each other. These dependent services require the presence of the antecedent services to function correctly. The data in this class is derived by the provider from the registry key: `System\CurrentControlSet\Control\GroupOrderList`
Win32_LogicalDisk	Represents a data source that resolves to an actual local storage device on a Windows system.
Win32_LogonSession	Describes the logon session or sessions associated with a user logged on to Windows NT or Windows 2000.
Win32_CacheMemory	Represents internal and external cache memory on a computer system.

Class	Description
`Win32_LogicalMemoryConfiguration`	Represents the layout and availability of memory on a Windows system. Beginning with Windows Vista, this class is no longer available in the operating system.
	Windows XP and Windows Server 2003: This class is no longer supported. Use the `Win32_OperatingSystem` class instead.
	Windows 2000: This class is available and supported.
`Win32_PhysicalMemoryArray`	Represents details about the computer system physical memory. This includes the number of memory devices, memory capacity available, and memory type, for example, system or video memory.
`WIN32_NetworkClient`	Represents a network client on a Windows system. Any computer system on the network with a client relationship to the system is a descendant (or member) of this class (for example, a computer running Windows 2000 Workstation or Windows 98 that is part of a Windows 2000 domain).
`Win32_NetworkLoginProfile`	Represents the network login information of a specific user on a Windows system. This includes but is not limited to password status, access privileges, disk quotas, and login directory paths.
`Win32_NetworkProtocol`	Represents a protocol and its network characteristics on a Win32 computer system.
`Win32_NetworkConnection`	Represents an active network connection in a Windows environment.
`Win32_NetworkAdapter`	Represents a network adapter of a computer running on a Windows operating system.
`Win32_NetworkAdapterConfiguration`	Represents the attributes and behaviors of a network adapter. This class includes extra properties and methods that support the management of the TCP/IP and Internetworking Packet Exchange (IPX) protocols that are independent from the network adapter.
`Win32_NTDomain`	Represents a Windows NT domain.
`Win32_NTLogEvent`	Used to translate instances from the Windows NT event log. An application must have `SeSecurityPrivilege` to receive events from the security event log; otherwise, "Access Denied" is returned to the application.
`Win32_NTEventlogFile`	Represents a logical file or directory of Windows NT events. The file is also known as the event log.
`Win32_OnBoardDevice`	Represents common adapter devices built into the motherboard (system board).
`Win32_OperatingSystem`	Represents an operating system installed on a computer running on a Windows operating system. Any operating system that can be installed on a Windows system is a descendant or member of this class. `Win32_OperatingSystem` is a singleton class. To get the single instance, use @ for the key.
	Windows Server 2003, Windows XP, Windows 2000, and Windows NT 4.0: If a computer has multiple operating systems installed, this class returns only an instance for the currently active operating system.

Class	Description
Win32_PageFileUsage	Represents the file used for handling virtual memory file swapping on a Win32 system. Information contained within objects instantiated from this class specify the runtime state of the page file.
Win32_PageFileSetting	Represents the settings of a page file. Information contained within objects instantiated from this class specify the page file parameters used when the file is created at system startup. The properties in this class can be modified and deferred until startup. These settings are different from the runtime state of a page file expressed through the associated class Win32_PageFileUsage.
Win32_DiskPartition	Represents the capabilities and management capacity of a partitioned area of a physical disk on a Windows system. Example: Disk #0, Partition #1.
Win32_PortResource	Represents an I/O port on a Windows computer system.
Win32_PortConnector	Represents physical connection ports, such as DB-25 pin male, Centronics, or PS/2.
Win32_Printer	Represents a device connected to a computer running on a Microsoft Windows operating system that can produce a printed image or text on paper or other medium.
Win32_PrinterConfiguration	Represents the configuration for a printer device. This includes capabilities such as resolution, color, fonts, and orientation.
Win32_PrintJob	Represents a print job generated by a Windows application. Any unit of work generated by the Print command of an application that is running on a computer running on a Windows operating system is a descendant or member of this class.
Win32_Process	Represents a process on an operating system.
Win32_Product	Represents products as they are installed by Windows Installer. A product generally correlates to one installation package. For information about support or requirements for installation of a specific operating system, visit *http://msdn.microsoft.com* and search for "Operating System Availability of WMI Components."
Win32_QuickFixEngineering	Represents system-wide Quick Fix Engineering (QFE) or updates that have been applied to the current operating system.
Win32_QuotaSetting	Contains setting information for disk quotas on a volume.
Win32_OSRecoveryConfiguration	Represents the types of information that will be gathered from memory when the operating system fails. This includes boot failures and system crashes.
Win32_Registry	Represents the system registry on a Windows computer system.
Win32_SCSIController	Represents a SCSI controller on a Windows system.
Win32_PerfRawData_PerfNet_Server	Provides raw data from performance counters that monitor communications using the WINS Server service.

Table F-2. Selected WMI Classes (continued)

Class	Description
Win32_Service	Represents a service on a computer running on a Microsoft Windows operating system. A service application conforms to the interface rules of the Service Control Manager (SCM), and can be started by a user automatically at system start through the Services Control Panel utility, or by an application that uses the service functions included in the Windows API. Services can start when there are no users logged on to the computer.
Win32_Share	Represents a shared resource on a Windows system. This may be a disk drive, printer, interprocess communication, or other shareable device.
Win32_SoftwareElement	Represents a software element, part of a software feature (a distinct subset of a product, which may contain one or more elements). Each software element is defined in a Win32_SoftwareElement instance, and the association between a feature and its Win32_SoftwareFeature instance is defined in the Win32_SoftwareFeatureSoftwareElements association class. For information about support or requirements for installation on a specific operating system, visit *http://msdn.microsoft.com* and search for "Operating System Availability of WMI Components."
Win32_SoftwareFeature	Represents a distinct subset of a product that consists of one or more software elements. Each software element is defined in a Win32_SoftwareElement instance, and the association between a feature and its Win32_SoftwareFeature instance is defined in the Win32_SoftwareFeatureSoftwareElements association class. For information about support or requirements for installation on a specific operating system, visit *http://msdn.microsoft.com* and search for "Operating System Availability of WMI Components."
WIN32_SoundDevice	Represents the properties of a sound device on a Windows computer system.
Win32_StartupCommand	Represents a command that runs automatically when a user logs on to the computer system.
Win32_SystemAccount	Represents a system account. The system account is used by the operating system and services that run under Windows NT. There are many services and processes within Windows NT that need the capability to log on internally, for example, during a Windows NT installation. The system account was designed for that purpose.
Win32_SystemDriver	Represents the system driver for a base service.
Win32_SystemEnclosure	Represents the properties that are associated with a physical system enclosure.
Win32_SystemSlot	Represents physical connection points including ports, motherboard slots and peripherals, and proprietary connection points.
Win32_TapeDrive	Represents a tape drive on a Windows computer. Tape drives are primarily distinguished by the fact that they can be accessed only sequentially.
Win32_TemperatureProbe	Represents the properties of a temperature sensor (e.g., electronic thermometer).

Class	Description
Win32_TimeZone	Represents the time zone information for a Windows system, which includes changes required for the Daylight Saving Time transition.
Win32_UninterruptiblePowerSupply	Represents the capabilities and management capacity of an uninterruptible power supply (UPS). Beginning with Windows Vista, this class is obsolete and not available because the UPS service is no longer available. This service worked with serially attached UPS devices, not USB devices.
	Windows Server 2003 and Windows XP: This class is available, but not usable because the UPS service fails. Windows Server 2003, Windows XP, Windows 2000, and Windows NT 4.0: This class is available and implemented.
Win32_UserAccount	Contains information about a user account on a computer running on a Windows operating system.
	Because both the Name and Domain are key properties, enumerating Win32_UserAccount on a large network can affect performance negatively. Calling GetObject or querying for a specific instance has less impact.
Win32_VoltageProbe	Represents the properties of a voltage sensor (electronic voltmeter).
Win32_VolumeQuotaSetting	Relates disk quota settings with a specific disk volume. Windows 2000/NT: This class is not available.
Win32_WMISetting	Contains the operational parameters for the WMI service. This class can only have one instance, which always exists for each Windows system and cannot be deleted. Additional instances cannot be created.

APPENDIX G

Selected COM Objects and Their Uses

As an extensibility and administration interface, many applications expose useful functionality through COM objects. While PowerShell handles many of these tasks directly, many COM objects still provide significant value.

Table G-1 lists a selection of the COM objects most useful to system administrators.

Table G-1. COM identifiers and descriptions

Identifier	Description
Access.Application	Allows for interaction and automation of Microsoft Access.
Agent.Control	Allows for the control of Microsoft Agent 3D animated characters.
AutoItX3.Control	(nondefault) Provides access to Windows Automation via the AutoIt administration tool.
CEnroll.CEnroll	Provides access to certificate enrollment services.
CertificateAuthority.Request	Provides access to a request to a certificate authority.
COMAdmin.COMAdminCatalog	Provides access to and management of the Windows COM+ catalog.
Excel.Application	Allows for interaction and automation of Microsoft Excel.
Excel.Sheet	Allows for interaction with Microsoft Excel worksheets.
HNetCfg.FwMgr	Provides access to the management functionality of the Windows Firewall.
HNetCfg.HNetShare	Provides access to the management functionality of Windows Connection Sharing.
HTMLFile	Allows for interaction and authoring of a new Internet Explorer document.
InfoPath.Application	Allows for interaction and automation of Microsoft InfoPath.
InternetExplorer.Application	Allows for interaction and automation of Microsoft Internet Explorer.
IXSSO.Query	Allows for interaction with Microsoft Index Server.
IXSSO.Util	Provides access to utilities used along with the IXSSO.Query object.
LegitCheckControl.LegitCheck	Provide access to information about Windows Genuine Advantage status on the current computer.
MakeCab.MakeCab	Provides functionality to create and manage cabinet (*.cab*) files.

Identifier	Description
MAPI.Session	Provides access to a MAPI (Messaging Application Programming Interface) session, such as folders, messages, and the address book.
Messenger.MessengerApp	Allows for interaction and automation of Messenger.
Microsoft.FeedsManager	Allows for interaction with the Microsoft RSS feed platform.
Microsoft.ISAdm	Provides management of Microsoft Index Server.
Microsoft.Update.AutoUpdate	Provides management of the auto update schedule for Microsoft Update.
Microsoft.Update.Installer	Allows for installation of updates from Microsoft Update.
Microsoft.Update.Searcher	Provides search functionality for updates from Microsoft Update.
Microsoft.Update.Session	Provides access to local information about Microsoft Update history.
Microsoft.Update.SystemInfo	Provides access to information related to Microsoft Update for the current system.
MMC20.Application	Allows for interaction and automation of Microsoft Management Console (MMC).
MSScriptControl.ScriptControl	Allows for the evaluation and control of WSH scripts.
Msxml2.XSLTemplate	Allows for processing of XSL transforms.
Outlook.Application	Allows for interaction and automation of your email, calendar, contacts, tasks, and more through Microsoft Outlook.
OutlookExpress.MessageList	Allows for interaction and automation of your email through Microsoft Outlook Express.
PowerPoint.Application	Allows for interaction and automation of Microsoft PowerPoint.
Publisher.Application	Allows for interaction and automation of Microsoft Publisher.
RDS.DataSpace	Provides access to proxies of Remote DataSpace business objects.
SAPI.SpVoice	Provides access to the Microsoft Speech API.
Scripting.FileSystemObject	Provides access to the computer's filesystem. Most functionality is available more directly through PowerShell, or through PowerShell's support for the .NET Framework.
Scripting.Signer	Provides management of digital signatures on WSH files.
Scriptlet.TypeLib	Allows the dynamic creation of scripting type library (.*tlb*) files.
ScriptPW.Password	Allows for the masked input of plain-text passwords. When possible, you should avoid this in preference of the Read-Host cmdlet with the -AsSecureString parameter.
SharePoint.OpenDocuments	Allows for interaction with Microsoft SharePoint Services.
Shell.Application	Provides access to aspects of the Windows Explorer Shell application, such as managing windows, files and folders, and the current session.
Shell.LocalMachine	Provides access to information about the current machine related to the Windows shell.
Shell.User	Provides access to aspects of the current user's Windows session and profile.
SQLDMO.SQLServer	Provides access to the management functionality of Microsoft SQL Server.

Table G-1. COM identifiers and descriptions (continued)

Identifier	Description
Vim.Application	(nondefault) Allows for interaction and automation of the VIM editor.
WIA.CommonDialog	Provides access to image capture through the Windows Image Acquisition facilities.
WMPlayer.OCX	Allows for interaction and automation of Windows Media Player.
Word.Application	Allows for interaction and automation of Microsoft Word.
Word.Document	Allows for interaction with Microsoft Word documents.
WScript.Network	Provides access to aspects of a networked Windows environment, such as printers, network drives, as well as computer and domain information.
WScript.Shell	Provides access to aspects of the Windows Shell, such as applications, short-cuts, environment variables, the registry, and operating environment.
WSHController	Allows the execution of WSH scripts on remote computers.

.NET String Formatting

String Formatting Syntax

The format string supported by the format (-f) operator is a string that contains format items. Each format item takes the form of:

```
{index[,alignment][:formatString]}
```

<index> represents the zero-based index of the item in the object array following the format operator.

<alignment> is optional and represents the alignment of the item. A positive number aligns the item to the right of a field of the specified width. A negative number aligns the item to the left of a field of the specified width.

<formatString> is optional and formats the item using that type's specific format string syntax (as laid out in Tables H-1 and H-2).

Standard Numeric Format Strings

Table H-1 lists the standard numeric format strings. All format specifiers may be followed by a number between 0 and 99 to control the precision of the formatting.

Table H-1. Standard numeric format strings

Format specifier	Name	Description	Example
C or c	Currency	A currency amount.	PS >"{0:C}" -f 1.23 $1.23
D or d	Decimal	A decimal amount (for integral types). The precision specifier controls the minimum number of digits in the result.	PS >"{0:D4}" -f 2 0002
E or e	Scientific	Scientific (exponential) notation. The precision specifier controls the number of digits past the decimal point.	PS >"{0:E3}" -f [Math]::Pi 3.142E+000

Table H-1. Standard numeric format strings (continued)

Format specifier	Name	Description	Example
F or f	Fixed-point	Fixed point notation. The precision specifier controls the number of digits past the decimal point.	`PS >"{0:F3}" -f [Math]::Pi` `3.142`

G or g	General	The most compact representation (between fixed-point and scientific) of the number. The precision specifier controls the number of significant digits.	`PS >"{0:G3}" -f [Math]::Pi`
			`3.14`
			`PS >"{0:G3}" -f 1mb`
			`1.05E+06`

N or n	Number	The human readable form of the number, which includes separators between number groups. The precision specifier controls the number of digits past the decimal point.	`PS >"{0:N4}" -f 1mb` `1,048,576.0000`
P or p	Percent	The number (generally between 0 and 1) represented as a percentage. The precision specifier controls the number of digits past the decimal point.	`PS >"{0:P4}" -f 0.67` `67.0000 %`

R or r	Round-trip	The Single or Double number formatted with a precision that guarantees the string (when parsed) will result in the original number again.	`PS >"{0:R}" -f (1mb/2.0)`
			`524288`
			`PS >"{0:R}" -f (1mb/9.0)`
			`116508.44444444444`

X or x	Hexadecimal	The number converted to a string of hexadecimal digits. The case of the specifier controls the case of the resulting hexadecimal digits. The precision specifier controls the minimum number of digits in the resulting string.	`PS >"{0:X4}" -f 1324` `052C`

Custom Numeric Format Strings

You may use custom numeric strings, listed in Table H-2, to format numbers in ways not supported by the standard format strings.

Table H-2. Custom numeric format strings

Format Specifier	Name	Description	Example
0	Zero placeholder	Specifies the precision and width of a number string. Zeroes not matched by digits in the original number are output as zeroes.	`PS >"{0:00.0}" -f 4.12341234` `04.1`
#	Digit placeholder	Specifies the precision and width of a number string. # symbols not matched by digits in the input number are not output.	`PS >"{0:##.#}" -f 4.12341234` `4.1`

Table H-2. Custom numeric format strings (continued)

Format Specifier	Name	Description	Example
.	Decimal point	Determines the location of the decimal separator.	`PS >"{0:##.#}" -f 4.12341234` `4.1`
,	Thousands separator	When placed between a zero or digit placeholder before the decimal point in a formatting string, adds the separator character between number groups.	`PS >"{0:#,#.#}" -f 1234.121234` `1,234.1`
,	Number scaling	When placed before the literal (or implicit) decimal point in a formatting string, divides the input by 1000. You may apply this format specifier more than once.	`PS >"{0:##,,.000}" -f 1048576` `1.049`
%	Percentage placeholder	Multiplies the input by 100, and inserts the percent sign where shown in the format specifier.	`PS >"{0:%##.000}" -f .68` `%68.000`
E0 E+0 E-0 e0 e+0 e-0	Scientific notation	Displays the input in scientific notation. The number of zeroes that follow the E define the minimum length of the exponent field.	`PS >"{0:##.#E000}" -f 2.71828` `27.2E-001`
'text' "text"	Literal string	Inserts the provided text literally into the output without affecting formatting.	`PS >"{0:#.00'##'}" -f 2.71828` `2.72##`
;	Section separator	Allows for conditional formatting. If your format specifier contains no section separators, then the formatting statement applies to all input. If your format specifier contains one separator (creating two sections), then the first section applies to positive numbers and zero. The second section applies to negative numbers. If your format specifier contains two separators (creating three sections), then the sections apply to positive numbers, negative numbers, and zero.	`PS >"{0:POS;NEG;ZERO}" -f -14` `NEG`
Other	Other character	Inserts the provided text literally into the output without affecting formatting.	`PS >"{0:$## Please}" -f 14` `$14 Please`

APPENDIX I

.NET DateTime Formatting

DateTime format strings convert a DateTime object to one of several standard formats, as listed in Table I-1.

Table I-1. Standard DateTime format strings

Format specifier	Name	Description	Example
d	Short date	The culture's short date format.	PS >"{0:d}" -f [DateTime] "01/23/4567" 1/23/4567
D	Long date	The culture's long date format.	PS >"{0:D}" -f [DateTime] "01/23/4567" Friday, January 23, 4567
f	Full date/short time	Combines the long date and short time format patterns.	PS >"{0:f}" -f [DateTime] "01/23/4567" Friday, January 23, 4567 12:00 AM
F	Full date/long time	Combines the long date and long time format patterns.	PS >"{0:F}" -f [DateTime] "01/23/4567" Friday, January 23, 4567 12:00:00 AM
g	General date/short time	Combines the short date and short time format patterns.	PS >"{0:g}" -f [DateTime] "01/23/4567" 1/23/4567 12:00 AM
G	General date/long time	Combines the short date and long time format patterns.	PS >"{0:G}" -f [DateTime] "01/23/4567" 1/23/4567 12:00:00 AM
M or m	Month day	The culture's MonthDay format.	PS >"{0:M}" -f [DateTime] "01/23/4567" January 23
o	Round-trip date/time	The date formatted with a pattern that guarantees the string (when parsed) will result in the original DateTime again.	PS >"{0:o}" -f [DateTime] "01/23/4567" 4567-01-23T00:00:00.0000000
R or r	RFC1123	The standard RFC1123 format pattern.	PS >"{0:R}" -f [DateTime] "01/23/4567" Fri, 23 Jan 4567 00:00:00 GMT

Table I-1. Standard DateTime format strings (continued)

Format specifier	Name	Description	Example
s	Sortable	Sortable format pattern. Conforms to ISO 8601, and provides output suitable for sorting.	PS >"{0:s}" -f [DateTime] "01/23/4567" 4567-01-23T00:00:00
t	Short time	The culture's ShortTime format.	PS >"{0:t}" -f [DateTime] "01/23/4567" 12:00 AM
T	Long time	The culture's LongTime format.	PS >"{0:T}" -f [DateTime] "01/23/4567" 12:00:00 AM
u	Universal sortable	The culture's UniversalSortable DateTime format applied to the UTC equivalent of the input.	PS >"{0:u}" -f [DateTime] "01/23/4567" 4567-01-23 00:00:00Z
U	Universal	The culture's FullDateTime format applied to the UTC equivalent of the input.	PS >"{0:U}" -f [DateTime] "01/23/4567" Friday, January 23, 4567 8:00:00 AM
Y or y	Year month	The culture's YearMonth format.	PS >"{0:Y}" -f [DateTime] "01/23/4567" January, 4567

Custom DateTime Format Strings

You may use custom DateTime format strings, listed in Table I-2, to format dates in ways not supported by the standard format strings.

 Single-character format specifiers are interpreted as a standard DateTime formatting string unless they are used with other formatting specifiers.

Table I-2. Custom DateTime format strings

Format specifier	Description	Example
d	Day of the month as a number between 1 and 31. Represents single-digit days without a leading zero.	PS >"{0:d dd ddd dddd}" -f [DateTime] "01/02/4567" 2 02 Fri Friday
dd	Day of the month as a number between 1 and 31. Represents single-digit days with a leading zero.	PS >"{0:d dd ddd dddd}" -f [DateTime] "01/02/4567" 2 02 Fri Friday
ddd	Abbreviated name of the day of week.	PS >"{0:d dd ddd dddd}" -f [DateTime] "01/02/4567" 2 02 Fri Friday

Table I-2. Custom DateTime format strings (continued)

Format specifier	Description	Example
dddd	Full name of the day of the week.	PS >"{0:d dd ddd dddd}" -f [DateTime] "01/02/4567" 2 02 Fri Friday
f	Most significant digit of the seconds fraction (milliseconds).	PS >"{0:f ff fff ffff}" -f [DateTime] "01/02/4567" 0 00 000 0000
ff	Two most significant digits of the seconds fraction (milliseconds).	PS >"{0:f ff fff ffff}" -f [DateTime] "01/02/4567" 0 00 000 0000
fff	Three most significant digits of the seconds fraction (milliseconds).	PS >"{0:f ff fff ffff}" -f [DateTime] "01/02/4567" 0 00 000 0000
ffff	Four most significant digits of the seconds fraction (milliseconds).	PS >"{0:f ff fff ffff}" -f [DateTime] "01/02/4567" 0 00 000 0000
fffff	Five most significant digits of the seconds fraction (milliseconds).	PS >"{0:fffff ffffff fffffff}" -f [DateTime] "01/02/4567" 00000 000000 0000000
ffffff	Six most significant digits of the seconds fraction (milliseconds).	PS >"{0:fffff ffffff fffffff}" -f [DateTime] "01/02/4567" 00000 000000 0000000
fffffff	Seven most significant digits of the seconds fraction (milliseconds).	PS >"{0:fffff ffffff fffffff}" -f [DateTime] "01/02/4567" 00000 000000 0000000
F	Most significant digit of the seconds fraction (milliseconds). Displays nothing if the number is zero.	PS >"{0:F FF FFF FFFF}" -f [DateTime]::Now 6 66 669 6696 PS >"{0:|F FF FFF FFFF|}" -f [DateTime] "01/02/4567" | |
FF	Two most significant digits of the seconds fraction (milliseconds). Displays nothing if the number is zero.	PS >"{0:F FF FFF FFFF}" -f [DateTime]::Now 6 66 669 6696 PS >"{0:|F FF FFF FFFF|}" -f [DateTime] "01/02/4567" | |
FFF	Three most significant digits of the seconds fraction (milliseconds). Displays nothing if the number is zero.	PS >"{0:F FF FFF FFFF}" -f [DateTime]::Now 6 66 669 6696 PS >"{0:|F FF FFF FFFF|}" -f [DateTime] "01/02/4567" | |

Table I-2. Custom DateTime format strings (continued)

Format specifier	Description	Example
FFFF	Four most significant digits of the seconds fraction (milliseconds). Displays nothing if the number is zero.	PS >"{0:F FF FFF FFFF}" -f [DateTime]::Now 6 66 669 6696 PS >"{0:|F FF FFF FFFF|}" -f [DateTime] "01/02/4567" | |
FFFFF	Five most significant digits of the seconds fraction (milliseconds). Displays nothing if the number is zero.	PS >"{0:FFFFF FFFFFF FFFFFFF}" -f [DateTime]::Now 1071 107106 1071068 PS >"{0:|FFFFF FFFFFF FFFFFFF|}" -f [DateTime] "01/02/4567" | |
FFFFFF	Six most significant digits of the seconds fraction (milliseconds). Displays nothing if the number is zero.	PS >"{0:FFFFF FFFFFF FFFFFFF}" -f [DateTime]::Now 1071 107106 1071068 PS >"{0:|FFFFF FFFFFF FFFFFFF|}" -f [DateTime] "01/02/4567" | |
FFFFFFF	Seven most significant digits of the seconds fraction (milliseconds). Displays nothing if the number is zero.	PS >"{0:FFFFF FFFFFF FFFFFFF}" -f [DateTime]::Now 1071 107106 1071068 PS >"{0:|FFFFF FFFFFF FFFFFFF|}" -f [DateTime] "01/02/4567" | |
%g or gg	Era (i.e., A.D).	PS >"{0:gg}" -f [DateTime] "01/02/4567" A.D.
%h	Hours, as a number between 1 and 12. Single digits do not include a leading zero.	PS >"{0:%h}" -f [DateTime] "01/02/4567 4:00pm" 4
hh	Hours, as a number between 01 and 12. Single digits include a leading zero. Note: This is interpreted as a standard DateTime formatting string unless used with other formatting specifiers.	PS >"{0:hh}" -f [DateTime] "01/02/4567 4:00pm" 04
%H	Hours, as a number between 0 and 23. Single digits do not include a leading zero.	PS >"{0:%H}" -f [DateTime] "01/02/4567 4:00pm" 16
HH	Hours, as a number between 00 and 23. Single digits include a leading zero.	PS >"{0:HH}" -f [DateTime] "01/02/4567 4:00am" 04
K	DateTime.Kind specifier that corresponds to the kind (i.e., Local, Utc, or Unspecified) of input date.	PS >"{0: K}" -f [DateTime]::Now.ToUniversalTime() Z

Table I-2. Custom DateTime format strings (continued)

Format specifier	Description	Example
M	Minute, as a number between 0 and 59. Single digits do not include a leading zero.	PS >"{0: m}" -f [DateTime]::Now 7
mm	Minute, as a number between 00 and 59. Single digits include a leading zero.	PS >"{0:mm}" -f [DateTime]::Now 08
M	Month, as a number between 1 and 12. Single digits do not include a leading zero.	PS >"{0:M MM MMM MMMM}" -f [DateTime] "01/02/4567" 1 01 Jan January
MM	Month, as a number between 01 and 12. Single digits include a leading zero.	PS >"{0:M MM MMM MMMM}" -f [DateTime] "01/02/4567" 1 01 Jan January
MMM	Abbreviated month name.	PS >"{0:M MM MMM MMMM}" -f [DateTime] "01/02/4567" 1 01 Jan January
MMMM	Full month name.	PS >"{0:M MM MMM MMMM}" -f [DateTime] "01/02/4567" 1 01 Jan January
s	Seconds, as a number between 0 and 59. Single digits do not include a leading zero.	PS > "{0:s ss t tt}" -f [DateTime]::Now 3 03 A AM
ss	Seconds, as a number between 00 and 59. Single digits include a leading zero.	PS > "{0:s ss t tt}" -f [DateTime]::Now 3 03 A AM
T	First character of the a.m./p.m. designator.	PS > "{0:s ss t tt}" -f [DateTime]::Now 3 03 A AM
tt	a.m./p.m. designator.	PS > "{0:s ss t tt}" -f [DateTime]::Now 3 03 A AM
Y	Year, in (at most) 2 digits.	PS >"{0:y yy yyy yyyy yyyyy}" -f [DateTime] "01/02/4567" 67 67 4567 4567 04567
yyy	Year, in (at most) 3 digits.	PS >"{0:y yy yyy yyyy yyyyy}" -f [DateTime] "01/02/4567" 67 67 4567 4567 04567
yyyy	Year, in (at most) 4 digits.	PS >"{0:y yy yyy yyyy yyyyy}" -f [DateTime] "01/02/4567" 67 67 4567 4567 04567
yyyyy	Year, in (at most) 5 digits.	PS >"{0:y yy yyy yyyy yyyyy}" -f [DateTime] "01/02/4567" 67 67 4567 4567 04567
Z	Signed time zone offset from GMT. Does not include a leading zero.	PS >"{0:z zz zzz}" -f [DateTime]::Now -7 -07 -07:00
zz	Signed time zone offset from GMT. Includes a leading zero.	PS >"{0:z zz zzz}" -f [DateTime]::Now -7 -07 -07:00
zzz	Signed time zone offset from GMT, measured in hours and minutes.	PS >"{0:z zz zzz}" -f [DateTime]::Now -7 -07 -07:00

Table I-2. Custom DateTime format strings (continued)

Format specifier	Description	Example
:	Time separator.	PS > "{0:y/m/d h:m:s}" -f [DateTime] "01/02/4567 4:00pm" 67/0/2 4:0:0
/	Date separator.	PS > "{0:y/m/d h:m:s}" -f [DateTime] "01/02/4567 4:00pm" 67/0/2 4:0:0
"text" 'text'	Inserts the provided text literally into the output without affecting formatting.	PS >"{0:'Day: 'dddd}" -f [DateTime]::Now Day: Monday
%c	Syntax allowing for single-character custom formatting specifiers. The % sign is not added to the output.	PS >"{0:%h}" -f [DateTime] "01/02/4567 4:00pm" 4
Other	Inserts the provided text literally into the output without affecting formatting.	PS >"{0:dddd!}" -f [DateTime]::Now Monday!

Index

We'd like to hear your suggestions for improving our indexes. Send email to *index@oreilly.com*.

About the Author

Lee Holmes is a developer on the Microsoft Windows PowerShell team and has been an authoritative source of information about PowerShell since its earliest betas. His vast experience with Windows PowerShell lets him integrate both the "how" and the "why" into discussions. Lee's integration with the PowerShell and administration community (via newsgroups, mailing lists, and blogs) gives him a great deal of insight into the problems faced by all levels of administrators and PowerShell users alike.

Colophon

The animal on the cover of *Windows PowerShell Cookbook* is a box turtle (*Terrapene carolina carolina*). This box turtle is native to North America, specifically northern areas in the Unites States and northern parts of Mexico. The average male turtle is about six inches long and has red eyes; the female is a bit smaller and has yellow eyes. This turtle is omnivorous as a youth but largely herbivorous as an adult. It has a domed shell that is hinged on the bottom and snaps tightly shut if the turtle is in danger (once its head, tail, and limbs are safely inside). Box turtles usually stay within the same area they were born, rarely leaving a 750 foot radius. During mating rituals, male turtles will sometimes shove and push each other to win the female's attention. During copulation, it is possible for the male turtle to fall backward, be unable to right himself, and starve to death.

Although box turtles can live for more than 100 years, their habitats are being seriously threatened by land development and roads. Turtles need loose, humid soil to lay eggs and burrow during their long hibernation season. Box turtles are also highly susceptible to contracting diseases from household pets. Experts strongly discourage taking turtles from their native habitat—not only will it disrupt the community's breeding opportunities, but the turtle will become extremely stressed when outside of its known habitat and perish quickly.

The cover image is from *Dover Picotorial Images*. The cover font is Adobe ITC Garamond. The text font is Linotype Birka; the heading font is Adobe Myriad Condensed; and the code font is LucasFont's TheSans Mono Condensed.

Related Titles from O'Reilly

Windows Administration

Active Directory Cookbook, *2nd Edition*

Active Directory, *3rd Edition*

DNS on Windows Server 2003, *3rd Edition*

Essential Microsoft Operations Manager

Essential SharePoint

Exchange Server Cookbook

Learning Windows Server 2003, *2nd Edition*

MCSE Core Elective Exams in a Nutshell

MCSE Core Required Exams in a Nutshell, *3rd Edition*

Monad (AKA PowerShell)

Securing Windows Server 2003

SharePoint Office Pocket Guide

SharePoint User's Guide

Windows Server 2003 in a Nutshell

Windows Server 2003 Network Administration

Windows Server 2003 Security Cookbook

Windows Server Cookbook

Windows Server Hacks

Windows XP Cookbook

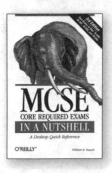

The O'Reilly Advantage

Stay Current and Save Money